Transforming the World?

Transforming the World?

The gospel and social responsibility

Edited by Jamie A. Grant and Dewi A. Hughes

APOLLOS (an imprint of Inter-Varsity Press)
Norton Street, Nottingham NG7 3HR, England
Email: ivp@ivpbooks.com
Website: www.ivpbooks.com

First published 2009

British Library Cataloguing in Publication Data
A catalogue record for this book is available from the British Library.

UK ISBN: 978-1-84474-374-2

Set in Monotype Garamond 11/13pt
Typeset in Great Britain by Servis Filmsetting Ltd, Stockport, Cheshire
Printed and bound in Great Britain by Ashford Colour Press Ltd, Gosport, Hampshire

Inter-Varsity Press publishes Christian books that are true to the Bible and that communicate
the gospel, develop discipleship and strengthen the church for its mission in the world.

Inter-Varsity Press is closely linked with the Universities and Colleges Christian Fellowship, a
student movement connecting Christian Unions in universities and colleges throughout Great
Britain, and a member movement of the International Fellowship of Evangelical Students.
Website: www.uccf.org.uk.

CONTENTS

CONTRIBUTORS

David L. Baker is Senior Lecturer in Old Testament at Trinity Theological College, Perth, Western Australia.

M. Daniel Carroll R. (Rodas) is Distinguished Professor of Old Testament at Denver Seminary in Denver, the United States, and adjunct professor at El Seminario Teológico Centroamericano, Guatemala City, Guatemala.

Tim Chester is a church planter with The Crowded House in Sheffield, UK, and Director of the Northern Training Institute.

Jamie A. Grant is Lecturer in Biblical Studies at the Highland Theological College, Dingwall, Scotland.

Peter Heslam is director of Transforming Business, a research project in the University of Cambridge which focuses on enterprise solutions to poverty.

Jason B. Hood is a PhD candidate in New Testament at the Highland Theological College, Dingwall, Scotland.

Dewi Hughes is Theological Advisor to Tearfund, UK.

I. Howard Marshall is Emeritus Professor of New Testament Exegesis in the University of Aberdeen.

C. René Padilla is Director of *Ediciones Kairos*, Buenos Aires, Argentina.

Anna Robbins is Vice-Principal and Lecturer in Theology and Contemporary Culture at the London School of Theology.

David Smith is Lecturer in Urban Mission and World Christianity at International Christian College, Glasgow, Scotland.

Melvin Tinker is vicar of St John Newland Church, Kingston upon Hull, England.

Alistair Wilson is Principal of Dumisani Theological Institute, King William's Town, South Africa and an Extraordinary Associate Professor in New Testament of the Faculty of Theology, North-West University, Potchefstroom, South Africa.

Christopher J.H. Wright is International Director of the Langham Partnership International, London.

ABBREVIATIONS

AB	Anchor Bible
ABD	*Anchor Bible Dictionary*, ed. D. M. Freedman, 6 vols. (New York, 1992)
BCOTWP	Baker Commentary on the Old Testament Wisdom and Psalms
BECNT	Baker Exegetical Commentary on the New Testament
BET	Beiträge zur biblischen Exegese und Theologie
Bib Int	*Biblical Intepretation*
DJG	*Dictionary of Jesus and the Gospels*, eds. J. B. Green, S. McKnight and I. H. Marshall (Downers Grove and Leicester: IVP, 1992)
DLNTD	*Dictionary of the Later NT and its Developments*, eds. R. P. Martin and P. H. Davids (Downers Grove and Leicester: IVP, 1997)
DOTP	*Dictionary of the Old Testament: Pentateuch,* eds. T. D. Alexander and D. W. Baker (Leicester: IVP, 2003)
DPL	*Dictionary of Paul and His Letters*, eds. G. F. Hawthorne, R. P. Martin and D. G. Reid (Downers Grove and Leicester: IVP, 1994)
ESV	English Standard Version
ET	English translation
EuroJTh	*European Journal of Theology*
ExpTim	*Expository Times*
FRLANT	Forschungen zur Religion und Literatur des Alten und Neuen Testaments
ICC	International Critical Commentary

JETS	*Journal of the Evangelical Theological Society*
JNES	*Journal of Near Eastern Studies*
JSNT	*Journal for the Study of the New Testament*
JSOT	*Journal for the Study of the Old Testament*
KJV	King James Version
LHBOTS	Library of Hebrew Bible/Old Testament Studies
LXX	Septuagint
NAC	New American Commentary
NASB	New American Standard Bible
NDBT	*New Dictionary of Biblical Theology*, eds. T. D. Alexander and B. S. Rosner (Leicester and Downers Grove: IVP, 2000)
NIB	The New Interpreter's Bible
NICNT	New International Commentary on the NT
NICOT	New International Commentary on the OT
NIDNTT	*New International Dictionary of New Testament Theology*, ed. C. Brown, 4 vols. (Carlisle: Paternoster, 1988)
NIGTC	New International Greek Testament Commentary
NIV	New International Version
NIVAC	NIV Application Commentary
NJB	New Jerusalem Bible
NRSV	New Revised Standard Version
NSBT	New Studies in Biblical Theology
OT/NT	Old/New Testament
REB	Revised English Bible
RSV	Revised Standard Version
SJT	*Scottish Journal of Theology*
TDOT	*Theological Dictionary of the Old Testament*, eds. G. J. Botterweck and H. Ringgren, 8 vols. (Grand Rapids, 1978–96), ET of *Theologisches Wörterbuch zum Alten Testament* (Stuttgart, 1970–)
TEV	Today's English Version
TNIV	Today's New International Version
TNTC	Tyndale NT commentary
TOTC	Tyndale OT commentary
TWOT	Theological Wordbook of the Old Testament
VTSupp	*Vetus Testamentum* Supplements
WBC	Word Bible Commentary
WJT	*Westminster Theological Journal*
WUNT	Wissenschaftliche Untersuchungen zum Neuen Testament
ZAW	*Zeitschrift für die alttestamentliche Wissenschaft*

INTRODUCTION

Jamie A. Grant and Dewi A. Hughes

Evangelical Christianity has long been plagued by a dichotomy. In the last century liberals reduced the mission of God to social action and in response evangelicals reduced it to making individual converts by proclaiming the 'gospel'. This was a case, common in the history of theology, of a bad argument being countered by an equally bad one. Even great theologians are not immune from this sort of thing. The sixteenth-century Jesuit theologian Robert Bellarmine argued that Protestantism could not be of God because Protestants did not engage in converting the heathen. Calvin countered by arguing that the Great Commission (Matt. 28:19–20) had been fulfilled in apostolic times and was no longer binding on Christians, and thus stymied the development of a robust Calvinistic missionary theology for 200 years. Theologians bear a heavy responsibility sometimes! The polarization of evangelism and social action was hardly ever complete but enough heat and suspicion was generated for social action to be damned by many evangelicals for its association with liberalism and for proselytizing evangelism to be damned by liberals for its association with obscurantist fundamentalism. From the evangelical side theologians have been trying to exorcize the demon of associating social action with liberalism for over half a century and will probably have to continue doing so. This book is not just another attempt to exorcize the demon, but its background is the debate about whether evangelicals should attempt to make this world a better place in tune with God's will as well as prepare people for life in a better world.

As we hope this volume will make entirely clear, there is no tension between the task of evangelism and the Christian's obligation to care for those in need. The issue should never have been one of 'either/or' but rather should always have been voiced in terms of 'both/and'. The Bible's teaching regarding the believer's responsibilities towards those in need makes it absolutely plain that God's salvific work is both spiritual and physical. Therefore, the church – as God's representatives on this earth – should be characterized as those who bring a message of salvation that deals with humanity in its every aspect, practical as well spiritual.

This collection of articles helps to illustrate the holistic gospel message that we find in the Scriptures. Whilst still no more than an overview, the first seven articles try to give the reader a fuller understanding of the Christian's responsibility towards those who are in need. The three opening chapters paint in broad brushstrokes an image of the Old Testament's teaching on care for the weak, poor and voiceless in society.

David Baker addresses the Pentateuch's emphasis on care for the vulnerable as it is expressed in the law. He points out that protection of the weak and underprivileged is unmistakably ingrained in the foundational laws of the Old Testament. What is more, these regulations are not addressed primarily to Israel's leaders but towards the covenant community as a whole. 'It is noteworthy that these laws are addressed primarily to the covenant community, not the king. Social care is seen as the responsibility of individuals and families within the community rather than as a state provision' (p. 31).

Danny Carroll goes on to examine the prophetic teaching on social care and there can be no mistaking the centrality of social justice themes in the writings of the Old Testament prophets. 'The Old Testament prophetic literature is replete with the demands of God for social and economic justice . . . The prophets have left us harsh words – penetrating exposures and compelling condemnations that should compel the people of God to call for justice today' (p. 48). However, Carroll goes on to point out that the prophetic message is not just one of judgment and condemnation but it also contains a voice of hope: eternal hope, certainly, but also a message of hope for the 'here and now'.

In the third of the Old Testament papers, Jamie Grant examines the wisdom literature's teaching on social care. Clearly, the law binds God's people to protect the vulnerable and the prophets bring a message of judgment when his people fail in this duty. The wisdom literature encourages the reader *to exceed* the minimum standards legislated in the law. 'The quest for wisdom in the Old Testament is really a search for that lifestyle which is most pleasing to God . . . It is absolutely plain from what we have seen that such a lifestyle must include an attitude and habitual practice of care for those in need' (p. 65). To live a life pleasing to God means that we will care for the needy.

Chris Wright's chapter on biblical paradigms of redemption straddles the testaments. In his examination of the exodus and jubilee as archetypal acts of salvation in the Old Testament, Wright notes the profoundly physical and practical implications of both. The question, therefore, naturally arises: do we make a mistake if we view Christ's work on the cross as entirely and uniquely spiritual? 'I do *not* reject or reduce the terribly serious spiritual realities of sin and evil that the New Testament exposes, or the glories of the spiritual dimension of God's redemptive accomplishment in the cross and resurrection of Jesus of Nazareth. I simply deny that these truths of the New Testament *nullify* all that the Old Testament has already revealed about God's comprehensive commitment to every dimension of human life, about his relentless opposition to all that oppresses, spoils and diminishes human well-being, and about his ultimate mission of blessing the nations and redeeming his whole creation' (p. 77).

This is followed by three chapters that consider how the New Testament addresses the whole question of care for the weak and vulnerable. First, Alistair Wilson takes a look at Jesus' attitude towards the marginalized in his society in the Gospel narratives of Matthew, Mark and John. He argues that any Gospels-centred view of compassion must take into account the twinned themes of the word and deed: 'As we observe Jesus' priorities in the Gospel narratives, we find him devoting himself to the proclamation of the kingdom of God at least as much as he devotes himself to dealing with illness or hunger (see Matt. 9:35). Thus, recognition of the centrality of the message of the gospel is a significant aspect of what it means to have compassion as Jesus had compassion. We also note that prayer to the "Lord of the harvest" recognizes that God's ability to act for the good of those in need far exceeds what any human being may be able to accomplish. Yet, we see in Matthew 10:5 that the disciples become the answer to their own prayer and so devotion to prayer to the sovereign God must not be detached from willingness to respond to the call of God to show compassion in action' (p. 109).

Then I. Howard Marshall discusses the prominence of care for the poor in the writings of Luke. He concludes that, 'Luke has a theology of a God who is generous and compassionate ... The faithful proclamation of the gospel includes its element of judgment on the selfish rich and the call to share with the needy. It also includes the expression of God's compassion and care for the sick and disabled and the calling to account of rulers and "the mighty" to practise righteousness (which includes compassion)' (pp. 126–127).

Finally, in our examination of the biblical material, Jason Hood considers the practical implications of the collection for the poor in Jerusalem that is so often referred to in the Pauline writings. While it would be fair to say that Paul is perhaps not as well known for his teaching on social care as, for example, Luke or James, Hood points out that this repeated emphasis on the collection gives us an example of care for the needy worked out in practice in the setting of Christian community. 'Paul does not present an abstract theology of social concern; he dramatizes his message through his life, challenging those who lead and teach that generosity, sacrifice and the sharing of *koinōnia* with others in God's family is not optional but integral to the call to Christian life in community' (p. 144).

Once you have read the seven chapters which discuss the Bible's teaching regarding the social responsibilities of the community of faith, it is our hope that the tensions mentioned in the opening paragraph of this introduction will become a relic of the past (if this is not already the case).

The second part of the volume explores the theme of world transformation from the perspective of theological disciplines such as social ethics, systematic theology and church history. The first chapter in this second part, 'The Servant solution: the coordination of evangelism and social action' by Melvin Tinker, develops a new approach to the relationship between 'evangelism' and 'social action' built on the assumption that it is not a question of whether Christians should engage in social action but '*how* that action might appropriately be expressed and upon what theological basis it should proceed' (p. 148). Tinker's contention is that the correct relationship between evangelism and social action comes to light when the roots of Jesus' teaching in Matthew 5:1–16 in the Servant Songs of Isaiah is properly appreciated. He then tests this solution by applying it to the life of the early church in Acts and concludes his chapter by examining briefly the impact of Christian beliefs and actions on the Graeco-Roman world. In his final remarks he strongly endorses David Wells' statement that '[p]ostmoderns want to see as well as hear, to find authenticity in relationship as the precursor to hearing what is said. This is a valid and biblical demand. Faith, after all, is dead without works, and few sins are dealt with as harshly by Jesus as hypocrisy. What postmoderns want to see, and are entitled to see, is believing and being, talking and doing, all joined together in a seamless whole.'[1]

Dewi Hughes in the next chapter, entitled 'Understanding and overcoming poverty', explores the roots of poverty in human hearts that are deeply flawed because of their rebellion against the Creator, and the solution to poverty in God's redemptive action that reaches its culmination in Jesus Christ. Applying this biblical story to our context he contends that we should prioritize resisting consumerism and appreciating afresh the significance of church. So, 'bringing the plight of the poor to the attention of those who listen to us should be an essential component of our attempt to counter the great lie of consumerism. The best way to do this is to face up to the difficult challenge of living in simplicity' (p. 182). And also, 'if the thousands, if not millions, of evangelical

---

1.   David F. Wells, *Above All Earthly Pow'rs: Christ in the Post Modern World.* (Leicester: IVP, 2005), p. 315. See also Kevin Vanhoozer, 'The world well staged', in *First Theology* (Leicester: Apollos, 2002), p. 334.

churches were anything like what the New Testament envisages churches should be, the impact on world poverty would be immense' (p. 186).

René Padilla, one of the elder statesmen of the evangelical world, whose strong advocacy of holistic mission since the first Lausanne Congress in 1974 has made a very significant contribution to evangelical theology and practice, distils much of his acquired wisdom into a chapter entitled 'The biblical basis for social ethics'. Beginning with his struggle as an IFES worker to support Latin American university students wrestling with the challenge of Marxism in the 60s, he argues for a contextualized theology based on a hermeneutic that includes, but goes beyond, the historical-grammatical approach that he learnt at Wheaton College. The 'Christ event' is at the heart of his understanding but he contends that '[w]ithout the political meaning of that story, Christians are left without the narrative through which the Spirit of God enables them to live as the servant people "on whom the ends of the ages have come" (1 Cor. 10:11), called by God to be the salt of the earth and the light of the world' (p. 201).

With Anna Robbins' chapter, 'Public execution: the atonement and world transformation', we move into the realm of systematic theology. The context of this chapter is the contemporary awakening of social action among young people and the debate about the nature of the atonement. Building on the foundation that 'the cross is the moral centre of our faith' (p. 207) and contending that reconciliation is the key purpose of the atonement, she explores the significance of the themes of 'satisfaction', 'regeneration' and 'triumph' for Christian social ethics. The section on 'satisfaction' addresses the current debate about the atonement and concludes that if we have no patience with concepts such as God's satisfaction, holiness and justice we will 'miss the ethical implications of what the cross means for God' (p. 214) and fail to be truly counter-cultural as Christians.

The systematic theology focus is retained in Tim Chester's 'Eschatology and the transformation of the world: contradiction, continuity, conflation and the endurance of hope'. The link between eschatology and world transformation has been an important theme in the last four decades. Chester critically examines the various ways this link has been conceived under the headings of contradiction (Moltmann), continuity (Volf) and conflation (Wolterstorff). He concludes by emphasizing the endurance of hope as explained by Calvin. 'For Calvin,' he contends, 'the patience of hope is always connected with the work of faith and labour of love. The faith that arises from hope "is an earnest faith, full of power, so that it shirks no task when our neighbours are in need of help"[2] (p. 243).

David W. Smith moves us into the realm of church history with his

---

2. John Calvin, *Commentary on 1 Thessalonians 1:3*.

'Evangelicals and society: the story of an on-off relationship'. His thesis is that throughout their history there have been two main ways in which evangelicals have conceived the way in which their faith impacts the world. On the one hand there is the world-transformative stream. Rooted in the Calvinistic, Reformed and Puritan tradition this stream manifests itself in the work and attitudes of evangelical nonconformists such as William Gadsby, and also in John Wesley and the legacy which he left for his more radical inheritors such as William Booth. On the other hand there is the world-avertive stream, which became particularly evident as a result of the French revolutionary wars, and was popular among evangelicals of the upper classes in that period. Their strong belief that there was nothing wrong with the British social order made possible the sort of pietism seen in the Keswick movement in which 'a tattling tongue, angry looks, viciousness on the croquet lawn [and] impatience with servants' were seen as the more serious sins to be overcome (see p. 262).

The final chapter by Peter Heslam, 'An appeal to moral imagination and commercial acumen: transforming business as a solution to poverty', takes us into the realm of practical or applied theology. Evangelicals from the Majority World, such as René Padilla, are very critical of the current world economic order dominated by free-market capitalism, and see the World Bank and the International Monetary Fund as instruments of oppression under the dominance of the rich and powerful West. Heslam argues that the free market is not all bad and that even big business can be a force for good when driven by a strong sense of social responsibility. In tune with Smith's article Heslam makes a case for attempting to transform business so that blessing the poor and needy becomes as important as profit.

Both the chapters that are specifically focused on the Bible, and a number of the historical and theological chapters, make a very strong case that there is no tension between the spiritual and the practical in the Scriptures. God's salvation encompasses humanity in its every aspect. So our proclamation of that salvation must address both the desperate spiritual need of a sinful humanity and the (often) desperate physical need that is all too apparent in the world in which we live. But that is not the end of the story. Some of the implications of accepting this clear biblical mandate are also explored in the historical and theological chapters. Whatever else we learn from these chapters we learn that there is theoretical and practical work yet to be done as we think and work under the dominion of he who as a result of his death and resurrection has been given all authority in heaven and earth. Our prayer is that this volume will be used to encourage the people of the Way to go further and higher in their service of the King of kings.

1. PROTECTING THE VULNERABLE: THE LAW AND SOCIAL CARE

David L. Baker

Two of the most important factors affecting prosperity in ancient Israel[1] were family relationships and access to land. Society was structured around the extended family, rather than the state; and in an agrarian society it was vital to own or have the use of agricultural land. Every member of the covenant community belonged to a family; and every family had land, allocated to the tribes and clans at the time of the Israelite occupation of Canaan.

If someone fell on hard times, another member of the family – designated as next of kin or 'redeemer' (*gō'ēl*) – was responsible for providing assistance (e.g. Lev. 25:25, 47–49; Ruth 2:20; 3:9; cf. Num. 5:8; 35:19; Jer. 32:7–8). Normally this would have been the nearest male relative, but others could take on the role by mutual agreement (Ruth 3:12–13; 4:1–12). If someone needed an emergency loan, another member of the covenant community was expected to help, without requiring interest and with sensitivity in asking for security (Exod. 22:25–27;[2] Lev. 25:35–38; Deut. 15:7–8; 23:19–20; 24:6, 10–13). If someone had to 'sell' part of their land, the law insisted that this could only be in the form of

---

1. I am using the term 'ancient Israel' to denote the society implied in the laws and described in the historical books of the OT, without entering into debates about the historicity of this society.

2. Verses 24–26 in Hebrew. In this article I use the verse numbering conventional in

a lease, as the land must be restored to its original owner in the jubilee year (Lev. 25:13–17, 25–28). If things got so bad that someone was unable to support his household, it was possible to pay a debt or raise capital by surrendering a family member to another household as a temporary slave, with guaranteed freedom after six years (Exod. 21:2–6). Alternatively, the household head, together with his family, could become a bonded labourer, with guaranteed freedom and restoration of land in the jubilee year (Lev. 25:39–43, 47–55). In these ways, the laws sought to provide for the present needs of impoverished farmers, and to ensure the eventual restoration of their ancestral land.[3]

However, even the best socio-economic system works imperfectly because there are people who do not fit into the system and so struggle for survival. In a patriarchal society, women and children who lose the head of their family are in a particularly vulnerable position. Widows and orphans are frequently mentioned together in the Old Testament (e.g. Job 22:9; 24:3; Ps. 68:5; 109:9; Isa. 1:17, 23; 9:17; Jer. 49:11; Lam. 5:3), often alongside resident aliens (Exod. 22:21–24; Deut. 10:18; 14:29; 16:11, 14; 24:17–21; 26:12–13; 27:19; Ps. 94:6; 146:9; Jer. 7:6; 22:3; Ezek. 22:7; Zech. 7:10; Mal. 3:5). They are also mentioned in conjunction with other vulnerable people such as Levites (Deut. 14:29; 16:11, 14; 26:12–13), hired workers (Mal. 3:5), and the poor in general (Job 24:3–4, 9; 29:12–13; 31:16–21; Isa. 10:2; Zech. 7:10). Before discussing the laws which regulate social care, it may be helpful to say a little more about the people for whom this care is intended.

Vulnerable people

A *widow* (*'almānâ*) in ancient Israelite society had not only lost her marriage partner, but as a result had lost her protector and source of sustenance. It appears widows had no inheritance rights and so were dependent on the goodwill of the extended family and the local community. While some widows did own property, or at least had use of it until their death (Job 24:3; Prov. 15:25), others were almost destitute (1 Kgs 17:10–12). Even if she was wealthy,

Footnote 2 (*Continued*)
English translations of the Bible, assuming that readers who know Hebrew will be aware of the differences.

3. For a more detailed study of the laws discussed in this chapter, together with ancient Near Eastern parallels and including many more references to secondary literature, see Baker, *Tight Fists or Open Hands?*

a widow would have been vulnerable to exploitation by the unscrupulous and needed special protection. If a widow had no sons, she would be in an especially precarious position (2 Sam. 14:4–7; 1 Kgs 17:20; cf. Luke 7:12). The law of levirate marriage (Deut. 25:5–10) was concerned primarily with producing an heir for a man who died without sons, to continue his line and inherit his land, and only secondarily to provide for the needs of the childless widow.[1]

The Hebrew word for *orphan* (*yātôm*) is generally taken to mean a child without a father, whether or not the mother is still alive, and so sometimes translated 'fatherless'. While the presence of a mother would be very important for a child's emotional well-being, the father would have been primarily responsible for provision of physical needs and so his death would leave a child in a particularly vulnerable position. Moreover, without their family head to represent them at the 'gate' (the local law-court in ancient Israel), widows and orphans could easily fail to receive their due share of the inheritance or be disadvantaged in other ways. In principle, another male from the extended family might take responsibility for them; but in practice, support from the extended family is likely to be less than from a husband and father.[2]

The term *resident alien* is the conventional scholarly translation of the Hebrew word *gēr* (e.g. NRSV; REB; cf. NIV; NJB). In fact, no single English word adequately covers the semantic range of the Hebrew. 'Stranger' (KJV) and 'foreigner' (TEV) are too general and say nothing about residence. 'Sojourner' (RSV) conveys the idea of temporary residence, but misses the hint of foreignness in the original and sounds quaint in modern English. One attractive suggestion is 'immigrant', which covers quite a few cases, but not that of Israelites who go to live in a different part of their own country, nor that of Canaanites who continue to live among the people of Israel. Another is 'refugee', but this implies an element of compulsion that is absent from the Hebrew. To use current terminology, these people might be described as 'ethnic minorities', who have distinctive racial or cultural traditions and are vulnerable to exploitation or discrimination by dominant groups in the population. This may be the best term when referring to groups, but it has no convenient singular form. Therefore, in the absence of any entirely satisfactory substitute, I use the conventional term 'resident alien'. I understand it to denote a free person who resides outside their native country or region, being

---

1. On widows in ancient Israel, see Hoffner, '*'almānâ*'; Hiebert, '"Whence Shall Help Come to me?"'; Carroll R., 'Widow'; Steinberg, 'Romancing the Widow'; Weisberg, 'The Widow of our Discontent'; Galpaz-Feller 'The Widow in the Bible'.
2. On orphans, see Ringgren, '*yātôm*'; Carroll R., 'Orphan'.

accepted by the host community and having certain rights but not regarded as a full citizen.[3]

Levites are distinct from the rest of the people of Israel: on the one hand because of their consecration to the service of God (Exod. 32:29; Num. 3:41, 45; Deut. 10:8; 33:8–10); and on the other because they receive no allotment of land (Num. 18:23b–24; 26:62; Deut. 10:9; 18:1–2) except for the pasture surrounding their cities (Num. 35:1–8; Lev. 25:32–34). Because they have relatively little land, they are to be supported by a share of the tithes and offerings of the people (Num. 18:21–24; Deut. 12:5–19; 14:22–29; 18:1–8; 26:12–13). This is probably implicit too in the instructions to include the Levites when celebrating the festivals (Deut. 16:11, 14; 26:11).[4]

Hired workers would generally be landless people, dependent on the availability of employment and reliant on fair treatment by employers (Deut. 24:14–15; cf. Lev. 25:6, 40, 50, 53). In an agrarian society they would be much more vulnerable than landowners (1 Sam. 2:5; Job 7:1–2; Jer. 22:13; Zech. 8:10; Mal. 3:5). Often work would be seasonal (Ruth 2), or dependent on a major building project (2 Chr. 24:12), or risky (Judg. 9:4; 2 Sam. 10:6; Jer. 46:21). Judging by the prohibition on taking part in Passover (Exod. 12:45), such workers may often have been foreigners.[5]

The *poor* are denoted in the laws by several Hebrew words.[6] These words do not refer to a clearly-defined social group, but simply to those in particular need of help from more prosperous members of the covenant community. Their situation is also recognized in ceremonial laws which provide alternatives for those who cannot afford the stipulated sacrifices and offerings (e.g. Lev. 5:7–13; 14:21–32).[7]

---

3. For a detailed discussion of the Hebrew terminology, see Baker, *Tight Fists*, ch. 7.1.b. On resident aliens, see Kellermann, '*gûr*'; van Houten, *The Alien in Israelite Law*; Bultmann, *Der Fremde im antiken Juda*; Burnside, 'The Status and Welfare of Immigrants'.

4. On Levites, see Nurmela, *The Levites*; Garrett, 'Levi, Levites'.

5. On hired workers, see Lipiński, '*śākar*'.

6. Especially '*ebyôn* ('poor, needy') and '*ānî* ('poor, humble, afflicted'), and occasionally *dal* ('poor, helpless') and *mûk* ('become poor').

7. I do not discuss here slaves and semi-slaves (temporary slaves, concubines, and bonded labourers). Although these groups of people in ancient Israel were vulnerable, they lived and worked within a particular household and the household-head was responsible for their welfare, so they did not need *social* care. Various laws were designed for their protection, on which see Baker, *Tight Fists,* chs. 5–6. There

Protection from abuse

The care of widows, orphans and resident aliens is dealt with in several Old Testament laws. According to the Book of the Covenant, God is concerned for the vulnerable and he warns Israelites of dire consequences if they do not show a similar concern. For example:

> You shall not oppress a resident alien, for you have been resident aliens in the land of Egypt. You shall not abuse any widow or orphan. If you do abuse one of them, and they cry out to me, I will certainly hear their cry. My anger will rage, and I will kill you with the sword; and your wives will become widows, and your children orphans[8] (Exod. 22:21–24).

First, the law prohibits oppression of resident aliens (v. 21), a prohibition which is repeated at the end of a section on judicial practice in Exodus 23 (vv. 1–3, 6–9). Whether in everyday life (22:21) or in a law-court (23:9), oppression on ethnic grounds is quite unacceptable. God's command is followed by a reminder of Israel's own experience of oppression as resident aliens in Egypt (cf. Exod. 3:9; Deut. 26:7). The exodus tradition made a lasting impression on the people of Israel, and resulted in a particular concern for ethnic minorities in their laws, unparalleled elsewhere in the ancient Near East. The descendants of Jacob had once been aliens in a foreign country. Over the centuries, their situation changed from a warm welcome to open hostility and ruthless exploitation. By God's mercy they were granted freedom and a land of their own; now they must be sympathetic to anyone else in a similar situation far from home. A parallel law is found in the Holiness Code (Lev. 19:33–34), which also cites Israel's experience in Egypt as the primary motivation for

---

were also other marginal people, for whom there are no specific laws of protection, such as infertile women (e.g. Gen. 11:30; 25:21; 29:31; Job 24:21), divorced women (Lev. 21:7, 14; 22:13; Num. 30:9; Ezek. 44:22), defiled women and prostitutes (Lev. 21:7, 14), illegitimate children (Judg. 11:1), and refugees. Israelites often became refugees in other countries (e.g. Gen. 27:41–28:5; Ps. 42:6; 1 Sam. 27:1–4; 1 Kgs 11:40; 2 Kgs 25:26; Jer. 40:11–12; 43:5–7) and there is one mention of foreign refugees in Israel (Jer. 50:28), but no laws relate specifically to their situation, apart from that on fugitive slaves (Deut. 23:15–16). Presumably these people would have been included in the general provisions for the poor.

8. I have made my own translations of Old Testament texts quoted in this article. For notes on these translations, see Baker, *Tight Fists*.

protecting resident aliens within the covenant community. Kindness cannot be enforced – since it is impractical to punish those who are unkind unless they break a specific law – so the motive clause is of great importance. (How far historical motivation like this is effective is another matter, and it is not uncommon for peoples who have suffered terribly to later turn and inflict suffering on others.)

The majority of resident aliens in Israel will have left their homes and moved to a new place because of hardship – famine or plague, oppression or war. On arrival, they will have had to find some way of making a living, and may have faced problems such as learning a new language and cultural adjustment. In general they are counted among the poor (cf. Lev. 19:10; 23:22), and are often the recipients of charity, though occasionally they seem to be well off (Lev. 25:47; cf. Deut. 28:43). In many ways resident aliens are integrated into the covenant community, but they remain marginal in two important respects: they own no land and so have no regular source of sustenance, and they have no family network to whom they can turn in a crisis. It would be convenient to ignore the needs of these people, but they are to be loved just like other members of the community (Lev. 19:18, 34), mirroring God's love for the vulnerable (Deut. 10:17–19).

Next, Exodus 22 turns to widows and orphans (vv. 22–24). There is a brief prohibition of abuse, followed by a warning that if abuse does occur and the abused cry to God, he will hear them, be angry, and punish the abuser. The Hebrew is quite emphatic, with a series of three infinitive absolutes (abuse, cry, hear). A loving God will be angry when those he loves are harmed; and the punishment he inflicts will fit the crime, as in the principle of *talion* (cf. Exod. 4:22–23; 21:23–25). A similar motive for keeping the law is given in Exodus 22:27, and in Deuteronomy 15:9 and 24:15.

At the time of the exodus, God is said to have heard the cry of the Israelites in Egypt (Exod. 2:23–25; 3:7–8), and in the messianic age he will take action against various crimes, including oppression of widows and orphans (Mal. 3:5). When Israel was oppressed, God took up her cause; but if Israelites become oppressors, they will make themselves enemies of God (cf. Prov. 22:22–23). According to Proverbs, God is concerned to maintain the boundaries of land belonging to widows and orphans (15:25; 23:10–11), and in the Psalms he is called the 'father of orphans and protector of widows' (Ps. 68:5; cf. 10:14, 18; 146:9). In an address to the divine council, God demands justice for orphans and other needy people (Ps. 82:3–4). The teaching of Jesus ben Sirach on prayer gives the assurance that God will not ignore the pleas of a widow or orphan who is wronged (Sirach 35:13–20).

Impartial justice

Threats and promises about divine judgment are only effective if people take them seriously and consider the long-term consequences rather than the short-term benefits of their behaviour. In practice, it seems, fear of God needs to be supplemented by human strategies for achieving a just society, and a key element in this is a sound legal system. Several Old Testament laws are concerned with judicial practice, often with particular emphasis on the need to protect the poor, since they are likely not to have the financial or intellectual resources to protect themselves. For example, we read in the Book of the Covenant as follows:

> You shall not pervert the justice [due to] the poor among you in their lawsuits. Keep far from a false charge; do not condemn the innocent and righteous, for I will not acquit the guilty (Exod. 23:6–7).

Three clauses prohibit perverting the course of justice (v. 6), accepting a false charge (v. 7a), and condemning the innocent (v. 7b). The first clause is concerned particularly with protection of the poor from abuse of legal power. The second clause is close in meaning to the prohibition of false testimony in verses 1–2 of the present chapter, but is addressed to the judge rather than the witness, instructing him to have nothing to do with a false charge. The third clause elaborates the dire consequences of perverting justice by making false charges and showing partiality in judgment. In ancient Israel, where capital punishment applied to many crimes, to convict an innocent person would often have been to condemn them to death (cf. Lev. 19:16; Deut. 27:25).

Finally, there is a brief motivation clause: 'I will not acquit the guilty' (v. 7c). This may be a warning to any judge who ignores this law, playing fast and loose with the truth, that he will one day have to face the divine Judge (cf. Prov. 17:15; Isa. 5:18–23). However, it could also be understood as an appeal to Israelite judges to be cautious in their sentences. In the absence of conclusive evidence, it is better to acquit someone who may be guilty than to condemn someone who may be innocent, since God himself will ensure that justice eventually prevails (cf. 1 Kgs 8:32; Mal. 3:1–5).

Some have claimed on the basis of texts like this that God is on the side of the poor, and it is true that the implementation of justice as envisaged here would be of great benefit to the poor and needy. However, it is more accurate to say that the biblical lawgiver portrays God as on the side of justice, and this rules out partiality both to the rich and the poor. This is stated explicitly a few verses earlier: 'And you shall not be partial to the poor[9] in their lawsuits' (Exod. 23:3); and also in the Holiness Code: 'You shall not act corruptly in judging [lawsuits]; you shall not show favouritism towards the poor, nor partiality towards the rich; with righteousness you shall judge your fellow' (Lev. 19:15). While there is clear divine authority for defending the rights of the poor, that does not mean they are always in the right. Judges and witnesses must be strictly impartial, and compassion for the poor is no justification for allowing them to break the law with impunity.

The book of Deuteronomy is also concerned with ensuring justice for the poor, specifically widows, orphans, and resident aliens. For example:

> You shall not pervert the justice [due to] a resident alien or orphan; and you shall not take a widow's garment as security for a loan. Remember that you have been a slave in Egypt, and the LORD your God has redeemed you from there; that is why I am commanding you to do this (Deut. 24:17–18).

Basic principles for just lawsuits – concerning witnesses, impartiality, and bribery – have already been made clear in Deuteronomy 16:18–20 and 19:15–21, and so are not repeated here. This law simply emphasizes the importance of implementing these principles for the benefit of the vulnerable. Orphans, widows and resident aliens have a right to both justice (v. 17a) and compassion (v. 17b). While it is reasonable for a creditor to ask for security on a loan, this has to be balanced with compassion for the poor person who needs the loan (cf. vv. 12–13). Like Exodus (22:21; 23:9) and Leviticus (19:34), Deuteronomy reminds Israel of their Egyptian experience as motivation for social care in their own society (v. 18; cf. 5:15; 10:19; 15:15; 16:12; 24:22).

However, the most fundamental theological basis for care of widows and orphans in the Deuteronomic laws is the nature of God. He is omnipotent and gracious, strong and loving, as emphasized in the introduction:

---

9. Some commentators have suggested emending 'and the poor' (*wdl*) in verse 3 to 'the great' (*gdl*). In view of the Book of the Covenant's concern to protect the weak, the prohibition of partiality to the poor is perhaps surprising, but the Bible often surprises its readers. There is no textual evidence for this emendation and therefore no good reason to emend a perfectly intelligible text just because it says something unexpected.

The LORD your God is God of gods and Lord of lords, the great God, mighty and awesome, who ... sees justice done for orphans and widows; and loves resident aliens, giving them food and clothing (Deut. 10:17–18).

Those who fail to imitate him in the matter of justice are subject to a curse, as noted in the conclusion: 'Cursed be anyone who perverts the justice [due to] a resident alien, orphan, or widow' (Deut. 27:19).

Provision of needs

In a predominantly agrarian society like ancient Israel, almost everyone was dependent on the land and its produce for survival. The equitable distribution of land at the outset of Israel's life in Canaan, and the restoration of mortgaged land to its original owners every fifty years, were designed to ensure that members of the covenant community could provide for the needs of their families. Inevitably, though, at the margins of society there were landless people who depended on work opportunities and charity provided by landowners to keep body and soul together. So the biblical laws encourage landowners to be generous with their produce, sharing it with those in need.

For example, in the Book of the Covenant, the law of the sabbatical year stipulates:

Six years you shall sow your land, and gather its produce; but the seventh [year] you shall let it rest and lie fallow so that the poor among your people may eat, and what they leave the wild animals may eat. You shall do the same with your vineyard and your olive grove (Exod. 23:10–11).

As human beings and animals rest on the seventh day (v. 12), so the land is to rest in the seventh year. While regular fallow years would have been essential to preserve the fertility of the land before the introduction of artificial fertilisers, efficient agriculture is not the main purpose of this law, at least in its canonical context. Rather, the specific purpose stated here is to provide food for the poor (v. 10). Another implied purpose is probably to honour God as the ultimate owner of the land (cf. Lev. 25:2, 4, 23). It may also be seen as a return of the land to its natural state, before human beings disturbed it by agriculture, when nomadic people and wild animals would have wandered freely to look for food.

Another example is the law of gleaning in the Holiness Code:

> When you reap the harvest of your land, you shall not reap to the very edge of your
> field; or gather the gleanings of your harvest. You shall not strip your vineyard bare,
> and the fallen grapes of your vineyard you shall not glean; you shall leave them for
> the poor and the resident alien. I am the LORD your God (Lev. 19:9–10; cf. 23:22).

The law consists of two double prohibitions, concerning fields and vineyards respectively. The first part of each prohibition instructs the farmer to deliberately leave part of his crop unharvested; the second part forbids him to go back after harvesting to gather grain or grapes which have been unintentionally missed. Next the purpose of the law is explained – to provide for the poor and the resident alien. Although such people have no land of their own, this law entitles them to a share of the harvest. Finally there is the characteristic theological refrain of the Holiness Code: 'I am the LORD your God.' The relevance of this refrain here may be seen by reference to Proverbs 22:23: 'For the LORD will plead their cause; and rob of life those who rob them.'

The same idea is expressed in greater detail in Deuteronomy 24:19–22, where the beneficiaries are to be resident aliens, orphans and widows. Farmers are given instructions on harvesting grain, olives, and grapes – the raw materials for the vital products of bread, oil, and wine (cf. Num. 18:12; Deut. 7:13; 11:14; 12:17; 14:23; etc.). The law concerning olives is unique to Deuteronomy, but the principle is the same as for grain and grapes. Two theological reasons are given for observing this law. First, looking to the future, those who are generous to others are promised the blessing of God in their own lives (v. 19b; cf. 14:29; 15:10, 18; 23:20). The second reason, looking to the past, is remembrance of slavery in Egypt (v. 22; cf. v. 18; also 15:15; 16:12). The Lord had mercy on the people of Israel, giving them freedom and a land to call their own; so they must always remember that the land and its harvest are theirs as a gift rather than a right. It follows that they too should be merciful to people in need, sharing the blessing they receive with others.

The right of the landless to glean, and the duty of landowners to facilitate this, is stipulated in both the Holiness Code and the Deuteronomic laws. This provision for the poor involves recipients in the work of gleaning, maintaining a balance between generosity and dignity. Landowners are not burdened with extra work in being generous to the poor, and the poor have the privilege of working to supply their needs. Donors do not decide who will receive their donation, as normally happens with modern charitable giving, but it is left to the poor to come and collect produce from the fields as they need. Some commentators have suggested that this passivity on the part of the donor is intended to emphasize that the land belongs to God, who has entrusted it to the whole covenant community for their sustenance, and therefore the landless have as much right to benefit from it as the land-owners (cf. Lev. 25:23).[10] They are entitled to a share of the harvest, not as charity, but because it is intended by God for them. In practice, however, most owners of land are likely to view its produce as their personal property, and the gleaning laws encourage them to be generous in sharing their harvest with those who have no land.

A third example is the Deuteronomic law of the triennial tithe:

> At the end of [every] three years you shall bring out all the tithe of your produce in that year; and you shall store it in your towns. Then the Levites may come, for they have no portion or inheritance with you, and the resident aliens and the orphans and the widows in your towns, and they shall eat and be satisfied; so that the LORD your God may bless you, in all the work of your hands which you do (Deut. 14:28–29; cf. 26:12–13).

Every third year the tithe is not to be taken to the central sanctuary, but stored in the towns (v. 28) and enjoyed by those who do not have land to grow their own food, specifically Levites, resident aliens, orphans and widows (v. 29a). The reference to storing implies that farmers would not distribute the whole tithe immediately, but rather keep it separate from their own supplies, perhaps in a public storehouse, and distribute it as required. In the arid climate of Palestine grain, wine and olive oil could be stored for several years (cf. Gen. 41:47–57; Lev. 25:20–22). In this way the poor would have provisions during the three-year period until the next 'year of the tithe'. As with other expressions of kindness to the poor in Deuteronomy, the people are assured that obedience to this rule will bring blessing in their own lives (v. 29b; cf. 15:4–5, 10, 18; 23:20; 24:19; 26:15).

Perhaps to avoid the impression that the holy institution of tithing has been secularized, the law is supplemented by a stipulation that after the farmer has distributed the tithed produce in accordance with the law (26:12), he must make a solemn declaration in the presence of God, probably at the central sanctuary on his next pilgrimage (v. 13). This declaration is completed by an assurance that the tithe has not been contaminated by improper handling (v. 14), and a prayer for God's continued blessing on his people as they live in the promised land (v. 15).

The triennial tithe was a major innovation compared with the conventional understanding of tithes in the ancient Near East and the Bible. In the ancient Near East tithes were taxes payable to the palace (Ugarit) or temple (Babylon), and none of the extant documents picture them as welfare. Almost all the other

---

10. Loewenberg, *From Charity to Social Justice*, pp. 93–94.

biblical references to tithing are concerned with gifts or payments to sanctuaries and their personnel (Gen. 14:20; 28:22; Lev. 27:30–33; Num. 18:21–32; 2 Chr. 31:4–21; Neh. 10:35–39; 12:44; 13:5, 12–13; Amos 4:4; Mal. 3:8–10).[11] But once every three years there is to be something quite different, and the tithe becomes the first known tax instituted for the purpose of social welfare.

This use of the tithe for social purposes is not secularization, but rather a recognition that one way of serving God is to serve the poor. Like other tithes and offerings, the triennial tithe in Deuteronomy is closely bound to the faith of Israel, even though it has no link with formal worship. So those who give the tithe thereby acknowledge God as the giver of the land; whereas those without an inheritance receive – as their share in the produce of the land – the 'holy portion' (Deut. 26:13) normally devoted to God.

Yet another example of the obligation to share harvest produce with the poor is given in Deuteronomy 23:24–25:

> When you go into your neighbour's vineyard, you may eat as many grapes as you wish to satisfy your hunger; but you shall not put [any] into your bag. When you go into your neighbour's standing grain, you may pluck ears with your hand; but you shall not put a sickle to your neighbour's standing grain.

In this unique law, undocumented in any other ancient Near Eastern sources, permission is given to eat food growing in a neighbour's vineyard or cornfield. The only limitation is that it must be to satisfy immediate hunger and produce is not to be taken home. The word 'neighbour' here refers to a fellow-Israelite, another member of the covenant community. It seems the law takes for granted the right of people to pass through others' fields and vineyards. Apparently this was not considered trespass, so long as no damage was caused (cf. Exod. 22:5–6).

This law would have obvious practical value for the poor. Landless people could eat as much as they want in the fields and vineyards, so long as they don't use a sickle or fill a vessel to remove produce from field. In this way all the riches of the land are made available to them, and all should have enough to eat. The needs of the hungry take precedence over the rights of private property, though not without limits.

However, the law also protects property owners. Limits are set on the prac-

---

11. The only exception is Samuel's warning about royal tithe-taxes, which are portrayed negatively and should not in any case be equated with the tithes prescribed in the laws (1 Sam. 8:15, 17).

tice of showing hospitality to passers-by, so that people do not take advantage of it to rob their neighbours. Privileges can be exploited, and this law forbids the removal of food from the vineyards and fields, thus recognizing farmers' property rights. They have worked hard to produce the harvest and – while they should be generous with it – they are not to be deprived of the bulk of it.

As with many other laws, the practicalities are humanitarian but the motivation is theological. The freedom to eat the produce of a neighbour's land is an illustration of the principle that the fruit of the land is a divine gift rather than a human right. The generosity expected of landowners is appropriate for members of the covenant community who have received their land from God and are dependent on his grace for its fruitfulness. As he blesses them, they are expected to share the blessing with others and in doing so they reflect something of God's own character.

Holidays and celebrations

As we have seen in the previous section, various Old Testament laws encouraged landowners in ancient Israel to share their harvest produce with those less fortunate than themselves. If these laws were obeyed, no-one would have gone hungry. However, the laws are not only concerned with ensuring physical survival. For example, they also recognize the importance of rest and worship.

First, everyone – including slaves, resident aliens, and even animals – is entitled and obliged to take a weekly day of rest:

> Remember the sabbath day, to keep it holy. Six days you shall labour, and do all your work. But the seventh day is a sabbath to the LORD your God; you shall not do any work, you or your son or your daughter, your male or female slave or your livestock, or your resident alien who is in your town (Exod. 20:8–10; cf. 23:12; Deut. 5:12–14).

Two main purposes are stated for sabbath observance. First, it is a holy day, dedicated to God, and so has a religious function. From this perspective, the cessation of work ensures that no-one is distracted from divine worship by other activities. Second, it is a holiday, providing rest and refreshment for tired workers, and so has a social function. Looked at in this way, work is stopped so that all may take a break from their labours and be renewed for the coming week. This aspect is designed primarily for the benefit of the poor, who need to work to earn a living or are forced to do so because of their status as slaves, rather than the wealthy who are free to choose when they work and how much time they spend on leisure activities.

Further, as repeatedly emphasized in the Deuteronomic laws, religious and agricultural celebrations should be enjoyed by all, not just the wealthy:

> You shall rejoice before the LORD your God – you, and your sons and your daughters, and your male and female slaves; and the Levites who [are] in your towns, because they have no portion or inheritance among you (Deut. 12:12; cf. v. 18).

> You shall rejoice before the LORD your God – you, and your son and your daughter, and your male and female slave, and the Levite who [is] in your town, and the resident alien and the orphan and the widow who [are] in your midst – in the place which the LORD your God chooses as a dwelling for his name (Deut. 16:11; cf. v. 14).

> You shall rejoice in all the good [things] that the LORD your God has given to you and to your household – you, and the Levite, and the resident alien who [is] in your midst (Deut. 26:11).

The whole community is to be involved in celebrating holidays and festivals: male and female, old and young, slave and free, clergy and lay people, native born and resident alien. In every case there is an emphasis on rejoicing, which includes both worship of God and a hearty communal meal (see also 12:7; 14:23, 26; 15:20; 27:7). Whereas Leviticus focuses primarily on the religious significance of sacrifices and festivals, Deuteronomy is particularly concerned with their social benefits. Holidays are not only for the elite, but to be enjoyed by slaves and other vulnerable people such as resident aliens, orphans and widows. There is a particular concern for the Levites in outlying towns, who have no allotment of agricultural land (10:9; 18:1–2) and are dependent on the generosity of others for their livelihood (cf. 12:19; 14:27, 29; 26:12), unlike the levitical priests at the central sanctuary who are provided for in the sacrificial system (18:1–8).

The specific celebrations mentioned are bringing first fruits of the harvest (26:1–11); tithes of produce, first born of livestock, and other offerings (12:10–12, 17–18); and the festivals of Weeks (16:9–12) and Booths (16:13–15). The main celebration which does not include specific reference to the vulnerable is Passover (16:1–8), though it is evident from the institution of this festival in Exodus that it was intended to include all members of the covenant community (12:3, 47; cf. Num. 9:10–13), including resident aliens and household slaves so long as they have been circumcised (Exod. 12:19, 44, 48–49; cf. Num. 9:14).

It is evident from these laws that both the weekly sabbath and the annual festivals are intended for the well-being of all members of the covenant community, alongside their primary purpose of facilitating the worship of God. There is a clear contrast in this matter between Israel and other parts of the ancient Near East. Although people would presumably have stopped work for the purpose of religious observance, no extant law collection outside the Old Testament actually legislates for holidays. Without such legislation, it is likely that many poor people elsewhere would have continued to work while the wealthy enjoyed their celebrations.

Conclusion

Ideally the role of the extended family in ancient Israel, and the distribution of land to all the tribes and clans, would have ensured that basic essentials for living were available to everyone in the community. Nevertheless, Old Testament law is realistic. Aware that there are inevitably marginal people who slip through the net of the socio-economic system, it includes a number of principles for social care:

- vulnerable individuals such as widows, orphans and resident aliens must be protected from oppression and abuse;
- justice should be administered impartially, irrespective of the litigant's social status and ability to pay;
- landowners are to be generous with their harvests, in order to provide for the needs of the poor;
- everyone, rich or poor, is entitled to enjoy a weekly day of rest and to participate in community celebrations.

It is noteworthy that these laws are addressed primarily to the covenant community, not the king. Social care is seen as the responsibility of individuals and families within the community rather than as a state provision. Kings are responsible for ensuring that justice is done (Ps. 72:1–14; cf. 2 Sam. 8:15; 14:4–11; 1 Kgs 3:9, 16–28; Prov. 29:14; Jer. 21:12), and expected to keep the laws themselves (Deut. 17:18–20), but are not portrayed as benefactors. King David once distributed food, but this was for a celebration and included all the people, not just the poor (2 Sam. 6:19).

How far these laws and principles were put into practice in ancient Israel is hard to tell. On the one hand, the impression we gain from the prophets is that it was common for widows and orphans, resident aliens and the poor, to be abused by the powerful (Jer. 7:6; 22:3; Ezek. 22:7; Zech. 7:10) and refused justice (Isa. 1:17, 23; 10:2; Jer. 5:28).[12] On the other hand, there may well have been many individuals who did practise social justice and show compassion to those in need, like Josiah (Jer. 22:15–16) and Nehemiah (Neh. 5). An example of gleaning is recounted in Ruth 2, and there are allusions to the practice elsewhere (Judg. 8:2; Jer. 6:9; 49:9). No records survive of the implementation of the triennial tithe, but there is one reference to a sabbatical year (Neh. 10:31). The right to eat produce when passing through other people's fields is not mentioned in Old Testament narratives, but it is certainly recognized in New Testament times (Matt. 12:1–8 par.). There are many references to observance of sabbath and other celebrations, but nothing specific to indicate how far the vulnerable were included. Evidently, there is much we do not know about the successes and failures of Israel in keeping their laws and maintaining a just and compassionate society.

However, more important than assessing Israel's track record in social care is to consider the contemporary relevance of these biblical principles. Vulnerable people such as the elderly, children and ethnic minorities still need protection from oppression and abuse. Even though the principle of impartial justice is acknowledged in theory, in practice social status and financial resources can have a significant effect on the outcome of legal proceedings, particularly in some countries. There may well be landowners who would like to be generous with their harvests, sharing them with the poor, but all too often agricultural policies make this difficult, especially in Europe.[13] Leisure time has expanded enormously in the modern world, but the divinely-ordained pattern of work and rest has been ignored. In Britain, for example, it is increasingly difficult to observe Sunday as a holy day, and many shops and businesses are now opening on national and religious holidays. While wealthy executives can take holidays when they choose, ordinary workers are often expected to work unsocial and irreligious hours.[14] These examples highlight some of the ways in which the Old Testament laws on social care are relevant to the societies in which we live today. Clearly, the principles enshrined in these biblical laws still need implementation in the twenty-first century.

---

12. For further discussion of the prophets and social care, see the following chapter in the present book.
13. See Baker, 'To Glean or Not to Glean', pp. 409–410, and references there.
14. See <http://www.keepsundayspecial.org.uk>.

Bibliography

BAKER, D. L., 'To Glean or Not to Glean . . .', *ExpTim* 117 (2006), pp. 406–410.

——, *Tight Fists or Open Hands? Wealth and Poverty in Old Testament Law* (Grand Rapids: Eerdmans, 2009).

BRIN, G., *Studies in Biblical Law: From the Hebrew Bible to the Dead Sea Scrolls* (JSOTSup, 176; Sheffield: Sheffield Academic, 1994).

BULTMANN, C., *Der Fremde im antiken Juda: Eine Untersuchung zum sozialen Typenbegriff ₂ger‹ und seinem Bedeutungswandel in der alttestamentlichen Gesetzgebung* (FRLANT, 153; Göttingen: Vandenhoeck & Ruprecht, 1992).

BURNSIDE, J. P., *The Status and Welfare of Immigrants: The Place of the Foreigner in Biblical Law and its Relevance to Contemporary Society* (Cambridge: Jubilee Centre, 2008).

CARROLL R., M. D., 'Orphan' and 'Widow' in *DOTP*, pp. 619–621 and 890–893.

DOMERIS, W. R., *Touching the Heart of God: The Social Construction of Poverty among Biblical Peasants* (Library of Hebrew Bible/Old Testament Studies, 466; New York and London: T&T Clark, 2007).

FENSHAM, F. C., 'Widow, Orphan, and the Poor in Ancient Near Eastern Legal and Wisdom Literature', *JNES* 21 (1962), pp. 129–139; repr. in J. L. CRENSHAW (ed.), *Studies in Ancient Israelite Wisdom* (New York: Ktav, 1976), pp. 161–171.

GALPAZ-FELLER, P., 'The Widow in the Bible and in Ancient Egypt', *ZAW* 120 (2008), pp. 231–253.

GARRETT, D. A., 'Levi, Levites', in *DOTP*, pp. 519–522.

HIEBERT, P. S., '"Whence Shall Help Come to me?" The Biblical Widow', in P. L. Day (ed.), *Gender and Difference in Ancient Israel* (Minneapolis: Fortress, 1989), pp. 125–141.

HOFFNER, H. A., "*almānâ*', in *TDOT*, vol. 1, 1972, pp. 287–291.

HOPPE, L. J., *There Shall Be No Poor among You: Poverty in the Bible* (Nashville: Abingdon, 2004); revision and expansion of *Being Poor: A Biblical Study* (Wilmington: Glazier, 1987).

VAN HOUTEN, C., *The Alien in Israelite Law* (JSOTSup, 107; Sheffield: Sheffield Academic, 1991).

KELLERMANN, D., '*gûr*', in *TDOT*, vol. 2, 1973, pp. 439–449.

LIPIŃSKI, E., '*śākar*', in *TDOT*, vol. 14, 1992, pp. 128–135.

LOEWENBERG, F. M., *From Charity to Social Justice: The Emergence of Communal Institutions for the Support of the Poor in Ancient Judaism* (New Brunswick: Transaction, 2001).

LOHFINK, N. L., 'Poverty in the Laws of the Ancient Near East and of the Bible', *Theological Studies* 52 (1991), pp. 34–50.

NURMELA, R., *The Levites: Their Emergence as a Second-Class Priesthood* (South Florida Studies in the History of Judaism, 193; Atlanta: Scholars, 1998).

PLEINS, J. D., *The Social Visions of the Hebrew Bible: A Theological Introduction* (Louisville: Westminster John Knox, 2001).

PORTEOUS, N. W., 'The Care of the Poor in the Old Testament', in J. I. McCORD and T. H. L. PARKER (eds.), *Service in Christ* (Barth Festschrift; London: Epworth, 1966), pp. 27–36; repr. in *Living the Mystery* (Oxford: Blackwell, 1967), pp. 143–155.

RINGGREN, H., '*yātôm*', in *TDOT*, vol. 6, 1982, pp. 477–481.

SCHLUTER, M., 'Welfare', in M. SCHLUTER and J. ASHCROFT (eds.), *Jubilee Manifesto: A Framework, Agenda & Strategy for Christian Social Reform* (Leicester: IVP, 2005), pp. 175–195.

STEINBERG, N., 'Romancing the Widow: The Economic Distinctions between the *'almana*, the *'iššā-'almana* and the *'ešet-hammet*', in J. H. ELLENS *et al.* (eds.), *God's Word for Our World*, vol. 1 (de Vries Festschrift; JSOTSup, 388; London: T&T Clark, 2004), pp. 327–346.

WEISBERG, D. E., 'The Widow of Our Discontent: Levirate Marriage in the Bible and Ancient Israel', *JSOT* 28 (2004), pp. 403–429.

VAN WIJK-BOS, J. W. H., *Making Wise the Simple: The Torah in Christian Faith and Practice* (Grand Rapids: Eerdmans, 2005).

2. FAILING THE VULNERABLE: THE PROPHETS AND SOCIAL CARE

M. Daniel Carroll R.

The prophetic literature has long been recognized as a source for social concern. In the late nineteenth and early twentieth centuries, some argued that the original message of the Old Testament prophets was best understood as essentially the demand for justice. This, they claimed, represented the purest form of faith in God. It was an 'ethical monotheism', defined by the transcendent moral ideals of Yahweh and unencumbered by ritual.[1] This position is now understood to be incomplete, but it does demonstrate a keen awareness of the centrality of morality in the work and words of the biblical prophets. Today, it is not uncommon to characterize a ministry or preaching as 'prophetic' if these activities emphasize issues of justice. Modern theological movements, such as Latin American and African-American liberation theologies, also have appealed to the prophets to ground their critique of society and their hope for a different tomorrow.

This chapter explores the message of social concern in the prophetic literature and is divided into three parts. The first provides evidence of the comprehensiveness of the social, economic and political interests in these books. The second section emphasizes the centrality of ethics for the worship

---

1. An early articulation of this position is Wellhausen, *Prolegomena*. Note, e.g., pp. 55–60, 470–488.

of Yahweh. God will not accept a religion from a people who do not demonstrate compassion for the needy or who allow national ideologies to skew their understanding of his person. Third, and last, we turn to the future hope of the prophets. Theirs was a vision of justice and peace for the people of God and for the entire world. It was, in other words, an ethical hope.

The breadth of the prophetic concerns

Prophets and prophetic oracles were not unique to Israel. Across Mesopotamia these types of figures played a prominent role in the religion and politics of many nations. Archaeological discoveries, particularly at Mari (eighteenth century BC) and several sites in ancient Assyria (seventh century BC), have established multiple parallels with the kinds of things that we read about God's prophets in the Old Testament. Nevertheless, there is a major difference between the prophets of these other cultures and those of Israel, and this distinction lies precisely at that point which is the topic of this essay. The Hebrew prophets are matchless in the fundamental priority of social concern in their message. This is not to say that there was no critique of sociopolitical structures and economic oppression in other places; there was.[2] It is to maintain, however, that there is no comparing their prominence in the consciousness of Israel's prophets.

There are several well-known passages that demonstrate the centrality of social justice for the prophets.[3] Perhaps the most celebrated is Amos 5:24: 'But let justice roll on like a river, righteousness like a never-failing stream!' Others include, for example, Isaiah 1:16–17, Jeremiah 22:15–16, Hosea 6:6 and Micah 6:8. Each in its own way powerfully conveys that Yahweh expects his people – especially the leadership – to care for the needy and not to exploit their helplessness for personal gain. 'Expects' is too bland a description; 'demands' surely is more fitting. A strong commitment to these matters permeates the prophetic corpus. The repeated challenges to heed God in these matters or face divine judgment are communicated with startling passion and pathos.[4]

---

2. For examples of social concern, see the letters of Nur-Sîn to Zimri-Lim (A.1121 + A. 2731 and A. 1968) in Nissinen, *Prophets and Prophecy*, pp. 17–22.

3. For full treatments see, e.g., Sicre, '*Con los pobres de la tierra*'; Dempsey, *Hope Amid the Ruins*. It should be noted that Dempsey is quite critical of certain aspects of the message of the prophets.

4. The classic expression of this is Heschel, *The Prophets*; cf. Carroll R., 'A Passion for Justice and the Conflicted Self'.

Social sensitivity and obligation, in other words, are not an ancillary part of what the prophets spoke about. They are a substantive part of their message, which arises from the very core of their soul. We ignore this at our peril.

One readily accessible means of grasping the importance of these issues is through a study of significant terms like 'justice' (*mišpāṭ*) and 'righteousness' (*ṣĕdāqâ*).[5] The insistence on 'justice' and 'righteousness' is ubiquitous, and the two terms often are paired (e.g., Isa. 33:5; Jer. 9:23–24). Both are grounded in the conviction that the proper ordering of society should reflect God's moral constitution of life itself. Equitable laws, humane socioeconomic structures, right behaviour, and attitudes of mercy, incarnate divine demands in diverse ways. In other words, 'justice' and 'righteousness' are not abstract notions, divorced from the realities of everyday life. It was the duty of Israel's kings to rule according to this vision (Jer. 21:11–12; 22:1–5, 13–17) and of society to reflect this ethos in all of its interactions and relationships. That is why the various victims of injustice also are prominent in prophetic texts: the widow, orphan, alien (or resident foreigner), and the poor.[6] Once again, pertinent terms occur together repeatedly. The combination 'widows and orphans' appears, for instance, in Isaiah 1:17, 23; 9:17. Aliens are listed with them as another vulnerable group that is unable to withstand the vicissitudes of fate and circumstance (Jer. 7:6; 22:3; Ezek. 22:7, 29; Zech. 7:10; Mal. 3:5).

To list these kinds of verses is a helpful exercise for becoming more acquainted with the heart of the prophets and of God. An awareness of the sheer number of these passages, the force of their rhetoric and the breadth of people within their compass alerts the reader to the vital importance of social justice. But, there is much more that can be gleaned from these books. Recent research has explored other key dimensions of the prophetic message that can contribute to our appreciation of what God insists on in this arena. The following discussion mentions two: sociological studies, which attempt to identify the systemic mechanisms of injustice in ancient Israel, and virtue ethics.

Sociological approaches to prophetic social concern

In the last three decades a number of scholars have attempted to uncover with more specificity those political policies and socioeconomic structures that generated the inequities that the prophets decry. Their goal has been to explore

---

5. See, e.g., Gossai, *Justice, Righteousness and the Social Critique*; Nardoni, *Rise Up, O Judge*.
6. There are several terms for the poor in Hebrew, each of which, some argue, has a different nuance. See Pleins, 'Poor, Poverty'; Schwantes, *Das Recht der Armen*, pp. 16–52; Domeris, *Touching the Heart of God*, pp. 14–26.

the possible concrete, interrelated factors – both national and international – that eventually brought the judgment of God and led to the demise of Judah and Israel. What were the tangible dynamics that led to this immoral state of affairs? Knowledge of them would provide a more realistic backdrop to the prophets' words. They could provide greater precision to more general terms, like 'injustice', 'exploitation', and 'oppression'.

Different models have proposed a variety of explanations of how the economy in fact worked in ancient Israel, the identity and conditions of social classes, and the role of the monarchy and its bureaucracy. Social science theories and archaeological data play a prominent role in these efforts.[7] Of course, these are all tentative reconstructions. We are at a far remove from that time, place and culture. This is not the venue to evaluate these hypotheses, but it can be illuminating to cite some of the features of that ancient world that the studies highlight.

To start with, it is important to recognize that the shape of government changed over the centuries. The biblical text recounts a long history and offers hints of the social changes that arose over time. Moral problems and dilemmas would vary at different points of this trajectory. Clearly, the creation of the monarchy forever changed life in Israel. With David and Solomon came a growing complexity in government quite unlike the undeveloped regime of Saul. What had once been a tribal coalition became a formal state. A professional standing army was formed and mercenaries hired (2 Sam. 23:8–39), a bureaucracy employed (2 Sam. 8:15–18; 1 Kgs 4:1–6), a taxation system set up (1 Kgs 4:7–19; 12:4), and forced labour instituted for building projects (1 Kgs 9:15–23; 12:4, 18). David took Jerusalem, and with Solomon began to transform it into a classic ancient Near Eastern capital, complete with palaces and a national central sanctuary – the temple (1 Kgs 5 – 8). International trade began to grow (1 Kgs 9:26–28; 10:14–15, 22–29). Eventually, the need for exports probably led to crop specialization (such as for the production of olive oil) and the growth of *latifundia* (large agricultural estates), the birth of markets, the rise of influential merchants, and international trade agreements. Economic developments and political decisions profoundly shaped the social realities of Israel before and after the division of the united monarchy. This 'progress' often brought negative consequences, which would have exacerbated the recurring

---

7. For summaries and evaluations from different perspectives, see Fleischer, *Von Menschenverkäufern, Baschankühen und Rechtsverkehren*; Gottwald, *Politics of Ancient Israel*, pp. 185–235; Houston, *Contending for Justice*, pp. 18–51; Domeris, *Touching the Heart of God*.

hardships wrought by drought, pestilence or disease that were so common in the ancient world. Configurations of power, influence and wealth very unlike what had characterized the people of God at the beginning of their sojourn in the land now became the realities of life. The peasants would have been the ones to suffer most acutely from these developments.

Foreign policy also had an effect. Judah and Israel fought a series of wars and endured invasions. The cost – both monetarily and in human life – of these armed conflicts was huge: the destruction of cities and the national infrastructure, the pressures of paying annual tribute, the loss of life, the maiming of able-bodied men and the suffering of those left behind (the widows and orphans), the influx of refugees, and the negative impact on agriculture and the rest of the economy. Of course, the poor bore a disproportionate share of this privation.

The book of Amos, from the middle of the eighth century BC, wrestles with many of these issues.[8] What is denounced in its pages covers a spectrum of abuse. Those unable to repay loans are sold into debt slavery (2:6; 8:6). The courts are rife with corruption, as justice goes to the highest bidder (2:7; 5:10, 12). The collectors of taxes profit from what is extracted from the general population (5:11), and creditors seize the distraints of the powerless and flaunt their gain (2:8b). The wealthy live a life of indulgence at the expense of others (2:8a; 3:15–4:1; 6:4–7; 8:4–6).[9] Israel appears to have been engaged in border wars, fighting off attacks from several directions in the recent past or during the days of Amos himself (1:3–13; 4:10). Whatever victories the monarchy might have trumpeted were insignificant (6:13; cf. 7:2, 5). Any national ideology of victory was a mockery of the actual state of affairs. The condemnation of warfare is not limited to what Israel initiated or endured. God also is exercised by the cruelty exhibited by the surrounding peoples: torture (1:3), the trafficking of those captured in battle as slaves (1:6, 9), the unrestrained viciousness of combat (1:11, 13), and the lack of respect for the dead (2:1).

It is difficult to identify the perpetrators of this host of injustices within Israel. The fact that the royal citadels of Samaria are singled out for judgment would indicate that at the very least those in the government administration are

---

8. Sicre, 'Con los pobres de la tierra', pp. 87–168; Houston, Contending for Justice, pp. 58–73. Social ethics has long been a key topic in Amos research; for a survey see Carroll R., Amos – The Prophet and His Oracles.

9. 6:4–7 most likely portrays a marzēaḥ feast, a ritual of excess that was widespread in the ancient world. For the marzēaḥ, see especially McLaughlin, The Marzēaḥ in the Prophetic Literature.

involved (3:9–11).[10] This is not surprising in terms of military decisions and tax collection. The denunciation of the judicial process most likely points to corrupt judges or elders at the city gates. Certain merchants or wealthy land-owners could very well have been the ones manipulating prices of goods, and they and some in government employ may have benefited from the defaulted loans and foreclosures to expand their own land holdings. It is even possible that a few of those lower down the social scale were taking advantage of others below them – the desperate times had tainted everyone. The victims are equally hard to identify with certainty. They are labelled the 'righteous' (2:6; 5:12), the 'poor' and 'needy' (2:6–7; 4:1; 5:11). Many of them could have been landless peasants or others on the brink of disaster for any number of reasons.

The language of injustice in the book of Amos is quite emotive: 'trample' (2:7; 8:4), 'unrest' (3:9, ESV 'tumults'), 'hoard plunder and loot' (3:10), 'crush' (4:1), 'oppress' (4:1; 5:12, ESV 'afflict'). Justice had been turned into 'bitter-ness' (5:7, ESV 'wormwood') and 'poison' (6:12). For the most part, those who violate Yahweh's ethical values are nameless. They are associated with actions, as 'they', 'those who', or 'you' (2:6–8; 3:10; 4:1; 5:7, 10–12; 6:1, 3–7; 8:4–6); that is, these individuals stand out because of what they do more than for who they are. This terminology also implies more than destructive actions; it reflects prejudicial attitudes towards the less fortunate and the lust for prestige and prosperity.

What can be gleaned from all of this? First, to speak about and to try to deal with issues of social justice requires realism. Injustice and inequalities arise from tangible socioeconomic and political decisions, practices and organiza-tions, as well as from governmental policies at home and abroad. The prophets mention all of these factors. They were not social scientists or political ana-lysts, so they do not provide as much detail of the particulars of oppression that we would like. Nonetheless, there is no doubting that the prophets were struck by the cruel contradictions of their world and by the cries of the des-titute and powerless. They knew that what they saw and heard did not please God and would bring his wrath.

A second, and interesting, legacy that can be drawn from the prophets concerns their literary style.[11] While the vague descriptions of their targets can

---

10. The most detailed study of the officials who are the target of the prophet is Jaruzelska, *Amos and the Officialdom*.

11. The concern here is distinct from those rhetorical studies that focus on the strategies used to persuade the original audiences (see Möller, *A Prophet in Debate*, pp. 2–60). For the continuing impact of the literary features of the Old Testament,

be frustrating, at the same time that very imprecision allows their relevance to extend beyond their day. The mechanisms of twenty-first-century injustice are very unlike those of ancient Israel in their details, but the moral vision remains. The 'they', 'you' and 'those who' have different faces and names today, and oppression takes dissimilar forms. But, oppression is still oppression, and exploitation remains exploitation. Equally, the divine demands continue, even if they must be expressed and lived out in other ways in our modern context. The prophetic books serve to attune our conscience to God's values and to those whom he champions.

Virtue ethics and prophetic social concern

God desires that humanity in general and his people in particular deal justly with those in need. Yet, the expectation for those who claim to follow him entails more than *doing justice*; they also must be *a just people*. This understand-ing of prophetic social concern turns our attention to what has been called virtue ethics.

Unlike other currents within philosophical ethics, which tend to concen-trate on decision-making and behaviour, virtue ethics focuses on character.[12] The purpose of a virtue ethics is to shape the habits, attitudes and intentions of a person or a people so that they will be able to live a singular kind of life, one marked by integrity and consistency. With this firm foundation, these persons are equipped to discern the best course of action within a specific circumstance. There are at least three components of this view of ethics that are pertinent to the topic of this chapter.

First is the concept of the 'good'. The 'good' is that supreme and abso-lute end that should define our existence as individuals – or as the people of God. To achieve this transcendent good is to realize the supreme purpose in life. A second element that requires definition is the term 'virtue'. Virtues are those dispositions which one must possess in order to embody the 'good'.

---

note, e.g., Brueggemann, *Theology of the Old Testament*. Narrative ethics and its view of the role of the text in ethical formation is useful for prophetic literature as well (Parry's *Old Testament Story and Christian Ethics* is a good introduction to the combination of a careful literary reading with narrative ethics). For reflections on Amos, see Carroll R., *Contexts for Amos*, pp. 140–175, 278–306; *Amos – The Prophet and His Oracles*, pp. 53–72.

12. For helpful introductions to virtue ethics from a Christian perspective, see Hauerwas, *Peaceable Kingdom*; Murphy, Kallenberg and Thiessen Nation (eds.), *Virtues and Practices*; Gilman, *Fidelity of the Heart*.

Historically, the virtues have been classified into two groups: the four cardinal virtues (prudence, justice, courage and temperance) and the three theological virtues (faith, hope and charity – or love). To possess these virtues is to have acquired the requisite skills of moral reasoning and to be able to exhibit those habits of behaviour commensurate with the 'good'. These are not natural traits. They are the fruit of a process of education in the virtues and their sustained practice. The third and last component is the setting of the community. Every community, or social grouping, decides for itself what the 'good' is for its members and moulds them in accordance to it. The community trains its people in how to think, feel and live. Character for religious communities is oriented by an established set of traditions and sacred texts, which explain what life is like and what is its end. Furthermore, every community has exemplars which it holds up for others to emulate. These are those individuals who serve as the best models of the desired attitudes and actions.

Each of these three features finds its counterpart in the prophetic message. Amos is a case in point.[13] Twice the 'good' is mentioned (5:14–15). Israel is called to 'seek' it and 'love' it. At one level, the 'good' is defined by its opposite: it is not 'evil'. In the immediate context, this evil is the injustice of dishonest judicial proceedings and irregular tax collections (5:10–13). In the broader scope of the book all the other injustices would be included. The connection of the 'good' with God is underscored in the passage by the repetition of the extended divine name and title, 'LORD God Almighty'. The counterpart to 5:14–15 within 5:1–17 is 5:4–6, where the people are commanded to seek Yahweh.[14] This reinforces the fundamental fact that God is their true good, and he is the one behind the moral good that should distinguish Israel's society.

Justice is one of the cardinal virtues, and it is central to the message of Amos. In the original Hebrew, the famous text of 5:24 is structured as a chiasm, a literary device that draws attention to its centre: 'and let roll down like water *justice*, and *righteousness* like an ever-flowing stream.' The visual picture generated by these words also is significant. In a land where ravines and river beds are dry for long stretches, Yahweh declares that justice should surge like a flow of water that never runs dry. 'Justice' and 'righteousness' occur together again in 5:7 and 6:12. The structure of both of these verses in Hebrew is chiastic as well. Instead of highlighting what God intends as in 5:24, these

---

13. Carroll R., 'Seeking the Virtues among the Prophets'.

14. 5:1–17 is a chiasm, or inverted structure. Vv. 14–15 parallel vv. 4–6. For a thorough discussion of chiasm and other literary structures in Amos, see Möller, *A Prophet in Debate*, pp. 47–103.

two verses describe and structurally emphasize Israel's perversion of justice: 'Those who turn to wormwood *justice*, and *righteousness* to the ground throw' (5:7); 'For they turn to poison *justice*, and the *fruit of righteousness* to bitterness' (6:12). Justice is no longer regarded as desirable or valuable; it is detested and disregarded. This attitude is supremely evident in the treatment of the poor by those with means and status.

The book of Amos again and again recalls the traditions of Israel, especially the exodus.[15] This event was the greatest manifestation of God's grace (2:10); it should have motivated the nation to obey him and replicate that mercy towards others. Now that momentous event will be used against them. They are without excuse (3:1–2). Election did not render them immune from judgment! That experience also did not mean that Yahweh was not involved in the histories of other peoples (9:7). What is more, he had sent them exemplars, the prophets and Nazirites, but the nation had tried to silence the one and compromise the other (2:11–12; cf. 3:7). Amos himself was rejected and accused of sedition by the high priest, Amaziah – he who, above all, should have been most sensitive to the voice of Yahweh (7:10–13). Israel had not acted according to the will of God and was not the kind of people they had been chosen to be.

Virtue ethics makes it clear that, then as now, appropriate social concern is more than determining what should be done on behalf of the less fortunate. Communities of faith must grasp the nature of the good, pursue the virtues and plumb the Scripture in order to know better what it means to be a people pleasing to God. Within their midst will be those who will show the way toward that flowing stream of justice.

The centrality of social ethics for worship

The prophets are vociferous in their critique of worship, especially in its relationship to social morality.[16] Important passages include Isaiah 1:10–20;

---

15. In addition to historical traditions, the prophets appealed to the covenant and law, wisdom, and the cult. Scholars disagree as to which traditions lie behind each prophetic message. The classic study of these traditions in the prophetic literature is von Rad, *Old Testament Theology*. For Amos, see Carroll R., *Amos – The Prophet and His Oracles*, pp. 12–18.

16. For what follows, see Dempsey, *Hope Amid the Ruins*, pp. 107–117; Wright, *Old Testament Ethics*, pp. 45–46, 374–378; Williams, '"La justicia seguirás"'; Carroll R., 'Can the Prophets Shed Light on Our Worship Wars?'.

58:1–14; Jeremiah 7:1–29; Hosea 6:4–6; Amos 4:4–13; 5:4–6, 18–27; and Micah 6:6–8. All of these denounce religious celebrations for the lack of concern for the needy. Why is ethics connected to worship?

The antagonism of the prophets towards ritual is not based on some sort of anti-clerical or anti-liturgical bias. Religion without ritual, holy places and religious personnel would have made no sense in the ancient world. Instead, the key for appreciating their point of view is to recognize the crucial role that religion can play in how people perceive and organize their social world. This is evident in at least two ways. On the one hand, through its ceremonies and symbols at its holy places a religion can serve to legitimate a certain worldview, a society's institutions and socioeconomic structures, and its government's ideology and policies. These arrangements thereby appear to the people not only as natural but also as sanctified by the deity. God wills that things be the way they are. On the other hand, religion can also be compartmentalized and disconnected from other areas of life. It then becomes just a duty to perform without any reflection on whether it relates at all to social life, or it is reduced to a personal sensory experience that meets human religious inclinations.

These dimensions of religious life and practice serve to explain why the prophets attack so harshly the religious ideas and activities of the people of God. This society claimed Yahweh as its national god. They were convinced that he was committed to blessing and protecting the life they knew. The problem was that God abhorred what was going on inside that world. He 'hated' and 'despised' any religious activity divorced from justice (Amos 5:21). To praise Yahweh as the one who supposedly upheld and defended this detestable state of affairs was a mockery and a contradiction. It was ultimately to worship another deity – to be sure, one who carried the same name, but one who was very different from the true God. This set of beliefs, the abuses it permitted, and its effects on the disadvantaged drew his outrage. It was the worst form of idolatry.[17]

Theirs was a religion disconnected from what was happening all around them, from the concrete problems of the real world. Worshippers were convinced that they were meeting Yahweh at the sanctuaries and celebrated his goodness, but their adoration was more about satisfying their own religious impulses than pleasing God. They did not know him as he actually is (Amos 4:4–13). On several occasions the prophets condemn a comprehensive list of

---

17. It is common to limit idolatry to the worship of other gods. That aspect of idolatry, which is also condemned by the prophets, is not the topic of this essay. For a thoughtful discussion on idolatry, see Wright, *The Mission of God*, pp. 136–188.

religious activities: all kinds of sacrifices, the prayers and singing. None of these were acceptable in Yahweh's sight; they were but misguided gestures offered to a false god, who did not demand care for the poor (Isa. 1:11–15; Amos 5:21–23). For many – the elite as well as the masses – the experiences at the sanctuaries, above all the principal shrines such as those at Jerusalem and Bethel, seemed to reinforce gloriously that God was on their side and behind their king (Jer. 7:1–11; Amos 7:10–13). But such was not the case. He had decreed judgment, and this would begin at the sanctuaries themselves (Jer. 7:12–15; 26:1–9; Amos 5:4–6; 8:3–6; 9:1). The prophets railed against the religious leaders, too, for they led the people horribly astray, never questioning the optimistic national ideology of victory and the injustices of the status quo (Isa. 1:21–31; Jer. 6:13–15; Amos 7:16–17; Mic. 3:5–12).

Yahweh was willing even to destroy the religious life of his people and their places of worship rather than to allow the charade to continue and his person to be misrepresented. His name was at stake. The prophets looked forward to a time when worship would be made new in an exalted Zion. Then the entire world would come to learn the ways of Yahweh and praise him. Peace and plenty finally would come with the universal reign of Almighty God (Isa. 2:1–5; 12:1–6; 66:18–24; Ezek. 40 – 44; Hag. 2:6–9; Zech. 14:16–21).

From the prophetic point of view, it is impossible to profess to worship Yahweh and not exhibit care for others. In addition, to blindly accept that God supports socioeconomic and political policies and systems without question, simply because a people take for granted that they are better than others or that they are believers blessed of God, and to praise him accordingly, are at profound odds with divine revelation. In a day when worship can focus so much on feelings and personal problems or desires, to the exclusion of severe social conditions and world crises, the clarion call of those ancient spokespersons of Yahweh needs to be heeded. Only then can worship be directed properly to and – more importantly – be accepted by God. The hope of the Old Testament is that one day all will worship in spirit and truth to his glory.

The hope for a better world

The allusion to the future provides a transition to this third section. Believers always have demonstrated a keen interest in what lies ahead. Of course, the prophets do, too, but not surprisingly their view of the future has a decidedly ethical emphasis.

In the prophetic literature we generally find announcements of two distinct futures – a near future of doom that is looming on the horizon, which will be

God's punishment primarily on his people, and a more distant future of world judgment to be followed by the restoration of his people and the entire globe. The imminent disaster which the prophets proclaim is God's negation of the present situation. It is the divine pronouncement that the economic injustices, social oppression, judicial corruption, and political machinations at home and abroad are intolerable. The society, government and religious life as Israel knows it will not be allowed to continue. This vision of the proximate future, in other words, reveals in a very graphic way the essential ethical commitments of God. His judgment is a moral one.

There are multiple examples of this truth. For instance, Isaiah pronounces a series of woes upon those who wrongly aggrandize their property and arrogantly pervert justice, and heralds Yahweh's punishment (5:8–30; cf. 10:1–2). Micah declares a woe on those who illegally gain riches (2:1–5) and censures those who heartlessly mistreat others and overturn any semblance of morality. Because of these transgressions, bloody Jerusalem will suffer at the hands of a cruel invader (3:1–4, 9–12; 6:9–7:6). By proclaiming that Yahweh roars from Zion in Judah and not from Samaria, Israel's capital, and the northern sanctuaries, the opening lines of Amos affirm that that oppressive society and its monarchy are illegitimate (1:2). Israel, like all the other nations, will suffer defeat and exile (2:14–16; 3:9–4:3; 5:14–20, 27; 6:1–7). Whatever hope exists for the nation cannot lie with the dynasty of Jeroboam (7:7–17; cf. 9:11–15).

In a series of publications Walter Brueggemann has developed the concept of the 'prophetic imagination'.[18] This prophetic imagination has two primary tasks. The first is to offer the kind of discourse that allows for the pain of the oppressed and the anger of God to be voiced. This is the articulation of disillusionment and reproof. The many metaphors for God (such as the lion or the disappointed parent and spouse)[19] and the impassioned accusations of the prophets are expressions of the prophets' responsibility to critique the dominant socioeconomic and political reality, which controlled the way the people understood the world and its workings. This first task is exemplified in the observations of the preceding paragraph.

18. Note his foundational work *The Prophetic Imagination*, as well as *Theology of the Old Testament*, pp. 622–649; cf. Carroll R., 'The Power of the Future in the Present.'

19. Work on metaphor in the prophetic literature has been prominent in books such as Hosea. Note, e.g., Landy, 'In the Wilderness of Speech'; Oestreich, *Metaphors and Similes for Yahweh*. For an accessible discussion with detailed notes, see Sandy, *Plowshares and Pruning Hooks*; cf. Brueggemann, *Theology of the Old Testament, passim*.

The other aspect of the prophetic imagination is to present visions of an alternative reality, where all will be made right. This view of a world beyond the oppressive present and after the coming disaster can energize the faithful with hope and encourage them to persevere until the end. This imaginative construal pushes the people of God past the grim present and the unsettling prospects of what is soon to occur, to a brighter time. The vision is an ethical one. Yet, whereas the message of impending judgment portrays God acting against injustice, the proclamation of this more glorious age shows him reversing human misery and affliction and bringing peace and plenty into every realm of human existence.

The biblical text very self-consciously contrasts this divine hope with what the people of God were experiencing at the time. The book of Isaiah, for instance, conveys some of these expectations. Chapter six presents an impressive scene with Yahweh seated on a throne. He is the unrivalled celestial King, who commands hosts of angels that wait to do his bidding (6:1–4; cf. 66:1). Yet the surrounding chapters mention other kings as well. There is the notice that Uzziah, one of the more successful kings of Judah, has died (6:1). His grandson Ahaz now rules, but he is lacking in faith and is not strong enough either to trust in God or face his enemies. He is under attack from the kings of Israel and Syria-Aram (7:1–9; cf. 2 Kgs. 16). According to Yahweh's sovereign will, Ahaz's refusal to believe in Yahweh's protection and his appeal to Assyria ensure that the armies of that evil empire under the command of its proud king will come and devastate the land (7:10–8:8). In chapters 6 – 11 there is the mention of still another king – the future Davidic king, who is described in impressive terms (9:6–7). This king will be full of the Spirit of God, and one day this One from the 'stump of Jesse' shall rule as the earthly representative of the heavenly King. Unlike the feckless Ahaz, the minor kings of the surrounding petty states, or the cruel Assyrian, this One will reign in justice and peace (11:1–6).

This future of full harmony is portrayed as a time when wild animals will lie down beside the helpless (11:6–9). These same words are picked up again at 65:20–25. There it is declared that in the future children will survive infancy (good news for peasants who would have seen so many die of disease, hunger and misfortune) and that everyone will be able to live in their own homes and tend their farms without the fear of displacement in wartime (an incredible dream for those accustomed to the constant threat of armed conflict). Clearly, Isaiah's is a comprehensive ethical hope: familial, social, economic and political. It is the hope of a world very unlike the present, and it is a certainty because the plan of Yahweh – the only true God – has already been set in motion and cannot be thwarted (14:24–27; 25:1; 37:26; 41:21–29; 46:8–11).

Jeremiah speaks of the future Davidic king, too. The righteous Branch will 'reign wisely and do what is just and right' (23:5) unlike the unjust kings of Judah, who have taken advantage of their subjects and not obeyed Yahweh (22:11–30). Amos 9:11–15 is a sharp contrast with the rest of the book. These verses predict a Davidic king, not one from Israel's monarchy (v. 11), promise food and drink in contradistinction to the people's hunger and thirst (v. 13; cf. 4:6–9), describe the rebuilding of the ruined cities in peace (v. 14a; cf. 2:14–16; 3:13–15; 4:3; 6:8–11), and the return to the land from forced exile (vv. 14b–15; cf. 4:3; 5:5, 27; 6:7; 7:17). These kinds of passages in the prophetic literature could be multiplied. All are powerful reminders of the ethical hope that lies before the people of God and which is sure in his sovereign hand. Life will be different. Justice will be done, and 'nation will not take up sword against nation, nor will they train for war any more' (Isa. 2:4). The poor will no longer cry out in vain, nor will the widow and orphan live in helplessness.

Conclusion

The Old Testament prophetic literature is replete with the demands of God for social and economic justice. There is no realm of life that does not come under their penetrating gaze. Social relationships, economic structures, political decisions, foreign policy and religious practices – and especially those who are leaders in these multiple arenas – must reflect concern for the disadvantaged. The prophets have left us harsh words – penetrating exposures and compelling condemnations that should compel the people of God to call for justice today. But censure and judgment is not their final word. Hope lies beyond all the tragedy. As we seek justice in the present, may we never forget the promise of Messiah and his kingdom. That kingdom has come in Jesus. The church should proclaim and model that new life and world in the 'in-between' time until his coming again.

Bibliography

BRUEGGEMANN, W., *The Prophetic Imagination* (Minneapolis: Fortress, ²2001).

_____, *Theology of the Old Testament: Testimony, Dispute, Advocacy* (Minneapolis: Fortress, 1997).

CARROLL R., M. D., *Contexts for Amos: Prophetic Poetics in Latin American Perspective* (JSOT Supplement Series 132; Sheffield: Sheffield Academic Press, 1992).

____, 'Seeking the Virtues among the Prophets: The Book of Amos as a Test Case', *Ex Auditu* 17 (2001), pp. 77–96.

____, *Amos – The Prophet and His Oracles: Research on the Book of Amos* (Louisville: Westminster John Knox Press, 2002).

____, 'The Power of the Future in the Present: Eschatology and Ethics in O'Donovan and Beyond', in C. BARTHOLOMEW, A. WOLTERS and J. CHAPLIN (eds.), *A Royal Priesthood: The Use of the Bible Ethically and Politically* (Scripture & Hermeneutics Series 3; Grand Rapids: Zondervan, 2002), pp. 116–143.

____, 'Can the Prophets Shed Light on Our Worship Wars? – How Amos Evaluates Religious Ritual', *Stone-Campbell Journal* 8.2 (2005), pp. 215–227.

____, 'A Passion for Justice and the Conflicted Self: Lessons from the Book of Micah', *Journal of Psychology and Christianity* 25.2 (2006), pp. 169–176.

DEMPSEY, C. J., *Hope Amid the Ruins: The Ethics of Israel's Prophets* (St. Louis: Chalice, 2000).

DOMERIS, W. R., *Touching the Heart of God: The Social Construction of Poverty among Biblical Peasants* (LHBOTS 466; London: T. & T. Clark, 2007).

FLEISCHER, G., *Von Menschenverkäufern, Baschankühen und Rechtsverkehren: Die Sozialkritik des Amosbuches in historisch-kritischer, sozialgeschichter und archäologischer Perspektive* (Bonner biblischer Beiträge 74; Frankfort am Maim: Athenäum, 1989).

GILMAN, J. E., *Fidelity of the Heart: An Ethic of Christian Virtue* (Oxford: Oxford University Press, 2001).

GOSSAI, H., *Justice, Righteousness and the Social Critique of the Eighth-Century Prophets* (American University Studies; Series VII: Theology and Religion, 141; New York: Peter Lang, 1993).

GOTTWALD, N. K., *The Politics of Ancient Israel* (Library of Ancient Israel; Louisville: Westminster John Knox, 2001).

HAUERWAS, S., *The Peaceable Kingdom: A Primer in Christian Ethics* (London: SCM, 1984).

HESCHEL, A., *The Prophets* (Perennial Classics; New York: HarperCollins, 2001). Originally published in two volumes (1969, 1971).

HOUSTON, W. J., *Contending for Justice: Ideologies and Theologies of Social Justice in the Old Testament* (LHBOTS 428; rev. edn, London: T. & T. Clark, 2008).

JARUZELSKA, I., *Amos and the Officialdom in the Kingdom of Israel: The Socio-Economic Position of the Officials in the Light of the Biblical, the Epigraphic and Archaeological Evidence* (Seria Socjologia 25; Poznań: Wydawnictwo Naukowe Uniwersytetu im. Adama Mickiewicza, 1998).

LANDY, F., 'In the Wilderness of Speech: Problems of Metaphor in Hosea', *Bib Int* 31.1 (1995), pp. 35–56.

McLAUGHLIN, J. L., *The Marzeah in the Prophetic Literature: References and Allusions in Light of the Extra-Biblical Evidence* (VTSupp 86; Leiden: Brill, 2001).

MÖLLER, K., *A Prophet in Debate: The Rhetoric of Persuasion in the Book of Amos* (JSOT Supplement Series 372; London: Sheffield Academic Press, 2003).

MURPHY, N., KALLENBERG, B. J. and THEISSEN NATION M. (eds.), *Virtues & Practices in the Christian Tradition: Christian Ethics after MacIntyre* (Harrisburg: Trinity Press International, 1997).

NARDONI, E., *Rise Up, O Judge: A Study of Biblical Justice in the Biblical World*, transl. S. C. MARTIN (Peabody: Hendrickson, 2004).

NISSINEN, M., *Prophets and Prophecy in the Ancient Near East* (Writings from the Ancient World 12; Atlanta: Society of Biblical Literature, 2003).

OESTREICH, B., *Metaphors and Similes for Yahweh in Hosea 14:2–9 (1–8)* (Friedensauer Schriftenreihe: Theologie 1; Frankfurt am Main: Peter Lang, 1998).

PARRY, R. A., *Old Testament Story and Christian Ethics: The Rape of Dinah as a Case Study* (Paternoster Biblical Monographs; Milton Keynes: Paternoster, 2004).

PLEINS, J. D., 'Poor, Poverty', *ABD* vol. 5, pp. 402–414.

SANDY, D. B., *Plowshares and Pruning Hooks: Rethinking the Language of Biblical Prophecy and Apocalyptic* (Downers Grove and Leicester: IVP, 2002).

SCHWANTES, M., *Das Recht der Armen* (BET 4; Frankfurt am Main: Peter Lang, 1977).

SICRE, J. L., *'Con los pobres de la tierra': La justicia social en los profetas de Israel* (Madrid: Sígueme, 1984).

VON RAD, G., *Old Testament Theology, vol. 2: The Theology of Israel's Prophetic Traditions*, transl. D. M. G. STALKER (New York: Harper & Row, 1965).

WELLHAUSEN, J., *Prolegomena to the History of Ancient Israel* (Atlanta: Scholars Press, 1994; reprint of 1885 edn.).

WILLIAMS, G., '"La justicia seguirás": Prioridades bíblicas y prioridades evangélicas', in O. CAMPOS (ed.), *Teología evangélica para el contexto latinoamericano. Ensayos en honor al Dr. Emilio A. Núñez* (Buenos Aires: Ediciones Kairós, 2004), pp. 127–170.

WRIGHT, C. J. H., *Old Testament Ethics for the People of God* (Downers Grove and Leicester: IVP, 2004).

_____, *The Mission of God: Unlocking the Bible's Grand Narrative* (Downers Grove and Nottingham: IVP, 2006).

3. 'WHY BOTHER WITH THE VULNERABLE?': THE WISDOM OF SOCIAL CARE

Jamie A. Grant

The Christian Aid website carries the following tag line: 'We believe in life before death. Working in more than fifty countries, helping people regardless of religion or race to improve their own lives and to tackle the causes of poverty and injustice.'[1]

This statement carries many of the hallmarks of Old Testament wisdom. Firstly, a nice twist on a known concept makes us stop and think – clearly, Christians believe in life *after* death, but the twist gives pause for thought . . . what about life *before* death? Secondly, there is an internationality about the wisdom literature (WL) just as there is in the aims of Christian Aid. While the ideology that we see in the books of Job, Proverbs and Ecclesiastes[2] is firmly grounded in the worldview of the Old Testament faith community, at the same time Old Testament wisdom is part of an international dialogue about principles that are true for all humanity.[3] Thirdly, Christian Aid desires to

---

1. <http://www.christian-aid.org.uk>, accessed 17 June 2006.
2. These three poetic books are traditionally classed as the Old Testament's 'wisdom literature'.
3. These international aspects of the WL led some scholars to assume that it was neither particularly Israelite nor particularly religious in its content (see, for example, James L. Crenshaw, *Old Testament Wisdom: An Introduction* [Louisville:

'improve people's lives' which, again, is typical of the Old Testament wisdom writers' view of our existence. Craig Bartholomew writes, 'Wisdom in the Old Testament is about how to negotiate life successfully in God's good but fallen world . . . The Old Testament wisdom books are written in order to help God's people find the way of wisdom amidst all the challenges of life in the world.'[4] There is a sense in which Old Testament wisdom is all about learning to live life well – to improve one's life – and the authors (like the charity) seek to help us, the reader, to reach that aim. Finally, Christian Aid aims to 'tackle the causes of poverty and injustice'. Here our discussion comes into sharp relief: how is the issue of poverty and its relief addressed in the WL? On one hand, the WL speaks a great deal about wealth as the reward for wisdom. So is poverty to be understood as evidence of the lack thereof? On the other hand, Qoheleth, the teacher of Ecclesiastes, tells us not to be surprised when we see 'the poor oppressed . . ., and justice and rights denied' (Eccl. 5:8), so is the WL somehow fatalistic about the continuance of oppressions of all sorts in our fallen world? Or do the sages also expect all those who read their books to confront poverty and injustice as evidence of a life lived wisely? This is the question that we seek to answer.

Wisdom and ethics

The starting point for any answer to the question of how the WL views issues of poverty must be rooted in a right understanding of the concept of wisdom

---

Footnote 3 (*Continued*)

WJKP, 1998], p. 184). As has been widely documented in recent years, such a view fails to take account of the profound significance of such concepts as 'the fear of the Lord' in Israel's wisdom teaching. Although the wisdom books do not focus explicitly on the same conversation points as the rest of the OT (covenant, salvation history, cult, etc.), clearly all of these are accepted and assumed by the wisdom writers and often these concepts provide essential background to the discussions found in the WL. See Raymond C. Van Leeuwen, 'The Book of Proverbs: Introduction, Commentary and Reflections', in Leander Keck *et al.* (ed.), *The New Interpreter's Bible: A Commentary in Twelve Volumes* (NIB vol. 5; Nashville: Abingdon Press, 1997, pp. 26–27) and Jamie A. Grant, 'Wisdom and Covenant: Revisiting Zimmerli', *EuroJTh* 12.2 (2003), pp. 103–113 for further discussion.

4. Craig G. Bartholomew, *Reading Proverbs with Integrity* (Cambridge: Grove Books, 2001), p. 8.

itself. It is often noted that the WL is markedly different in its foci and emphases from the rest of the biblical literature found in the Old Testament. Murphy, for example, comments that, 'The most striking characteristic [of the WL] is the absence of elements generally considered to be typically Israelite: the promises to the patriarchs, the Exodus experience, the Sinai covenant etc.'[5] Scholars also point out that it is less overtly religious than the rest of the OT, or at least that it is less explicitly concerned with religious matters. How does the different nature of the WL impact our interpretation of the message of these books?

Wisdom is not law, as we would find in the Pentateuch. It is different from the history books that record God's interventions in this world. It does not make the same claim of divine origin and authority as the prophets do.[6] Somewhat cryptically, the WL has been described as being about 'the art of steering'.[7] The teaching purpose of the wisdom books is focused on the question of how best to live our lives given the vagaries of this world. There are so many options and so many life choices. Daily we are faced with a conundrum of possibilities in the midst of our normal routine. Each and every one of the choices that we make will have repercussions for our life and for the lives of others round about us, so it is important to choose well. Wisdom is designed to help us navigate our way through the labyrinth of life. 'So you want to live life well? Here are some thoughts on how to do so', the wisdom writers tell us.

Why is this discussion of the fundamental nature of wisdom so important to our discussion of poverty and social responsibility in this section of the Old Testament? It is important to realize what type of material we are dealing with, because – while the law prescribes the bare minimum standards to which every one in Yahweh's community must adhere – Old Testament wisdom does something quite different. Wisdom looks beyond the lowest common denominator and points us towards *ideal standards* by which we should live our lives. The teaching of the sages moves from the realm of law, which provides the foundation and backdrop to their deliberation, into the sphere of ethics.

---

5. Roland E. Murphy, 'Wisdom in the OT', in *ABD* vol. IV, p. 927.

6. Michael V. Fox, *Proverbs 1–9: A New Translation with Introduction and Commentary* (AB; New York: Doubleday, 2000), p. 7.

7. Walther Zimmerli, 'The Place and Limit of Wisdom in the Framework of the Old Testament Theology', *SJT* 17 (1964), pp. 148–149. Zimmerli's description of the WL picks up on the Hebrew word *taḥbûlôt* which is translated 'guidance' or 'plans' in the English versions (see Prov. 1:6; 11:14; 12:5; etc.). However, the root of the word *taḥbûlôt* seems to be a nautical term implying 'sailing' or 'navigation' (see TWOT 596a), hence the idea of wisdom as 'the art of steering'.

Law is the line that we must not cross; the ethical standards described in the Old Testament wisdom books move us to the heights that are as far *above* that line as we can imagine.

So it is important to realize what to look for as we investigate the teachings on poverty and social responsibility found in Job and Proverbs.[8] This is where we will find examples of the heights to which we should all aspire. However, the exemplary nature of these texts and discussions in no way lets the reader off the hook. We are not meant to think that we can get away with a lot less. As mentioned above, wisdom takes a broad perspective on how life is *best* lived – both for the individual reader and for the created order within which we live. The teaching of the sages is about what is best for us. It is also about what is best for the world in which we live. These two loci are inseparable if our lives are going to be 'lived well'.

As we will see, social care and responsibility for the poor play a significant part in the exemplary paradigms of Job and Proverbs.[9] As readers of these texts, we are meant to aspire to the application of these ideals in our own setting. The examples that we read are purposefully general – specific contexts and settings are not given. The reason for that is so that we can take the axiomatic principles that we read about in these books and apply them to the specifics of our own life settings. We are not Job, but we can learn from the literary figure and apply in our own setting the lessons that he uncovered. We do not know the specific life setting that gave rise to the authorship of the proverbs that we read, indeed the authors are purposefully vague about questions of background because historical specificity limits application. We do not need to know the specifics. The lessons learned by the authors of these maxims are presented in general terms, so that we can readily apply them in our own life setting. The WL is aspirational. It takes us beyond the bare minimums of law, and challenges us to dream of a better life for ourselves as individuals and a better world for everyone around us. The point of the WL is that doing what is wise makes life better. Wisdom applied in daily reality has an impact. So the ethical paradigms that we read in Job and Proverbs reflect lifestyles that are to be pursued with a passion if our lives are to be full and this world is to be good.

---

8. Limited space means that we cannot do justice to Qoheleth's meditations on wealth and poverty in Ecclesiastes, so our focus will be on the two remaining wisdom books.

9. Typically, discussion of poverty and social care in Ecclesiastes is more enigmatic in its tone.

Common humanity, common Judge

There is no doubt that the WL sees social care and responsibility for those who are in need as an important characteristic of the life well-lived. We read of exemplary paradigms in the lives of Job and the 'Proverbs 31 woman' that inspire us towards lifestyles of care.[10] This is the right thing to do – the wise thing to do. There is a sense in which the WL roots our responsibilities towards others in the attitude that says, 'all humanity is one family'. There is no pride or sense of superiority in the attitudes of social care encouraged by the sages. Rather, there is an awareness that we all share a common humanity and, therefore, a common responsibility (see Prov. 14:31 and 22:2 or, as discussed more fully below, Job 31:15). The flip-side of the coin of a shared humanity is the fact that we also share a Judge (see Prov. 22:22–23 or Job 31:14). The WL encourages the realization that one day we will all give account for the way in which we treated our fellows who are all created in the image of God.

In the book of Proverbs we come across several interesting expressions of this idea, especially in the ancient wisdom of the sages found in Proverbs 22 – 24.[11] Proverbs 23:10–11, for example, gives this advice:

> Do not move an ancient boundary stone
> or encroach on the fields of the fatherless,
> For their Defender is strong;
> he will take up their case against you.

---

10. We will look more fully at these paradigmatic examples below.
11. Many scholars point out the similarity between the collection of proverbs found in Prov. 22:17 – 24:22 and the ancient Egyptian collection called the *Instruction of Amenemope*. This association is partially based on similarities of content and partly based on their common reference to 'thirty sayings'. (*Amenemope* is a collection of thirty proverbial meditations and Prov. 22:20 may also refer to 'thirty sayings' – there is some doubt over how to translate the word *šilšôm* ['thirty' or 'previously'] in 22:20). *Amenemope* is clearly ancient wisdom (probably second millennium BC) and the proverbs found in this section of Proverbs reflect ancient wisdom discussions. See Derek Kidner, *The Wisdom of Proverbs, Job and Ecclesiastes: An Introduction to the Wisdom Literature* (TOTC; Leicester: IVP, 1985), pp. 31–32 and Tremper Longman III, *Proverbs* (BCOTWP; Grand Rapids: Baker Academic, 2006), pp. 45–48, 415–416 for further discussion of the similarities and differences between Prov. 22:17 – 24:22 and *Amenemope*.

The imagery of these verses speaks against easy exploitation of the weak. Ancient boundary stones safeguarded one person's territory from incursion by others. Moving this stone would imply the theft of some or all of another's property. To move a boundary stone was a serious thing because it would – in a largely agrarian society – impact upon that person's ability to maintain their livelihood and, therefore, to survive. In ancient Israel not even a king was allowed to simply take land that belonged to someone else (see the incident involving Naboth the Jezreelite and King Ahab in 1 Kgs 21). Such prohibitions are common in the wisdom literatures of the ancient Near East. There is a sense in which it was broadly acknowledged that no society could work well on a human level if such excesses were allowed. So, on a human and societal level, moving these stones was a big deal. When it did occur it would normally be because the one changing the boundaries felt that they could get away with their deed. To move a boundary stone was an act of exploitation of the weak in society.[12]

However, the illegal appropriation of land was not only an attack on societal order, it was also seen as an attack on God's divinely-ordained order. '[T]he historically established social order – though human and flawed – was also seen as a work of God inasmuch as it protected the weak and powerless and fostered justice and righteousness. For the sake of the vulnerable, bound-ary markers came under God's protection (see ... 15.25; 23.10–11).'[13] This is typical of the tone of the WL's teaching on social care and the protection of the weak. Societally, this is the wise thing to do – it is good and right and creates a society that is both strong and caring. Spiritually, attacks on this social order are attacks against the divinely-ordained structures of the created order. Exploitation of the weak is an offence against God's design for this earth. Such an attitude sticks in the gullet because it goes against the grain of 'the way this world should be'.

Lack of care for the voiceless in society is wrong because of our common humanity, but Proverbs 23:10–11 also makes it clear that neglect of this type is culpable in God's eyes. The imagery of this teaching is rich. Those who would exploit always do so because they believe that they can get away with it. Probably implied in Proverbs 23:11 is the idea that the ruthless will exploit orphans because the latter will have no recourse against such actions. What are they going to do? They cannot speak at court nor can they afford an advocate

---

12. See the discussion of Prov. 22:28 in Longman III, *Proverbs*, pp. 418–419 and Van Leeuwen, 'Proverbs', p. 205.

13. Van Leeuwen, ibid.

who will take the bully to task. The irony of this wisdom saying is that, ultimately, the greatest of all advocates will take up the cause of the oppressed!
Exploitation is not just an affront against our shared humanity; it is an offence
against God and he will ultimately call for reparation.

We can chart this dual message throughout the WL. Any strong society will
care for the poor because we are all one in God's eyes, all created in his image,
and 'righteousness exalts a nation' (Prov. 14:34). So, to care for the weak in any
generation and community is the good, wise and right thing to do. However,
we should also remember that such care is not just a cultural expectation, it is
a divine imperative that we ignore at our peril (Prov. 14:31; 22:22–23[14]). Also
we should never forget that this is a universal imperative in the WL. We cannot
deflect responsibility onto those with power and influence. Any individual who
can benefit one who is poor, honours God by doing so. Bruce Waltke, in his
discussion of Proverbs 14:31, writes:

> The poor and needy have an exalted status together with all humanity by reason of
> their Creator (see also 17:5; 22:2; 29:13), whose honor is inseparably connected with
> his workmanship (cf. Job 31:15; Matt. 25:40, 45; Jas. 3:9; 1 John 3:17, 18). The one
> who humiliates God will not go unpunished, and the person who gives him honor
> will not go unrewarded (3:9–10). *Proverbs that commend generosity toward the poor (14:21,*
> *31; 19:17; 22:9; 28:27) are addressed to anyone who is able to help the destitute and save them from*
> *starvation.* In 28:3 a poor man slanders and/or oppresses another poor man![15]

Looking after those who are weak – in any way and at any level – honours
God. Exploiting the voiceless dishonours God and will ultimately receive his
punishment. On the level of a shared humanity, good societies are those that
care for the ones who would otherwise be forgotten. We do not have to be a
Bill Gates or a J. K. Rowling before such responsibility falls upon us. It is wise
to be generous with *whatever* we have, regardless of how much that may be
when compared with others. The WL of the Old Testament also provides us
with some 'worked examples' of these principles in the figure of Job and the

---

14. Hoppe says of Prov. 22:22–23, 'This is as strong an identification of God's concern
    for the cause of the poor as one sees in the biblical tradition' (Leslie J. Hoppe, *There
    Shall Be No Poor Among You: Poverty in the Bible* [Nashville: Abingdon, 2004], p. 107).
15. Bruce K. Waltke, *The Book of Proverbs: Chapters 1–15* (NICOT; Grand Rapids:
    Eerdmans, 2004), p. 607 (emphasis added). Note that the NIV wrongly translates
    geber roš as 'ruler'. It should rather be 'a poor man' (see ESV, RSV, NASB and Longman
    III, *Proverbs*, p. 488).

'noble woman' of Proverbs 31. Turning our attention to look at these figures will further illuminate the WL's presentation of the wisdom of social care.

Paradigms of social care

Picking up on the idea of the WL as exemplary, it is important to consider the implications of positive examples that we find within the books of Job and Proverbs. It is interesting to note that care for the poor is a theme that is, in some sense, paradigmatic for each of these books.

Job and the question of care for the poor

The whole issue of caring for the poor is a central and repeated notion in the circular debates of the speech cycles in the book of Job. Essentially, in an attempt to find a rationale for Job's present suffering, his friends cannot see beyond a retributive view of justice. In their minds, for Job to suffer so greatly, he must have sinned equally greatly. For Eliphaz, Bildad and Zophar the only way of justifying the righteousness of God is to establish that Job is unrighteous. Ultimately, they are declared wrong in their logic, therefore their attempt to defend God is unnecessary, however, it is worth noting how significant care for the poor is in the debates about Job's righteousness.[16] It is acknowledged by all parties to the speech cycles (Job and each of his friends) that failure to care for the poor would be a moral lapse of such significance as to merit serious punishment from God. Here are just a few of the assertions found in the speech cycles that illustrate this point:

> [God] saves the needy from the sword in their mouth; he saves them from the clutches of the powerful. So the poor have hope, and injustice shuts its mouth (Job 5:15–16, Eliphaz speaking).

> For he has oppressed the poor and left them destitute; he has seized houses he did not build. Surely he will have no respite from his craving; he cannot save himself by his treasure (20:19–20, these are the words of Zophar).

> You gave no water to the weary and you withheld food from the hungry, though you were a powerful man, owning land – an honoured man, living on it. And you sent

---

16. See Job 42:7–9 and John E. Hartley, *The Book of Job* (NICOT; Grand Rapids: Eerdmans, 1988), pp. 538–539.

widows away empty-handed and broke the strength of the fatherless (22:7–9, Bildad addressing Job).

Job consistently denies these accusations throughout the speech cycles of Job 4 – 27. His habitual practice is summarized in his epic defence in chapters 29 – 31. For example, in Job 29:11–12, he gives an account of his own life prior to the tragic events presently debated: 'Whoever heard me spoke well of me, and those who saw me commended me, because I rescued the poor who cried for help, and the fatherless who had none to assist him.' The root of Job's popularity was grounded in his attitude towards those in need in his society. So, a major part of Job's defence against the accusations of his friends (both implied and explicit) is grounded in his habit of care for the voiceless and oppressed round about him. However, before we go on to look at Job's defence as an example of the type of care that every truly wise believer should show, we should pause to take note of the unanimity of opinion displayed by the three friends and Job himself.

It is broadly acknowledged that Job is a book of international character. Although Hebraic in its worldview, the literary Job is not a Hebrew and neither are his friends. The book has a decidedly transnational flavour and it is often assumed that each of the 'friends' is sent as the foremost sage of his country.[17] So, we have the best and the brightest wisdom scholars from throughout the ancient world gathering to provide comfort for their friend (Job 2:11). They do so in their week of silent mourning with Job (Job 2:13). The problems begin when the friends try to find root causes that would explain the severity of Job's suffering. While this is not the place to discuss the ins and outs of the debate that ensues, one thing becomes absolutely clear that serves the purposes of this essay. Care for the poor is an absolute to be expected of any wise person who seeks to please God. As the above verses make plain, anyone failing to care for the poor, let alone actively oppressing them, would place themselves under the just punishment of God. This 'dream team' of the world of wisdom is in absolute agreement: lack of proactive care for the weak is a denial of godly lifestyle. Speaking of Job 20:19 (above), Clines writes that:

> [I]t is of unmistakable significance that the crime that comes most readily to
> Zophar's mind as the quintessence of wickedness is a social and economic crime.
> Not a sin against God, nor a cultic offence, not the infringement of some state

---

17. See Francis I. Andersen, *Job* (TOTC; Leicester: IVP, 1976), pp. 94–95.

law, but the perhaps perfectly legal exploitation of the poor. 'Attitudes and actions towards the underprivileged is a fundamental gauge of integrity and righteousness in Job (Habel). . .'[18]

However, the archetypal paradigm of care for the needy is found in Job's ethical defence in chapter 31. Here we discover not only the bare minimum standard of care that falls upon everyone in the community of biblical faith, but we read of an exemplary standard of care – one to which we are meant to aspire and which we should emulate. This should not be taken as referring to an ideal that is unattainable. Rather, Job's defence presents the readers with a picture of the ethical heights which it is possible to attain in our attitude towards others if we truly follow the patterns of biblical wisdom. Job 31 outlines this paradigm of social responsibility using a method of legal defence by way of self-imprecation called 'negative confession'.[19] The way in which this worked is that the accused makes his appeal not to human judicial institutions but directly to God – he attests to his right behaviour and calls on the Almighty to visit him with an appropriate punishment if his assertion of innocence is in any way false. As such Job 31 stands as one of the great statements of ethics in the Old Testament. How does this statement of biblical ethics address the issue of social responsibility?

Firstly, Job affirms his care for his own servants:

If I have denied justice to my menservants and maidservants when they had a grievance against me, what will I do when God confronts me? What will I answer when called to account? Did not he who made me in the womb make them? Did not the same one form us both within our mothers? (Job 31:13–15)

The ethical essence of this statement is based in Job's awareness of the folly of injustice. He may in some sense profit now, but he is fully aware that ultimately he would not because he will face the judgment of the God who made both

---

18. David J. A. Clines, *Job 1–20* (WBC; Dallas: Word Books, 1989), p. 491. In a similar vein Andersen comments on the same verse that, 'Zophar reflects common Israelite belief in highlighting neglect of the poor as the worst failing of the rich' (*Job*, p. 196). Whilst we in the West often try to immunize ourselves from such labels, if we stop to take stock of the world stage in which we participate, there can be no doubt that 'rich' is precisely what we are. Therefore, we too bear the expectations placed upon 'the rich' in the WL.

19. Andersen, *Job*, p. 238.

servant and master. The equation is simple: from an eternal perspective no short-term gain by means of injustice can possibly outweigh the ultimate cost of a declaration of guilt in the eyes of the God who made both servant and master.[20] Not only is social injustice 'wrong' morally-speaking, it is folly from the wisdom perspective. Every human being, in Job's eyes, is created by God and therefore instilled with the same innate dignity. Such a moral wrong against those made in his image would receive God's wrath. Therefore, Job states that such injustice is both 'wrong' and 'wrong-headed'.

Secondly, Job describes his refusal to exploit the underprivileged:

> If I have denied the desires of the poor or let the eyes of the widow grow weary, if I have kept my bread to myself, not sharing it with the fatherless – but from my youth I reared him as would a father, and from my birth I guided the widow – if I have seen anyone perishing for lack of clothing, or a needy man without a garment, and his heart did not bless me for warming him with the fleece from my sheep, if I have raised my hand against the fatherless, knowing that I had influence in court, then let my arm fall from the shoulder, let it be broken off at the joint. For I dreaded destruction from God, and for fear of his splendour I could not do such things (31:16–23).

On one level this seems to be a straightforward declaration of the help Job had provided those who found themselves in dire straits. In an ancient society without the safety net of a welfare system, Job declares that he has not only fed the poor (v. 17) but also invested himself in the lives of others (v. 18). As he has provided food, so he has also given clothing to keep warm those who would otherwise have suffered privation (v. 19). However, Job's confession goes beyond the provision of necessities. He is also well aware of the different types of exploitation that the influential in any given society can visit upon the voiceless of that community and declares his innocence of such selfishness. Those who have the ear of a society's 'movers and shakers' can do much to attain their own ends even at a cost to others. Job makes it clear that he was not that type of rich man. Again, his active care and his willing restraint are inspired by an awareness of the divine justice that he would face should he visit injustice on others.[21]

---

20. Clines comments, 'Job has never dismissed out of hand a call for justice by one of his servants or slaves. He would not have dared risk God's calling him to account over such a matter, he says. In any case, slaves also have their rights, according to Job: they are as much human beings as he is, created by the same God' (*Job 21–37* [WBC; Nashville: Thomas Nelson, 2006], p. 1019).

21. See Andersen, *Job*, pp. 242–243.

Thirdly, we read Job's declaration that wealth has never been an end in itself for him:

> If I have put my trust in gold or said to pure gold, 'You are my security,' if I have rejoiced over my great wealth, the fortune my hands had gained, if I have regarded the sun in its radiance or the moon moving in splendour, so that my heart was secretly enticed and my hand offered them a kiss of homage, then these also would be sins to be judged, for I would have been unfaithful to God on high (31:24–28).

Having wealth, as we will see again later when we consider the 'Proverbs 31 woman', is nowhere condemned in the WL. Indeed, it is sometimes presented as a sign of God's blessing on an individual who seeks to honour the Lord (Prov. 10:22). However, wrong attitudes towards money are roundly condemned in the Old Testament and the WL in particular (see, for example, Deut. 17:17; Job 22:23–26; Prov. 22:16). Here Job declares that wealth has never become the object of his trust. God has always come first in Job's life and he has acknowledged that the only true source of security is found in relationship with Yahweh.[22] The cryptic verses 26–27 probably refer to some sort of idolatry, and it is interesting that even in ancient times we see a thought connection being made between wrong attitudes towards wealth and false worship;[23] just as we see today, when gold becomes god, failure to worship the true God inevitably follows.

Fourthly, Job was *proactive* in his care even for those whom he did not know:

> . . . if the men of my household have never said, 'Who has not had his fill of Job's meat?' – but no stranger had to spend the night in the street, for my door was always open to the traveller . . . (31:31–32).

These verses seem to echo Job's self-imprecation of vv. 16–23, yet the aspect that is added in this declaration of innocence here is that he *sought out* opportunities to provide help and care. His sense of social responsibility extended beyond his own household (servants, vv. 13–15) and even beyond the broader community of those who were known to him (vv. 16–23). Here he presents an image of compassion extended to the stranger in need, as was the expected

---

22. Hartley comments that, 'Resolutely Job disputes Eliphaz's insinuation that he has raised gold above God as his first love (22:24–25). To the contrary, he knows that he has always remembered that God himself is the one who gave him the strength and the wisdom to earn his abundance (Deut. 8:17–18)' (*Job*, p. 418).

23. See Andersen, *Job*, p. 243; and Hartley, *Job*, p. 418.

norm of ancient Near Eastern hospitality.[24] In the Middle East this would be seen as normal behaviour, rather than an example of a higher ethic, but the point is that Job was assiduous in his hospitality. He did not assume that others would provide shelter for the sojourners found within the city gates that night, rather he sent out his men to ensure that everyone was accommodated. Equally, it was meat that was on offer at Job's table and this was normally a luxury reserved for feast days and special occasions. So Job did what was expected in his care of others but he did so scrupulously and generously.

Finally, Job's attitude of social care extends even to the seriousness with which he viewed his responsibilities towards the environment as a landowner.

> . . . if my land cries out against me and all its furrows are wet with tears, if I have devoured its yield without payment or broken the spirit of its tenants, then let briers come up instead of wheat and weeds instead of barley (31:38–40).

Care for the environment and social responsibility for people are often treated as separate issues, yet Job as a landowner knows that they are closely linked. Hartley comments:

> In Job's day there must have been regulations regarding the use of the land, for he acknowledges that a bond exists between the land and its owner's deeds. If the owner abuses his workers by withholding their wages or shortens the life span of his servants by demanding excessive production under poor working conditions, the land and all its furrows will cry out against the lord on behalf of those oppressed.[25]

So Job provides the reader with a holistic pattern of social care, one that we, as readers, are meant to see as a challenge to our own lives and to which we should conform our own practices.

The 'noble woman' of Proverbs 31 and care for the poor

More briefly, we see a similar example of care in the acrostic poem that acts as a summary of the diverse teaching of the book of Proverbs (Prov. 31:10–31).[26]

---

24. Hartley, *Job*, p. 420; Clines, *Job II*, pp. 1028–1029.
25. Hartley, *Job*, p. 423.
26. There has been much debate about the identity of 'the Proverbs 31 woman', about why she is a woman, about whether she is real and many other tangential issues regarding this passage. This is not the place to discuss these issues in depth. Bartholomew, *Reading Proverbs*, pp. 15–17 provides a helpful overview of the

'Proverbs 31:10–31 is deliberately placed at the conclusion, in order to give us a picture of what wisdom looks like in practice.'[27] The woman presented in this concluding poem serves as a 'worked example' of what wisdom might look like in the midst of the realities of daily life. She is described as *ḥayil* in the Hebrew – a woman of strength, valour or significance, depending on which nuance of the word one seeks to emphasize. And these characteristics shine through in her omnicompetence in every area of life. The noble woman is industrious in providing for her family (vv. 13–15). She is prepared for every eventuality, even those that are not terribly common (v. 21).[28] Perhaps unusually in an ancient oriental culture, she is seen as competent to invest in real estate (v. 16) and to engage in trade (v. 24); the implication seems to be that she does so in her own right and with her own money.[29] Rather than focusing on the woman's physical beauty (as did many ancient Near Eastern poems dedicated to women), this composition eulogizes her good character and her abilities (vv. 25–26, 30). However, primarily, the life of this woman is celebrated because she lives life in the fear of the Lord (31:30). The 'fear of the Lord' is the WL's shorthand for a life lived in proper relationship with God – a life that accepts God's holistic claim on our lives and responds wholeheartedly to that claim.[30] The noble woman lives in right relationship with Yahweh and this, rather than the pursuit of wealth or a vain attempt to find security, drives her lifestyle.[31]

However, it is interesting to note that in the poetic presentation of another paradigmatically 'wise' lifestyle, once again, care for the poor is seen as a significant element in right living. This is seen partly in the noble woman's provision for all of her household, not just her family (v. 15), but much more explicitly in the pivotal verses 19–20. These verses lie at the centre of the poem, where

---

Footnote 26 (*Continued*)

passage and Al Wolters, *The Song of the Valiant Woman: Studies in the Interpretation of Proverbs 31:10–31* (Carlisle: Paternoster, 2001) gives a much more far-reaching treatment of the passage and its interpretation.

27. Bartholomew, *Reading Proverbs*, p. 15.

28. Longman III, *Proverbs*, p. 545.

29. Wolters, *Song of the Valiant Woman*, p. 11.

30. Van Leeuwen, 'Proverbs', p. 33.

31. Longman comments, 'The verse does not mean that a noble woman is abrasive and ugly; it simply contrasts these relatively worthless traits (charm, beauty) with what is truly important: fear of Yahweh. This is true of all people, male and female, but here there is a reminder that a woman who deserves to be called noble is motivated by a proper relationship with her God' (*Proverbs*, p. 548).

we see a chiastic word play focused on the woman's 'hands'. As Van Leeuwen comments, 'The hands that grasp to produce, open wide to provide.'[32] The image is one that speaks of productivity and generosity. The woman works hard to provide but *refuses* to hoard. 'The sages have taught that the wise must be generous to the poor (11:24; 28:27; 29:7, 14). Here the "noble woman" shows her wisdom by being concerned about the needs of the destitute.'[33]

So speak the paradigmatic examples of the wisdom literature. The WL is designed to give us something to aim at, to present examples that we should follow and apply in our own circumstances. Therefore, clearly, care for the poor is the 'wise' thing to do. Anyone who walks in the fear of the Lord (i.e., in right relationship with God) must be generous in their care for those who have less. But what does that mean for people living, as I suspect many of us do, in the twenty-first-century Western world?

Conclusion

Clearly there is much more that can be said on the topic at hand, but our consideration is limited by space. We have not even considered such matters as the WL's emphasis on simplicity of life and how right lifestyle is worth more than great wealth (Prov. 3:14; 8:19; 15:16, etc.). We do not have the opportunity to consider the sometimes fatalistic tone of Ecclesiastes when it comes to the poor (Eccl. 5:8; 9:15–16). However, although there is much that remains to be discussed, we have seen enough to draw two general principles from the WL's discussion of how we should respond to the underprivileged in society.

Wisdom and social care are inseparably linked
The quest for wisdom in the Old Testament is really a search for that lifestyle which is most pleasing to God. Life is so full of flux and difficulty and shades of grey that, even with the best will in the world, it is difficult to know *how* to live life well and in a manner that pleases God. Hence, the purpose of the WL is to teach what it means to live a godly lifestyle on a daily basis. It is absolutely plain from what we have seen that such a lifestyle *must* include an attitude and habitual practice of care for those in need. The teachings of Proverbs make it clear that failure to care for the poor is anathema to God, the Creator of all humanity

---

32. Van Leeuwen, 'Proverbs', p. 262. See also Paul E. Koptak, *Proverbs* (NIVAC; Grand Rapids: Zondervan, 2003), pp. 682–683.
33. Longman III, *Proverbs*, p. 545.

(Prov. 14:31). We should remember that the WL encourages us to go beyond the minimums dictated by law to practices that far exceed our 'legal' responsibility. The exemplars found in Job and the Proverbs 31 woman emphasize the central importance of proactive social care if we are to live a life pleasing to God.

Wealth and wisdom are not incompatible

It is often suggested that God favours the poor over the rich. The underlying idea is that those without things are forced to trust in God in a way that becomes more ambiguous for those who *have* things. The poor trust in God alone. The risk faced by the rich is that they end up trusting in things other than God. God's favour towards the poor is often mentioned in the Scriptures (e.g. Isa. 41:17; Luke 6:20; Jas 2:5–6) and this sometimes leads to the mistaken conclusion that God is pro-poor and anti-rich.[34] The examples that we read in Job and Proverbs 31 make it plain that wealth in and of itself is not wrong. Job's wealth is presented as a sign of God's blessing on a life well-lived (Job 1:1–3; 42:12–17). The industry of the Proverbs 31 woman brings wealth to herself and her family and this is laid out to the reader as an example to be followed (Prov. 31:14–19). So contrary to popular belief, God is not anti-wealth. The issue is not whether one is wealthy or not, the issue that comes under scrutiny in the WL is what one does with one's wealth. Proverbs 28:8 is a good example of this principle: 'He who increases his wealth by exorbitant interest amasses it for another, who will be kind to the poor.' It is not the wealth in itself that is the problem, but the wealth without social justice that is roundly condemned in the wisdom books. Industry is encouraged, but as shown by the central verse (20) of the Proverbs 31 acrostic poem, hearty care for the poor must be central to our industry and its benefits.

So, the teaching of the WL with regard to issues of wealth and poverty and social responsibility is clear. A lifestyle pleasing to God is a lifestyle marked by generosity to those who have less than us. Godliness and selfishness are incompatible. Industry is encouraged and wealth not viewed as intrinsically wrong. Rather, wealth that results from hard work provides an opportunity to bring help and blessing to others. When it comes to the language of wealth and poverty we are

---

34. God's care for the poor is mentioned explicitly in the biblical text because they are the ones normally forgotten and his people need to be reminded of their duty of care for all those created in his image. Lohfink makes the point well that God's preoccupation with the poor should be held in balance with the biblical imagery that describes Yahweh as a God of 'plenitude and riches' (Norbert F. Lohfink, S. J., *Option for the Poor: The Basic Principle of Liberation Theology in the Light of the Bible*, transl. Linda M. Maloney [Berkley: Bibal, 1987], pp. 10–12).

always inclined to look up the ladder at those who have so much more than we do. The teaching of the Old Testament's wisdom books encourages us to look down the ladder and see how much more *we* have when compared to others. Whatever we have, a *wise* life is marked by generous care for anyone who has less.

Bibliography

ANDERSEN, F. I., *Job* (TOTC; Leicester: IVP, 1976).

BARTHOLOMEW, C. G., *Reading Proverbs with Integrity* (Cambridge: Grove Books, 2001).

CLINES, D. J. A., *Job 1–20* (WBC; Dallas: Word Books, 1989).

_____, *Job 21–37* (WBC; Nashville: Thomas Nelson, 2006).

CRENSHAW, J. L., *Old Testament Wisdom: An Introduction* (Louisville: WJKP, 1998).

FOX, M. V., *Proverbs 1–9: A New Translation with Introduction and Commentary* (AB; New York: Doubleday, 2000).

GRANT, J. A., 'Wisdom and Covenant: Revisiting Zimmerli', *EuroJTh* 12.2 (2003), pp. 103–113.

HARTLEY, J. E., *The Book of Job* (NICOT; Grand Rapids: Eerdmans, 1988).

HOPPE, L. J., *There Shall Be No Poor Among You: Poverty in the Bible* (Nashville: Abingdon, 2004).

KIDNER, D., *The Wisdom of Proverbs, Job and Ecclesiastes: An Introduction to the Wisdom Literature* (Leicester: IVP, 1985).

KOPTAK, P. E., *Proverbs* (NIVAC; Grand Rapids: Zondervan, 2003).

LOHFINK, N. F., *Option for the Poor: The Basic Principle of Liberation Theology in the Light of the Bible*, transl. L. M. MALONEY (Berkley: Bibal, 1987).

LONGMAN III, T., *Proverbs* (BCOTWP; Grand Rapids: Baker Academic, 2006).

McCANN, J. C., *A Theological Introduction to the Books of Psalms: The Psalms as Torah* (Nashville: Abingdon Press, 1993).

MURPHY, R. E., 'Wisdom in the OT', in *ABD*, vol. IV, pp. 920–931.

SARNA, N. M., *On the Book of Psalms: Exploring the Prayer of Ancient Israel* (New York: Schocken Books, 1993).

VAN LEEUWEN, R. C., 'The Book of Proverbs: Introduction, Commentary and Reflections', in L. KECK *et al.* (ed.), *The New Interpreter's Bible: A Commentary in Twelve Volumes* (NIB vol. 5; Nashville: Abingdon Press, 1997).

WALTKE, B. K., *The Book of Proverbs: Chapters 1–15* (NICOT; Grand Rapids: Eerdmans, 2004).

WOLTERS, A., *The Song of the Valiant Woman: Studies in the Interpretation of Proverbs 31:10–31* (Carlisle: Paternoster, 2001).

ZIMMERLI, W., 'The Place and Limit of Wisdom in the Framework of the Old Testament Theology', *SJT* 17 (1964), pp. 146–158.

4. BIBLICAL PARADIGMS OF REDEMPTION: EXODUS, JUBILEE AND THE CROSS

Christopher J. H. Wright

A biblical understanding of social theology requires (as does a biblical theology of anything), a holistically biblical worldview. That in turn demands that we take the whole Bible, with both testaments, into account, and acknowledge the foundational nature of the grand narrative that it renders to us. It has become commonplace to articulate the biblical worldview or meta-narrative in the form of four main segments of a storyline, or four great acts within a drama: creation, fall, redemption in history, and new creation. This scheme, in my view, is no less valuable for having become commonplace, and I find it frequently fruitful in thinking biblically through any topic. Given constraints of time and space, however, this essay will omit the first and the fourth of these great themes and focus in particular on three biblical paradigms of redemption and how they inform our thinking about the gospel and our social responsibilities as Christians.[1]

---

1. Fuller discussion of the implications of the complete paradigm of analysis (creation, fall, redemption and new creation) can be found in my *The Mission of God: Unlocking the Bible's Grand Narrative* (Nottingham: IVP, 2006), esp. pp. 265–323.

The fall

Before we move on to examine the full implications of God's patterns of redemption, we must first consider some of the effects of the entrance of sin into the world. To understand God's patterns of redemption we need to understand what it is that we are redeemed from. Just as our theology of mission must embrace a holistic understanding of creation and humanity, so it must work with a radical and comprehensive understanding of sin and evil. The profound simplicity of the narratives of Genesis 1 – 11 show us at least three things about sin that must be taken into account in a biblical social theology.

Sin affects every dimension of the human person

The portrait of the human being that we find in the early chapters of Genesis is of an integral, single person, but with different dimensions of life and relationship. Rather than speaking of a human being 'having a body and a soul', it seems preferable to speak adjectivally of the human person as living with a fully integrated combination of different dimensions. At least four aspects of human life are seen in these early accounts. Human beings are *physical* (they are creatures in the created physical world), *spiritual* (they have a unique intimacy of relationship with God), *rational* (they have unique powers of communication, language, addressability, consciousness, memory, emotions and will), and *social* (their gender complementarity reflects the relational dimension of God and underlies all human relationships). All of these dimensions – physical, spiritual, rational and social – are combined in the integrated human person described in Genesis 2:7 as a 'living being'.[2] Romans 1 and 2 is Paul's incisive commentary on the universal reign of sin in human life and society. Reading his searing analysis there, we can see all of the same four dimensions of human personality involved in human sin and rebellion. There is no part of the human person that is unaffected by sin.

Sin affects human society and history

Sin spreads *horizontally within society* and sin propagates itself *vertically between generations*. It thus generates contexts and connections that are laden with

---

2. This fourfold perspective on the dimensions of the whole human person is also adopted as a framework for biblical holistic mission by Jean-Paul Heldt, 'Revisiting the "Whole Gospel": Toward a Biblical Model of Holistic Mission in the 21st Century', *Missiology* 32 (2004), pp. 149–172.

collective sin. Sin becomes endemic, structural, and embedded in history. Thus, the Old Testament historians observe how whole societies become addicted to chaotic evil (as the book of Judges portrays with its slow crescendo of vile behaviour) or as seen in Isaiah's attacks on those who legalize injustice by passing laws that give structural legitimacy to oppression (Isa. 10:1–2).

We need to be careful here, of course. Some people are very reluctant to speak of 'structural sin' – arguing that only *people* can sin. Sin is a personal choice made by free moral persons. Structures cannot sin in that sense. With that I agree. However, no human being is born into, or makes his or her moral choices in the context of, a clean sheet. We all live within social frameworks that we did not create. They were there before we arrived and will remain after we are gone, even if individually or as a whole generation we may engineer significant change in them. Those frameworks are the result of other people's choices and actions over time – all of them riddled with sin. So although structures may not sin in the personal sense, structures do embody myriad personal choices, many of them sinful, that we have come to accept within our cultural patterns.

So if our mission is bringing good news into every area of human life, then it calls for some research and analysis as to what exactly constitutes the bad news, horizontally in the structures of a given society and vertically in its history. Many factors will be uncovered in the process. But only as they are uncovered can the cleansing, healing and reconciling power of the gospel undo their dismal effects.

Sin affects the whole environment of human life

When human beings chose to rebel against their Creator, their disobedience and fall affected the whole of their physical environment. This is immediately clear from God's words to Adam, 'cursed is the ground because of you' (Gen. 3:17). But in view of the connections between human beings and the rest of creation, it could not have been otherwise. Richard Bauckham expresses the inevitable effects well:

> How does the fall affect nature? Is it only in human history that God's creative work is disrupted, necessitating a redemptive work, whereas in the rest of nature creation continues unaffected by the fall? This cannot be the case, because humanity is part of the interdependent whole of nature, so that disruption in human history must disrupt nature, and since humanity is the dominant species on earth human sin is bound to have very widespread effects on nature as a whole. The fall disturbed humanity's harmonious relationship with nature, alienating us from nature, so that we now

experience nature as hostile, and introducing elements of struggle and violence into our relationship with nature (Gn. 3:15, 17–19; 9:2).[3]

The apparent simplicity, then, of the narratives of creation and fall, contain enormous depths of truth about the triangle of relationships between God, humanity and the whole created order. It is clear that the Bible offers us a very radical assessment of the effects of our wilful rebellion and fall into disobedience, self-centredness and sin. It is not just that every dimension of the human person is affected by sin. It is not just that every human person is a sinner. It is also the case that the totality of our social and economic relationships with each other, horizontally and historically, and of our ecological relationship to the earth itself have all been perverted and twisted. So, having described the complex effects of sin, we should turn our attention to the wholeness of God's redeeming work.

Paradigms of redemption: the exodus

The exodus is the first and foundational account in which the God of the Bible is presented as redeemer – as it is celebrated in the Song of Moses (Exod. 15:13, 16). If we are to develop a biblical understanding of the meaning of redemption (which, as we have said, is essential to developing a biblical understanding of the meaning of mission), we must start here and explore all that these narratives have to tell us about the situation from which God redeemed Israel, the reasons for which he did so, and the changed reality into which their redemption led them.

The political dimension
The Israelites in Egypt were an immigrant, ethnic minority people. They had originally come to the host country as famine refugees and had been welcomed and given the asylum they sought.[4] However, with a change of dynasty had come a change of policy toward them, and Exodus 1:8–10 portrays how

---

3. Richard Bauckham, 'First Steps to a Theology of Nature', *Evangelical Quarterly* 58 (1986), p. 240.
4. A fact which was not forgotten. Even though the predominant memory of Egypt in the Old Testament is of the oppression, one law at least skips over that and recalls the fact that Egypt had given succour to the family of Jacob as aliens in need (Deut. 23:7–8).

vulnerable they were to being made the target of irrational fear, political cunning and unjust discrimination. They had no political freedom or voice within the Egyptian state, even though they had grown in numbers. In fact their numerical growth is cited as one of the major reasons for the Egyptian hostility. This is a story with modern echoes.

The economic dimension

The Israelites were being exploited as slave labour (Exod. 1:11–14). They did not own the land they lived on (mind you, neither did the Egyptians, ironically because of the actions of Joseph generations earlier, but that's another story). But rather than being able to use that land for their own benefit as it had originally been given, their labour is now being siphoned off to the benefit of the host nation for its own economic advantage. Israelite labour is being exploited for Egyptian agriculture and construction projects. An ethnic minority does the dirty and heavy work for the king of Egypt. The modern echoes continue.

Among the explicit promises of God in advance of the exodus was that he would give to the Israelites a land of their own (Exod. 6:8). The economic dimension of their liberation is thus built into it, both in historical reality and in the metaphoric use of the *gō'ēl* institution to describe it. For it was particularly in circumstances of economic threat and loss that the *gō'ēl* was expected to act in order to restore economic viability to the needy.[5] Rescuing the Israelites from slave-labour was the very heart of the exodus redemption.

The social dimension

The rest of Exodus chapter 1 goes on to describe the escalating state violence against the Israelites by a government that piles brutality on stupidity. Failing to subvert the community from within, because of the midwives' respect for life and their courageous combination of wit and disobedience, the Pharaoh embarks on state-sponsored genocide – inciting 'all his people' to a murderous campaign against Israelite male babies. So the people suffer intolerable violation of fundamental human rights and aggressive interference in their family lives. Israelite families are made to live in constant fear – nine months of fear as every pregnant mother waited for the news that should normally have brought great joy ('It's a boy!'), but would now bring terror and grief (Exod. 2:1–2).

In the ensuing narrative, the plagues 'strike back' with increasing violence at a regime that has sunk to such depravity. The climactic death of Egypt's own

---

5. See David Baker's 'Protecting the Vulnerable: The Law and Social Care', in this volume.

first-born sons mirrors their destruction of Israel's (Exod. 4:23). The Passover forever reminds Israel of the social and family nature of God's redemption and the precious delivery out of such demented evil. And when Israel is established as a new kind of society in covenant relationship with Yahweh, the sanctity of human life and the preservation of social justice are among the key elements in their social and legal structures.

The spiritual dimension

While the narrator highlights the political, economic and social dimensions of Israel's plight in Exodus 1–2, once Yahweh appears as a character in the drama, we become aware of a further dimension. The Israelites' slavery to Pharaoh is a massive hindrance to their worship and service of the living God, Yahweh. One way in which the story makes this point is a simple play on a single Hebrew verb and noun. *'ābad* means to serve – that is to work for another; *'ăbodâ* means service or slavery. Thus the Israelites cried out to God 'because of their slavery' (2:23). But the same words can be used for worship, the service of God. And of course, Israel's destiny was to serve and worship Yahweh. How could they, however, as long as they were chained in slavery to Pharaoh? The point is made most sharply in Exodus 4:22, where Moses is told to tell Pharaoh on behalf of Yahweh, 'Israel is my firstborn son ... let my son go that he may worship me (*'ābad*)'. English translations vary between 'that he may worship me', and 'that he may serve me'. The truth is, Yahweh was asking for both and Pharaoh was preventing both.

This is illustrated in the spiritual nature of Israel's bondage and their redemption, by the presentation of the conflict as a power encounter between the true divine power of Yahweh and the usurped divine claims of Pharaoh and 'all the gods of Egypt' (12:12). The sequence of plagues was not just a series of natural phenomena, though of course the natural order was catastrophically affected. All of them were directed at aspects of what Egyptians regarded as divine power – especially the first (the attack on the Nile) and the last but one (darkness, blotting out the sun). The Nile and the sun were among the foremost of all Egypt's deities. Yahweh proves his devastating sovereignty over both.[6]

The exodus demonstrates who is truly God. Yahweh stands alone and incomparable. And as a result of his decisive victory over all that opposed him and resisted his will, Israel is to know that Yahweh is God and there is no

---

6. Cf. M. Louise Holert, 'Extrinsic Evil Powers in the Old Testament', unpublished MTh thesis, Fuller Theological Seminary, 1985, pp. 55–72.

other (Deut. 4:35, 39), and to celebrate that 'the LORD will reign for ever and ever' (Exod. 15:18). The spiritual dimension of the exodus, then, is that God makes it clear his purpose in the whole process is that it should lead to the *knowledge, service* and *worship* of the living God. The implication is that all three of these were difficult, if not impossible, as long as they were in the depths of bondage to Pharaoh.

The Bible's first account of God in action as redeemer, then, is broad and deep and dynamic. In the exodus God responded to *all* the dimensions of Israel's need. God's momentous act of redemption did not merely rescue Israel from political, economic and social oppression and then leave them to their own devices to worship whom they pleased. Nor did God merely offer them spiritual comfort of hope for some brighter future in a home beyond the sky while leaving their historical condition unchanged. No, the exodus effected real change in the people's real historical situation and at the same time called them into a real new relationship with the living God. This was God's total response to Israel's total need.

The exodus and mission

What are we to take from our survey of the exodus narrative for our social theology and our practice of mission? We have seen that the exodus must be taken as a whole in all its dimensions. In this great event, as rendered to us through the biblical narrative, God *redeemed* Israel. The Bible tells us so. We have no liberty to extract some part of the whole and define redemption more narrowly or even exclusively in those terms. Exodus 15:13 celebrates the whole event under the metaphor of Yahweh as redeemer. The exodus, of course, was not God's only redeeming act, or even (in a full biblical perspective) his greatest. But it is the first that is described as such in the Bible, and the rest of the Bible clearly takes it as paradigmatic. That is, the exodus models for us the contours of what God himself means by redemption even if, of course, it was not yet all he planned to do in his redemptive purpose for humanity and creation.

If then, redemption is biblically defined in the first instance by the exodus, and if God's redeeming purpose is at the heart of God's mission, what does this tell us about mission as we are called to participate in it? The inevitable outcome surely is that *exodus-shaped redemption demands exodus-shaped mission*. And that means that our commitment to mission must demonstrate the same broad totality of concern for human need that God demonstrated in what he did for Israel. And it should also mean that our overall motivation and objective in mission be consistent with the motivation and purpose of God as declared in the exodus narrative. It is a basic biblical perception that *our* mission must be derived from *God's* mission. And the mission of God is expressed with exceptional clarity and repeated emphasis throughout the whole exodus narrative. The whole story is shaped and driven by God's agenda.

Two interpretative options fall short of a holistic missional hermeneutic of the exodus. One is to concentrate on its spiritual significance and marginalize the political, economic and social dimensions of the narrative. The other is to concentrate so much on its political, economic and social dimensions that the spiritual dimension is lost from sight. My critique in what follows is not meant to take sides by affirming that one is right and the other wrong. For both do have strong biblical support for the positive aspects of what they advocate. My point rather is that either approach, if its one-sided reductionism is driven too far, ends up in an unbalanced, less than fully biblical, missiological position. Both approaches may be accused of putting asunder what God has joined together, when what we need to do is to hold together the integrated totality of the narrative's impact.

A spiritualizing interpretation

This approach pays close attention to the way the New Testament uses the exodus as one model for explaining the significance of the death of Christ for the believer. Those who take this approach are fully right and justified in doing so, for this is clearly part of the New Testament's rich catalogue of explanatory models for the cross. Indeed, well before the cross, the exodus is used by all Gospel writers in their portrayal of the life, teaching and ministry of Jesus.[7] The problem is that, having rightly affirmed this spiritual and Christocentric interpretation of the exodus in the New Testament, popular preaching of the exodus then tends to dismiss or ignore the historical reality that constituted the original event for Israel – namely the actual deliverance out of real, earthy, injustice, oppression and violence.

---

7. The use of the exodus (and new exodus) theme in the New Testament is well documented by many scholars, e.g., F. F. Bruce, *This Is That: The New Testament Development of Some Old Testament Themes* (Exeter: Paternoster and Grand Rapids: Eerdmans, 1968); Rikki Watts, *Isaiah's New Exodus in Mark* (Grand Rapids: Baker, 1997); David Pao, *Acts and the Isaianic New Exodus* (Grand Rapids: Baker, 2000); Richard D. Patterson and Michael Travers, 'Contours of the Exodus Motif in Jesus' Earthly Ministry', *Westminster Theological Journal* 66 (2004). This last is an excellent compact summary of all relevant biblical material, and a helpful survey of scholarship on the theme.

The implication for mission follows. If the exodus narrative has anything to contribute to mission, it lies in the imperative to evangelize. For only through evangelism can we bring people deliverance from their slavery to sin, which is their deepest problem and is basically spiritual. This can be linked to the wonderful narrative of Moses' missionary call; for just as God sent Moses with the good news that God was going to save the Israelites from slavery to Pharaoh, so God sends us with the good news of how people can be saved from sin. My difficulty with this position and its missiological outcome is not in what it *affirms* (for I recognize its valid biblical foundations), but in what it simultaneously *omits*. I am not suggesting that it is not biblical, but that it is not biblical enough. Several reasons may be given for this.

First, the parallel between exodus and cross, at least in the popular form of expressing it, does not quite fit. Being delivered from slavery to our own sin is not quite parallel to the deliverance the Israelites experienced. For the exodus was decidedly not deliverance *from their own sin*. Now the Old Testament does know what it means to be delivered from the results of God's wrath on one's own sin. That is what the return from exile is all about. Nothing could be clearer than that Israel ended up in exile in Babylon because of the anger of God against their persistent wickedness over many generations. And equally the prophets interpret the return from exile not merely as deliverance from Babylon but as the blotting out of the sin that put them there. But there is no hint whatsoever that Israel's suffering in Egypt was God's judgment on their sin. The exodus, then, was indeed deliverance from slavery to sin – not Israel's own sin, but *the sin of those who oppressed them*.

The exodus was a climactic victory for Yahweh against the *external* powers of injustice, violence and death. In the exodus God brought his people up and out from under the enslaving power to which they were in bondage. When we grasp this, it would seem more appropriate to link the exodus to the cross, not so much in terms of release from slavery to our own sin (which of course is gloriously also part of its reality), but in terms of release from slavery to all that oppresses human life and well-being and opposes God. The cross, like the exodus, was the victory of God over his enemies, and through the cross God has rescued us from slavery to them. There is plenty of New Testament support for this reading of the cross as cosmic victory and of our salvation as rescue from bondage. Paul probably makes an exodus allusion as he thanks God the Father 'for he has rescued us from the dominion of darkness and brought us into the kingdom of the Son he loves, in whom we have redemption, the forgiveness of sins' (Col. 1:13–14). Later he speaks of Christ's triumph on the cross over all powers and authorities (Col. 2:15). Hebrews rejoices that the death of Christ is the means by which he has been able to 'free those who all their lives were held in slavery by their fear of death' (Heb. 2:15).

Secondly, a simplistic spiritualized interpretation of the exodus seems to me to presuppose a quite remarkable change in the character and concerns of God. Now, of course, the prophets are not afraid to speak of God changing his plans in response to Israel's (or any nation's) response to him. There is progression and development also in the biblical grand narrative. But this is much more radical than that. The spiritualizing way of interpreting the Bible, and the missiological implications that go with it, requires us to imagine that for generation after generation, century after century, the God of the Bible was passionately concerned about social issues – political arrogance and abuse, economic exploitation, judicial corruption, the suffering of the poor and oppressed, the evils of brutality and bloodshed. So passionate, indeed, that the laws he gave and the prophets he sent give more space to these matters than any other issue except idolatry, while the psalmists cry out in protest to the God they know cares deeply about such things.[8]

Somewhere, however, between Malachi and Matthew, all that changed. Such matters no longer claim God's attention or spark his anger. Or if they do, it is no longer our business. The root cause of all such things is spiritual sin, and that is now all that God is interested in, and that is all that the cross dealt with. A subtle form of Marcionism underlies this approach. The alleged God of the New Testament is almost unrecognizable as the Lord God, the Holy One of Israel. This alleged God has shed all the passionate priorities of the Mosaic law, and has jettisoned all the burdens for justice that he laid on his prophets at such cost to them. The implications for mission are equally dramatic. For if the pressing problems of human society are no longer of concern to God, they have no place in Christian mission – or at most a decidedly secondary one. God's mission is getting souls to heaven, not addressing society on earth. Ours should follow suit. There may be an element of caricature in the way I have sketched this view, but it is not unrepresentative of a certain brand of popular rhetoric.

I do *not* reject or reduce the terribly serious spiritual realities of sin and evil that the New Testament exposes, or the glories of the spiritual dimension of God's redemptive accomplishment in the cross and resurrection of Jesus of Nazareth. I simply deny that these truths of the New Testament *nullify* all that the Old Testament has already revealed about God's comprehensive commitment to every dimension of human life, about his relentless opposition

---

8. See the chapters in this volume written by David Baker and M. Daniel Carroll R.

to all that oppresses, spoils and diminishes human well-being, and about his ultimate mission of blessing the nations and redeeming his whole creation. Deriving our own missional mandate from this deep source precludes the kind of spiritualized reductionism that can read the exodus narrative, discern one vital dimension of its truth, and yet bypass the message that cries out from its pages as loudly as the Israelites cried out in their bondage.

A politicizing interpretation

At the other end of the hermeneutical spectrum are those who are drawn to the exodus narrative precisely *because* of its robust affirmation of Yahweh's passionate concern for justice, and his execution of that justice on a rogue state that first exploited the weak and then turned against them with murderous ferocity. They see this as the prime meaning of the exodus story: Yahweh is the God who hates oppression and acts decisively against it. The political, economic and social dimensions of Israel's plight, and the matching dimensions of God's deliverance, are thus explored to the full and built into a theology, an ethic, and a missiology of committed advocacy for the weak and marginalized of the world.

The most well-known protagonists of such a hermeneutic in the modern era,[9] of course, have been the different brands of liberation theology that emerged in Latin America and then spread to other parts of the world. In some (though by no means all) of these, the position is taken that God is at work redemptively wherever there is struggle against injustice and oppression. The biblical God declares himself, through the exodus story, to be on the side of all who are oppressed, so any action to throw off that oppression and to bring liberty and justice is, by its very nature, redemptive, saving – whether or not anybody comes to faith in Jesus Christ as Lord and Saviour, whether or not churches are planted. So we have the opposite of the first error, which was to emphasize the spiritual interpretation of the exodus in the New Testament and overlook its societal dimensions; in this case it is to emphasize the social justice dimension of the exodus while overlooking both its own inbuilt spir-

---

9. I say, 'in the modern era', in recognition of the fact that both Jews and Christians through the centuries have found in the exodus story powerful dynamics for political, social and economic struggle against the forces of oppression in many previous generations. See, e.g. Michael Walzer, *Exodus and Revolution* (New York: Basic Books, 1985). See also (but with a more subverting perspective on the normal liberationist reading of Exodus), J. David Pleins, *The Social Visions of the Hebrew Bible: A Theological Introduction* (Louisville: Westminster John Knox, 2001), ch. 4.

itual purpose as well as its explicit New Testament connection to the saving work of Christ. An exclusively political interpretation of the exodus, however, is as biblically deficient as an exclusively spiritual one. As before, my objection is not to the main case that such interpretations build (namely that the God of the Bible is committed to social justice and so should we be), but rather when the whole exodus tradition is reduced to that dimension alone, or severed from its spiritual and evangelistic implications.

My objection to the politicized interpretation of the exodus is not that it is hermeneutically wrong to use the exodus as evidence for God's passionate concern for justice and for human rights and dignity in wider society or the international arena (any more than the spiritual interpretation is wrong to use the exodus as a picture of the victory of the cross). The problem is not with what it says but where it stops. An interpretation which limits the relevance of the exodus to the political, social and economic realm, or prioritizes such issues at the expense, or even to the exclusion, of the spiritual question of whether or not people come to know the one living God, and to worship and serve him in covenant commitment and obedience, is simply not handling the text as a whole and is therefore seriously distorting it.

For we have seen that the goal of the exodus in the biblical story was clearly *not* confined to political liberation. Indeed, 'liberation' (with its modern sense of achieving freedom or independence), is not even the best word to describe the whole narrative. In various texts in Exodus, God or Moses speak of Yahweh's intention to 'bring out', 'rescue', 'redeem' or 'save' Israel from the Egyptians (e.g. 6:6; 14:13, 30). They do not talk merely of finding freedom in the modern sense of independence or self-determination. Rather, the purpose of the exodus was to bring Israel out of slavery (*'ăbodâ*) to Pharaoh so that they could properly enter the service/worship (*'ăbodâ*) of Yahweh. Israel's problem was not just that they were slaves and ought to be free. It was that they were *slaves to the wrong master and needed to be reclaimed and restored to their proper Lord.*

The exodus does not take Israel from serfdom to the freedom of independence but from service of one lord to service of another. Freedom in Scripture is the freedom to serve Yahweh. This dynamic suggests another direction in which we might need to reframe the emphases of liberation theology.[10]

So to work for political reform, the replacement of tyranny with democratic freedoms, to devise programmes of economic uplift and community development, to campaign for redistribution of resources, social justice, the restraint

---

10. John Goldingay, *Old Testament Theology, vol. 1: Israel's Gospel* (Downer's Grove: IVP, 2003), p. 323.

of state-sponsored violence or genocide, etc., are all positive things in themselves and Christians who engage in them can assuredly motivate their efforts
by reference to the character and will of God as revealed prominently throughout Scripture. But to *confine* oneself to such an agenda, without also seeking to
lead people to know God through repentance and faith in Christ, to worship
and serve him in covenant love, faithfulness and obedience (in other words
without effective evangelism and discipling), simply cannot be considered an
adequate expression of exodus-shaped redemption and is certainly not holistic, exodus-shaped mission.

Furthermore, to focus exclusively on the exodus as the biblical foundation
for a theology and mission of socio-political engagement is unbalanced in that
it ignores the rest of the biblical history of Israel. The people who enjoyed the
great benefit of Yahweh's redeeming intervention, who were delivered from
political discrimination, economic exploitation and social violence, went on to
allow all these things to poison their own life as a society in the centuries that
followed. And the wrath of God's judgment bore in upon rebellious Israel just
as severely as it had on the Egyptians – even more so. So the story that began
with the exodus ended with the exile. And this is a story which proved, as the
prophets and psalmists perceived, that Israel's deepest problem was the same
as that which afflicts all the rest of humanity – their own sinful rebellion, their
hardness of heart, their blindness to God's acts, their deafness to God's word,
their congenital unwillingness to do the one thing he asked – to fear the Lord,
walk in his ways, love him, serve him and obey him (Deut. 10:12).

And so, from the death and despair of exile, comes the voice that tells
Israel that although, yet again, God will indeed intervene in their national
history with another exodus (this time out of Babylon), their real need is not
just restoration to Jerusalem but *restoration to God*. What Israel needed was not
just the ending of their exile, but also the forgiveness of their sin. Both are
contained in the prophets' vocabulary of salvation (e.g. Isa. 43:25; Jer. 31:34;
Ezek. 36:24–32). Cyrus as God's agent could take care of the first, but only
the suffering Servant of the Yahweh would accomplish the second.[11] So the

---

11. 'One does not want to make a false distinction between the material and the
    spiritual, but in some sense the man of war can effect the former kind of
    restoration, but only the suffering servant the latter. A military victor can bring the
    Jews back to Jerusalem; but their history has exposed the depth of the problem of
    their sin, and it will take a suffering servant to bring them back to God.' John
    Goldingay, 'The Man of War and the Suffering Servant: The Old Testament and
    the Theology of Liberation', *Tyndale Bulletin* 27 (1976), p. 104.

spiritual dimension of Israel's (and humanity's) need, and the spiritual dimension of God's ultimate redemptive goal, are both recognized within the Old Testament itself. The New Testament did not add a spiritual dimension to an otherwise materialistic Old Testament understanding of redemption. It tells the story of how God accomplished that deepest dimension in the climactic work of Christ. Nor is it the *replacement* of the Old by the New, but a recognition of where the Old Testament's insights eventually must lead if the fullness of God's redeeming purpose was to be realized. [12]

An integral interpretation
My plea, then, is that if we are to regard the exodus as the prototype of God's redemption, as the Bible assuredly does in both testaments, we must apply the wholeness of its message and meaning to our practice of mission. Reducing our missional mandate to either pole of the whole model will result not only in hermeneutical distortion, but worse, in practical damage and deficiency in the fruit of our mission labours. Walter Brueggemann warns us, rightly in my view, against such reductionism in either direction:

> There is no doubt that the Old Testament witness concerns real socioeconomic and political circumstances, from which Yahweh is said to liberate Israel. There is also no doubt that the rhetoric of the New Testament permits a 'spiritualizing' of Exodus language, so that the liberation of the gospel is more readily understood as liberation from sin, in contrast with concrete socioeconomic-political bondage. It is not necessary here to reiterate the arguments concerning the genuine material forms of rescue presented in the New Testament. It is important to recognize, however, that already in the Old Testament, the witnesses to Yahweh understood that real, concrete, material bondage is authorized and enacted by 'the powers of death' that actively resist the intention of Yahweh. Thus we must not argue, in my judgement, that deliverance is material rather than spiritual or that salvation is spiritual rather than material. Rather, either side of such dualism distorts true human bondage and misreads Israel's text . . . The issue of the Bible, in both Testaments, is not one of either/or but of both/and. It will not do to be

---

12. 'The drift of the New Testament is along the line hinted at by Exodus and developed by Isaiah 40–55. In particular, the motifs of exodus, redemption, and liberation become predominantly spiritual; redemption from sin is the central idea, because man's weakness and wilfulness is his deepest problem, without which his political, social, and economic problems cannot be solved' (Goldingay, 'Man of War', p. 105).

reductionist in a materialist direction. Conversely it is simply wrong to refuse the material dimension of slavery and freedom in a safer spiritualizing theology, to which much Christian interpretation is tempted.[13]

To think that social action is all there is to mission, while failing to lead people to the knowledge, worship and service of God in Christ, is to condemn those whom we may, in one way or another, 'lead out of slavery' to repeat the history of Israel. For the Israelites experienced the political, social and economic effects of God's redemption, but many of them failed to enter into the spiritual requirements of the God who redeemed them. They would not acknowledge him as God alone. They repeatedly went astray in the worship of other gods. They chose to serve other nations in alliances that were spiritually and politically calamitous. They experienced God as redeemer – the Old Testament affirms that persistently. But they would not submit to God as king and walk in his ways. So in more ways than one, they perished.

The social, political and economic dimensions of God's redeeming work were real, vital and they still remain as pressing priorities for God – as every prophet testified. But they did not constitute the totality of what God intended by a covenant relationship with this people. Without covenant faith, covenant worship and covenant obedience, Israel stood as much under the severity of God's wrath as any other nation. A change of political or economic or geographical landscape, a change of government, a change of social status, may all be beneficial in themselves but they will be of no eternal benefit unless the spiritual goals of exodus are also met. So to change people's social or economic status without leading them to saving faith and obedience to God in Christ leads no further than the wilderness or the exile, both places of death.

But on the other hand, to think that spiritual evangelism is all there is to mission, is to leave people vulnerable in other ways that are also mirrored in Israel. 'Spiritual evangelism' means that the gospel is presented only as a means of having your own sins forgiven and having assurance of a future with God in heaven – without either the moral challenge of walking with personal integrity in the world of social, economic and political society around us, or the missional challenge of being actively concerned for issues of justice and compassion for others. The result is a kind of privatized pietism, or one that is cosily shared with like-minded believers, but has little cutting edge or prophetic relevance in relation to wider society. One can then be a Christian

---

13. Walter Brueggemann, *Theology of the Old Testament: Testimony, Dispute and Advocacy* (Minneapolis: Fortress, 2003), p. 180.

on the way to heaven, and even make a virtue out of paying little attention to the physical, material, familial, societal and international needs and crises that abound on every side. These latter things can then be all too easily relegated to such a non-priority status that they drop below the radar of mission recognition altogether.

Israel fell victim to this temptation too. The prophets saw a people whose appetite for worship was insatiable but whose daily lives were a denial of all the moral standards of the God they claimed to worship. There was plenty of charismatic fervour (Amos 5:21–24), plenty of atonement theology in the blood of multiple sacrifices (Isa. 1:10–12), plenty of assurance of salvation in the recitation of sound-bite claims for the temple (Jer. 7:4–11), plenty of religious observance at great festivals and conventions (Isa 1:13–15). But beneath their noses and under their feet, the poor were uncared for at best and trampled on at worst. Spiritual religion flourished amidst social rottenness. And God hated it. God longed for somebody to shut down the whole charade (Mal. 1:10), and finally he wiped it out of his sight.

Mission that claims the high spiritual ground of preaching only a gospel of personal forgiveness and salvation without the radical challenge of the full biblical demands of God's justice and compassion, without a hunger and thirst for justice, may well expose those who respond to its partial truths to the same dangerous verdict. The epistle of James seems to say as much to those in his own day who had managed to drive an unbiblical wedge between faith and works, the spiritual and the material. If faith without works is dead, mission without social compassion and justice is biblically deficient.

Paradigms of redemption: the jubilee

Elsewhere I have argued for a paradigmatic approach to handling the laws of the Old Testament as Christians, in order to discern their ethical implications in the contemporary world.[14] This means identifying the coherent body of principles on which an Old Testament law or institution is based and which it embodies or instantiates. To do this, it is helpful once more to move around our three angles and consider how Israel's paradigm, in the particular case of the jubilee institution (see Lev. 25), speaks to Christian ethics and mission.

---

14. Christopher J. H. Wright, *Old Testament Ethics for the People of God* (Leicester: IVP, 2004), ch. 9.

The economic dimension

The jubilee existed to protect a form of land tenure that was based on an equitable and widespread distribution of the land, and to prevent the accumulation of ownership in the hands of a wealthy few. This echoes the wider creation principle that the whole earth is given by God to all humanity, who act as co-stewards of its resources. There is a parallel between, on the one hand, the affirmation of Leviticus 25:23, in respect of *Israel*, that 'the land is mine', and on the other hand, the affirmation of Psalm 24:1, in respect of *all humanity*, that 'the earth is the LORD's and everything in it, the world and all who live in it'. The moral principles of the jubilee are therefore universalizable on the basis of the moral consistency of God. What God required of Israel in God's land reflects what in principle he desires for humanity on God's earth – namely broadly equitable distribution of the resources of the earth, especially land, and a curb on the tendency towards accumulation with its inevitable oppression and alienation.

The jubilee thus stands as a critique not only of massive private accumulation of land and related wealth, but also of large-scale forms of collectivism or nationalization which destroy any meaningful sense of personal or family ownership. It still has a point to make in modern Christian approaches to economics. The jubilee did not, of course, entail a redistribution of land, as some popular writings mistakenly suppose. It was not a redistribution but a restoration. It was not a free handout of bread or 'charity', but a restoration to family units of the opportunity and the resources to provide for themselves again. In modern application, that calls for some creative thinking as to what forms of opportunity and resources would enable people to do that, and to enjoy the dignity and social involvement that such self-provision entails.[15] The jubilee, then, is about restoring to people the capacity to participate in the economic life of the community, for their own viability and society's benefit. There is both ethical and missional relevance in that.

The social dimension

The jubilee embodied practical concern for the family unit. In Israel's case, this meant the extended family, the 'father's house', which was a sizeable group of related nuclear families descended in the male line from a living progenitor,

---

15. Interesting and creative applications of the jubilee and other aspects of Old Testament economics are found in John Mason, 'Biblical Teaching and Assisting the Poor', *Transformation* 4.2 (1987), and Stephen Charles Mott, 'The Contribution of the Bible to Economic Thought', *Transformation* 4.3–4 (1987).

including up to three or four generations. This was the smallest unit in Israel's kinship structure, and it was the focus of identity, status, responsibility and security for the individual Israelite. It was this social unit, the extended family, that the jubilee aimed to protect and periodically to restore if necessary.

Notably the jubilee law pursued this objective, not by merely 'moral' means (i.e. appealing for greater family cohesion or admonishing parents and children to greater exercise of discipline and obedience respectively). Rather, the jubilee approach was immensely practical and fundamentally *socioeconomic*. It established specific structural mechanisms to regulate the economic effects of debt. Family morality was meaningless if families were being split up and dispossessed by economic forces that rendered them powerless (cf. Neh. 5:1–5). The jubilee aimed to restore social dignity and participation to families through maintaining or restoring their economic viability.[16]

Debt is a huge cause of social disruption and decay, and tends to breed many other social ills, including crime, poverty, squalor and violence. Debt happens, and the Old Testament recognizes that fact. But the jubilee was an attempt to limit its otherwise relentless and endless social consequences by limiting its possible duration. The economic collapse of a family in one generation was not to condemn all future generations to the bondage of perpetual indebtedness. Such principles and objectives are certainly not irrelevant to welfare legislation or indeed any legislation with socioeconomic implications. And indeed, taken to a wider level still, the jubilee speaks volumes to the massive issue of international debt. Not for nothing was the worldwide campaign to see an ending of the intolerable and interminable debts of impoverished nations called *Jubilee 2000*. And many Christians have instinctively felt a moral imperative to support the campaign, not only out of compassion for the poor, but out of a biblically rooted sense of justice and what God requires of us.

The theological dimension
The jubilee was based upon several central affirmations of Israel's faith, and the importance of these should not be overlooked when assessing its relevance to Christian ethics and mission. As we observed with the exodus, it would be

---

16. A thorough attempt to apply the relevance of the Old Testaments patterns regarding the extended family to modern Western society is made by Michael Schluter and Roy Clements, *Reactivating the Extended Family: From Biblical Norms to Public Policy in Britain* (Cambridge: Jubilee Centre, 1986). See further, Michael Schluter and John Ashcroft (eds.), *Jubilee Manifesto: A Framework, Agenda and Strategy for Christian Social Reform* (Leicester: IVP, 2005), ch. 9.

quite wrong to limit the challenge of the jubilee to the socioeconomic realm and ignore its inner spiritual and theological motivation. From a holistic missiological point of view, each is as important as the other, for all are fully biblical and all fully reflect the character and will of God. The following points stand out in the text.

Like the rest of the sabbatical provisions, the jubilee proclaimed the *sovereignty of God* over time and nature, and obedience to it would require submission to that sovereignty. That is, his people were to keep the jubilee as an act of obedience to God. This Godward dimension of the matter is why the year is deemed holy, 'a sabbath to Yahweh' (Lev. 25:4), and why it was to be observed out of the 'fear of Yahweh' (v. 17).

Furthermore, observing the fallow year dimension of the jubilee would also require faith in *God's providence* as the one who could command blessing in the natural order and thereby provide for basic needs (vv. 18–22).

Additional motivation for the law is provided by repeated appeals to the knowledge of *God's historical act of redemption,* the exodus and all it had meant for Israel. The jubilee was a way of outworking the implications within the community of the fact that all Israelites were simply the former slaves of Pharaoh, now the redeemed slaves of Yahweh (vv. 38, 42–43, 55).

And to this historical dimension was added the cultic and 'present' *experience of forgiveness* in the fact that the jubilee was to be proclaimed on the Day of Atonement (v. 9). To know yourself forgiven by God was to issue immediately in practical remission of the debt and bondage of others. Some of the parables of Jesus spring to mind.

And the inbuilt future hope of the literal jubilee blended with an *eschatological hope* of God's final restoration of humanity and nature to his original purpose. There is a strong theological pulse beating in this chapter of Leviticus.

To apply the jubilee model, then, requires that people obey the sovereignty of God, trust the providence of God, know the story of the redeeming action of God, experience personally the sacrificial atonement provided by God, practise God's justice and put their hope in God's promise for the future. Now if we summon people to do these things, what are we engaging in? Surely these are the very fundamentals of evangelism.

It is no wonder, as we shall see in a moment, that the jubilee itself became a picture of the new age of salvation that the New Testament announces. It is an institution that models in a small corner of ancient Israelite economics the essential contours of God's wider mission for the restoration of humanity and creation. When appropriately set in the light of the rest of the biblical witness, *the wholeness of the jubilee model embraces the wholeness of the church's mission, its personal and social ethics and its future hope.*

Jesus and the jubilee

The future orientation of the jubilee serves additionally as a bridge to seeing how it influenced Jesus, and helps us answer questions as to whether our insistence on a holistic understanding of mission is sustained in the New Testament.

Looking to the future

Even at a purely economic level in ancient Israel, the jubilee was intended to have a built-in future dimension. Anticipation of the jubilee was supposed to affect all present economic values (including the provisional price of land). It also set a temporal limit on unjust social relations – they would not last forever. The jubilee brought hope for change. It was proclaimed with a blast on the trumpet (the *yôbēl,* from which its name derives), an instrument associated with decisive acts of God (cf. Isa. 27:13; 1 Cor. 15:52). However, as time went by, and even when the jubilee probably fell into disuse in practice, its symbolism remained potent. We have seen that the jubilee had two major thrusts: release/ liberty and return/restoration (from Lev. 25:10). Both of these were easily transferred from the strictly economic provision of the jubilee itself to a wider metaphorical application. That is, these economic terms became terms of hope and longing for the future, and thus entered into prophetic eschatology.

There are allusive echoes of the jubilee particularly in the later chapters of Isaiah. The mission of the Servant of Yahweh has strong elements of the restorative plan of God for his people, aimed specifically at the weak and oppressed (Isa. 42:1–7). Isaiah 58 is an attack on cultic observance without social justice, and calls for liberation of the oppressed (v. 6), specifically focus-ing on people's own kinship obligations (v. 7). Most clearly of all, Isaiah 61 uses jubilee images to portray the one anointed as the herald of Yahweh to 'evangelize' the poor, to proclaim liberty to the captives (using the word *dĕrôr* which is the explicitly jubilary word for release), and to announce the year of Yahweh's favour (almost certainly an allusion to a jubilee year). The hope of *redemption and return* for God's people are combined in the future vision of Isaiah 35, and set alongside the equally dramatic hope of a transformation of nature. Thus, within the Old Testament itself, the jubilee had already attracted an eschatological imagery, alongside its ethical application in the present. That is to say, the jubilee could be used to portray *God's* final intervention for mes-sianic redemption and restoration; but it could still function to justify ethical challenge for *human* justice to the oppressed in the present.

Looking to Jesus

How, then, was the institution of jubilee taken up by Jesus and applied in the New Testament to the age of fulfilment that he inaugurated? How, in other words, did jubilee relate to the wider sense of Old Testament promise that Jesus fulfilled? Jesus announced the imminent arrival of the eschatological reign of God. He claimed that his people's hopes for restoration and for messianic reversal were being fulfilled in his own ministry. To explain what he meant, he used imagery from the jubilee circle of ideas (among others, of course).

The 'Nazareth manifesto' (Luke 4:16–30) is the clearest programmatic statement of this. It is the closest Jesus comes to a personal mission statement, and it quotes directly from Isaiah 61, which as we have seen was strongly influenced by jubilee concepts. Most commentators observe this jubilee background to the prophetic text and Jesus' use of it. It certainly builds a holistic dimension into the mission that Jesus sets out for himself by reading this scripture and claiming to be its embodiment.

Luke will not allow us to interpret this jubilee language as flowery metaphors or spiritual allegories: Jesus fulfilled the jubilee that he proclaimed. His radical mission was the very mission of God found in the Old Testament proclamation of jubilee. It is presented in Luke's Gospel as holistic in four aspects:

1. It is both proclaimed and enacted.
2. It is both spiritual and physical.
3. It is both for Israel and the nations.
4. It is both present and eschatological.[17]

Other examples of the influence of the jubilee on Jesus' thinking are suggested by Robert Sloan and Sharon Ringe. Sloan observed that Jesus' use of the word for 'release', *aphesis*, carries both the sense of *spiritual* forgiveness of sin and also literal and *financial* remission of actual debts. Thus, the original jubilee background of economic release has been preserved in Jesus' challenge concerning ethical response to the kingdom of God. If we are to pray the Lord's prayer, 'release for us our debts', we must be willing to release others from theirs. It is not a matter of deciding between a spiritual and a material meaning, for both can be included as appropriate.[18]

Ringe traces the interweaving of major jubilee images into various parts of the Gospel narratives and the teaching of Jesus. There are echoes of jubilee in the beatitudes (Matt. 5:2–12), in Jesus' response to John the Baptist (Matt. 11:2–6),

---

17. Paul Hertig, 'The Jubilee Mission of Jesus in the Gospel of Luke: Reversals of Fortunes', *Missiology* 26 (1998), pp. 167–179, pp. 176–177.

18. Robert B. Sloan Jr., *The Favorable Year of the Lord: A Study of Jubilary Theology in the Gospel of Luke* (Austin: Schola, 1977).

in the parable of the banquet (Luke 14:12–24), in various episodes of forgiveness and especially teaching on debts (Matt. 18:21–35, etc.).[19] The evidence is broad, and conforms to the pattern already observed in the Old Testament. At the level of fairly explicit allusion and implicit influence, the jubilee serves both as a *symbol of future hope* and also as an *ethical demand in the present.*

Looking to the Spirit

The book of Acts shows that the early church had a similar combination of future expectation and present ethical response. The jubilee concept of eschatological restoration is found in the otherwise unique idea of 'complete restoration'. The unusual word for this, *apokatastasis*, occurs in Acts 1:6 and 3:21, where it speaks of God's final restoration of Israel and all things. It seems Peter has taken the core of the jubilee hope (restoration) and applied it, not just to the restoration of land to farmers, but to the restoration of the whole creation through the coming Messiah.

Significantly, however, the early church responded to this future hope not merely by sitting waiting for it to happen. Rather, they put into practice some of the jubilee ideals at the level of mutual economic help. Luke almost certainly intends us to understand that in doing so they were fulfilling the sabbatical hopes of Deuteronomy 15. Acts 4:34, with its simple statement that 'there were no needy persons among them', is virtually a quotation of the Greek Septuagint translation of Deuteronomy 15:4, 'there will be no needy person among you'. The new community of Christ, now living in the eschatological era of the Spirit, is making the future hope a present reality in economic terms. Or to put it another way, the church by its internal practice was erecting a signpost to the reality of the future. The new age of life in the Messiah and in the Spirit is described in terms that echo the jubilee and its related sabbatical institutions.[20] And the effect was a community in mission, marked by an integral combination

---

19. Sharon H. Ringe, *Jesus, Liberation, and the Biblical Jubilee: Images for Ethics and Christology* (Philadelphia: Fortress, 1985). For a concise survey of various interpretations of the way Luke uses Isaiah 61 here, see also Robert Willoughby, 'The Concept of Jubilee and Luke 4:18–30', in Anthony Billington, Tony Lane and Max Turner (eds.), *Mission and Meaning: Essays Presented to Peter Cotterell* (Carlisle: Paternoster, 1995), pp. 41–55.

20. In addition to my own work, already referred to, a full and helpful account of the way Jesus and the rest of the New Testament related to the rich scriptural traditions of the land is David E. Holwerda, *Jesus and Israel: One Covenant or Two?* (Grand Rapids: Eerdmans and Leicester: Apollos, 1995), pp. 85–112.

of verbal proclamation (the evangelistic preaching of the apostles), and visible attraction (the social and economic equality of the believers). Not surprisingly, the church grew in numbers, strength, maturity and mission.

The ultimate paradigm of redemption: the cross

For any social theology of mission to claim to be biblical it must have at its core that which is at the very core of biblical faith – the cross of Christ. So if we are to establish that a truly biblical understanding of mission is holistic, integrating all the dimensions we have been surveying hitherto, then we must ask how all of that coheres around the cross.

A mission-centred theology of the cross

God's mission has many dimensions as we trace the theme of his saving purpose through the different strands of Scripture. But every dimension of that mission of God led inexorably to the cross of Christ. *The cross was the unavoidable cost of God's mission.* Think for a moment of some of the great contours of God's redemptive purpose. The following items (at least) would probably have been included by Paul in what he called 'the whole counsel (or purpose) of God' (Acts 20:27, ESV). I list them as minimally as possible although every point deserves a theological discourse of its own (and each has generated many).

It was the purpose or mission of God:

- *To deal with the guilt of human sin*, which had to be punished for God's own justice to be vindicated. And at the cross God accomplished this. God took that guilt and punishment upon himself in loving and willing self-substitution through the person of his own Son. For 'the LORD has laid on him the iniquity of us all' (Isa. 53:6), and 'Christ himself bore our sins in his body on the tree' (1 Pet. 2:24). The cross is the place of personal pardon, forgiveness and justification for guilty sinners.
- *To defeat the powers of evil,* and all the forces (angelic, spiritual, 'seen or unseen'), that oppress, crush, invade, spoil and destroy human life, whether directly or by human agency. And at the cross God accomplished this, 'having disarmed the powers and authorities . . . triumphing over them by the cross' (Col. 2:15). The cross is the place of defeat for all cosmic evil and seals its ultimate destruction.
- *To destroy death,* the great invader and enemy of human life in God's world. And at the cross God did so, when by Christ's death he destroyed 'him who holds the power of death – that is, the devil' (Heb. 2:14). The

cross, paradoxically the most terrible symbol of death in the ancient world, is the fount of life.

- *To remove the barrier of enmity and alienation between Jew and Gentile,* and by implication ultimately all forms of enmity and alienation. And at the cross God did so: 'For he himself is our peace, who has made the two one and has destroyed the barrier . . . to create . . . one new humanity out of the two, thus making peace, and in this one body to reconcile both of them to God through the cross, by which he put to death their hostility' (Eph. 2:14–16, TNIV). The cross is the place of reconciliation, to God and one another.
- *To heal and reconcile his whole creation,* the cosmic mission of God. And at the cross God made this ultimately possible. For it is God's final will 'through [Christ] to reconcile to himself all things, whether things on earth or things in heaven, by making peace through his blood, shed on the cross' (Col. 1:20). The 'all things' here must clearly mean the whole created cosmos, since that is what Paul says has been created by Christ and for Christ (vv. 15–16), and has now been reconciled by Christ (v. 20). The cross is the guarantee of a healed creation to come.

So then, all these huge dimensions of God's redemptive mission are set before us in the Bible. All of these together constitute the mission of God. And all of these led to the cross of Christ. *The cross was the unavoidable cost of God's total mission* – as Jesus himself accepted, in his agony in Gethsemane: 'not my will, but yours, be done'.

A full biblical understanding of the atoning work of Christ on the cross (of which the above points are the merest sketch), goes far beyond (though, of course, it includes) the matter of personal guilt and individual forgiveness. That Jesus died in my place, bearing the guilt of my sin, as my voluntary substitute, is the most gloriously liberating truth, to which we cling in glad and grateful worship with tears of wonder. That I should long for others to know this truth and be saved and forgiven by casting their sins on the crucified Saviour in repentance and faith, is the most energizing motive for evangelism. All of this must be maintained with total commitment and personal conviction. But there is more in the biblical theology of the cross than individual salvation, and there is more to biblical mission than evangelism. The gospel is good news for the whole creation (to whom, according to the longer ending of Mark, it is to be preached, Mark 16:15; cf. Eph. 3:10). To point out these wider dimensions of God's redemptive mission (and therefore of our committed participation in God's mission), is *not* 'watering down' the gospel of personal salvation, (as is sometimes alleged). Rather, we set that most precious personal good news for the individual firmly and affirmatively within its full biblical context of *all* that God has achieved, and will finally complete, through the cross of Christ.

A cross-centred theology of mission

So, the cross was the unavoidable cost of *God's* mission. But it is equally true, and biblical, to say that the cross is the unavoidable centre of *our* mission. All Christian mission flows from the cross – as its source, its power, and as that which defines its scope. It is vital that we see the cross as central and integral to every aspect of holistic, biblical mission – that is, of all we do in the name of the crucified and risen Jesus. It is a mistake, in my view, to think that, while our evangelism must be centred on the cross (as of course it has to be), our social engagement and other forms of practical mission work, have some other theological foundation or justification. The fact is that sin and evil constitute bad news in every area of life on this planet. The redemptive work of God through the cross of Christ is good news for every area of life on earth that has been touched by sin – which means every area of life. Bluntly, we need a holistic gospel because the world is in a holistic mess. By God's incredible grace we have a gospel big enough to redeem all that sin and evil has touched. And every dimension of that good news is good news utterly and only because of the blood of Christ on the cross.

Ultimately all that will be there in the new, redeemed creation will be there because of the cross. And conversely, all that will *not* be there (suffering, tears, sin, Satan, sickness, oppression, corruption, decay and death), will not be there because they will have been defeated and destroyed by the cross. That is the length, breadth, height and depth of God's idea of redemption. It is exceedingly good news. It is the heart of biblical social theology. It is the font of all our mission.

So it is my passionate conviction that holistic mission must have a holistic theology of the cross. That includes the conviction that the cross must be as central to our social engagement as it is to our evangelism. There is no other power, no other resource, no other name, through which we can offer the whole gospel to the whole person and the whole world, than Jesus Christ crucified and risen.

Bibliography

BAUCKHAM, R., 'First Steps to a Theology of Nature', *Evangelical Quarterly* 58 (1986), pp. 229–244.

BRUCE, F. F., *This Is That: The New Testament Development of Some Old Testament Themes* (Exeter and Grand Rapids: Paternoster and Eerdmans, 1968).

BRUEGGEMANN, W., *Theology of the Old Testament: Testimony, Dispute and Advocacy* (Minneapolis: Fortress, 2003).

GOLDINGAY, J., *Old Testament Theology, vol. 1: Israel's Gospel* (Downer's Grove: IVP, 2003).

_____, 'The Man of War and the Suffering Servant: The Old Testament and the Theology of Liberation', *Tyndale Bulletin* 27 (1976), pp. 79–113.

HELDT, J.-P., 'Revisiting the "Whole Gospel": Toward a Biblical Model of Holistic Mission in the 21st Century', *Missiology* 32 (2004), pp. 149–172.

HERTIG, P., 'The Jubilee Mission of Jesus in the Gospel of Luke: Reversals of Fortunes', *Missiology* 26 (1998), pp. 167–179.

HOLERT, M. L., 'Extrinsic Evil Powers in the Old Testament', unpublished MTh thesis, Fuller Theological Seminary, 1985.

HOLWERDA, D. E., *Jesus and Israel: One Covenant or Two?* (Grand Rapids and Leicester: Eerdmans and Apollos, 1995).

MASON, J., 'Biblical Teaching and Assisting the Poor', *Transformation* 4.2 (1987), pp. 1–14.

MOTT, S. C., 'The Contribution of the Bible to Economic Thought', *Transformation* 4.3–4 (1987), pp. 25–34.

PAO, D., *Acts and the Isaianic New Exodus* (Grand Rapids: Baker, 2000).

PATTERSON, R. D. and TRAVERS, M., 'Contours of the Exodus Motif in Jesus' Earthly Ministry', *Westminster Theological Journal* 66 (2004), pp. 25–47.

PLEINS, J. D., *The Social Visions of the Hebrew Bible: A Theological Introduction* (Louisville: Westminster John Knox, 2001).

RINGE, S. H., *Jesus, Liberation, and the Biblical Jubilee: Images for Ethics and Christology* (Philadelphia: Fortress, 1985).

SCHLUTER M. and ASHCROFT J. (eds.), *Jubilee Manifesto: A Framework, Agenda and Strategy for Christian Social Reform* (Leicester: IVP, 2005).

SCHLUTER, M. and CLEMENTS, R., *Reactivating the Extended Family: From Biblical Norms to Public Policy in Britain* (Cambridge: Jubilee Centre, 1986).

SLOAN Jr., R. B., *The Favorable Year of the Lord: A Study of Jubilary Theology in the Gospel of Luke* (Austin: Schola, 1977).

WALZER, M., *Exodus and Revolution* (New York: Basic Books, 1985).

WATTS, R., *Isaiah's New Exodus in Mark* (Grand Rapids: Baker, 1997).

WILLOUGHBY, R., 'The Concept of Jubilee and Luke 4:18–30', in BILLINGTON, A., LANE, T. and TURNER, M. (eds.), *Mission and Meaning: Essays Presented to Peter Cotterell* (Carlisle: Paternoster, 1995), pp. 41–55.

WRIGHT, C. J. H., *Old Testament Ethics for the People of God* (Leicester: IVP, 2004).

_____, *The Mission of God: Unlocking the Bible's Grand Narrative* (Nottingham: IVP, 2006).

5. THE COMPASSION OF THE CHRIST

Alistair I. Wilson

> Whereas first-century Judaism spoke primarily of the holiness of God, Jesus spoke primarily of the compassion of God.[1]

Did Jesus speak, 'primarily of the compassion of God', as Marcus Borg claims? Borg has been one of the champions of the view that Jesus' ministry was primarily about compassion. And who would want to challenge such a view? In fact, we might wish to go further than Borg and ask, 'Did Jesus *embody* compassion in the way in which he dealt with people?' D. L. Parkyn answers affirmatively, 'Compassion is demonstrated in the life of Jesus, and it is also part of the instruction he gave to those who inquired how they might follow him', drawing attention to Matthew 9:36 and also to the parable of the Good Samaritan in Luke 10.[2]

In seeking to answer the question regarding the place of compassion in Jesus' ministry, we are faced with the surprising fact that the term 'compassion' is used relatively infrequently in English translations of the canonical

---

1. M. Borg, *Jesus, A New Vision* (London: SPCK, 1987), p. 130.
2. D. L. Parkyn, 'Compassion', in D. J. Atkinson, D. H. Field, O. O'Donovan and A. F. Holmes (eds.), *New Dictionary of Christian Ethics and Pastoral Theology* (Leicester: IVP, 1995), p. 244.

Gospels, but we have to remember that the concept may be expressed using more than one term or even by means of a demonstration of the concept without the use of key terms at all. Even if we establish that compassion is an important concept for understanding Jesus, what does that say about him and what implications does it have? What does it mean to say that Jesus was 'a man of compassion'?

Scope, method and outline

This essay is one of several papers dealing with the New Testament. I have been asked to consider the theme of Jesus' compassion, which means that I must turn to the four canonical Gospels as my primary source material. Another essay, however, will deal with Luke-Acts, which happen to contain a significant number of relevant and important texts. So as to avoid unnecessary duplication, I will therefore make only passing reference to Luke's writings.

Methodologically speaking, it is important to avoid the danger of some older 'word study' approaches which focused particularly on a set of specific terms. This approach tended to equate particular terms with the concept the terms described. Recent studies have recognized that a concept (in our case, compassion) can be represented in a text even where there is no use of particular key terms. Likewise, it is as important to consider the records of the acts of Jesus as it is to consider the records of his words. On the other hand, careful attention paid to passages where key terms are used may take us to the heart of this discussion.

Since I have been asked to consider the compassion of Jesus rather than the treatment of the theme by a canonical document, I will feel free to draw on any of the canonical Gospels (largely excepting Luke, as explained above), but I do not intend to discuss the authenticity of recorded sayings or actions. I am going to assume (as I believe) that the canonical records accurately reflect the sayings and actions of Jesus.

In this paper I intend to begin by formulating a working definition of 'compassion'. Then I will proceed to consider a small selection of texts which either explicitly identify compassion as a quality of Jesus, or which present Jesus as acting in a way that may be described as compassionate. These will be taken both from two of the synoptic evangelists, Matthew and Mark, and from John's Gospel. We will see that there is a variety of different circumstances in which Jesus demonstrates compassion.

Definition

As we begin to consider the issue of 'compassion' in the Gospels, we are faced with the fundamental question of how we are to define this term. One modern English dictionary defines the term as 'pity inclining one to be helpful or merciful'[3] but, in order to do justice to the biblical presentation, we must look at the linguistic data from the Greek New Testament and its background in the Old Testament and at the way these terms are actually employed by the authors of the Gospels.

Terminology

Louw-Nida's *Lexicon* identifies a group of Greek words which relate to 'love, affection, compassion' (25.33–25.58). Included in this group are the following terms:

- *phileō*, defined as 'to have love or affection for someone or something based on association'.
- *agapaō*, defined as 'to have love for someone or something, based on sincere appreciation and high regard – to love, to regard with affection, loving concern, love'.
- *splanchnizomai*, defined as 'to experience great affection and compassion for someone – to feel compassion for, to have great affection for, love, compassion'.
- *embrimaomai*, defined as 'to have an intense, strong feeling of concern, often with the implication of indignation – to feel strongly, to be indignant'. This term is probably relevant to our theme, but its precise nuance in John 11:33 is the subject of much debate.[4]

Of these terms, *splanchnizomai* is particularly significant and will receive particular attention in this paper. However, while we note the importance of these key terms, we should not limit our study to these linguistic data. It is also possible to recognize Jesus' compassion in texts which do not explicitly mention it. An obvious example (apparently, at least) is John 11:35 where Jesus weeps at the tomb of Lazarus; a passage to which we shall return later.

---

3. *The Concise Oxford Dictionary* (Oxford: Clarendon Press, 1984), p. 191.
4. See the discussion in A. Köstenberger, *John* (BECNT; Grand Rapids, Baker, 2004), pp. 339–340.

The humanity of Christ

We may begin our definition by recognizing that 'compassion' is a human emotion and therefore Jesus' compassion highlights the reality that he shared in human emotion. The classic essay on this topic is that of B. B. Warfield, who opens his essay with the claim, 'It belongs to the truth of our Lord's humanity, that he was subject to all sinless emotions.'[5]

More particularly, Warfield continues, 'The emotion which we should naturally expect to find most frequently attributed to that Jesus whose whole life was a mission of mercy, and whose ministry was so marked by deeds of beneficence that it was summed up in the memories of his followers as a going through the land "doing good" (Acts xi. 38), is no doubt "compassion." In point of fact, this is the emotion which is most frequently attributed to him.'[6]

How frequently, in fact, is 'compassion' attributed to Jesus in the Gospels? A quick search of the English Standard Version (an 'essentially literal'[7] translation) using BibleWorks 7 reveals the following verses which use the term 'compassion':

Matthew 9:36: 'When he saw the crowds, he had compassion (*esplanchnisthe*[8]) for them, because they were harassed and helpless, like sheep without a shepherd.'

Matthew 14:14 (cf. Mark 6:34): 'When he went ashore he saw a great crowd, and he had compassion (*esplanchnisthe*) on them and healed their sick.'

Matthew 15:32 (cf. Mark 8:2): 'Then Jesus called his disciples to him and said, "I have compassion (*splanchnizomai*) on the crowd because they have been with me now three days and have nothing to eat. And I am unwilling to send them away hungry, lest they faint on the way."'

Mark 9:22: 'And it has often cast him into fire and into water, to destroy him. But if you can do anything, have compassion on us and help us.'

---

5. B. B. Warfield, 'The Emotional Life of Our Lord', in *The Person and Work of Christ* (Phillipsburg: P&R, 1950), p. 93. See also M. A. Elliott, *Faithful Feelings: Emotion in the New Testament* (Leicester: IVP, 2005 and Grand Rapids: Kregel, 2006), pp. 249–250, who confirms Warfield's findings.

6. Warfield, 'Emotional Life', p. 96.

7. <http://www.esv.org/translation/philosophy> (accessed 18 May 2007).

8. A form of the root verb *splanchnizomai*.

Luke 7:13: 'And when the Lord saw her, he had compassion (*esplanchnisthe*) on her and said to her, "Do not weep."'

Luke 10:33: 'But a Samaritan, as he journeyed, came to where he was, and when he saw him, he had compassion (*esplanchnisthe*).'

Luke 15:20: 'And he arose and came to his father. But while he was still a long way off, his father saw him and felt compassion (*esplanchnisthe*), and ran and embraced him and kissed him.'

A comparison of the ESV and the NIV shows that these two representative modern translations generally translate forms of *splanchnizomai* using the term 'compassion', but that each of them sometimes deviate from this translation of this particular verb (NIV uses 'pity' in Matt. 18:27; Mark 9:22; Luke 10:33: 'heart went out' in Luke 7:13; ESV uses 'pity' in Matt. 18:27; 20:34; Mark 1:41:). Likewise, the KJV translates forms of *eleeō* with 'compassion' in two cases where modern translations translate more precisely with 'mercy'. Yet the concept of mercy may indeed be quite closely related to that of compassion. This is seen in the way that Yahweh reveals his character to Moses in Exodus 33:19: 'And he said, "I will make all my goodness pass before you and will proclaim before you my name 'The LORD'. And I will be gracious to whom I will be gracious, and will show mercy on whom I will show mercy."' (NIV: 'I will have mercy on whom I will have mercy, and I will have compassion on whom I will have compassion.')[9] Thus we can see that there is a measure of overlap between 'compassion', 'pity' and 'mercy'.

It is striking that there are no occurrences of explicit 'compassion' language in the Gospel of John (in English or Greek), although we have already noted that this does not necessarily imply the absence of the concept and we will have to look at this more closely later.[10]

---

9. On the OT background to the concept of mercy, based on a study of *hesed*, see particularly F. I. Andersen, 'Yahweh, the Kind and Sensitive God', in P. T. O'Brien and D. G. Peterson (eds.), *God Who Is Rich in Mercy: Essays Presented to D. B. Knox* (Homebush West: Lancer, 1986), pp. 41–88. Andersen comments that 'the earliest revelations of God's character (or "name") highlight his *hesed* as primal, elemental, enduring and associated with his love, grace, compassion, rather than with justice'.

10. The only reference made to John's Gospel in D. J. William's article on 'mercy' in *DJG*, pp. 542–543, is a fleeting reference to John 10:17–18 which is not developed.

The centrality of compassion

While it is possible to get a sense of the definition of any crucial term from the linguistic background, it is also important to consider the context in which the term is used, which may indicate something of the way the author understands it. R. T. France provides the following helpful reflection on the meaning of our key term, based on a discussion of Jesus' response to the crowds in Matthew 9:36:

> His response is described by the strongly emotional Greek verb *splanchnizomai*, which speaks of a warm, compassionate response to need. No single English term does justice to it: compassion, pity, sympathy, and fellow feeling all convey part of it, but 'his heart went out' perhaps represents more fully the emotional force of the underlying metaphor of a 'gut response.' A further feature of this verb appears through a comparison with its other uses in Matthew (14:14; 15:32; 18:27; 20:34). In each case there is not only sympathy with a person's needs, but also a practical response which meets that need; emotion results in caring and effective action, in this case the action of sending out his disciples among the people. It is a verb which describes the Jesus of the Gospel stories in a nutshell.[11]

Interestingly, the NIV does adopt precisely France's preferred translation ('his heart went out') but only in one instance (Luke 7:13). Thus we may define compassion, based on the usage we see in the Gospels, as a strong emotion, motivated by awareness of the suffering of others, which leads to action intended to deal with that suffering.

An alternative approach to the definition of compassion, based particularly on Matthew 5:48/Luke 6:36, is provided by Marcus Borg. This is a particularly important text in Borg's thinking. Borg draws attention to the Old Testament background of the concept of compassion, noting that the root of the key term refers to the womb. He then states, 'Thus the Hebrew Bible speaks frequently of God as compassionate, with resonances of "womb" close at hand.'[12] He goes on to say, 'And so Jesus' statement, "Be compassionate as God is compassionate" is rooted in the Jewish tradition. As an image for the central quality of God, it is striking. To say that God is compassionate is to say

---

11. R. T. France, *The Gospel of Matthew* (NICNT; Grand Rapids: Eerdmans, 2007), p. 373.

12. M. J. Borg, *Meeting Jesus Again for the First Time* (San Francisco: HarperSanFrancisco, 1995), p. 48.

that God is "like a womb," is "womblike," or to coin a word that captures the flavour of the original Hebrew, "wombish".[13]

But what might this mean? Borg defines this term according to associations of the womb: 'In its sense of "like a womb", *compassionate* has nuances of giving life, nourishing, caring, perhaps embracing and encompassing.' He then gives the term a virtually all-encompassing definition: to be compassionate is 'to feel what God feels and to act as God acts: in a life-giving and nourishing way. "To be compassionate" is what is meant elsewhere in the New Testament by the somewhat more abstract command "to love." According to Jesus, compassion is to be the central quality of a life faithful to God the compassionate one.'[14] While one might question whether Borg places undue emphasis on the etymology of Hebrew terminology with this specific proposal, it is helpful to note that these verses do call Jesus' followers to reflect the character of God himself and that there is ample evidence of God's compassion in the OT.[15]

The South Africa-based theologian Isabel Phiri agrees with Borg's reading of the Lukan text, saying, 'It is a command that we "be compassionate as God is compassionate".'[16] Later, Borg writes, 'The ethos of compassion led to an inclusive table fellowship, just as the ethos of purity led to a closed table fellowship.'[17] Again he writes, 'An interpretation of scripture faithful to Jesus and the early Christian movement sees the Bible through the lens of compassion, not purity.'[18]

While Borg has arguably highlighted an important aspect of the Gospels' presentation of Jesus, it appears from the manner in which he emphasizes the inclusive nature of compassion that he may wish to erect an unnecessary gulf between compassion and purity or holiness. Witherington certainly appears to think so when he comments, 'It becomes clear in this latest book that Borg sees compassion as so central to Jesus' teaching that it is categorically impossible to contemplate a Jesus . . . who might demand moral purity.'[19]

---

13. Borg, *Meeting Jesus*, p. 48.

14. Borg, *Meeting Jesus*, p. 49.

15. See, for example, Exod. 33:19; 34:6; Deut. 4:31 and the lengthy list of texts cited by S. McKnight, *A New Vision for Israel* (Grand Rapids: Eerdmans, 1999), p. 65.

16. Professor Isabel A. Phiri in a sermon preached on 24 February 2005 entitled 'Compassion', drawing on Matt. 25:31–46 and Luke 6:36; <http://www.yale.edu/ism/marquand/marqsermonpdf/022405PhiriSermon.pdf> (accessed 24 November 2008).

17. Borg, *Meeting Jesus*, p. 56.

18. Borg, *Meeting Jesus*, p. 59.

19. B. Witherington III, *The Jesus Quest* (Carlisle: Paternoster, 1995), p. 103.

It is only fair to note that Borg does not set compassion and holiness as mutually incompatible characteristics: 'The issue was not whether God was compassionate or holy, but concerned which of these was to be the central paradigm for imaging God and for portraying the life of the faithful community.'[20] Yet, though he does guard against ignoring the holiness of God, there is a distinct risk that making compassion 'the central paradigm for imaging God' may lead to distortion unless the notion of compassion is faithful to the total character of Jesus' teaching and ministry.

Borg speaks of the 'politics of compassion', which he describes under the headings of 'banqueting with outcasts', 'association with women', 'good news to the poor', 'peace party' and the 'spiritualization of central elements'.[21] That is to say, Jesus ate with those who 'threatened the survival' of the people of God: tax collectors and sinners (Mark 2:15). Borg claims, 'the simple act of sharing a meal had exceptional religious and social significance in the world of Jesus'. It challenged 'the politics of holiness' and presented a picture of what Israel was to be: 'an inclusive community reflecting the compassion of God'.[22]

We may also ask whether the desire to identify 'compassion' as *the* defining characteristic of Jesus' ministry sometimes leads to pressing the evidence. The translation of Luke 6:36 adopted by I. Phiri in her sermon is supported by only one translation, the New Jerusalem Bible ('Be compassionate just as your Father is compassionate'). All other translations surveyed translate 'be merciful'. Now, in this case, there is probably no substantial difference between the two translations. What intrigues me is that Phiri seems to choose an uncommon translation and it makes me wonder whether she feels that she gains something in terms of the implications of the wording by that choice.

Jesus' compassion

Scott McKnight comments that, 'In the Gospels, no one but Jesus is described as having "compassion," except the characters of Jesus' parables of the good Samaritan (Luke 10:29–37) and the prodigal son (Luke 15:11–32)'.[23] The two passages which McKnight mentions lie outside the scope of this chapter, but we may note in passing that both of the figures

---

20. Borg, *Jesus*, p. 130.
21. Borg, *Jesus*, p. 131–141.
22. Borg, *Jesus*, pp. 131–133.
23. McKnight, *A New Vision*, p. 66.

which demonstrate compassion (the Samaritan in Luke 10 and the father in Luke 15) are easily understood to point towards the attitude of Jesus and God, respectively.

It is now important to see how the compassion of Jesus was expressed in the actual circumstances of his dealings with people. We will look at two key texts – one found in both Matthew and Mark and one unique to John.

The compassion of the true shepherd (Matt. 9:36/Mark 6:34)

> When he saw the crowds, he had compassion on them, because they were harassed and helpless, like sheep without a shepherd.

> *Idōn de tous ochlous esplanchnisthē peri autōn, hoti ēsan eskylmenoi kai errimmenoi hōsei probata mē echonta poimena.*

Several texts could have been chosen from Matthew and Mark. For example, we might have considered some of the miracle narratives – G. H. Twelftree suggests that Mark includes so many miracle accounts in his Gospel because of 'the compassion that is portrayed in Jesus' healings'.[24] Similarly, with regard to the parables, France comments regarding the master of Matthew 18:27,

> [The master's] decision derives not from calculation but from his 'heart going out' (traditionally, 'compassion'), that quality which we have seen to be characteristic of Jesus himself when confronted with the need of those who cannot help themselves (9:36; 14:14; 15:32; 20:34). The parable thus speaks of the totally unmerited grace of God which forgives his people more than they could ever imagine because they are unable to help themselves.[25]

The text we have chosen is particularly important, however, for several reasons. Firstly, it includes the first occurrence in Matthew of the verb *splanchnizomai* and its cognates, typically translated as 'compassion' in English versions. Secondly, it comes at a decisive moment in Matthew's presentation of Jesus' ministry as he is about to draw his disciples into his ministry in a new way, a way which is apparently motivated by his compassion. Thirdly, the text appears to function as part of a summary statement (cf. the similar passage in

---

24. G. H. Twelftree, *Jesus the Miracle Worker* (Downers Grove: IVP, 1999), p. 95.
25. France, *Matthew*, p. 706.

4:23–25) which serves to highlight not simply one occasion in Jesus' ministry but that which is characteristic of his approach.[26] Thus France comments, 'This transitional paragraph serves both as a summary of the ministry in word and deed which has been depicted in chs. 5–9 and as an introduction to the theme of mission which follows.'[27]

We may identify several key elements in this short account, as helpfully noted by McKnight, who writes, 'When the Gospels describe Jesus as one who had "compassion," a clear pattern emerges. First, a situation of serious need emerges . . . Second, Jesus is filled with compassion . . . Third, and often overlooked, a contrast is made with someone or some group that does not show the needed compassion . . . Finally, the compassion of Jesus leads him to alleviate the need . . .'[28]

In this particular case, this pattern is worked out as follows. First, Jesus is actively engaged in ministry to the needy throughout 'all the cities and villages', dealing with various physical and spiritual needs in the people he meets ('curing every disease and every sickness'). At the heart of this work lies the act of 'proclaiming the good news of the kingdom': the declaration that God's kingly rule has come near in the person of Jesus himself. He is thus busy engaging in the work of the kingdom which his Father sent him to do and the compassion which is ascribed to him arises from that faithful obedience. In the course of this work, he perceives a particular need. This need is not, however, identified as the diseases but rather the experience of being 'harassed and helpless, like sheep without a shepherd'. Secondly, this situation draws forth a heart-felt response from Jesus, which we might translate, following France, as 'his heart went out to them'.

But before we proceed, it is important that we clarify the nature of the need which Jesus identifies. This phrase 'like sheep without a shepherd' recalls language found in the Old Testament, particularly in Numbers 27:16–17, where Moses says to the Lord, 'May the LORD, the God of the spirits of all mankind, appoint a man over this community to go out and come in before them, one who will lead them out and bring them in, so the LORD's people will not be like *sheep without a shepherd*'. Likewise in 1 Kings 22:17 (cf. 2 Chr. 18:16), Micaiah the prophet picks up the same language as he addresses Ahab, king

26. So F. D. Bruner, *The Christbook: Matthew 1–12* (Grand Rapids: Eerdmans, 2004), p. 47; C. S. Keener, *A Commentary on the Gospel of Matthew* (Grand Rapids: Eerdmans, 1999), p. 308.

27. France, *Matthew*, p. 706.

28. McKnight, *A New Vision*, p. 65.

of Israel: 'And he said, I saw all Israel scattered on the hills, like sheep without a shepherd, and the LORD said, "These people have no master. Let each one go home in peace".'[29]

This phrase thus contrasts the sorry state of the people of God 'when lacking God appointed leaders'[30] with the care which is provided by the true shepherd who is God himself (see Ezek. 34:11–16 and Ps. 23). So Hagner correctly identifies the root of Jesus' compassionate response to the crowds when he writes, 'What causes Jesus' deep compassion at this point is not the abundance of sickness he has seen but rather the great spiritual need of the people, whose lives have no center, whose existence seems aimless, whose experience is one of futility. The whole Gospel is a response to just this universal need.'[31]

On this basis, we can now see that the third element which McKnight correctly highlights above – the contrast with someone who does not show compassion – is, in this text, an implied contrast between Jesus who shows compassion and those who should have been shepherding the people of God.[32] As Keener says, 'This implies that the religious leaders of Israel who purported to be their shepherds had failed to obey God's commission.'[33]

Finally, we see McKnight's fourth element: the readiness to act. Nolland notes, 'Compassion involves so identifying with the situation of others that

---

29. Cf. also Ezek. 34:1–10.

30. Keener, *Matthew*, p. 308.

31. D. A. Hagner, *Matthew 1–13* (WBC; Dallas: Word, 1993), p. 260.

32. Though it is perhaps debatable whether this aspect of the text is as 'often overlooked' as McKnight suggests, since most commentators pick this up, including the following sample: W. D. Davies and D. C. Allison Jr. ('The scribes and the Pharisees and the others in positions of power have, for Matthew, not performed properly', *Commentary on Matthew VIII-XVIII: A Critical and Exegetical Commentary on the Gospel According to Saint Matthew* [International Critical Commentary, vol. 2; London: T&T Clark, 1991], p. 148); Craig L. Blomberg ('[Jesus'] compassion increases because Israel lacks adequate leadership, despite the many who would claim to guide it,' *Matthew* [NAC, 22; Nashville: Broadman & Holman Publishers, 1992], p. 166); J. Nolland ('it is likely that Matthew intends an oblique criticism of the Jewish leaders here,' *The Gospel of Matthew* [NIGTC; Grand Rapids: Eerdmans and Bletchley: Paternoster, 2005], p. 407). The same issue is also picked up by D. A. Carson, 'Matthew', in Frank E. Gaebelein (ed.), *Expositor's Bible Commentary*, vol. 8 (Grand Rapids: Zondervan, 1984), p. 235; David E. Garland, *Reading Matthew* (New York: Crossroad, 1993), p. 109; and France, *Matthew*, pp. 372–373.

33. Keener, *Matthew*, p. 308.

one is prepared to act for their benefit.'[34] In this case, we have already read of Jesus' actions in Matthew 9:35, in terms of his teaching and healing activities, prior to the reference to his compassion. Now, the action which Jesus takes as a result of his compassion appears to be to establish what we might call a 'mission' (ch. 10). Yet, in fact, he does not tell the disciples to do anything (yet). Rather, he lays before them a vision of the scale of the need – and indeed the opportunity – and calls them to pray. It seems that Jesus is seeking to awaken in his disciples a similar compassion for the needs of the lost sheep (although he has now changed the metaphor) to that which has gripped him. While a call to prayer may appear to be a rather quietist approach to need from a modern activist's perspective, Jesus does not equate prayer with inactivity. Instead, he expects that prayer will lead to a change in circumstances because God, to whom the disciples are to pray, is 'Lord of the harvest'. Yet he does not anticipate that God will act in the lives of the crowds in an unmediated manner. He calls the disciples to pray for the Lord to send out (*ekballō*, 9:38) workers. And what the reader of Matthew's narrative will learn just a few lines later is that Jesus will send out (*ekballō*, 10:1) this very same group of disciples to be those workers. That is to say, Jesus (who, interestingly, seems now to take on the role of the 'Lord of the harvest') commissions his disciples to carry out a similar ministry to his own by which means he may address the crying need which he perceives in the people. This presumably involved the balance of proclamation and healing which Jesus himself exercised according to 9:35 (see 10:1 and 10:7–8). Thus, assuming the disciples heeded Jesus' call in 9:38, they become the answer to their own prayers! As Bruner comments, 'The first reason for Christian mission is the fellow feeling of Jesus, which we can formally call Jesus' compassion (from the Latin *cum*, "with," and *passio*, "suffer," "suffering with").'[35]

The compassion of the true friend (John 11:33)

When Jesus saw her weeping, and the Jews who had come along with her also weeping, he was deeply moved in spirit and troubled.

Iēsous oun hōs eiden autēn klaiousan kai tous synelthontas autē Ioudaious klaiontas, enebrimēsato tō pneumati kai etaraxen heauton.

---

34. Nolland, *Matthew*, p. 407.
35. Bruner, *Christbook*, p. 448.

'Not once is Jesus spoken of as manifesting pity or compassion.'[36] This statement may be true in terms of explicit terminology in the Gospel of John, but it does not seem to reflect the reality of the picture of Jesus in the fourth Gospel. In fact there are several places where we may interpret Jesus' actions as demonstrating compassion in some sense or other without the presence of the explicit terminology. For example, the miraculous production of wine in John 2:3–10 responds to a family crisis which might have brought great shame upon the family and, in John 4, Jesus' dealings with the Samaritan woman in a manner which affirms her dignity, despite all that he knows to be true about her, seem to display what can reasonably be called compassion.

In John 11, we see a particularly moving expression of Jesus' compassion in the account of the death of Lazarus. In this narrative, the language used is not of 'compassion' or 'mercy' but 'love', using two of the Greek words for love. First, we note John 11:3, where Lazarus is described to Jesus as 'the one you love (*phileis*)'. Then, in John 11:5, we are told that 'Jesus loved (*ēgapa*) Martha and her sister and Lazarus'. This highlights the fact that these two verbs may be used virtually interchangeably[37] and is a warning against drawing too hard and fast distinctions (particularly in the famous passage in John 21).[38] Commentators generally recognize the raising of Lazarus as one of the 'signs' that Jesus performed (although it is not explicitly identified as such) and therefore that it is a means of displaying his power and God's glory, but this does not exclude the possibility that Jesus is deeply involved in the whole event.

Although Jesus' apparent lack of urgency in making his way to Bethany might give the impression of a lack of personal involvement, several features in the text suggest the opposite. First, in John 11:33, John tells us that Jesus *enebrimēsato*. The translation of this verb varies considerably between the different versions: 'was deeply moved' is favoured by both the ESV and the NIV, and this would certainly seem to be in the semantic domain of 'compassion'. Köstenberger, however, suggests that 'Jesus is shown here not so much to express empathy or grief as to bristle at his imminent encounter with and assault on death'.[39] If this is the correct reading, it may well be the case that

---

36. E. Day, 'The Jesus of the Fourth Gospel', *Biblical World* 34.6 (1909), pp. 410–416.

37. So D. A. Carson, *The Gospel According to John: An Introduction and Commentary* (Pillar New Testament Commentary: Grand Rapids: Eerdmans, 1991), p. 406.

38. See the discussion in D. A. Carson, *Exegetical Fallacies* (Grand Rapids: Baker, 1996), pp. 30, 51–54.

39. A. Köstenberger, *John*, pp. 339. Köstenberger notes that the verbal form is deponent rather than passive and thus would favour an active meaning.

Jesus is angry at the reality of death or of the realm of Satan or the unbelief of the mourners,[40] yet this does not rule out the aspect of compassion. The addition of 'was troubled' also suggests an emotional response.

Secondly, the fact that Jesus weeps in 11:35 is very difficult to dissociate from the death of his friend. Köstenberger claims that 'the object of Jesus' grief is not so much the death of his friend (whom he is about to raise) as it is the presence of death itself. Yet, he then immediately affirms H. Ridderbos's viewpoint when he adds that 'Beyond this, Jesus, by weeping at the tomb of his friend, identifies with humanity by experiencing and participating "in the grief of all whose loved ones have gone to the grave"'.[41] It is quite true that Jesus does not grieve without hope,[42] just as that is true of any modern Christian whose theology is firmly founded in Scripture. But the tears of a Christian who compassionately shares in the grief of a Christian brother or sister who has lost a loved one seem to be very much in harmony with the tears shed by Jesus at Lazarus' grave.[43]

In passing, it is striking to note that as Jesus talks with Martha, the grief-stricken sister of Lazarus (11:21–27), a significant aspect of his dealing with her is to sort out her theological convictions ('Do you believe this?', v. 26). When she has come to the point of applying the confession of verse 27 to the circumstances she faces, she will see them in a different light.

On the basis of these remarks, I would suggest that there is sufficient evidence to argue that Jesus is by no means presented as devoid of compassion in John's Gospel.

Implications

Commenting on the compassion of Jesus described in Matthew 9:36, Davies and Allison write, 'Undoubtedly, in this, as in so much else, Jesus is implicitly being presented as a model for Christian behaviour. The community is to perceive outsiders with love and compassion and should be moved to act on their behalf.'[44]

---

40. See Köstenberger, *John*, pp. 339–340 for discussion of the various proposals which have been presented by commentators.

41. Köstenberger, *John*, p. 341, citing H. Ridderbos, *The Gospel According to John*, transl. J. Vriend (Grand Rapids: Eerdmans, 1997), p. 402.

42. So Carson, *John*, pp. 416–417.

43. C. S. Keener, *The Gospel of John* (Peabody: Hendrickson, 2003), p. 847.

44. Davies and Allison, *Matthew VIII-XVIII*, p. 147, n. 13.

Beyond saying that Jesus is a model for Christian behaviour, how may we apply the texts we have considered? Let me make several suggestions:

Firstly, we must recognize that compassion for Jesus resulted as much in declaration of the kingdom as in meeting of physical needs. Living and working, as I do, in the Eastern Cape of South Africa where the results of poverty, Aids, discrimination and exclusion are all too evident, it is (relatively) easy for a Christian's compassion to lead to social action and the alleviation of need. C. J. H. Wright presents one aspect of the situation starkly,

> Unquestionably the greatest emergency facing the human family today is the HIV/ AIDS virus. It is devastating human life on a scale that can scarcely be grasped. Imagine twenty Boeing 747 airliners crashing to earth every day, killing all passengers. At least that many people (approximately 7,000–8,000) die every day from AIDS-related illness. The great majority of these are in sub-Saharan Africa (home to over 70 percent of all HIV/AIDS cases, deaths and new infections).[45]

A pastor could spend all day seeking to care for the sick or to provide aid to those who can barely subsist on a negligible income. And would it not seem immoral to neglect such activities in favour of taking time to read the biblical texts and to reflect prayerfully on them with a view to proclaiming the word of God in church or elsewhere? Wright highlights elements of a response to HIV/Aids, commenting that 'such holistic evil demands a holistic response'. The first element which he identifies is, 'Sheer compassionate care for the sick and dying. No disciple of Jesus should need to be persuaded of this.'[46] One can hardly argue with this, and in fact I gladly affirm it. But of the eight elements of a 'holistic missional response' which Wright identifies, only the last seems to involve specific presentation of the biblical presentation of the gospel: 'Sensitive evangelistic witness to the new and eternal life that can be ours in Christ, with the forgiveness of sin, the hope of resurrection, and the certainty that death will not have the final word.' Now, given that a great proportion of Wright's important book is biblical exposition, I have no doubt that he assumes the vital importance of the biblical foundation he has laid in that earlier work. It is also the case that he explicitly emphasizes the need for both practical care and proclamation: 'Mission may not always *begin* with

---

45. C. J. H. Wright, *The Mission of God: Unlocking the Bible's Grand Narrative* (Nottingham: IVP, 2006), p. 433. Wright has an extended discussion of the horror of this disease which makes for sobering reading.

46. Ibid., p. 438.

evangelism. But mission that does not ultimately *include* declaring the word and the name of Christ, the call to repentance, and faith and obedience has not completed its task. It is defective mission, not holistic mission.'[47] And it is certainly possible, as Wright warns, for a pietistic emphasis on evangelism to lead to a complete lack of action, which is a travesty of the gospel. But a compassionate pastor, faced with the horror of HIV/Aids must, along with practical care for those who are suffering, devote himself to sufficient careful reflection on the biblical materials so that he has something of *God's perspective* on the problem and does not risk heart-felt but wrong-headed reactions. Effective biblical instruction must be the foundation of a church's response to the human tragedy it faces. As we observe Jesus' priorities in the Gospel narratives, we find him devoting himself to the proclamation of the kingdom of God at least as much as he devotes himself to dealing with illness or hunger (see Matt. 9:35). Thus, recognition of the centrality of the message of the gospel is a significant aspect of what it means to have compassion as Jesus had compassion. We also note that prayer to the 'Lord of the harvest' recognizes that God's ability to act for the good of those in need far exceeds what any human being may be able to accomplish. Yet, we see in Matthew 10:5 that the disciples become the answer to their own prayer and so devotion to prayer to the sovereign God must not be detached from willingness to respond to the call of God to show compassion in action.

Secondly, it is essential that Christians recognize the need to be involved in the lives of those who are going through the painful experiences of life. Jesus was able to show compassion to the crowds and to Martha and Mary because he came close to them. Those who never become engaged with the lives of others need not be surprised if opportunities to display compassion are relatively infrequent. This will require determination. Most of us feel a measure of reluctance to be confronted with the trials of others. In our own context, it is traumatic to see many poor Xhosa people living in inadequate housing, receiving inadequate education for their children and healthcare for their sick. Likewise, it is tough to come close to those who struggle with the physical pain of illness or the emotional pain of bereavement. We would naturally choose to turn to someone who is experiencing joy and success because our encounter may then be full of light and joy. But it is only when we come close to those in trying circumstances that we may share something of Jesus' compassion. And only then may we be moved to act in a way which makes a difference in Jesus' name.

---

47. Ibid., p. 319.

Finally, in drawing these two themes together, we may note that whatever compassion Jesus' followers may show (rightly) as they seek to follow his example, it is only Jesus' compassion which offers hope of an ultimate change of circumstances. A compassionate Christian may make a difference to the Aids-sufferer or the homeless person or to the hungry child, and so they should whenever the opportunity is available. Yet Jesus' compassion led him to the cross where he defeated the powers which held humanity in chains and thus opened up the hope for his people of a day when there will be no more tears and no more pain. Thus, to lead someone to the risen Jesus, who alone has the power and authority to bring an ultimate and everlasting end to the distress of a human being, is surely the greatest act of compassion which one human being can perform for another.

Bibliography

ANDERSEN, F. I., 'Yahweh, the Kind and Sensitive God', in O'BRIEN, P. T. and PETERSON, D. G. (eds.), *God Who Is Rich in Mercy: Essays Presented to D. B. Knox* (Homebush West: Lancer, 1986), pp. 41–88.

BLOMBERG, C. L, *Neither Poverty nor Riches* (NSBT; Leicester: Apollos, 1999).

____, *Matthew* (NAC 22; Nashville: Broadman & Holman, 1992).

BORG, M., *Jesus, A New Vision* (London: SPCK, 1987).

____, *Meeting Jesus Again for the First Time* (San Francisco: HarperSanFrancisco, 1995).

BRUNER, F. D., *The Christbook: Matthew 1–12* (Grand Rapids: Eerdmans, 2004)

CARSON, D. A., *The Gospel According to John: An Introduction and Commentary* (Pillar New Testament Commentary; Grand Rapids: Eerdmans, 1991).

____, *Exegetical Fallacies* (Grand Rapids: Baker, 1996).

____, 'Matthew', in F. E. GAEBELEIN (ed.), *Expositor's Bible Commentary*, vol. 8 (Grand Rapids: Zondervan, 1984).

DAVIES, W. D. and ALLISON, D. C., Jr., *Commentary on Matthew VIII-XVIII: A Critical and Exegetical Commentary on the Gospel According to Saint Matthew* (International Critical Commentary, vol. 2; London: T&T Clark, 1991).

DAY, E., 'The Jesus of the Fourth Gospel', *Biblical World* 34.6 (1909), pp. 410–416.

ELLIOTT, M. A., *Faithful Feelings: Emotion in the New Testament* (Leicester: IVP, 2005 and Grand Rapids: Kregel, 2006).

ESSER, H.-H., 'Mercy, Compassion', *NIDNTT* 2, pp. 593–601.

FRANCE, R. T., *The Gospel of Matthew* (NICNT; Grand Rapids: Eerdmans, 2007).

GARLAND, D. E., *Reading Matthew* (London: SPCK, 1993).

HAGNER, D. A., *Matthew 1–13* (WBC; Dallas: Word, 1993).

HENGEL, M., *Earliest Christianity* (London: SCM, 1986).

HERZOG, III, W. R., *Jesus, Justice and the Reign of God* (Louisville: WJKP, 2000).

KEENER, C. S., *A Commentary on the Gospel of Matthew* (Grand Rapids: Eerdmans, 1999).

_____, *The Gospel of John* (Peabody: Hendrickson, 2003).

KÖSTENBERGER, A., *John* (BECNT; Grand Rapids, Baker, 2004).

NOLLAND, J., *The Gospel of Matthew* (NIGTC; Grand Rapids: Eerdmans and Bletchley: Paternoster, 2005).

McKNIGHT, S., *A New Vision for Israel* (Grand Rapids: Eerdmans, 1999).

PARKYN, D. L., 'Compassion', in ATKINSON, D. J., FIELD, D. H., O'DONOVAN, O. and HOLMES, A. F. (eds.), *New Dictionary of Christian Ethics and Pastoral Theology* (Leicester: IVP, 1995), p. 244.

TIDBALL, D., *Skilful Shepherds* (Leicester: IVP, 1986).

TWELFTREE, G. H., *Jesus the Miracle Worker* (Downers Grove: IVP, 1999).

WARFIELD, B. B., 'The Emotional Life of Our Lord', in *The Person and Work of Christ* (Phillipsburg: P&R, 1950), pp. 93–145.

WILLIAM, D. J., 'Mercy', in *DJG*, pp. 542–543.

WITHERINGTON, III, B., *The Jesus Quest* (Carlisle: Paternoster, 1995).

WRIGHT, C. J. H., *The Mission of God: Unlocking the Bible's Grand Narrative* (Nottingham: IVP, 2006).

6. LUKE'S 'SOCIAL' GOSPEL:
THE SOCIAL THEOLOGY OF LUKE-ACTS

I. Howard Marshall

Unpacking the title

The most helpful way to introduce the topic of this essay may be to unpack the wording of the title assigned by the editors of this symposium to the present author.

The theme is a '*social*' gospel. I assume that this is to be distinguished from a 'political' gospel that might deal with the ways in which the world – or the part of it that forms the context of our daily life – is governed. We are concerned with social issues in a narrower sense of the conditions in which people live their daily lives, and this means essentially issues regarding wealth and poverty. It is not that these issues can be separated from politics, but our focus will exclude such matters as war and weapons and attitudes to the state.

A '*gospel*' is a message of good news for those whose situation is bad (whether or not they realize it), intimating that something is happening that can change it. At the same time, the Christian gospel definitely includes a strong element of challenge and demand in order to deal with the causes of the problem. Good news for the poor may well be bad news for the rich. The oppressive rich, whose wealth may be due to their maltreatment of the down-trodden poor, are challenged to repent and amend their ways. So whereas the gospel is often understood to be the good news of salvation, it includes the announcement of

God's judgment, a call to repentance, and a programme for a new life for the 'saved' that may sharply challenge their former, sinful way of life.

A social *theology* is an underlying understanding of things that gives rise to this gospel with its call to repentance. It may not be spelled out fully in the gospel, but it gives the understanding of the basis for the good news. To speak in these terms implies that there is a deliberate, conscious attitude to social matters on the part of the author rather than that there is no attitude or that the attitude is ill-thought out (though it might be), so that the attitude is perhaps something that is uncritically assumed. So an opening question might be whether Luke has a social theology, just as one might ask whether he has a theology of what it means to be 'in Christ' (a Pauline phrase never used by Luke).

The prominence of the theme in Luke's writings certainly suggests that he has a social *agenda*. This is most clearly seen from the fact that Acts is fundamentally about a mission that offers salvation, summed up as forgiveness of sins and the gift of the Spirit through incorporation into the people of God of Jew and Gentile alike. But while Luke tells us very little about the inner life of the groups of people of God that developed through this mission, the little that he does say has quite a lot to do with the question of poverty. Similarly, in the Gospel he uses the language of poverty more than the other evangelists and we find it occurring in strategic locations (Luke 4:18; 6:20).[1]

Consequently, there is general agreement that questions of wealth and poverty are more prominent in Luke-Acts than elsewhere in the Gospels and that he is self-conscious about this issue, although it can readily be seen that what he says rests on traditions about Jesus (and also about the early church) shared with other New Testament writers and not on his own theologizing and historicizing (by which I mean the expression of his ideas in the fictional form of appropriate narratives).[2]

---

1. Luke 4:18; 6:20; 7:22; 14:13, 21; 16:20, 22; 18:22; 19:8; 21:2–3; synonymous terms also figure prominently (Luke 1:52–53).

2. Thus the story of the rich ruler is taken from tradition as recorded already in Mark. Such a parable as the story of the rich fool is unparalleled elsewhere in the Gospels, and some regard it as a creation by Luke. M. D. Goulder, 'Characteristics of the Parables in the Several Gospels', *JTS* ns 19 (1968), pp. 51–69, thought that only the parables in Mark were genuine and those in the other Gospels showed clearly the marks of composition by the authors of the respective Gospels; see, however, A. Gendy, 'The Parables of Matthew or the Parables of Jesus', unpublished PhD Thesis, University of Aberdeen, 2001.

Luke and Acts are clearly meant to be read as *two parts of one work*, even though they are separated in the New Testament by the Gospel being placed alongside the other Gospels (and by never being put as the last one in the collection).[3]

Luke-Acts tells the story of Jesus and his disciples as they are engaged in God's mission to bring salvation to people everywhere. The primarily spiritual character of this salvation is evident: it is concerned with the spiritual blessings of forgiveness of sins, the creation of a right relationship with God as children of a heavenly Father and impartation of the gift of the Spirit. All this takes place in the context of the establishment of the kingdom of God in the world. But such spiritual changes entail changes in people that affect their social life, and hence a social element is built into the gospel and its effects.

We shall begin with what we find in Acts, and then see how this may be related to the material in the Gospel.

Social issues in Acts

The mission and the new life

In Acts the central emphasis lies upon making known the word and calling people to repentance, belief and baptism. No other mission is given to the church. But people who accept the call to repent live differently from the way that they did previously (Acts 26:20). So alongside the new relationship to God we note that the lives of believers are ideally filled with good works (Acts 9:36).

Sharing of possessions

There is selling of property by believers in Jerusalem and a sharing of the proceeds with the needy in some kind of communal life (Acts 2:44–45). My proposal for understanding this problematical text is that, when the believers came together for the purposes described in verse 42, they shared together in a way that was intended to break down the barriers between the rich and the

---

3. The question of whether we should read Luke and Acts together canonically continues to be debated (most recently in a study group at the British New Testament Conference, 2006), largely on the grounds that they are never placed together in early canonical collections. This argument is surely fallacious in view of the way in which Acts is clearly introduced by its author as a sequel to the Gospel.

poor.[4] They held their goods at the disposal of the community as needed, but they did not abandon their homes or their daily work and income.

This would, of course, fit in with the pattern in Judaism. Here there was great stress on almsgiving as a mark of piety. Special approval attached to works of love as opposed to mere fulfilment of legal requirements. The Qumran community evidently shared possessions, at least within the monastic set-up at Qumran.[5]

The point is repeated in Acts 4:32–37. Here the story of Barnabas is singled out for possibly three reasons: the size of his donation suggests a specially generous act of renunciation; the episode serves to introduce one who will become a key figure later in the story and to give some indication of his spiritual stature; this specific example of generosity acts as a foil to the immediately following story of the named couple Ananias and Sapphira who tell lies about what proportion of their property they were actually giving to the Lord (Acts 5:1–11).

Care for the needy

Within the early church care is provided in this and other ways for the needy, including specifically the widows in Jerusalem (Acts 6:1–4). Another group of widows is apparently cared for by Tabitha/Dorcas; at any rate she is commended for making 'robes and other clothing' which (it is clearly implied) were given to them, and they mourned the loss of their benefactor (Acts 9:36–39).

Preaching and healing

The mission of preaching is accompanied by various miraculous acts of healing that bring a new dimension to the life of those healed. The lame beggar in Acts 3 no longer needs to beg but can live a normal life and presumably earn his keep. Sick people and demon-possessed are healed by Peter (Acts 5:15–16), Stephen (Acts 6:8, though the nature of his acts is not described) and Philip (Acts 8:7); even the dead or seeming-dead are raised by Peter (Acts 9:40–41). Similarly, Paul heals a lame man (Acts 14:8–10), casts out an evil spirit (Acts 16:16–18), heals generally (Acts 19:11–12; 28:1–10), and raises Eutychus (Acts 20:9–12).

---

4. This is the issue that became problematic at Corinth.

5. K.-J. Kim argues that the communal living in Jerusalem was modelled not on the Qumran community but on the town-based Essene communities, and that Christian almsgiving stands in contrast to the benefaction in Graeco-Roman society through its radical nature that went beyond reciprocity; *Stewardship*, pp. 234–252.

Gifts

The forecasting of a famine leads the believers in Antioch to collect money for the aid of the believers in Judaea (Acts 11:27–30).[6]

Paul commends his own practice of caring for his own needs and those of others, described as 'the weak', rather than coveting what other people have. He backs up his example by appeal to the saying of Jesus that it is more blessed to give than to receive (Acts 20:34–35). Paul brings 'alms' for his nation (Acts 24:17), here presented as an accompaniment to the offerings that he makes at the temple on behalf of his colleagues who were fulfilling a vow. The gift is here highlighted as an example of Jewish piety that should have been acceptable to the people, a sign that Christian Jews were not abandoning their ethnic loyalties. Hence the elements accented in Paul's own references to the collection are downplayed.

Non-Christian care

Such qualities and actions are not peculiar to Christian believers. They are also related of pious Jews or God-fearers (Cornelius, Acts 10:2) and also of non-believers (Julius, Acts 27:3; the people of Malta and Publius, Acts 28:1–10).[7]

Acts as paradigm

This summary demonstrates that doing good to others by caring for their needs is recognized and practised as good behaviour by both Jews and Gentiles, and therefore all the more it is to be practised by Christian believers. Such conduct reflects that of God himself, who provides rain and crops (Acts 14:17), the implicit point being that his people should follow his example. For Christians it is further supported by the saying of Jesus (Acts 20:35). Such actions spring from and are part of religion. The border between actions like prayer and Bible study and social actions is a fluid one; both can be mentioned in the same breath since caring for the needy is seen as a general religious obligation.

In the church miraculous acts of healing accompany the preaching. The accent is no doubt primarily on the way in which through these God gives visible testimony of the power of the message and the grace that it incarnates, but the significant point is that these are not just demonstrations of power

---

6. Clearly the money was to enable them to buy whatever food was available, despite the carping objection that money is not much help when it is food that is in short supply.

7. For a brief survey of benefaction in the Graeco-Roman world, see Kim, *Stewardship*, pp. 253–283.

(such as 'signs in heaven above'), still less destructive signs (though note the temporary blinding of Elymas, Acts 13:8–11, and the threat to Simon, Acts 8:20–24), but rather the replacement of evil by good and of sorrow by joy. The evil effects of sin are undone.

Within the company of believers there is mutual care. It appears to have been voluntary, though the peer pressure may have been intense. We appear to have the natural expression of love for one another (though Luke does not so call it in Acts), but like anything else this needs to some extent to be organized and regulated for efficiency, and it is important that the congregation and its leaders did something towards this.

In the early days of the church in Jerusalem there was a voluntary sharing of goods which involved a theoretical openness to make everything available for use by the community, but this fades out after chapter 5 and we hear no more of it. Tension has been found between the picture of a community where they 'had everything in common' (Acts 2:44; 4:32) and the way in which individuals apparently made voluntary gifts.[8] Moreover, the apostles made gifts to the poor as each had need, which most naturally means that the gifts became their own property. The picture of the giving at Antioch in Acts 11 is more reminiscent of each disciple giving what they could to help the poor in Jerusalem than a communal gift from the church; it is clearly not the case that each disciple had given everything to a common fund and had nothing left from which to make the individual gifts here described.

Although parallels have been seen with the system at Qumran where individuals gave up all their possessions to the community after a period of probation, this does not seem to have been the case in Jerusalem, not least because joining a monastic order in the wilderness is rather different from continuing family life in an urban environment. Scholars tend to argue that Luke has described the situation in terms of a Hellenistic ideal of sharing that was not fully put into operation. I have suggested that the solution is that Luke is describing what happened when the believers met together: in their meetings rich and poor met on equal terms and shared with one another. Certainly the original daily meetings and fellowship are likely to have been at a high pitch of spiritual fervour that could not be maintained indefinitely (compare how couples who can hardly bear being out of each other's company in the first flush of marriage learn to cope with having to be separated from one another

---

8. It seems probable that the sin of Ananias and Sapphira was not that they kept back something for themselves but that they pretended that what they were giving the church was the whole proceeds of the sale.

for sizable periods of time). Further, the sharing of goods was voluntary and a matter of willingness to give what was necessary rather than a total handing over of everything.

We are not explicitly told that the same 'togetherness' was practised elsewhere, but in view of the importance that Luke manifestly attaches to it, it is fair to assume that something similar continued in other Christian groups, and the way in which the congregation at Antioch was able to respond to the needs in Jerusalem clearly shows that the same basic spirit existed.[9]

Bearing this in mind, we may want to ponder whether the arrangements in Acts 6 are intended by Luke to provide a paradigm that was intended to be practised more widely. Two concerns that were surely ongoing emerge: first, to ensure that nobody who requires aid is overlooked or excluded; second, to ensure that the provision of aid does not distract the Twelve from what they regard as the priority of the ministry of the word of God. The priority may be based on the fact that the Twelve had a special function that could be carried on by nobody else, in that they were eye-witnesses of the resurrection and there was no way of adding to their ranks (apart from the initial replacement of Judas by Matthias).

Significantly the task to be done is also called a ministry; it is administered by people of the highest spirituality, and the Seven also shared in the apostolic

---

9. L. T. Johnson, *Sharing Possessions*, pp. 117–132, is strongly critical of the community of possessions as the appropriate pattern for the church to follow, and he commends almsgiving as a better alternative. T. E. Schmidt holds that the non-mention of community of possessions after ch. 4 is not because it was a failure or was purely a temporary measure to help itinerant pilgrims who left Jerusalem when hopes of an immediate parousia were disillusioned, but rather it was because believers failed to live up to their original high ideals (*DLNTD*, p. 1051). Our suggestion is that Luke makes it clear enough that the ideal was intended to be upheld and practised elsewhere, though not necessarily in the same precise manner. Having emphasized what happened in Jerusalem, Luke had no need to repeat himself later; he expects his readers to take certain things 'as read'.

T. D. Hanks notes the total absence of the 'poor' vocabulary in Acts compared with the Gospel (where there are eleven occurrences), and also the relative stress on the poor in the first half of Acts compared with the second, particularly the lack of attention to Paul's 'collection' for the poor in Jerusalem. He explains the latter difference by noting that Acts 13 – 28 is more concerned with the admission of the marginalized Gentiles and that the communal nature of Christian life has been amply explained in Acts 1 – 12 (*ABD* V, p. 417).

tasks of preaching and witness. It would follow that the work of the Seven was not 'inferior', but the Twelve by nature of their peculiar status had to make preaching their priority. It is often assumed that the relationship of the Twelve and the Seven reflects the later distinction between overseers and deacons, although the Seven are not specifically given this title.[10] But the combination of overseers and deacons is unusual, and the co-working of the Twelve and the Seven may have served as a model or a secondary justification for it.[11] The testimony elsewhere to caring for widows (Acts 9:39; 1 Tim 5:3–16; Jas 1:27) shows that the concern expressed in Acts 6 continued.

A social programme?

We now have evidence for various kinds of social action within the Christian community together with the accompaniment of the proclamation of the word by healings and other signs. Is it right to speak of social concern or a social gospel? Was there a social programme that went wider? The following factors are relevant:

1. Care for widows (and orphans) was probably taken for granted as a duty in a religious community. There was no state provision, and once separated from Judaism no religious care from the synagogue.
2. Action to deal with unusual disasters is also natural.
3. However, action to bring about wider social change (e.g. social amelioration) is not indicated. It would have been unusual in the ancient world, possibly beyond their horizon.
4. While we do hear of state officials and military leaders becoming believers and continuing their functions, there is no evidence of believers taking part in politics or local government.
5. Consequently, we do not hear either of attempts to reform society at large.
6. The political and social commentary given by the prophets in the Old Testament is mostly lacking. Yet Paul does speak about righteousness, judgment and self-control with Felix (Acts 24:25; cf. 26:20), implying

---

10. It was possible in the ancient world to refer to a group of people simply by a number, 'the Twelve' (the supplement 'apostles' is rarely used, and 'apostles' functions rather as an alternative title), occasionally called 'the Eleven' (+ apostles, Acts 1:26), the 'Seven'; cf. the 'Triumviri' (a group of three Roman politicians) or the Four Hundred in Athens.
11. Discussions of overseers and deacons tend to focus on the origins of each separately; but the question of the origin of the *combination* also requires attention.

that the preaching of the gospel does include making people aware of their sins and judgment.

7. There is an implicit subordination by Christians of the Emperor (and hence of his representatives) or of earthly kings beneath 'another king, Jesus'. This is compatible with acceptance of the authority and dictates of earthly leaders (cf. Paul and the high priest) provided that they do not come into conflict with the dictates of this other king.

There is no 'programme' of social mission here, but the social implications of the gospel are made plain.

Back to the Gospel

It is now time to consider the Gospel of Luke to see whether it provides a basis for the thinking and practice of the early church.

Political language and the kingdom

The opening scenes portray the effect of the coming of the Messiah in a manner that looks like political and social upheaval:

> He has brought down rulers from their thrones, but has lifted up the humble. He has filled the hungry with good things but has sent the rich away empty . . . Salvation from our enemies and from the hand of all who hate us . . . to rescue us from the hand of our enemies, and to enable us to serve him without fear in holiness and righteousness before him all our days (Luke 1:52–53, 71, 74–75).

But, as I have argued elsewhere, this political language is not fulfilled literally by a reversal in society and the destruction of enemies; rather, there comes One who announces the rule of God and brings about a small, but growing, new community which practises the values of the kingdom. If change in society depends upon forceful action by military means, this is not the way of Jesus; nor is there any cataclysmic intervention from on high. Yet the words are true in that God's blessings are brought to the humble and the poor, whereas those who are rich and self-sufficient get nothing. It is not that the rich are excluded, but they are called to repentance and many of them cannot face it. The new society is formed peaceably.[12]

---

12. Marshall, 'Political and Eschatological Language'.

The danger of wealth

Luke certainly emphasizes those aspects of the teaching of Jesus that warn people against trusting in wealth and possessions, and he inculcates the importance of giving. It is more important to feed on the words of God than to have plenty of bread to eat (Luke 4:4). There are blessings promised to those who give (Luke 6:38), but these are evidently not necessarily material blessings. There are warnings against the deceit of riches (Luke 8:14). The rich are told to use their wealth in a way that will provided a welcome for them into the eternal dwellings (Luke 16:9)

The poverty of Jesus and his disciples

Luke retains the picture of Jesus as a poor man, brought up in a family that could not be called rich but was not destitute, in a culture where shepherds were welcome; he is a wanderer who does not work for his living but is supported by his friends and those who respond to his message. No especial emphasis is laid on his poverty, the point in Luke 9:58 is more the lack of welcome that he receives (cf. the immediately preceding pericope). The gospel is good news for the poor.

The missions of the disciples in Luke 9 and 10 are concerned with the proclamation of the advent of the kingdom of God and rest upon an authority conferred upon them to cast out demons and cure diseases (Luke 9:1–2, 6; 10:9, 17). The disciples are given the authority of Jesus himself for their task (Luke 10:16). Since the disciples go out penniless to do their work (Luke 9:3; 10:4; but see also 22:35–37), being dependent on the hospitality that they receive, they are not involved in giving to the poor, despite the fact that almsgiving is commended in the Gospel and the evidence elsewhere (John 13:29) that they practised charitable giving.[13]

---

13. The response of Peter to the lame beggar is not a refusal to give alms to the needy but rather a rhetorical way of indicating the superlative value of what he did have to offer (Acts 3:6). (It also confirms that the disciples were not so well-off that to say 'Silver and gold have I none' would have been palpably untrue.)

    John 13:29 is evidence that there was nothing unusual in the disciples giving to the poor even though the common purse may not have held much money. Compare how even poor people today may give their spare small change to charity. Mark 14:5 and 7 are omitted by Luke, presumably because he has a story that might be regarded as functionally equivalent to this one elsewhere in the Gospel. This pericope also indicates a positive attitude to charitable giving.

Radical poverty?

The way of life described here has been characterized as '*Wanderradikalismus*', a life of poverty based on trust in God to provide the bare necessities of life (but nothing more), and this has been contrasted with the way in which elsewhere in the New Testament there is a less radical attitude: the wealthy in this world can become believers, but they must use their wealth charitably. They are not called to poverty. These two attitudes are not so far apart as all that. On the one hand, it is clear that historically most of the first followers of Jesus were not wealthy; they were at home in a rural society where there was not much money, and those who followed Jesus were largely poor, but not exclusively so. On the other hand, there would be richer disciples and believers as the gospel took root in the towns, and they were not called to give up their homes and their jobs. But there can be a way of life that uses wealth in acceptable ways. In modern terms, there is a difference between giving up one's capital and one's source of income to be totally poor, and therefore to become a liability to other people, and retaining the capital and source of income, but making use of the resulting income in ways that prevent you from being a burden to other people and yet allow for surplus income to be used for the good of others. Paul's teaching in 1 and 2 Thessalonians points in this direction.

Misuse of wealth and proper use

The rich farmer who builds more barns is condemned because he is apparently using his wealth selfishly instead of being wealthy towards God, in other words, charitable (Luke 12:16–21). To give to the poor is what makes a person 'clean' rather than religious ritual concerned with outward conformity and cleanliness (Luke 11:41).

Although it is not said overtly that the rich man in Luke 16:19–31 had misused his wealth, the very clear implication of the story is that he was condemned for being content to live in luxury while the beggars were only spared the crumbs from his table.

The Pharisees are criticized for their love of money (Luke 16:14–15; cf. 11:41); it is safe to assume that such material was intended to be used in the church as a criticism of 'Pharisaic' attitudes among its members. It has been plausibly argued that Luke was responding to the situation of a poor church (whether Caesarea or Antioch) faced with an influx of affluent members and thus tempted by the 'love of money' characteristic of the Pharisees.[14]

---

14. Hanks, *ABD* V, p. 417, citing H. Moxnes, *Economy of the Kingdom*, pp. 1–21.

The 'ruler' who seeks after eternal life is told not only to observe the Torah but also to sell all that he has and give the proceeds to the poor and then come and follow Jesus (Luke 18:18–29). This is radical, the implication being that the wealthy man is to join the ranks of the peasants and share in the life of the group of disciples. Commentator after commentator has tried to water down the requirement or to insist that this was a special case. Certainly it can be urged that there is no indication elsewhere that wealthy people were expected to give up all their capital in order to follow Jesus. Yet undoubtedly there were individuals who 'left all' to follow Jesus by joining the group of travelling disciples; in Luke's version they were supported by a large number of women who joined the travelling group but used their wealth to help to support the group (Luke 8:1–3).[15]

The contrast is provided by Zacchaeus who is wealthy and knows that he has acquired wealth unscrupulously. He adopts a new way of life in which he gives away 50% of his wealth to the poor and repays anybody whom he has cheated the full sum with 300% interest. This did not necessarily impoverish him, but is still a remarkable gesture (Luke 19:1–10). Joseph of Arimathea is portrayed positively, but he is wealthy enough to own a tomb that surely peasants could not have afforded (Luke 23:50–53). So also we note the generosity of the good Samaritan who has the money to provide for the needy victim (Luke 10:30–35).

Putting things together

Stewardship – a picture to be developed?

The question has been raised as to whether there is continuity and coherence between the Gospel and Acts. The former has been thought to condemn the rich and to develop an ideal of renunciation of possessions with which the picture in Acts of giving to deal with specific needs stands in some tension.[16]

This stark contrast stands in need of correction, like so many such contrasts which scholars draw between different parts of the New Testament. Our summary of the material in the Gospel has hopefully shown that the picture is more nuanced, and that Luke is more concerned with the dangers of wealth and the commendation of generosity.

---

15. There is a tension here with the command to go out 'with nothing for the journey' in Luke 9:3; 10:4 and trusting to the people whom they meet to provide for them, Luke 10:7.

16. Cf. the survey in Kim, *Stewardship*, pp. 13–32.

An important fresh contribution to the topic is found in the thesis of K.-J. Kim.[17] He argues that Luke sees the disciples of Jesus as falling into two types, the itinerant and the sedentary; the former forsook all that they possessed to travel for Jesus, while the latter provided hospitality for Jesus and his companions, and could be said to forsake the ownership of all that they possessed. Kim suggests that the better model for discipleship is not the teacher-pupil one, but the master-slave one. Within that relationship the believers are to behave as stewards who are provisionally in charge of their master's property and will be judged according to their faithfulness in so doing. 'A proper way for a Christian as steward to use his possessions is almsgiving in the interest of the poor and needy inside and outside the community.'[18] Such a way of life was motivated by genuine compassion for the poor and not simply by the desire to gain 'treasure in heaven'.

While, then, some disciples were called to forsake all to follow Jesus in his itinerant ministry, the rest (the majority) were called to beware of the dangers of wealth and to act as responsible stewards of what belongs to God rather than to themselves.

Kim's thesis is helpful in drawing attention to the concept of stewardship as an expression of the rationale in Luke. The term is found in the New Testament mostly in relation to spiritual goods and responsibilities (1 Cor. 4:1–2; 9:17; Eph. 3:2; Col. 1:25; 1 Tim. 1:12; Titus 1:7; 1 Pet. 4:10). But the term and the concept figure in parables of Jesus which liken disciples to servants left in charge of a household or resources by their master and required to manage property that is not their own and to give an account of their stewardship on the master's return (Luke 12:35–48; 16:1–14; 19:11–27). The metaphor is there waiting, as it were, to be developed, but it is not taken further.[19]

The emphasis on almsgiving demonstrates that Luke's concern is with helping the poor (rather than with renunciation of wealth as an ascetic practice) and paves the way for the kind of community concern that is displayed in Acts.

The organization of care
From Acts and the Gospel we conclude that the early church saw the need for some organization of care for the poor within its community, but it did not explicitly engage in what we might call social welfare for the world at

---

17. Ibid.
18. Ibid., p. 286.
19. It is also present in the similar material in the other Gospels, although they do not use the vocabulary of stewardship.

large. To be sure, the boundaries cannot have been set tightly; charitable care would surely extend to (let us say) the unbelieving husband of a believing wife. And the picture in Luke 14:13 is very important here. Believers saw their task as the proclamation of the gospel and part of that message involved repentance and a new way of life for its hearers in regard to their use of their possessions.

At the same time, the proclamation of the gospel included some element of judgment upon ways of life that fell short in terms of social justice and (presumably) compassion.

Care for those outside the congregation

We have seen how the Christian community organized care for its own poor. It seems clear that help to the world outside is understood more as being a part of evangelism/mission and a necessary outworking of the new lifestyle practised by Christians. The *organization* of believers (as believers or in conjunction with non-believers) to do good in society commends itself as an entirely appropriate means of doing such tasks better. The early church saw its care for others as part of its proclamation of the gospel. The healing of a lame man gave an occasion for preaching the gospel. In your preaching or personal evangelism you cannot very well compare the gospel message to an invitation to a banquet and then insist: 'But of course the banquet is purely spiritual!' (Luke 14:16–24).

The teaching in the Sermon on the Plain pronounces a woe on the rich and comfortable. The Old Testament background to the language makes it virtually certain that the rich are assumed to have gained their wealth at the cost of the poor, and similarly the term 'poor' probably carries the undertone that these are people who trust in God to provide for them. The admonition in Luke 6:27–36 is primarily about not treating other people in the bad way that they treat you but rather taking the initiative in doing good instead, even to the point of 'going the extra mile' (a metaphor found in Matthew rather than Luke). This involves the ideals of giving more than you are forced to give as an example of the goodness of God who is kind to the ungrateful and the wicked.[20] The instruction to the candidates for baptism in Luke 3:10–14 (peculiar to Luke) requires them to be content with a sufficiency for their needs and to share what is surplus to that with the needy.

---

20. Hence Christian giving goes beyond the reciprocity that seems to have been characteristic of at least some in the Graeco-Roman world; see Kim, *Stewardship*, p. 269–272.

Healings, exorcisms and medical care

The accompaniment of signs and wonders to preaching the gospel, by which healings and exorcisms are surely intended (but with the occasional miracle of judgment), indicates the presence of the power of God and acts, like the healing of the paralysed man, to indicate that the disciples have a message that is confirmed by God himself and brings good to the hearers. The healings/exorcisms have the threefold character of: demonstrating the power of God; overcoming evil; and bringing good to those healed. It is surely arguable that doing good by healing (medical missions) operates in the same way, certainly by bringing good to people but also in fact by demonstrating the powerful compassion of God in his inspiring people to do good (at personal cost – they could have done something else with their resources for their own selfish good). The element lacking is the 'materially-miraculous' (of doing things beyond ordinary human capability) as opposed to the 'spiritually-miraculous' (of changing the agents of the gospel from their selfishness and greed), but the possibility of the former is not to be ruled out. Moreover, in a world where much good is done from non-Christian motives by adherents of other religions (e.g. Red Crescent) or none (e.g. *Médicine Sans Frontières*) it cannot be helpful to the gospel if Christians do not go the extra mile in compassion and care.

Conclusion

Luke has a theology of a God who is generous and compassionate and condemns the way in which the rich make themselves rich at the expense of the poor. His Son Jesus was conspicuously poor and called his disciples to beware of wealth and its temptations, and to practise giving, regarding their property and income as being held in trust for the good of others as well as themselves. To this end the early Christians encouraged charity so that the church was a microcosm of a society in which all shared together, the rich helping the poor so that poverty was eradicated.[21] The faithful proclamation of the gospel

---

21. Above it has been noted that the term 'poor', which is conspicuous in the Gospel, is not carried over into Acts. Likewise the vocabulary of stewardship is not carried over; but, when believers no longer regard their possessions as their own but put them at the disposal of the congregation, this is tantamount to a recognition of themselves as stewards. Again, the element of expressing trust in God in the Gospel is not so evident in Acts where the stress is more on caring

includes its element of judgment on the selfish rich and the call to share with the needy. It also includes the expression of God's compassion in care for the sick and disabled and the calling to account of rulers and 'the mighty' to practise righteousness (which includes compassion).

Bibliography

BECK, B. E., *Christian Character in the Gospel of Luke* (London: Epworth, 1989).

CAPPER, B. J., 'The Interpretation of Acts 5.4', *JSNT* 19 (1983), pp. 117–131.

DAVIDS, P. H., 'Rich and Poor', *DJG*, pp. 701–710.

DEGENHARDT, H.-J., *Lukas – Evangelist der Armen: Besitz und Besitzverzicht in den lukanischen Schriften* (Stuttgart: Katholisches Bibelwerk, 1965).

DONAHUE, J. R., 'Two Decades of Research on the Rich and Poor in Luke-Acts', in KNIGHT, D. A. and PARIS, P. J. (eds.), *Justice and the Holy: Essays in Honor of Walter Harrelson* (Atlanta: Scholars Press, 1989), pp. 129–144.

HANKS, T. D., 'Poor, Poverty', *ABD* V, pp. 402–424 (good further bibliography).

JOHNSON, L. T., *The Literary Function of Possessions in Luke-Acts* (Missoula: Scholars Press, 1977).

_____, *Sharing Possessions: Mandate and Symbol of Faith* (London: SCM Press, 1986).

KIM, K.-J., *Stewardship and Almsgiving in Luke's Theology* (Sheffield: Sheffield Academic Press, 1998).

KVALBEIN, H., 'Jesus and the Poor', *Themelios* 12 (1987), pp. 80–87.

_____, 'Poor/Poverty', *NDBT*, pp. 687–691.

MARSHALL, I. H., *Luke: Historian and Theologian* (Exeter: Paternoster, ³1988), pp. 141–144, 206–209.

_____, *The Acts of the Apostles* (NT Guides; Sheffield: JSOT Press, 1992), pp. 78–81.

_____, 'Political and Eschatological Language in Luke', in C. G. Bartholomew *et al.* (ed.), *Reading Luke: Interpretation, Reflection, Formation* (Milton Keynes: Paternoster and Grand Rapids: Zondervan, 2005), pp. 157–177.

PILGRIM, W. E., *Good News to the Poor: Wealth and Poverty in Luke-Acts* (Minneapolis: Augsburg, 1981).

ROTH, S. J., *The Blind, the Lame, and the Poor: Character Types in Luke-Acts* (Sheffield: SAP, 1977).

SCHMIDT, T. E., *Hostility to Wealth in the Synoptic Gospels* (Sheffield: JSOT, 1987).

_____, 'Riches and Poverty', *DLNTD*, pp. 1051–1053.

---

for the needy in the community (Schmidt, *DLNTD*, 1051). These are trivial differences that do not substantially affect the picture.

SECCOMBE, D. P., *Possessions and the Poor in Luke-Acts* (Linz: Fuchs, 1982).

THEISSEN, G., *The First Followers of Jesus: A Sociological Analysis of the Earliest Christianity* (London, 1978).[22]

© I. Howard Marshall, 2009

---

22. The stream of literature on this topic flows unabated. The second revised
    edition of F. Bovon, *Luke the Theologian: Fifty-five Years of Research (1950–2005)* (Waco:
    Baylor University Press, 2006), discusses social ethics and the rich and the poor
    (pp. 546–551) and comments very briefly on the following works which I have
    not consulted:

    AYUCH, D. A., *Sozialgerechtes Handeln als Ausdruck einer eschatologischen Vision. Zum
    Zusammenhang von Offenbarungswissen und Sozialethik in den lukanischen Schlüsselreden*
    (Altenberge: Oros Verlag, 1998).

    BEYDON, F., *En danger de richesse. Le chrétien et les biens de ce monde selon Luc* (Aubonne:
    Éditions du Moulin, 1989).

    DEPNER, J. M., *Der Mensch zwischen Haben und Sein: Untersuchungen über ein
    anthropologisches Grundproblem für die Seelsorge* (Frankfurt am Main: Lang, 1998).

    GILLMAN, J., *Possessions and the Life of Faith: A Reading of Luke-Acts* (Collegeville:
    Liturgical Press, 1991).

    HORN, F. W., *Glaube und Handeln in der Theologie des Lukas* (Göttingen: Vandenhoeck
    und Ruprecht, ²1986).

    KATO, T., *La pensée sociale de Luc-Actes* (Paris: Presses Universitaires de France, 1997).

    MINESCHIGE, K., *Besitzverzicht und Almosen bei Lukas. Wesen und Forderung des
    lukanischen Vermögensethos* (Tübingen: Mohr Siebeck, 2003).

    MOXNES, H., *The Economy of the Kingdom: Social Conflict and Economic Relations in Luke's
    Gospel* (Fortress: Philadelphia, 1988).

    PETRACCA, V., *Gott oder das Geld: Die Besitzethik des Lukas* (Tübingen: Francke, 2003).

7. THEOLOGY IN ACTION:
PAUL AND CHRISTIAN SOCIAL CARE

Jason Hood

Introduction

The apostle Paul[1] is famous for his theology and his role in the formation of early Christianity. Most believers are familiar with his preaching, his church planting efforts, and his letters. Yet many Christians have little awareness of Paul's great passion for the poor, which is best seen in what one scholar calls 'Paul's *obsession* for nearly two decades': his 'collection for the saints'.[2] Paul's collection and other teaching on possessions and generosity occupy more space in his letters than his teaching on justification by faith. Yet Pauline scholars and contemporary church leaders often fail to give the collection the attention it deserves.[3] This study examines Paul's efforts for the poor, how the

---

1. In this essay the letters ascribed to Paul in the canon are treated as a unit deriving from a single author, the canonical Paul.

2. S. McKnight, 'Collection for the Saints', in *DPL*, p. 143, emphasis original. See D. Garland, *2 Corinthians* (NAC; Nashville: Broadman and Holman, 1999), pp. 386–390; M. J. Gorman, *Apostle of the Crucified Lord: A Theological Introduction to Paul and His Letters* (Grand Rapids: Eerdmans, 2004), pp. 312–318, 402: 'The hard-fought-for collection . . . to some extent consumed Paul for years.'

3. So Gorman, *Apostle*, p. 312. Contrast the almost total absence of the collection in

poor impacted his theology, and the significance of these observations for believers today.[4]

Paul's social concern: the collection

The collection for the poor provides an important window to Paul's own social concern. The first word we have of the collection in Paul's letters comes in Galatians 2:1–10.[5] As Paul and Barnabas are accepted as apostles to the Gentiles, the leaders in Jerusalem call them to 'remember the poor', and Paul professes that he and Barnabas were already eager to do whatever such a request required. No doubt Barnabas's track record made him a prime candidate to deliver and model this service (Acts 4:36–37). The 'poor' as the target of the collection probably were Christians in a state of material want due to some combination of natural or political disaster (food shortages could be caused by both) and loss of inheritance and family structure as social punishment for believing in Jesus as Messiah and joining with his followers. No doubt many among the believers were widows, the disabled, and other marginalized persons.

Footnote 3 (*Continued*)

(among other texts and studies) the *Anchor Bible Dictionary* and B. Witherington III, *The Paul Quest: The Renewed Search for the Jew of Tarsus* (Leicester: Apollos and Downers Grove: IVP, 2001).

4. Most aspects of Paul's life, letters, ministry and theology are contentious matters in contemporary scholarship; the collection is no exception. Full survey of the social implications of Paul's ministry, theology and the collection is beyond the scope of the present study. For fuller studies, see D. Georgi, *Remembering the Poor: The History of Paul's Collection for Jerusalem* (Nashville: Abingdon Press, 1992); S. Joubert, *Paul as Benefactor: Reciprocity, Strategy, and Theological Reflection in Paul's Collection* (WUNT 124; Tübingen: Mohr Siebeck, 2000); and commentaries by Garland; M. Thrall, *A Critical and Exegetical Commentary on the Second Epistle to the Corinthians*, vol. 2 (ICC; Edinburgh: T & T Clark, 2000).

5. Some scholars treat Paul's efforts over time separately. J. D. G. Dunn, for example, rules out Galatians 2:10 in his discussion of the collection (*The Theology of Paul the Apostle* [Grand Rapids and Cambridge: Eerdmans, 1998], p. 706). This study follows others who consider it appropriate to treat all of Paul's efforts under the same umbrella. See McKnight; Gorman, p. 312; Joubert, 'Collection, The,' in *New Interpreter's Dictionary of the Bible A-C*, vol. 1 (Nashville: Abingdon, 2006), p. 698; S. Hafemann, *2 Corinthians* (NIVAC; Grand Rapids: Zondervan, 2000), p. 330.

In addition to Galatians, Paul explicitly addresses the collection in his three largest letters. 1 Corinthians 16:1–4 includes instructions for gathering the collection weekly, according to one's ability. Romans 15:25–28, 30–31 discuses the collection as the reason for Paul's absence from Rome and addresses the obligation to give in terms of a 'debt' owed to Jews by Gentiles as a result of their spiritual indebtedness to the Jews. Paul also expresses some concern over whether the gift will be accepted or fully appreciated by those in Jerusalem. 2 Corinthians 8–9 is one of the longest sustained discussions on a single topic in Paul's letters. All three of these passages include references to other churches' participation in the collection, Paul's active role in collection and delivery, and 'the saints' as the recipients.

Other possible references in Paul's letters are less certain.[6] Acts, although largely outside the scope of this chapter, provides evidence of the collection as well. The collection is stimulated by a prophecy in Antioch regarding a famine, and Barnabas and Saul take the lead in delivering the subsequent gifts (Acts 11:27–30; 12:25). Many of Paul's companions mentioned in Acts are almost certainly representatives of the nations selected to participate in the transportation and delivery of the collection (see especially Acts 20:3–6).[7] Paul's insistence on returning to Jerusalem to fulfil his mission to deliver the collection, and the presence of Gentile co-workers aiding him in the delivery, would become one of the proximate causes leading to his arrest and imprisonment (Acts 21:10–33; 24:17).[8]

As Paul's mission grew so did his collection, and the shape of his life and ministry were dominated by the collection and its implications. McKnight summarizes, 'It is hard to imagine any campaign more embracing of the northern Mediterranean and any project that occupied Paul's attention more

---

6. D. J. Downs, '"The Offering of the Gentiles" in Romans 15.16', *JSNT* 29 (2006), pp. 173–186; L. Hurtado, 'The Jerusalem Collection and the Book of Galatians', *JSNT* 5 (1979), esp. pp. 53–57, believes Paul addresses the collection in Gal. 6:6–10. See C. Blomberg, *Neither Poverty Nor Riches: A Biblical Theology of Material Possessions* (NSBT 7; Leicester: Apollos, 1999), p. 178 n. 5 for moderate critique of Hurtado's argument.

7. I. H. Marshall, *Acts* (TNTC; Grand Rapids: Eerdmans, 1980), p. 323: 'these were probably the persons appointed by the churches to take their shares of the collection to Jerusalem'; cf. McKnight, 'Collection', pp. 143–144 and Thrall, *2 Corinthians*, pp. 561–562.

8. As the NIV translation of Acts 24:17 suggests. See Marshall, *Acts*, pp. 378–379; G. Fee, *The First Epistle to the Corinthians* (NICNT; Grand Rapids: Eerdmans, 1987), p. 804 n. 5; Garland, *2 Corinthians*, p. 386 n. 72; Dunn, *Theology*, p. 707.

than this collection for the saints.'[9] The collection even competes for Paul's attention with his church-planting efforts. Paul demonstrates a commitment to fundraising for those in need despite the dangers of such an enterprise; despite legitimate needs among donors themselves (2 Cor. 8:1–5), reluctance among some givers (2 Cor. 8:8; 9:1–5), and possibly the reluctance of some would-be recipients (Rom. 15:27; Acts 20:22); despite the planning and personnel required (2 Cor. 8:16–24; cf. Acts 20:3–6); despite the way in which Paul's dream of evangelizing all the way to Spain was postponed (Rom. 15:24–27); and despite the way in which the presence of his Gentile contributors contributed to his arrest and imprisonment (Acts 21:28–29).[10]

Theology in action: Paul's gospel and Paul's collection

Dunn notes that the collection holds a 'peculiar significance' for Paul, and 'sums up to a unique degree the way in which Paul's theology, missionary work, and pastoral concern were held together as a single whole'.[11] Such statements notwithstanding, the collection rarely plays such a role in scholars' articulations of Paul's ministry and theology. Still less frequently are the ethical implications of the collection addressed, although 2 Corinthians 8–9 is a favourite passage from which to derive inspirational slogans for church building campaigns and budgets. Because of the depth of Paul's concern with factors such as Jew–Gentile unity, some scholars address the collection almost entirely in terms of Paul's concern for the gospel project in which he was engaged, seemingly leaving no room for concern for the poor in their analysis of the purpose of the collection.[12] At the very least, however, it is clear that many factors motivated Paul, and concern for the poor was among them.[13] Paul desires *to assist the poor in such a way that the unity of the church is powerfully expressed.*

Paul's language concerning the collection reflects these diverse motiva-

---

9. McKnight, 'Collection', p. 144; see Joubert, 'Collection', p. 699, for similar comments.

10. McKnight, 'Collection', p. 146.

11. *Theology*, p. 707.

12. Some scholars question the relevance of poverty by itself, compared to more 'political' and social factors for the collection (J. Schneider, *The Good of Affluence: Seeking God in a Culture of Wealth* [Grand Rapids: Eerdmans, 2002], pp. 208–209, drawing on Jouette Bassler, *God and Mammon: Asking for Money in the New Testament* (Nashville: Abingdon, 1991), pp. 92–96; but contrast Garland, *2 Corinthians*, p. 387 n).

13. Gorman, *Apostle*, p. 313, helpfully offers seven reasons for the collection.

tions. The giving creates and sustains *koinōnia* (Rom. 15:26, 2 Cor. 8:4; 9:13), or family-like unity, fellowship or partnership with deep economic implications. Christian *koinōnia* and the collection are grounded in the good news that God redeems sinners and creates one new family – a unified new humanity in Christ.[14] Paul anticipates that in such a fellowship, the mutual obligation of loving unity across racial, geographic and cultural lines would work itself out in tangible acts of generosity, potentially flowing osmosis-like in both directions as needed (2 Cor. 8:13–15). Paul calls the collection a 'proof of love' (2 Cor. 8:8) and a 'service' to those in need (9:4; Acts 12:25). As proof of submission to the gospel (2 Cor. 9:13), the collection testifies to all willing to hear that God is Lord over the Gentiles.[15] The collection might provide evidence for the truth of the gospel to unbelievers and Jews sceptical of the law-free admission of Gentiles into God's family, the great 'mystery' at the centre of Paul's gospel (Eph. 2 – 3).[16] Above all, the collection is associated with 'grace'. Inspired by the grace given them in the past (2 Cor. 8:1; 9:14) and the grace awaiting them in the future (9:8), the recipients of grace should themselves give graciously.

The collection is also relevant as a concrete example of Paul's teaching on the ethical consequences of salvation. Throughout Paul's writings, divine salvation ('indicative') precedes the command to respond with 'good works' ('imperative'; see esp. Eph. 2:8–10; 4:28; 1 Tim. 2:9–10; Titus 2:8; 3:1, 8), no small part of which would have been care for those with various physical, relational and emotional needs. In a similar way there is a close relationship between Paul's gospel and Paul's collection, borne out by the pithy summary in 2 Corinthian 8:9: 'You know the grace of our Lord Jesus Christ, that though he was rich, yet for your sakes he became poor, so that through his poverty you might become rich.' The good news of Christ's self-sacrificial incarnation and his life and death on behalf of others is the motivation for participating in the collection and the model for Christian life lived in service to others. While biblical religion is often seen as a means to material benefit then as now (1 Tim. 6:5), Paul calls readers to the mutual benefit the whole church derives from charitable responses to God's gracious, costly acceptance of sinners.

---

14. Eph. 2 – 3; Gal. 3:27–29; Col. 3:10–11, 14–15.

15. The strategic place of the collection in Rom. 15 reinforces these points (see J. C. Beker, *Paul the Apostle: The Triumph of God in Life and Thought* [Philadelphia: Fortress, 1980], p. 72).

16. 'Social' aspects of Paul are often linked to the New Perspective(s) on Paul; the present reading neither requires nor opposes the presuppositions and exegesis associated with the NPP.

Rather than pitting various motives against one another, Paul sees them functioning in harmony and contributing to the ultimate goal of God's praise and glory (2 Cor. 9:11–15), which helps to explain his reference to the collection in priestly language (Rom. 15:27; 2 Cor. 9:12). Hafemann observes that 'the collection illustrates the significance of Paul's theology of grace both for the individual (having received from God, Christians give to others) and for the life of the church (having been accepted by God, Christians accept one another). Completing the collection would therefore be the theological capstone of Paul's apostolic service'.[17]

Finally, one should note that for Paul, care for the poor cannot be pitted against 'gospel ministry'. The return to Judea to deliver the collection takes priority over Paul's visit to Rome. As he explains to the Romans (Rom. 15), this visit was to be the great launch of gospel ministry in the western half of the Empire all the way to Spain. We do not know if Paul achieved this mission, but we do know that he delivered the collection.[18] *The collection was so vital that its delivery was at that moment a more urgent matter for Paul than his desire to evangelize and plant churches on the missionary frontier* among those who were 'without hope and without God in the world', as he describes them in Ephesians 2:12.[19]

Applying Paul in the preaching, teaching and practice of Christian social concern

The following section addresses some of the practical implications that can be drawn from what we know about Paul's collection and other teachings on Christian social concern. Paul has much to say that is relevant for our contemporary social concern, although there are areas of contemporary application where he is more or less silent.

The demands of social concern: Paul and the standard for Christian generosity

What does Paul teach us about the Christian's standard for generosity? In the first instance, Christians must give generously as they are blessed, not 'by the

---

17. Hafemann, *2 Corinthians*, p. 331.

18. McKnight, 'Collection', p. 143, correlates this plan with the data in Acts 20:16, 22.

19. Paul illustrates in his actions the approach espoused by C. J. H. Wright, *The Mission of God: Unlocking the Bible's Grand Narrative* (Nottingham: IVP, 2006), pp. 61, 316–323, on the relative importance of evangelism and mercy ministry.

numbers'. Paul has numerous opportunities to institute a quantitative guideline or tithe, yet he never does.[20] Nor does Paul ask for what people do not have.[21] Instead, Paul relies on altogether different standards.

Paul's most important ethical construct is summarized in Philippians 2:4 and the verses following. The principle, 'Let each of you look not only to your own interests, but to the interests of others', is followed by a description of the humble, sacrificial form of service seen in Jesus' incarnation and death. We have already addressed the examples of Jesus used in 2 Corinthians 8:9 and will later see Romans 15:7 employed to spur the Romans on to hospitality and community-creation that leads to mutual care and the breaking of cultural barriers. The former verse stands at the heart of Paul's elaboration on his collection for the poor in 2 Corinthians. Imitation of the cross suggests that the standard of Christian giving has no clear limit.[22] Moreover, when Paul does circumscribe limits to Christian generosity, he does so not for the sake of one's own security or comfort, but so as to prevent idleness and sin, and to avoid undue burdens on the churches (1 Tim. 5).

The call to imitate Jesus flows throughout Paul's letters: 'Imitate me as I imitate Christ.'[23] This practice of being shaped by the cross is not simply

---

20. Tithing was not practiced outside Palestine; it is anchored to the Promised Land in Deut. 26 and Malachi, and Tobit 1 – 2; cf. Paul's emphasis on the removal of OT legislation. See M. A. Powell, *Giving to God: The Bible's Good News about Living a Generous Life* (Grand Rapids: Eerdmans, 2006), pp. 161–162; Blomberg, *Neither Poverty Nor Riches*, p. 198–199 and his conclusion and autobiographical comments, pp. 241–253.

21. 1 Tim. 6:17–19; 1 Cor. 16:2; 2 Cor. 8:12; cf. Acts 11:29.

22. Perhaps the Macedonians (2 Cor. 8:1–5) have grasped this vision. On the cross as fundamental to Christian ethics, see R. Hays, *The Moral Vision of the New Testament: Community, Cross, New Creation; A Contemporary Introduction to New Testament Ethics* (San Francisco: Harper, 1999). On pp. 19–26 Hays lays out central foci for ethics in Paul which are similar to those presented here. Gorman brings out the relevant theme of 'cross imitation' in *Apostle* and in his earlier book, *Cruciformity: Paul's Narrative Spirituality of the Cross* (Grand Rapids: Eerdmans, 2001). This theme is often missing in evangelical treatments on the significance of the cross in the New Testament; see Hood, 'Bolting Our Crosses? Cross Imitation in Mark's Gospel, Redemptive History, and Contemporary Evangelicalism', *Evangelical Quarterly* (forthcoming, 2009).

23. Rom. 8:17; 15:2–7; 1 Cor. 4:8–17; 9; 11:1 (cited); 2 Cor. 4:7–18; 12:7–10, 15; 13:3–5; cf. Phil. 2:4–11; 3:10–11; Eph. 5:2; Col. 1:24; 1 Thess. 1:6–7; throughout 2 Tim.; cf. Acts 20:33–35.

responding to God's 'gracious gift of salvation'. Rather, being shaped by the cross requires the imitation of the pattern of life by which that salvation came through incarnation and the cross, *self-sacrifice which absorbed great costs for the benefit of others*, in hope of resurrection, new creation and exaltation. For Paul, the standard for Christian giving and all of life is not an amount; it is a Person, the *crucified* Lord. And Paul himself repeatedly holds out his own sacrificial example as a model for others, not least in the arena of personal finance.

This sacrificial standard is not unique to Paul, nor is it merely a New Testament phenomenon (1 John 3:16–18; Luke 14:25–33). Old Testament characters such as Abraham and Job provide fine examples of open-handedness before God and others.[24] Jewish tradition suggests that one important aspect of wickedness and unrighteousness is *disadvantaging others for one's own benefit* (e.g., Jer. 22:13–16). There is a tendency to take the essence of righteousness to be the result of keeping oneself from disadvantaging *others*. But the Old Testament, Jesus and Paul require more than avoiding unrighteousness. The truly righteous person *disadvantages himself or herself for the sake of the community*. Jesus' predecessors, no less than his followers, were required to exhibit righteousness of the sacrificial sort, just as he himself illustrated this righteousness perfectly.[25] Thus, Paul can appeal to Jesus as well as Old Testament texts in his call to righteous acts for the sake of others (Acts 20:33–35; Ps. 112:9 in 2 Cor. 9:9).

Paul also presents an often-overlooked benefit to such sacrificial Christian generosity. Given the sinful human state, such open-handedness is necessary to wage war against the idolatry of greed.[26] In various passages Paul addresses the way in which idolatry goes hand-in-hand with the possession or pursuit of wealth (Col. 3:5; Eph. 5:5; cf. Matt. 6:19–34). Rather than promising material blessings and prosperity as signs of God's favour, Paul requires believers to wage spiritual warfare against love of money and the desire for wealth (1 Tim.

---

24. On Abraham see especially John Calvin, *Institutes of the Christian Religion*, transl. Henry Beveridge (Grand Rapids: Eerdmans, 1990), 2.10.11; Heb. 11:8–10, 13–16; Jas 2:21–22.

25. B. Waltke with C. Yu, *Old Testament Theology: a Canonical and Thematic Approach* (Grand Rapids: Zondervan 2007), p. 289; Waltke, *Proverbs 1–15* (NICOT; Grand Rapids: Eerdmans, 2004), pp. 97–98; Waltke, 'Righteousness in Proverbs', *WTJ* 70 (2008), pp. 225–238; and the chapter by Grant in the current volume.

26. See B. Rosner, *Greed as Idolatry: The Origin and Meaning of a Pauline Metaphor* (Grand Rapids: Eerdmans, 2007); cf. S. E. Wheeler, *Wealth as Peril and Obligation: The New Testament on Possessions* (Grand Rapids: Eerdmans, 1995).

6:6–10). In their place, contentment with God's provision and grateful enjoyment thereof provide a balance which liberates resources to meet the needs of others (6:17–19). Paul's insistence on modelling a sacrificial lifestyle and Christ-sufficiency confirmed his own status as one free from the grasp of greed.

The director of social concern: a generous God and his generous people

This theme is related to Paul's use of Jesus as exemplar, and constitutes another aspect of the standard for Christian generosity. Paul connects God's generosity with human generosity by citing a passage on the way in which God provided manna in the Old Testament: 'As a matter of fairness your abundance at the present time should supply their need, so that their abundance may supply your need, that there may be fairness. As it is written, "Whoever gathered much had nothing left over, and whoever gathered little had no lack."'[27] There has been something of a backlash against earlier trends to interpret supernatural feeding miracles naturalistically as 'fable[s] about generosity' rendering the 'miracle' in Jesus' feedings of the thousands as 'generosity overcoming selfishness as everyone follows Jesus' example'.[28] Can human generosity be compared to God's unique goodness and supernatural power? Is there in fact biblical warrant for using God's miracles as a model for human generosity? Or are others correct in resisting the use of this passage as an ethical norm?[29] Answers can be found if we consider similar uses of God's generosity as a stimulus for human generosity.

2 Corinthians

Paul connects the generosity of the giver with God's own generosity in multiple places in 2 Corinthians, stating that believers are blessed by God so that they themselves can give (2 Cor. 9; 1 Tim. 6). As we have already seen, God's *spiritual* generosity (which of course includes future physical generosity when believers receive new bodies and the whole of the new creation) is to result in our *physical* generosity (2 Cor. 8:9). Scarcely a chapter later, Paul cites Psalm 112:9 in 2 Corinthians 9:9: 'He has scattered abroad his gifts to the poor; [therefore] his righteousness endures forever.' Many have taken this passage as a reference to God's own generosity and righteousness.[30] But the psalmist

---

27. 2 Cor. 8:13–15.
28. D. Turner, *Matthew* (BECNT; Grand Rapids: Baker, 2008), p. 369.
29. E.g., Schneider, *Good of Affluence*, pp. 208–210.
30. Thrall, *2 Corinthians*, pp. 580–583 for discussion and the correct conclusion; *pace* Garland, *2 Corinthians*, 410.

clearly speaks throughout Psalm 112 of 'the righteous man'. The canonical location of the psalm is instructive as the previous psalm speaks of God's own righteousness enduring forever, in part on the basis of his goodness to nature and humans, who receive covenant blessings such as food and 'inheritance'. From this bounty the righteous man gives generously (Pss. 111:3–6; 112:2–4, 9). In this way the psalmist ties human care for others to God's own righteous care. Paul's overall emphasis in the conclusion of the chapter fits elegantly with Psalms 111 and 112. God's gift, even if coming through human hands, redounds to his glory and for the benefit of the giver: 'To him belongs eternal praise' (111:10); the giver is 'blessed' and 'his horn will be lifted high in honour' (112:1, 9; cf. 2 Cor. 9:11–15).

Divine generosity and human generosity in Romans

There is also evidence from Paul outside 2 Corinthians. In Romans 15 Paul cites the hospitality and service of Christ as a theological foundation for believers' reception of others in Christ.[31] God's goodness to alien Gentiles must inevitably result in a response of goodness towards others, regardless of ethnic or cultural distinctions, in imitation of God's goodness. Hospitality, harmony and love (Rom. 15:1–7) requires believers to 'accept one another . . . as Christ accepted you'.[32] Again, God receives glory when his earthly family experiences the material, physical benefits from the destruction of segregating boundaries long in place (Eph. 2–3). The citation of Psalm 69 in Romans 15:3, widely used in the early church as a reference to Jesus, underscores the imitative response to divine hospitality required of believers.

Divine generosity and human generosity in the New Testament

Other New Testament passages suggest that Paul is not unique in coordinating divine and human generosity. In the synoptic tradition, Jesus makes much of the way in which God's own goodness and 'natural provision' must result in our own generosity (Matt. 5:38–48; Luke 6:27–36). If God's 'natural' provision leads to our own natural provision, it is surely no great step beyond this to see God's 'supernatural provision' as a model for human generosity. The Eucharist is juxtaposed with foot-washing in John 13; Jesus follows these acts of divine care and provision with instruction for his dis-

---

31. The ancient social principle of reciprocity, with God in Christ as the ultimate benefactor, is relevant here; see below.

32. Hospitality is linked to material care for the saints (see esp. Rom. 12:13).

ciples to learn from his own 'example' (13:12–17, 31–35; cf. 1 John 3:16–18). The correlation between God's provision in the Eucharist and Christ's sacrificial service which the Eucharist communicates adds to the awful irony of socio-economic segregation in the church in Corinth during the Lord's Supper (1 Cor. 11:17–34), segregation which incurs Paul's condemnation in no uncertain terms as they failed to 'accept one another . . . as Christ accepted [them]' (Rom. 15:3, 7).[33]

Eschatological divine generosity and human generosity

Finally, both miraculous and non-miraculous Christian generosity function as evidence of the work of God's Spirit. The Promised Land was a 'miraculous provision' anticipating a greater eschatological conclusion (Heb. 11:8–10, 13–16) and requiring a response of gratitude-fuelled generosity (Deut. 26:1–15). As Christians live in *koinōnia*-shaped generosity and kingdom community in the present, they respond to, anticipate, witness to, and share in the miraculous presence of God's abundant new creation wrought by the Holy Spirit. That which abundant life in the Promised Land anticipated (Heb. 11:8–10, 13–16) is already partially present, in advance of the great eschatological conclusion. God's guarantee of future generosity provides a stimulus for Christian generosity in the present, just as God's generosity in the past inspires present giving. Christian generosity in the present covenant community also represents God's *own* eschatological goodness to his people, for the Christian community is in fact his own new creation. Hafemann's comments on 2 Corinthians 8:13–15 tie these various threads together and suggest the relevance of this 'standard' of eschatological equality for contemporary Christian generosity:

> Equality . . . is being established *by the people themselves* through their *own* Spirit-led sharing. While God supplied Israel's physical needs with manna and quail but did not change their spiritual condition, under the new covenant God is meeting the spiritual needs of the Corinthians in order that *they* might meet the physical needs of others (cf. 2 Cor. 9:8–11). Paul's expectation in 8:11 is thus one more expression

---

33. See Blomberg's treatment in *Neither Poverty nor Riches* and R. Hays, *1 Corinthians* (Atlanta: John Knox Press, 1997), pp. 194–206. According to Fee, *First Corinthians*, p. 560, Chrysostom clearly understood the thrust of the passage, but 'sacramentalism' and 'pietistic' readings of this passage emphasized personal introspection and have led the church to downplay Paul's actual intention, which was more corporate than personal.

of his confidence in the transforming power of the presence of God under the new covenant (cf. 3:3, 6, 18). For this reason, Paul leaves the amount of their giving up to the Corinthians, convinced that, as a new creation in Christ (5:17), the quantity of their giving will match the quality of their changed hearts (5:15).[34]

The delimitation of Christian social concern

In addition to a call for generosity (1 Tim. 6:17–19), 'fair sharing' or 'equality' (NRSV and ESV, respectively, for *isotēs*, 2 Cor. 8:13–14), and 'liberality' (Rom. 12:8), Paul also provides restrictions on Christian social care. The Pastoral Epistles supply limits on organized church-based support for the needy, such as requiring recipients of aid to participate in merciful deeds of Christian *koinōnia* (1 Tim. 5:10); such deeds are part of the purpose of Christian work (Eph. 4:28). Under normal circumstances at least, one must rely on one's own work or one's family for support and not the church or illicit means of gain. The priority of work strongly suggests that Christian social care should exhibit a concern for human flourishing that includes employment. Paul called his disciples to follow his own model of contentment and care for self (Acts 20:35; 1 Thess. 1:6; 2:9–12; 1 Tim. 6:6–10).

In our day of democratic mass participation in the political process, Paul's readers can be expected to be interested in the political significance of his teaching on social concern. Paul's commitment to the lordship of Jesus over all (Rom. 14:11; Phil. 2:10) suggests that the political significance of his teaching is extensive. Yet it is probably not fair to press Paul for his opinion on political and social action outside the church. Martin Hengel explains: '[The first Christians] cannot give us a practicable programme of social ethics to solve the question of possessions, which has become so acute today.' In addition to the massive socio-political and economic differences between Paul's day and ours, 'the first Christians were a tiny minority, who were also politically suspect, [therefore] they could not strive in their ethical action for the social reform of the Roman empire of the time'. Hengel explains that this is the reason Paul focuses on the construction and care of the Christian community.[35] Nor

---

34. Hafemann, *2 Corinthians*, p. 341 (emphases original); see also p. 366. As Hafemann notes, Acts seems to share this vision (2:42–47 and 4:34–37; on which see n. 9 of Marshall's chapter in the present volume).

35. Hengel, *Property and Riches in the Early Church*, trans. J. Bowden (London: SCM and Philadelphia: Fortress, 1974), p. 41; Blomberg, *Neither Poverty Nor Riches*, p. 247; Hays, *Moral Vision*, p. 33: '[Paul] articulates no basis for a general ethic applicable to those outside the church.'

does Paul engage ecology, although Romans 8 is relevant for a theology of Christian stewardship.

But to note the difficulty in applying Paul's teaching universally or politically is not to say that Paul does not care about the unbelieving world or creation, or that Christians have no responsibility to those outside the church – far from it, as Galatians 6:10 and Romans 13:7 make clear. We must not mistake Paul's emphasis on care-within-the-church as *rejection* of various kinds of beneficence outside the ecclesial sphere.[36] The limits on Christian social concern taught in Paul's letters should not be pressed into service *against* Christian social obligation in the wider world. Paul offers no support for limiting assistance to unbelievers afflicted by violence, natural disasters and systemic injustice. Nor can Paul's limits be directly applied to require single mothers work *full-time* in order to receive government benefits, thus leaving children of single-parent families less well-attended. Paul's insistence on rendering taxes – used to accomplish a whole raft of objectives in the ancient world – contrasts with at least some of the ways in which contemporary conservative and libertarian impulses manifest themselves, especially in America. If Paul does not explicitly affirm such tax-producing enterprises, neither does he spend his energy condemning them.

So was Paul conservative or liberal politically? The question is anachronistic, and in Paul's letters we find that many of our most pressing questions regarding social and political concerns are effectively unaddressed. While there are grounds for exploring the broader implications of Paul's teaching, the present essay does not provide the opportunity to probe for such implications.[37]

However, the after-effects of Paul's efforts may well point to the wisdom of his focus on a massive *koinōnia*-engineering enterprise of his own. In just a few centuries, the church would rival the Empire itself as the fount of social care. Paul's collection and the *koinōnia* undergirding it formed a powerful counter-imperial critique, not through overt denigration, still less through open hostility, but through quiet counter-example.[38] Christian *koinōnia* attempts to reflect

---

36. The Christian standard of neighbour-love arguably demands such concerns.

37. See the relatively sophisticated treatment by M. Gornik, *To Live in Peace: Biblical Faith and the Changing Inner City* (Grand Rapids: Eerdmans, 2002), who uses his experience living and serving in a marginalized community to good effect (see also his 'The Rich and the Poor in Pauline Theology', *Urban Mission* 9 [1991], pp. 15–26).

38. The collection is often neglected in imperial and anti-imperial readings of Paul; see Wan, 'Collection for the Saints as Anticolonial Act: Implications of Paul's Ethnic Reconstruction', in K. Stendahl (ed.), *Paul and Politics: Ekklesia, Israel, Imperium, Interpretation* (Harrisburg: Trinity Press Intl., 2000), pp. 191–215.

God's true intentions for new humanity in a state of *šālôm* (Eph. 2:15) that is only possible in Christ, not in Caesar.

The dynamics of Christian giving: Paul and the rhetoric of generosity

Paul subverts the normal expectation for gift-giving in the ancient world. Forceful social rules in the ancient world meant that a gift would inevitably require the recipient to respond appropriately with a gift or kind words, so that generosity essentially functioned as an investment in one's future well-being. Givers often tried to outdo one another in order to earn honour in the court of public opinion. Paul is capable of using such social rules himself when it suited his purposes (e.g., 2 Cor. 8:1–5, 16–21; 9:1–2). But because God is the ultimate author of grace, and perhaps also considering that there may be little return on the 'investment' from Jewish Christians (Rom. 15:30–31), the apostle undercuts the normal expectation for reciprocal giving.[39] Paul expects that the Spirit-sealed (Eph. 2:18–22; 4:1–4) bonds of Christian *koinōnia* could potentially lead to reciprocal care, not simply on the basis of social rules, but on the basis of future need (2 Cor. 8:13–15).[40]

Consideration of the methods of communication and giving in the ancient world is crucial for those seeking to understand Paul. Suffice it to say that one must take care in pulling a word, phrase or verse from Paul on generosity and holding it up outside its cultural context as a universal truth. To take but one example, in the light of Paul's rhetoric throughout 2 Corinthians 8 – 9, it is doubtful that Paul's audience would have understood themselves to be completely free not to participate on the basis of 2 Corinthians 8:8 (Paul states he is not commanding their participation) and 9:7: 'Each of you must give as you have made up your mind, not reluctantly or under compulsion, for God loves a cheerful giver' (NRSV). An over-emphasis on freedom misses Paul's rhetoric in this passage, which would not have sounded 'optional' or 'free' to his audience.[41] Paul's rhetoric in the preceding verses constitutes an appeal to the Corinthians to do *what they had promised*, so that the sudden appearance of

---

39. See Joubert. D. deSilva offers a readable introduction to benefaction, patronage and reciprocity in *Honor, Patronage, Kinship and Purity: Unlocking New Testament Culture* (Downers Grove: IVP, 2000), pp. 95–156. He makes the case that when Paul engages in reciprocity, it is frequently *God* who is regarded as the primary benefactor (see especially pp. 153–156), rewarding those who give.

40. Paul *never thanks individuals for their service or their gifts*, only the God who stands behind their labours and gifts (cf. 2 Cor. 8:16; Phil. 1:3–6; Acts 28:15).

41. S. Hafemann, *2 Corinthians*, pp. 339, 358–359; *pace* Schneider, *Good of Affluence*.

fundraisers would not result in emergency, 'forced' preparations which would have embarrassed Paul and the Corinthians. Perhaps the flow of thought leads to the following translation of 9:7: 'Each of you must give as you have *previously* made up your mind.'

So while Paul does not compel precise amounts, participation in *koinōnia* cannot be said to be *merely* voluntary. After all, giving on the basis of personal pleasure is *not* opposed to 'debt' and reciprocity (Rom. 15:25–27); nor is personal readiness opposed to responsibility (Gal. 2:10). A variety of motives and inspirations stand side-by-side throughout Paul's discussions of the collection.

Notably, there is no embarrassment or shame when Paul mentions his needs or the needs of others, *including the need to contribute for the sake of others*. The same courage required in evangelism is required in calling believers to *koinōnia* and the appropriate economic response to God's good news. Courage and commitment are not only necessary at the beginning of Christian social concern. Paul also anticipates and warns against growing weary of 'doing good' (Gal. 6:9, ESV; 2 Thess. 3:11–13), and his lengthiest address on money, 2 Corinthians 8 – 9, was a follow-up letter and not an initial appeal for assistance.

The dimensions of Christian social concern

In Colossians Paul provides grounds for moving application beyond 'Jew-Gentile' relationships and into the realm of ethnicity more broadly. The unification of 'Greek . . . Jew . . . barbarian, Scythian' constitutes the one new humanity (3:9–10).[42] Not only was the collection cross-cultural, cross-ethnic and inter-continental in nature, it likely took place across something like modern denominational fault lines. The recipients of Paul's gifts were Torah-observant: that is, they were keeping Jewish diet and calendar, and at least some were insisting on circumcision. A number of them would have objected to Paul's 'Torah-free teaching' and Gentile communities. In the same way, many Gentiles likewise found Jewish practices repulsive. Accepting fellow believers – or their financial assistance – as one family across such religious, cultural

---

42. Crucially, this description arises in the context of ethical responsibility and treatment of others (Col. 3:5–17). The contemporary application of the collection advocated by G. Peterman, 'Social Reciprocity and Gentile Debt to Jews in Romans 15:26–27' (*JETS* 50 [2007], pp. 735–46), disappoints. He fails to consider adequately Paul's diverse motives, universalizes the work of the first generation of believing Jews, and fails to note the possible ongoing relevance of the collection for ethnic and cultural barrier-breaking. Paul thinks reciprocity should go both ways (2 Cor. 8:14)!

and ethnic barriers required a great deal of charity and no small amount of instruction in Christian sacrifice (for instance, Rom. 14–15; Acts 16:3). Like most denominations today, these Jewish believers would point to Scripture and tradition to fortify the distinctives that kept them separated. In this respect, Paul's collection could be compared to the collection of resources from wine-swilling, covenantal, amillennial, Pentecostal, Korean Presbyterians to be sent to a group of impoverished and marginalized teetotal, dispensationalist, cessationist, premillennial, pew-sitting, Baptist congregations in Eastern Europe. Such is *koinōnia*.

Conclusion: the drama of Christian social concern

Paul's collection for the poor provides a valuable glimpse into the manner of life required by the gospel. The power of Paul's theology and his crucial role as an evangelist and church planter tempt interpreters to focus only on these aspects of his teaching and ministry. But believers must not neglect what can be learned from this great advocate for Christian social concern. Paul does not present an abstract theology of social concern; he dramatizes his message through his life, challenging those who lead and teach that generosity, sacrifice and the sharing of *koinōnia* with others in God's family is not optional but integral to the call to Christian life in community. Thanks to the collection, students of Paul know more about his praxis of Christian social concern than that of any other early Christian, including those who offer comparatively fuller theologies on the poor and Christian social concern (such as James and Luke). In the collection we see the whole of Paul's theology in action, and we learn that Christian social concern was neither optional nor secondary for the apostle and his churches.

Bibliography

BASSLER, J., *God and Mammon: Asking for Money in the New Testament* (Nashville: Abingdon, 1991).

BEKER, J. C., *Paul the Apostle: The Triumph of God in Life and Thought* (Philadelphia: Fortress, 1980).

BETZ, H., *2 Corinthians 8 and 9: A Commentary on Two Administrative Letters of the Apostle Paul* (Hermeneia; Philadelphia: Fortress, 1985).

BLOMBERG, C., *Neither Poverty Nor Riches: A Biblical Theology of Material Possessions* (NSBT 7; Leicester: Apollos and Downers Grove: IVP, 1999).

DESILVA, D., *Honor, Patronage, Kinship and Purity: Unlocking New Testament Culture* (Downers Grove: IVP, 2000).

DOWNS, D. J., '"The Offering of the Gentiles" in Romans 15.16', *JSNT* 29 (2006), pp. 173–186.

DUNN, J. D. G., *The Theology of Paul the Apostle* (Grand Rapids and Cambridge: Eerdmans, 1998).

FEE, G., *The First Epistle to the Corinthians* (NICNT; Grand Rapids: Eerdmans, 1987).

GARLAND, D., *2 Corinthians* (NAC; Nashville: Broadman and Holman, 1999).

GEORGI, D., *Remembering the Poor: The History of Paul's Collection for Jerusalem* (Nashville: Abingdon Press, 1992).

GORMAN, M. J., *Cruciformity: Paul's Narrative Spirituality of the Cross* (Grand Rapids: Eerdmans, 2001).

____, *Apostle of the Crucified Lord: A Theological Introduction to Paul and His Letters* (Grand Rapids: Eerdmans, 2004).

GORNIK, M., *To Live in Peace: Biblical Faith and the Changing Inner City* (Grand Rapids: Eerdmans, 2002).

____, 'The Rich and the Poor in Pauline Theology', *Urban Mission* 9 (1991), pp. 15–26.

HAFEMANN, S., *2 Corinthians* (NIVAC; Grand Rapids: Zondervan, 2000).

HAYS, R., *1 Corinthians* (Atlanta: John Knox Press, 1997).

____, *The Moral Vision of the New Testament: Community, Cross, New Creation; A Contemporary Introduction to New Testament Ethics* (San Francisco: HarperSanFrancisco, 1999).

HENGEL, M., *Property and Riches in the Early Church*, transl. J. Bowden (London: SCM and Philadelphia: Fortress, 1974).

HOOD, J., 'Bolting Our Crosses? Cross Imitation in Mark's Gospel, Redemptive History, and Contemporary Evangelicalism', *Evangelical Quarterly* (forthcoming, 2009).

____, 'The Cross in the New Testament: Two Theses in Conversation with Recent Literature (2000–2007)', *WTJ* (forthcoming, 2009).

HURTADO, L., 'The Jerusalem Collection and the Book of Galatians', *JSNT* 5 (1979), pp. 46–62.

JOUBERT, S., *Paul as Benefactor: Reciprocity, Strategy, and Theological Reflection in Paul's Collection* (WUNT 124; Tübingen: Mohr Siebeck, 2000).

____, 'Collection, The', in *New Interpreter's Dictionary of the Bible A-C*, vol. 1 (Nashville: Abingdon, 2006), pp. 698–699.

MARSHALL, I. H., *Acts* (TNTC; Grand Rapids: Eerdmans, 1980).

McKNIGHT, S., 'Collection for the Saints', in *DPL*, pp. 143–147.

PETERMAN, G., 'Social Reciprocity and Gentile Debt to Jews in Romans 15:26–27', *JETS* 50.4 (2007), pp. 735–746.

POWELL, M. A., *Giving to God: The Bible's Good News about Living a Generous Life* (Grand Rapids: Eerdmans, 2006).

ROSNER, B., *Greed as Idolatry: The Origin and Meaning of a Pauline Metaphor* (Grand Rapids: Eerdmans, 2007).

SCHNEIDER, J., *The Good of Affluence: Seeking God in a Culture of Wealth* (Grand Rapids: Eerdmans, 2002).

THRALL, M., *A Critical and Exegetical Commentary on the Second Epistle to the Corinthians*, vol. 2 (Edinburgh: T & T Clark, 2000).

TURNER, D., *Matthew* (BECNT; Grand Rapids: Baker, 2008).

WAN, Sze-Kar, 'Collection for the Saints as Anticolonial Act: Implications of Paul's Ethnic Reconstruction', in K. STENDAHL (ed.), *Paul and Politics: Ekklesia, Israel, Imperium, Interpretation* (Harrisburg: Trinity Press Intl. 2000), pp. 191–215.

WALTKE, B., *Proverbs 1–15* (NICOT; Grand Rapids: Eerdmans, 2004).

WALTKE, B., with C. YU, *Old Testament Theology: a Canonical and Thematic Approach* (Grand Rapids: Zondervan 2007).

WHEELER, S. E., *Wealth as Peril and Obligation: The New Testament on Possessions* (Grand Rapids: Eerdmans, 1995).

WITHERINGTON III, B., *The Paul Quest: The Renewed Search for the Jew of Tarsus* (Leicester: Apollos and Downers Grove: IVP, 2001).

WRIGHT, C. J. H., *The Mission of God: Unlocking the Bible's Grand Narrative* (Nottingham and Downers Grove: IVP, 2006).

8. THE SERVANT SOLUTION: THE COORDINATION OF EVANGELISM AND SOCIAL ACTION[1]

Melvin Tinker

In his popular and penetrating theodicy *The Enigma of Evil*, John Wenham concludes his study with an attractive presentation of the character of God as revealed in the person of Jesus of Nazareth. He writes:

> Jesus was kind as well as severe – kind in an utterly unsentimental way, which combined depth of feeling with total self-giving. He pre-eminently showed the kindness of God to the world, for he taught God's love, he taught his followers to love and he demonstrated love by deeds and words and demeanour, and supremely by accepting his vocation to shed his blood for the remission of the sins of his enemies.[2]

Note the nature of that revelation: Jesus 'taught' God's love and his followers to love; a love 'demonstrated' by 'deeds' and 'words'. This, it would be argued by many, is sufficient justification for maintaining that it is the task of the church likewise to express the same divine love to a needy world by declaration and deed, evangelism and social action. So writes John Stott:

---

1. This chapter was originally presented as the John Wenham Lecture in July 2006, and was first published in *Themelios* 32.2 (2007), pp. 6–32.

2. J. Wenham, *The Enigma of Evil* (Leicester: IVP, 1985), p. 177.

It is exceedingly strange that any followers of Jesus Christ should ever need to ask
whether social involvement was their concern, and that controversy should have blown
up over the relationship between evangelism and social responsibility. For it is evident
that in his public ministry Jesus both 'went about . . . teaching and preaching' (Matthew
4:23; 9:35) and 'went about doing good and healing' (Acts 10:38). In consequence
evangelism and social action have been intimately related to one another throughout the
history of the church . . . Christian people have often engaged in both activities quite
unselfconsciously, without feeling the need to define what they are doing or why.[3]

Whether it is strange or not, the fact is that tensions and controversy do exist
amongst evangelicals on this matter. The controversy does not centre on *whether*
Christians should engage in social action, understood as acts to improve the
physical, psychological and social welfare of people[4]; but *how* that action might
appropriately be expressed and upon what theological basis it should proceed.[5]

Current issues

On one side of the debate may be placed Tim Keller: 'The ministry of mercy
is not just a means to the end of evangelism. Word and deed are equally necessary, mutually interdependent and inseparable ministries, each carried out with
the single purpose of the spread of the kingdom of God.'[6] On the other side
is Gary Meadors who argues, 'Jesus did not call Paul or present day Christians
to a primary task of changing the world-system, but to evangelise individuals,
to teach them all things he commanded, and to recognise that Satan is the
"god of this world" and that our only hope for ultimate political correction
is Jesus' second advent.'[7] But he is equally insistent that: 'We do not disagree

---

3. John R. W. Stott, *Issues facing Christians Today* (Basingstoke: Marshall, Morgan and
   Scott, 1984), p. 3.
4. This definition is put forward by John Woodhouse, 'Evangelism and Social
   Responsibility', in B. G. Webb (ed.), *Christians in Society* (Explorations 3; Homebush
   West, NSW: Lancer Books, 1988), p. 5.
5. See Robert K. Johnstone, *Evangelicals at an Impasse: Biblical Authority in Practice*
   (Louisville: John Knox 1979), p. 70.
6. Tim Keller, *Ministries of Mercy: The Call of the Jericho* Road (Phillipsburg: Presbyterian
   & Reformed, 1997), p. 106.
7. Gary T. Meadors, 'John R. W. Stott on Social Action', *Grace Theological Journal* 1.2
   (1980), p. 146.

that we should have compassion for starving people and for those who suffer from political injustice.'[8]

Answers to questions of priority and motivation in evangelism and social action are inevitably shaped by the theological framework in which they are viewed. It is understandable that some evangelicals have strongly reacted against theological models which, in their eyes, are remarkably reminiscent of the 'social gospel' which wreaked havoc in many Western churches from the late nineteenth century throughout the 1930s and well into the 1960s, not least when definitions of what constitutes the kingdom of God seem far removed from the way the New Testament writers use the term.[9] How, then, are evangelicals to react when they read such a statement as this: 'All the earth is the Lord's and so we trace the Spirit at work *beyond* the Church, especially in movements that make for human dignity and liberation.'[10] ? Anxiety and caution will be expressed by some, and disdain and outright opposition by others. The danger, however, for the more conservative evangelical, is over-reaction, a concern raised by Ranald Macaulay when he writes of the move in some quarters to 'place exclusive emphasis on evangelism'.[11]

Is it possible to coordinate evangelism and social action in such a way that it reflects faithfully the pattern of the New Testament; enabling each to reinforce the other while avoiding the extremes of exclusive gospel proclamation on the one hand and the collapsing of evangelism into social action on the other? The contention of this chapter is that such a course is possible and that it is to be found in the 'Servant solution' which lies behind Jesus' teaching in the Sermon on the Mount.[12]

We shall proceed to examine in detail the form that solution might take with special reference to Matthew 5: 13–16 and the metaphors of salt, light and a city on a hill. This will be followed by a consideration of the extent to which the

---

8. Ibid., p. 146.

9. J. N. D. Anderson warned against this at the 1967 Anglican Evangelical Conference at Keele University. See 'Christian Worldliness: the Need and Limits of Christian Involvement', in J. I. Packer (ed.), *Guidelines* (CPAS, 1967), p. 231.

10. Nigel Wright, *The Radical Evangelical* (London: SPCK, 1996), p. 112.

11. Ranald Macaulay, 'The Great Commissions', *Cambridge Papers* 2.7 (Cambridge, 1998).

12. For a full discussion on the historical developments and theological implications of evangelicals and social involvement see Melvin Tinker, 'Reversal or Betrayal? Evangelicals and Socio-Political Involvement in the Twentieth Century', in *Evangelical Concerns* (Fearne: Mentor, 2001), pp. 139–166.

early church implemented this teaching as recorded in the book of Acts. Brief reference will also be made to the impact Christianity made upon Graeco-Roman society by virtue of its distinctive beliefs and practices. Finally, some conclusions will be drawn regarding what lessons we might learn for today.

The Sermon on the Mount and its Isaianic background

Jesus' teaching in the section on the Sermon on the Mount, running from Matthew 5:13–16, in which he likens his disciples to salt and light, has frequently been drawn upon not only to provide a theological rationale for Christian social action but as being suggestive of the means. Thus, John Stott can write:

> Both images set the two communities (Christian and non-Christian) apart. The world is dark, Jesus implied, but you are to be its light. The world is decaying, but you are to be salt, and hinder its decay . . . Although Christians are (or should be) morally and spiritually distinct from non-Christians, they are not to be socially segregated. On the contrary, their light is to shine into darkness, and their salt to soak into the decaying meat . . . Before the days of refrigeration, salt was the best known preservative . . . Light is even more obviously effective; when the light is switched on, the darkness is actually dispelled. Just so, Jesus seems to have meant, Christians can hinder social decay and dispel the darkness of evil.[13]

Without wishing to deny that Christians can and do hinder social decay and dispel evil in a society, it is doubtful that this is the way Jesus intended these metaphors to function within the context of the address given from the mountain. What such interpretations as Stott's tend to do is to understand 'salt' and 'light' as universal metaphors and then read off their sense as presently understood (preservation and illumination) and assume that this is what Jesus meant. This carries the obvious danger of engaging in an anachronistic reading of the text. What is more, the metaphors tend to be detached from the wider canonical context and treated in isolation from the more immediate literary context without exploring whether there is any *theological* connection to be made between them. Also, there is often a failure to note that Jesus in fact uses *three*, not two pictures, for there is also a 'city on a hill'.

What is necessary is first, to consider how this part of Jesus' discourse relates to the immediate context; second to ask whether what is being said has Old

---

13. Stott, *Issues*, p. 65.

Testament associations and thirdly, to tease out how such metaphors function in relation to both considerations. This will then enable us to more precisely identify the meaning of Jesus' teaching and its significance for his followers given that it is actual and prospective disciples which are in view.

The wider picture

In Matthew's Gospel, the setting is the sermon delivered from the mountain-side. Parallels between Jesus and Moses have often been made at this point.[14] Without wishing to deny such allusions, we would suggest that they are second-ary to the more striking points of contact which exist with the heralding Servant in Isaiah 40 – 66. The identification of Jesus as this Servant has already been made explicit at his baptism (Matt. 3:17). Jesus is then presented by Matthew as the great fulfilment figure with the quotation from Isaiah 9 in 4:14–16 who begins his ministry by proclaiming the kingdom of heaven and the concomi-tant call to repent. This is in line with the mission of the Servant as found in the central sections of Isaiah, who is given the task of announcing the arrival of God's reign in salvation (Isa. 52:7), a salvation which is established through his teaching and suffering (Isa. 50:4–11; 51:4, 16; 52:13 – 53:12 *passim*).

Matthew's relating of the ministry of Jesus, which immediately precedes the Sermon on the Mount, also testifies to the fulfilment of the Isaianic vision (Matt. 4:23–25). There we observe that there is an *outward* movement in which Jesus heralds the good news amongst people who had no difficulty at all in rec-ognizing their needy downtrodden state. At the same time as announcing the kingdom he acted to lift people out of their needy situation, as evidenced by healing the sick and liberating the demon-possessed (Matt. 4:24). There might also be a hint of the wider ministry of Jesus as a 'light to the Gentiles' by the passing reference that news spread all over *Syria*. This is followed, in the second place, by an *inward* movement: the gathering of Israel as represented by the large crowds of verse 25 which came from 'Galilee, the Decapolis, Jerusalem, Judea and the region across the Jordan' (cf. Isa. 60:4–7).

The commencement of Jesus' programmatic ministry in his hometown synagogue by Luke is well known, with the assertion that the prophecy of Isaiah 61 had been fulfilled in the hearing of the congregation (Luke 4:16–21). What is not so readily recognized is that the same passage lies behind the

---

14. E.g. Vern S. Poythress, *The Shadow of Christ in the Law of Moses* (Phillipsburg: Presbyterian & Reformed, 1991), ch. 17.

commencement of Jesus public ministry in Matthew as represented by the Sermon on the Mount.

For example, a convincing case can be made that the first four beatitudes have their grounding in Isaiah 61:

'Blessed are the *poor* in spirit, for theirs is the kingdom of heaven' (Matt. 5:3).
'The Spirit of the Sovereign Lord is upon me because the Lord has anointed me to preach good news to the *poor*' (Isa. 61:1).

'Blessed are those who *mourn*, for they shall be *comforted*' (Matt. 5:4).
'He has sent me to bind up the broken hearted . . . to *comfort* all who *mourn*, and provide for those who grieve in Zion' (Isa. 61:2–3).

'Blessed are the meek, for they shall *inherit* the *earth*' (Matt. 5:5).
'Instead of their shame my people will receive a double portion and instead of disgrace they will rejoice in their *inheritance;* and so they will *inherit* a double portion in their *land*. . .' (Isa. 61:7).

'Blessed are those who hunger and thirst for *righteousness*, for they will be filled' (Matt. 5:6).
'They will be called oaks of *righteousness*, a planting of the Lord' (Isa. 61:3).[15]

It is to his immediate circle of disciples as distinct from the larger crowd that Jesus addresses his words.[16] These are they who are described as 'blessed'. In the LXX *makarios* renders the Hebrew comparative article *'ašrê*. It therefore functions as a *description* of a state of affairs rather than acting as a performative announcement which *brings into being* a state of affairs. As such the addressees are the 'enviable ones' who are in a prized position. The fortunate situation in which they find themselves relates somehow to 'the kingdom' – a term which constitutes the inclusio for the beatitudes in verses 2 and 10. Given that the opening beatitude and the closing beatitude define the members of the kingdom, it is to these we shall give some detailed attention.

---

15. W. J. Dumbrell has given some very helpful exegetical thoughts on the OT background to the Sermon on the Mount in *Seven Exegetical Studies in Matthew 5:1–17* (Sydney: Moore Theological College, [1980]). See also David Seccombe, *The King of God's Kingdom. A Solution to the Puzzle of Jesus* (Carlisle: Paternoster, 2002), p. 253.

16. Although given the response of the crowds to his teaching in 7:28, caution should be exercised against making any hard and fast distinction between his immediate followers who are called to himself and the larger gathering of potential disciples.

Jesus describes as enviable those who are 'poor in the realm of the spirit'. This is not a description of people lacking spiritual things as such (having a spiritual deficiency of some kind), but a description of someone's lower standing in relation to someone else. *Ptōchos* describes a person who is in a dependent-client relationship; it refers to the destitute who can only exist with the help of charitable assistance (e.g. Lazarus in Luke 16:20).[17] It is hardly likely that Jesus was applying this term to describe the physical poverty of his followers as by the standards of the day they were not poor at all, indeed, they carried a money bag and gave alms rather than received them.

The background again is Isaiah. While most certainly the Messiah is presented as one who will be concerned with the physical poor whose state of poverty is a result of oppression and injustice, as we see for example in Isaiah 11:4; 61:8; 49:13, the term poor/afflicted ones (*'ānî*) has been extended to describe the *whole* nation which finds itself destitute and beggar-like in exile as it stands in a dependent-client relationship with Yahweh, wholly dependent upon him for salvation. As Seccombe writes, 'Seeing Israel as poor became so intrinsic to national self-understanding that sectarian groups like the Qumran community could seize the title and actually name themselves "the Poor".'[18]

Thus the poor (*'āniyîm*, LXX *ptōchoi*) are those who are in a state of oppression and affliction; designated as being of lowly, humble status. This is the state which characterizes the true people of God.[19] But why should this be described as a fortunate position to be in? The answer is that to such is promised the 'kingdom'. With Isaiah 61 providing the theological backcloth to the beatitudes, what is being promised is the restoration of God's people – an end to exile[20] – and the announcement of the day of favour of Yahweh – the jubilee. While this is a teaching open to all, it only becomes effective for those who identify themselves with Jesus. This will entail suffering, which brings us to the final beatitude in Matthew 4:10 and its extended treatment in verse 11: 'Blessed are those who are persecuted because of righteousness, for theirs is the kingdom of heaven.'

---

17. See David Seccombe, *Possessions and the Poor in Luke-Acts* (Lintz: SNTU, 1983), p. 137.

18. Ibid., p. 162.

19. This is a position argued in detail by Warren Heard Northbrook II, 'Luke's Attitude Toward the Rich and the Poor', *A Puritan's Mind*, <http://www.apuritansmind.com>.

20. The most notable advocate of this view is N. T. Wright in *Jesus and the Victory of God* (London: SPCK, 1993). Also see, Mervyn Eloff, 'From the Exile to the Christ', unpublished PhD thesis, University of Stellenbosch, 2004).

This raises the question: what 'righteousness' did the prophets perform, and the disciples were about to perform, which leads to such opposition? In the Old Testament righteousness is that which is well pleasing to God, which receives approval in the heavenly court.[21] The connotation is not distributive justice, guaranteeing fairness so that each receives what is deserved, but acts on behalf of people who cannot help themselves. It is supremely in salvation, therefore, that God exhibits his righteousness (e.g. Isa. 46:13: 'I am bringing my righteousness near, it is not far away; and my salvation will not be delayed. I will grant salvation to Zion, my splendour to Israel.'). As with John the Baptist who, 'came to show you the way of righteousness' (Matt. 21:32) to 'turn many of the people of Israel to the Lord their God' (Luke 1:16, ESV), so is the 'saving righteousness' performed by all true prophets. It is this calling of people to covenant fidelity, a total way of life given over to the Creator-Redeemer God which fulfils the righteous saving purposes of God.[22]

It is noteworthy that the manner in which this persecution comes is 'insulting' and 'speaking evil'. The nature of the prophetic ministry is such that it is invariably met in this way. Why that should be so turns on what the nature of that ministry is, which, having just been touched on above, is elucidated further by the section which lies on the other side of Jesus 'salt and light' pericope, concerning 'the fulfilment of the law and the prophets' (Matt. 5:17–20.)

In verse 17 Jesus says to his disciples, 'Do not think that I have come to abolish the law and/or the prophets; I have not come to abolish them but to fulfil them.' The identical term, 'law and the prophets' is used again in 7:12, forming an inclusio for the whole of this section and so strongly intimating that Jesus is emphasizing continuity between former revelation and his present ministry, something which he goes on to expound at length. Also, from the fact that in verse 18 Jesus deals with the matter of the law alone, it would be legitimate to infer that the use of the term 'prophets' indicates that Jesus has in view the wider extension and application of the law, the 'spirit' as well as the 'letter', since it was the function of the prophets to correct the people's misapplication and neglect of their covenant obligations – as Jesus himself does in the remaining section running from 5:21 – 7:12.[23]

In what sense, therefore, do Jesus and his followers 'fulfil' *(pleroō)* the law and prophets? The word *pleroō* occurs sixteen times in Matthew. Twelve of

---

21. See S. Motyer, 'Righteousness by faith in the New Testament', in J. I. Packer (ed.), *Here We Stand* (London: Hodder, 1986), p. 35.

22. Ibid., pp. 36–37.

23. E.g. 2 Kgs 17:13.

these occur in relation to the fulfilment of prophecy. The other three occasions, not counting the one here in verse 17, indicate the completion and finality of something – the 'filling' of covenant obligations in baptism, the 'filling' of a net with fish, and the 'filling up' of God's judgment (Matt. 3:15; 13:48; 23:32). And so it would seem that the meaning in verse 17 is that in the new age of the Messiah amongst the Messiah's new community the final expression of the law will be manifest.[24] Theirs will be a righteousness which exceeds that of the Pharisees (v. 20), whose attitude was anticipated and condemned by Isaiah (Matt. 15:7) with their principle of 'minimum requirement' which is in the sights of much of Jesus' teaching in the following section. By way of contrast, Jesus in true prophetic style is concerned not only with outward action but inner attitude, motives as well as methods. He commends the principle of 'maximum application'. As the prophets in the past called God's people back to the true nature of their covenant obligations, not least in the realm of social justice, and were met with scorn and derision, so the followers of the Servant who exercise such a prophetic ministry will meet with the same.

To summarize: the Servant heralds good tidings from the mountain; it is the time when the exile is ended and restoration begins for the people of God. The state of those who recognize their afflicted situation is one of great fortune, for to them belong the kingdom. This paradoxical state of blessing/affliction will continue in the form of the persecution of those who carry out a prophetic ministry. This happened with the former prophets and will continually reoccur as people are called to covenant fidelity. In this sense Jesus and his new community stand in direct line with the prophets of old and the righteousness spoken of in Isaiah 61 begins to be fulfilled amongst his followers.

Furthermore, Isaiah 61 links back to chapter 60 and forward to chapter 62. Chapter 60:1–3 has the people gathering awaiting the return to Zion with the promise that 'Nations will come to your light, and kings to the brightness of your dawn'. Verses 4–11 picture the rebuilding of the city on a hill – Jerusalem. Towards the end in verses 21–22, we hear echoes of the Abrahamic covenant with references to the giving of the land and the growth of a mighty nation: 'Then will all your people be righteous and they will possess the land for ever. They are the shoot I have planted, the work of my hands for the display of my splendour. The least of you will become a thousand, the smallest a mighty

24. See Zoe Holloway, 'Understanding and Misunderstanding the Discontinuity that Christ Makes to the Moral Order and the Mosaic Law: A Conceptual Foundation for Using the Mosaic Law in Christian Ethics', unpublished thesis, Moore College, Sydney, 2005.

nation. I am the LORD; in its time I will do this swiftly.' In chapter 62 the blessings of the 'everlasting covenant' announced in 61:8 are elucidated further
with the note of righteousness to the fore: 'For Zion's sake I will not keep
silent, for Jerusalem's sake I will not remain quiet, till her *righteousness shines*
out like the dawn, her salvation like a blazing torch. The nations will *see* your
righteousness and all kings your glory' (Isa. 62:1).[25]

Isaiah is the only prophet who uses the light metaphor to any significant
extent. Motyer commenting on Isaiah 60 writes: 'When the Redeemer has
come to Zion, gathered his penitents (59:20) and appointed a covenant mediator to share the Lord's Spirit with them, it is not just that they are bathed in
light but that they are irradiated, inwardly charged with new, outshining life
. . .This subjective experience has an objective basis, *for your light has come.*'[26]
Furthermore, the presence of God as symbolized by the light metaphor and
its saving and transforming witnessing effect, is also closely associated with
the theme of 'righteousness' and the work of God's 'Anointed One' which is
dominant in Isaiah 62. The work of this divine agent, which has been set forth
in chapter 61, is to bring about a new status of righteousness before God, a
rescue from bondage (v. 1) and a visible righteousness of life (v. 2).[27]

Thus, the flow of the revelation in this section is the elevation of a new
Jerusalem, the formation of a people of righteousness who will become a light
to the nations. It will be a time of unprecedented covenant fidelity resulting in
an inward movement of peoples drawn to the light and an outward movement
of God's word/law. All of this has direct bearing on Matthew 5:13–16 and, in
turn, on our understanding of the relation between gospel proclamation and
social involvement.

Jesus speaking to his disciples (the 'poor' – afflicted ones who engage in
prophetic ministry), is emphatic: '*You are* the salt of the earth; *you are* the light of
the world.' Here we discover a correspondence with the structure of the beatitudes themselves: the first four describing the condition of the members of the
kingdom, the second four relating their activity. In other words, their 'doing' –
showing mercy, godliness (pure in heart); peacemaking and a prophetic ministry
of righteousness – arises out of their 'being'. This is also very much in line with
what we have just been discussing regarding the Zion of the last days. It is because
of the salvation experienced through God's servant that not only has a new status
of righteousness been bestowed, but a new life of righteousness is being lived.

---

25. All of this fulfils the eschatological vision in Isa. 2:2–3.

26. A. Motyer, *The Prophecy of Isaiah* (Leicester: IVP, 1993), p. 494.

27. Ibid., p. 506.

The sense and referent of the metaphors

'Salt of the earth'

Given the substantiated premise that Isaiah 40 – 66 stands behind the Sermon on the Mount, it is perhaps suggestive that the Servant of the Lord in Isaiah 42:6 is described as one who is sent 'to be a covenant for the people and a light to the Gentiles'. On the basis of the covenant renewal, the light goes forth to the ends of the earth. This was to be the task of Israel as symbolized by Mount Zion in Isaiah 2, a servant which failed and which became blind and deaf (Isa. 42:18) and so in as much in need as the Gentiles. This task has now been fulfilled by Jesus (Matt. 5:17ff) and, in turn, his gathered community. If the parallel is to be maintained, it follows that being the 'salt of the earth' is a symbolic reference to maintaining the covenant. This is an interpretation which is justified by a consideration of the Old Testament use of 'salt' in covenantal agreements.[28] Could not the way the metaphor functions be that just as salt has the quality of making something last which would otherwise decay, having a preserving quality, so there is a concern to preserve the covenant, thus making it last when otherwise it would not? When this metaphor is transferred to the work of the prophets we readily see how it would operate. The task of the prophetic ministry is to remind the people of the covenant and the way of life which is consistent with that covenant and so ensure its continuing operation. In this way the prophets acted as 'salt of the covenant', seeking to maintain the covenant's integrity amongst God's people.

For the disciples to fulfil their duty of being the salt of the earth they, like the prophets, have to remain distinctive and speak God's truth. *Prima facie,* therefore, if a strict parallel is to be maintained, we would contend that it is a proclamatory ministry which is being envisaged here as was the case with the Old Testament prophets.[29] Acting in a salt-like capacity involves calling people to be true to the way of life of the new covenant community, a way

---

28. E.g. Lev. 2:13; 2 Chr. 13:5.

29. Since this sermon constitutes the platform for Jesus' ministry in Matthew, with Jesus gathering his disciples to prepare them as his followers, and given the centrality of preaching in his own ministry (Mark 1:38), it would be most extraordinary to say the least, if *no* instruction were offered by Jesus on the proclamatory aspects of ministry. What is more, one of the main characteristics of the Servant in Isaiah is that he is one who proclaims God's word (Isa. 49:1–2, 52:7; 53:1; 61:1–2). This interpretation of the disciples being salt fills what would otherwise be an astonishing lacuna in the Sermon.

of life Jesus expounds in the rest of the Sermon. Such a ministry will invariably meet with resistance as Jesus has just warned. It is when faced with such opposition that his followers run the danger of losing their saltiness, either by adopting values and lifestyles indistinct from the people being addressed and/or by diluting the message being brought to bear and so in effect becoming a false prophet (Matt. 7:15–27). If this happens, as it did with Israel herself, there will be a 'trampling under foot' in judgment (cf. Isa. 5:5; 10:6; 22:5). The salt metaphor then, has little to do with 'penetrating society' and so 'preserving' it. It has much more to do with the followers of Jesus engaging in a 'prophetic' word ministry which brings people into covenant relationship with the one true God through Jesus Christ as well as a change of values and lives which flow from that covenant.[30]

'Light of the world' and the 'city on a hill which cannot be hidden' (Matt. 5:14)

In Isaiah it is Zion which is to be such a city, the community of the redeemed whose light and shining righteousness attracts the nations in the end times (60:1–3; 62:1–3). The 'irradiated', 'inwardly charged, new life' referred to by Motyer, which shines like a light, is, according to the prophets Ezekiel and Jeremiah, brought about by the pouring out of God's Spirit and the bestowal of new hearts on which are written God's law (Eze. 36:24–32; Jer. 31:31–34). But it would appear that Jesus is giving the symbols of light and a city a new referent, namely, the poor/prophetic community of his followers. In Isaiah 62:2, the nations (Gentiles) will 'see the righteousness' of the redeemed which shines out of them 'like the dawn', likewise, this new 'city' of the redeemed cannot be hidden and their righteous good works (which are to exceed those of the Pharisees), will be seen and result in the offering of praise to God the Father. It is by being salt within one's own circle – calling God's people to be true to his covenant and being true to it oneself – that the covenant community will influence the world in drawing others to the one true God. It is also from this community that God's law/word goes into the world as a source of blessing (cf. Isa. 2:3). This is the *raison d'être* of the community: just as a lamp placed on a stand is to illumine the whole house, a hidden lamp defeating its purpose, so there can be no retreat *from* the world for these kingdom people if they are to be a light *to* the world. It is 'before men' that such deeds are performed, so producing a desired doxological effect (Matt. 5:16).

It is not without significance that the same programmatic pattern established here at the beginning of his Gospel is repeated by Matthew at the end

---

30. The apostle Paul may be using the metaphor of salt in this way in Col. 4:6.

in chapter 28:16–20. On that mountain the Son of Man, who has received all authority and an everlasting kingdom (cf. Dan. 7:13), gathers his people in order to disperse them into the world with the specified task of proclaiming and demonstrating his rule. This involves making disciples of all people groups, baptizing them into his teaching[31] so that they will obey all that has been commanded (cf. Matt. 5:19). This is the calling of his people which they are to maintain until the end of the age when the reign of God which has been inaugurated will be consummated. What is anticipated and promised in Isaiah – a new heavens and new earth (66:22) – will finally be realized at the end of time. It is the renewed covenant community, the city on a hill, which is God's chosen vehicle for achieving these things.

Seccombe expresses well the relationship between the Servant, his gathered people and their mission:

> At the time of the Sermon on the Mount Jesus evidently did not see himself carrying out the Servant's mission as an isolated individual. We observe, how, having declared the gospel, he appeals to all who have ears to hear. This is a plea for response, and the nature of that response is to become his disciple and join him in his mission of suffering; he warns them that if they will not they will never see his kingdom. This is because first, the role of the Suffering Servant was Israel's role; secondly only in default did the task pass on to the disciples, and finally with their defection, to one individual. Thus Jesus calls upon all who heard him to join him in an active programme of outgoing love and generosity that would engage with others and demonstrate God's goodness. It would meet opposition with generosity, prayer, and a willingness to suffer. God was seeking to be reconciled with his enemies, and his sons were called to participate in the peacemaking initiative (Luke 6:27–38).[32]

The coordination of evangelism and social action

Now we are in a position to see how evangelism and social action are to be coordinated, arising out of, and modelled by, the Sermon on the Mount and shaped by the Isaianic motifs which lie behind it.

---

31. D. B. Knox presents a very strong case that this is the correct understanding of the use of 'baptism' in Matt. 28 in his chapter 'New Testament Baptism', in *D. B. Knox Collected Works*, vol. 11 (Kingsford, NSW: Matthias Media, 2002), p. 278.

32. Seccombe, *Possessions and the Poor*, p. 259. Similarly David Peterson, 'Jesus and Social Ethics', in Webb (ed.), *Christians and Society*, p. 92.

First, there is the heralding of the good news, the *euangelion*. The blessings themselves are evangelistic, declaring the good news of the year of the Lord's favour to his afflicted people (the *ptōchoi*) that the kingdom is theirs.[33] As the word of the Lord was to go out from Mount Zion in Isaiah's oracle, it now goes out from the 'new city on a hill' as represented here by Jesus' disciples. Evangelism is the priority ministry so that all nations will receive the blessing promised to Abraham (Gen. 12), hearing the news that there is now an appointed ruler of the house of David (2 Sam. 7) and his name is Jesus who is the Christ (Matt. 1:1). The time of exile is now over, God has come to dwell amongst his people in the form of the one who is called 'Emmanuel' (Isa. 7:14; Matt. 1:23). As the suffering Servant, he atones for the sins of his people (Matt. 1:21/Isa. 52:13–53:12). What was said of *the* Servant can also be said of *his* servants: 'How beautiful on the mountains are the feet of those who bring good news, who proclaim peace, who bring good tidings, who proclaim salvation, who say to Zion, "Your God reigns!"' (Isa. 52:7/Rom. 10:15).[34] Furthermore, given the cataclysmic nature of *not* responding to this message (Matt. 7:13, 23, 27) the urgency as well as the priority of gospel proclamation is underscored.

Secondly, as salt, the followers of Jesus are to engage in a prophetic ministry and so ensure that the new covenant remains operative. Here again is the priority of word ministry – declaring to people gospel truths. But these truths are not to be understood in a reductionist fashion, they embrace God's concern for justice and right living. Social relations lie at the heart of Jesus' prophetic application of the law (Matt. 5:21 – 7:12) as they did for Isaiah himself (Isa. 1; 2:6–18; 5:8–25 *passim*). At the centre of the great 'jubilee' passage of Isaiah 61 we find these words: 'For I, the Lord, love justice; I hate robbery and iniquity' (v. 8). If his followers are to be faithful to their calling as 'prophetic salt' in maintaining the integrity of the covenant, can they settle for anything less? Such ministry is costly and it is often from the professing

---

33. Those who have argued at length for the evangelistic character of the beatitudes are reviewed by Seccombe in his *Possessions and the Poor,* pp. 34f, 85f.

34. Note the priority of proclaiming God's truth 'justice' in the first servant song. Motyer writes: 'Justice is the leading idea in this first Servant Song, pointing to the scope of the servant's work, his reliability in its discharge and his perseverance through to its accomplishment. The word "mishpat" is versatile, but its sense is plain in this context . . . It is a summary word for his revealed truth (cf. in verse 4, the parallelism between justice and law/"teaching") and its requirements. In this wide sense the servant brings the truth of God to the world, a pointed contrast to their former situation.' *Prophecy of Isaiah,* p. 319.

religious people that opposition will most likely come (as Jesus and the apostles were soon to discover).

Thirdly, as a community of light, God's people are to embody and express the new life of the kingdom amongst themselves and outwards to others: being as prodigal in loving forgiveness as God is himself (Matt. 5:44); giving generously to those in need (6:1–4); refusing to serve Mammon and instead storing up treasures in heaven (6:19–21); learning contentment and eschewing judgmentalism (7:1–5). This is a community of light which will shine, whose deeds will impact upon a watching world and act as a witness to the reality of the breaking in of God's kingdom here on earth.

Salt, light and a city on a hill in Acts

We now turn to examine how the early Christians, as portrayed in the book of Acts, fulfilled this calling of Jesus.

It has been argued above that although the two metaphors are related they are nonetheless distinct; being salt and engaging in prophetic action is a necessary condition for being light and vice versa. This distinction is maintained in the book of Acts in relation to the proclamatory, evangelistic work of the apostles and the communal life of the Christian believers. This dichotomy also has bearing on the question as to whether it can legitimately be claimed that the church *qua* church actually has a 'mission'.

Blue[35] contends that there is a clear differentiation of activities in Acts between those which took place within the confines of a private domestic residence (the house church) and those which required a more open, public setting. He writes: 'Luke consistently pairs the public and private activities of the early church. On the one hand, the Temple precincts, synagogues, lecture halls, etc. served as platforms from which to preach the gospel. On the other, the converted hearers formed a community centred in the houses which were placed at the communities' disposal by affluent Christians.'[36]

In turning to Acts 5:42, he argues that the chiastic construction suggests the activity of the house churches was distinct from the public proclamation which took place in the temple precincts: 'Day after day, in the temple courts

---

35. Brad Blue, 'The Influence of Jewish Worship on Luke's Presentation of the Early Church', in I. H. Marshall and D. Peterson (eds.), *Witness to the Gospel: The Theology of Acts* (Grand Rapids: Eerdmans, 1998).

36. Ibid., p. 482.

and from house to house, they never stopped teaching and proclaiming the good news that Jesus is the Christ.' A parallel construction and so a similar distinction is found in Acts 20:20.[37]

This interpretation[38] could be applied to unravel the summary description of the activities of the early Christians in Acts 2:46:

Day after day

They steadfastly met together in the   In their houses breaking bread
temple courts

Place (public)   *Place* (private)

Sharing food with glad and generous hearts
Main clause: characteristic of private gatherings

Praising God   Having goodwill towards all the people
                                                    (*Echontes charin pros holon ton laon*)

Place (private)   *Place* (public)

The Lord added to their number those being saved
Main clause: results of the public activity

Day after day

Blue concludes:

> If we have rightly understood the Lukan presentation of early Christianity, both in Palestine and the Greco-Roman world, the gospel was first proclaimed in the publicly acceptable places. Subsequently, those who had responded were drawn together into house gatherings. Luke never even suggests that during these private meetings of believers the gospel message was preached for the purpose of converting the hearers. On the contrary, for Luke, these private house meetings were for the benefit of the Christian community alone.

It is being proposed here that this pattern of public proclamation and private gathering parallels the two functions of being salt and light. There is

---

37. See also I. H. Marshall, *Acts* (Leicester: IVP, 1980), p. 118.

38. Originally proposed by Klauck and cited by Blue, 'Influence of Jewish Worship', p. 486.

the ministry of the word in evangelism. On the day of Pentecost the redeemed community is gathered in an upper room (Acts 1:13). With the pouring out of the Holy Spirit the scene shifts as the group spills out into the public arena, the most natural setting being the temple precincts, which at that time of day would have been busy. It is here that Jesus is declared Lord and Christ, fulfilling the promise of Scripture (2:32). In response to the preaching of Peter, the people are called to repent and be baptized in the name of Jesus. The setting is Jerusalem – Mount Zion. The people are being called to a renewed covenant relation with God, as evidenced by the giving of the Spirit (Joel 2:28–32; Eze. 36:24–27). The gathering in of God's people to Zion has started from the diaspora, represented by the different language groups present (2:9–11). This continued on a daily basis (2:47; 3:1; 5:12–14). The everlasting covenant made to David is fulfilled in Jesus and offered to the people (3:24–26).

Not surprisingly, given Jesus' warning in Matthew 5:11, such 'salt activity' is soon met with opposition from the ruling authorities (Acts 4:1–21; 5:17–40). It was for 'acts of righteousness' that they suffer and, accordingly, they take Jesus' injunction literally when, having foretold of persecution because of him, they are to 'rejoice and be glad' (Acts 5:41). The most striking example in Acts of the exercise of prophetic ministry of which Jesus speaks and the consequent opposition is Stephen in Acts 6 and 7.

But the prophetic activity was also directed inwards to the redeemed community, the 'city on a hill'. This comes out most clearly in the Ananias and Sapphira episode (Acts 5:1–11). Their lying to the Holy Spirit was met with swift and deadly judgment such that 'a great fear seized the whole church and all who heard about such events' (5:11). The words of Peter are reminiscent of the words of the Old Testament prophets to Israel (Isa. 66:2b–5). Such behaviour was a denial of the new covenant and the renewed life which flows from it, and as such threatened its future existence.

All of this is matched by the 'light' motif. As the redeemed community, new values and generous lifestyles were to be adopted and expressed. For Luke it is the formation of a community of property which most markedly reflects these things, as indicated by its repetition in his first two summaries: Acts 2:44–45 and 4:32, 34. The statement of the last verse that, 'there were no needy persons (endeēs) among them', suggests the fulfilling of the Mosaic law of Deuteronomy 15:4.[39] What is envisaged here is a reversal of the corrupt

---

39. Deut. 15: 4, 'However, there should be no poor among you. . .' the LXX uses *endeēs*. For a comment on the significance of this see Brian Capper, 'Reciprocity and the Ethic of Acts', in *Witness to the Gospel*, p. 511.

Zion which Isaiah condemned and the inauguration of the eschatological community he foresaw. Instead of adding 'house to house' and 'field to field' in greed (Isa. 5:8), houses and fields were sold in order to meet need (Acts 4:34). Whereas in the former Jerusalem the cause of the widows was neglected (Isa. 1:23), in God's new Zion it is met (Acts 6:1–7).

We have said that the public and private activities of the early church can be distinguished, but we would also wish to maintain that the distinction is not a hard and fast one. It is highly unlikely that others in Jerusalem were unaware of the activities of the church in caring and sharing. What is more, the word ministry of the apostles to the people was accompanied by a ministry of healing miracles (Acts 5:12–16). Both would clearly constitute the 'good works' spoken of by Jesus and mirror the pattern of his own ministry (Matt. 4:23–25).

In the debate on the relation between evangelism and social action, both are often bracketed together as at least being different but complementary aspects of the Church's 'mission'. In recent years the suitability of this phrase has been brought into question. Here is Peter Bolt: 'The concept of the "mission of the church" ought to be laid to rest. Acts does not present "the Church" as an institution which is sent. A particular church may send individuals to do a particular work (cf. Acts 13:1–4), but the church itself is not sent.'[40] Similarly John Woodhouse comments,

> The New Testament does not contain this concept. The apostles are 'sent'. And one may suppose that evangelists are 'sent'. Perhaps in some sense all Christians are 'sent' (John 20:21). But the 'church' as the church is not 'sent'. Individuals are given *to* the church, 'sent' to the church if you like (Eph 4:11) and the church sends individuals (Acts 13:3). But we do not find the *church* with a mission. This is because the New Testament concept of 'church' is not of an institution. All the 'sending' has the gathering of God's people by the gospel as its goal. The gathering, the 'church', is not the means to some other goal.[41]

This is very much in accord with what we have already seen in Acts. The public proclamation of the gospel has as its *goal* the addition of people to the gathering/church (Acts 2:47). That is where they receive the apostles' teaching and experience fellowship as the redeemed community, thus actualizing in some measure the Zion of the last days spoken of by Isaiah, with nations coming to God's light (Isa. 60:3) and being taught his ways (Isa. 2:3). Individuals or groups

---

40. Peter Bolt, 'Mission and Witness', in *Witness to the Gospel,* p. 211.
41. Ibid., p. 22.

of individuals are sent out (as were the disciples in Matt. 10) but with a view to 'gathering in' (Acts 5:12–14). The priority of word ministry is asserted by the apostles in Acts 6:2 in response to the pending crisis amongst the Grecian Jewish widows that, 'It would not be right for us to neglect the ministry of the word of God in order to wait on tables', but nonetheless practical steps are taken so as not to neglect the needy provision of widows which would have undermined the ministry in a different way, for by denying the proper expression of the new covenant the salt would be in danger of losing its saltiness.

Being salt and light and the transformation of a society

The effect of the prophetic testifying to God's truth from which flows the good deeds of light amongst Christians in the first four centuries has been carefully documented by Rodney Stark.[42]

Stark shows how 'Christianity served as a revitalization movement that arose in response to the misery, chaos, fear and brutality of life in the urban Greco-Roman world'. That it

> revitalized life in Greco-Roman cities by providing new norms and kinds of social relationships able to cope with many urgent urban problems. To cities filled with the homeless and impoverished, Christianity offered charity as well as hope. To cities filled with newcomers and strangers, Christianity offered an immediate basis for attachments. To cities filled with orphans and widows, Christianity provided a new and expanded sense of family. To cities torn by violent ethnic strife, Christianity offered a new basis for social solidarity. And to cities faced with epidemics, fires and earthquakes, Christianity offered effective nursing services.[43]

In AD 260, during what was probably a massive measles epidemic, Dionysius Bishop of Alexandria wrote:

> Most of our brother Christians showed unbounded love and loyalty, never sparing themselves and thinking only of one another. Heedless of the danger; they took charge of the sick, attending every need and ministering to them in Christ, and

---

42. Rodney Stark, *The Rise of Christianity. A Sociologist Reconsiders History* (Princeton: Princeton University Press, 1996).

43. Ibid., p. 161. See also Alan Kreider, 'Conversion and Christendom: An Anabaptist Perspective', <http://www.c3.hu/~bocs/rcmenno.htm>.

with them departed this life serenely happy; for they were infected by others with the disease, drawing on themselves the sickness of their neighbours and cheerfully accepting their pains.[44]

Contrast that description with his account of the pagans: 'The heathen behaved in the very opposite way. At the first onset of the disease, they pushed the sufferers away and fled from their dearest, throwing them into the roads before they were dead and treated unburied corpses as dirt, hoping thereby to avert the spread and contagion of the fatal disease.' That this was not the hyperbolic license of a preacher, casting the 'opposition' in a bad light, is substantiated by a similar description of the activity of non-Christians in Athens by Thucydides in 431 BC.[45]

What was it that motivated such self-sacrificial action amongst Christians? Here is a report of Cyprian's instruction to his congregation at Carthage:

> The people being assembled together; he first of all urges upon them the benefits of mercy . . . Then he proceeds to add that there is nothing remarkable in cherishing merely our own people with the due attentions of love, but that one might become perfect who should do something more than heathen men or publicans, one who, overcoming evil with good, and practicing a merciful kindness like that of God, should love his enemies as well . . . Thus the good was done to all men, not merely to the household of faith.[46]

This is pure Sermon on the Mount – the salt ensuring that the community is light.[47]

Concluding remarks

At the mount of Matthew 5 we see the heralding Servant gathering his nascent servant community to himself, thus beginning to realize the great act of sal-

---

44. *Festival Letters,* quoted by Eusebius, *Ecclesiastical History* 7.22 (1965 edn).

45. Thucydides, *The Peloponnesian War* (London: Penguin, 1954), pp. 51–53.

46. Quoted by Stark, *Rise of Christianity,* p. 87.

47. In his remarkable book *The Real Heroes of the Inner City: It Can Be Done* (Cambridge: Lutterworth, 2000), Sir Fredrick Catherwood gives many examples in the UK where churches have followed this example in social action, leading not only to people being helped and communities transformed, but lives surrendered to Christ.

vation prophesied in Isaiah 40–66. The proclamatory prophetic ministry of the disciples, which entails suffering, is to the fore, acting as the salt of the covenant; but this cannot be separated from the new way of life created by the good news which in turn testifies to that gospel, for the prophetic ministry is one which not only calls people into a living covenantal relationship with God through Christ, but seeks to uphold its integrity by calling the redeemed people to act righteously and so shine like the city on a hill – Zion – as it was meant to be.

In his teaching, Jesus presents 'being salt' and 'being light' as two different but intrinsic and integrally related aspects of what it means to be members of his covenant community. While it may legitimately be argued that theologically, evangelism has priority for the church, for it is only the evangel which saves and brings people into the new covenant way of life; operationally, social action, as an expression of the community's 'light', cannot be neglected without bringing into question the church community's covenantal integrity, its saltiness.

The implications of this for Christians living in a postmodern setting have been powerfully presented by David Wells. He writes:

> The postmodern reaction against Enlightenment dogma will not be met successfully simply by Christian proclamation. Of that we can be sure. That proclamation must arise within a context of *authenticity*. It is only as the evangelical Church begins to put its own house in order, its members begin to disentangle themselves from all those cultural habits which militate against a belief in truth, and begin to embody that truth in the way that the Church actually lives, that postmodern scepticism might begin to be overcome. Postmoderns want to see as well as hear, to find authenticity in relationship as the precursor to hearing what is said. This is a valid and biblical demand. Faith, after all, is dead without works, and few sins are dealt with as harshly by Jesus as hypocrisy. What postmoderns want to see, and are entitled to see, is believing and being, talking and doing, all joined together in a seamless whole.[48]

May God in his mercy enable the church to be what it is called to be in our day, to the praise of his glory and the transformation of his world.

© Melvin Tinker, 2009

---

48. David F. Wells, *Above All Earthly Pow'rs: Christ in the Post Modern World* (Leicester: IVP, 2005), p. 315. See also Kevin Vanhoozer, 'The world well staged', in *First Theology* (Leicester: Apollos, 2002), p. 334.

9. UNDERSTANDING AND OVERCOMING POVERTY[1]

Dewi Hughes

The God of the Bible, the God of the law and prophets and apostles, is a God of transformations. As Amos says, God/Yahweh is he:

> . . . who made the Pleiades and Orion,
>   who turns blackness into dawn
>   and darkens day into night,
> who calls for the waters of the sea
>   and pours them out over the face of the land –
>   the LORD is his name –
> he flashes destruction on the stronghold
>   and brings the fortified city to ruin (Amos 5:8–9).

The fact that God is in control of transformations in nature – the coming and going of the seasons, the daily round of night and day and the ebb and flow of the tides – is called on as witness to the fact that he can also bring about change in human society. The world is full of ruined cities that were once magnificent testimonies to the ingenuity, invention and inhumanity of

---

1. For a much expanded version of the thesis of this chapter see Dewi Hughes, *Power and Poverty: Divine and Human Rule in a World of Need* (Leicester: IVP, 2008).

human beings and God claims that this fact has something to do with him and
with the way he desires human beings to relate to each other.

What is striking about Amos' message is that it is the fortified cities of
Israel, God's own covenant people, that are being threatened with ruin. In fact
this poetic description of the transforming God is a parenthesis in the middle
of God's charges against his people:

> You who turn justice into bitterness
>   and cast righteousness to the ground . . .
> you hate the one who reproves in court
>   and despise him who tells the truth.
> You trample on the poor
>   and force him to give you grain (Amos 5:7, 10–11).

God's message to Israel through Amos can be summed up very simply –
if you are not prepared to take my demand for social justice seriously then I
will transform your current prosperity and security into poverty and oppression. God's government of his people was a government based on social
justice and equity and since his people had been chosen as an example to all
nations they were to exemplify God's will by being a just society. They were
not meant to have any poor among them but even if they did they were to
treat them well.

As I have become very familiar with the reality of poverty through my link
with Tearfund, the very clear biblical revelation that God does not approve of
poverty has been a constant strength and inspiration. There are around a billion
people today living on less than $1 a day. This means that they are living in
absolute poverty without adequate nutrition, shelter, clothing, healthcare and
education. As I have on occasion picked my way through human excrement to
visit the poor in their unhygienic slums in the shadow of the smart houses of
the rich, or walked pathways through beautiful countryside to hovels where a
high proportion of children die of malaria because a £4 mosquito net is completely beyond their means, I find it impossible to ignore the insistent voice
within declaring that this is not right – that this is not how human beings were
meant to live. The more I study the Bible the more convinced I am that the
voice I hear is the transforming Spirit of God witnessing in my heart. Being in
the kingdom of God, which means being under God's rule, means that social
justice or caring for the poor must be one of our priorities. But in order to
care for the poor in a truly transformative way we need a biblical understanding of what poverty is and of the strategies that are available to us in order to
overcome it. This is the topic of this chapter.

Understanding poverty

Some will struggle with the whole idea of putting effort into trying to understand poverty. What need is there to do this when it is patently obvious that poverty is economic deficit? People lack basic necessities because they do not have the money to buy them. Answer – give them the money so that they can buy them and then they will not be poor any more. In many of the poorer and most deprived communities in the UK we now have a third generation of poor people that are dependent on this type of welfare handout. Throwing money at the problem is clearly not enough. It is true that Jesus in promising the kingdom to his little flock encourages us to sell our possessions and give to the poor (Luke 12:32–34), but I don't think that he meant us to throw the money at them without thought. Our aim should be to reflect the generosity of God that is a good and just generosity.

The spiritual roots of poverty

One sentence in Jim Wallis' *The Call to Conversion* has had a profound effect on the way that I think about poverty: 'The poor are not our problem; we are their problem.'[2]

Wherever I go there is always a proportion of the population that is more than adequately fed, clothed, housed, etc. In some countries that may be a small minority but everywhere a proportion of that small minority is fabulously wealthy, even by our Western standards. I suspect that if the wealth generated in any country was equitably distributed there would be enough for everyone's need. But even if this belief was not well founded there is no doubt at all that there is enough wealth in the world to more than satisfy everyone's basic needs. The problem seems to be that we find it very difficult as human beings to judge what is enough, so that the more we have the bigger our needs become. It would be easy here to knock the world's more than 300 billionaires for possessing as many assets as 2.5 billion of the world's poor, while forgetting that someone on an average salary in the UK is earning

---

2. *The Call to Conversion: Why Faith is Always Personal But Never Private* (London: Monarch, 2006), p. 46. Cf. Susan George, *How the Other Half Dies* (Harmondsworth: Penguin, 1976), p. 289: 'Here comes one of the most important sentences in this chapter: *study the rich and powerful, not the poor and powerless* . . . Let the poor study themselves. They already know what is wrong with their lives and if you want truly to help them, the best you can do is to give them a clearer idea of how their oppressors are working now and can be expected to work in the future.'

maybe a hundred times more than the average earnings in many of Africa's poorest countries.

There are many explanations for the huge gulf between the rich industrialized states and the poor Majority World countries, ranging from the belief in 'manifest destiny' of the political right wing to the dependency theories of the left. It is not within the scope of this chapter to expound and critique these theories. Rather what I am going to attempt is some biblical reflection that shows why a tendency to inequality has become deeply embedded in the spirit and psyche of mankind. I have become convinced that the reason for the unjust inequality in the world is to be found ingrained in our fallen nature as human beings. If this is the case, then, overcoming poverty calls for profound spiritual transformation.

Without the sort of intimacy with God pictured by life in the Garden of Eden, human beings became preoccupied with themselves and their survival. With their relationship with God, each other and the earth disrupted, life for Adam and Eve became much more insecure. There were those among their descendants that hankered after intimacy with their Creator but the overwhelming majority followed Cain's way of wandering further and further away from God. The fact that Cain finds it impossible to see any fault in himself is clear evidence of this. He cannot understand why God should have approved his brother Abel's offering while rejecting his. He blames the rejection on his brother and, despite being warned about the danger of his jealousy and hatred, kills him. He shows no remorse whatever for the murder and complains about God's very lenient sentence and promise of protection. His sentence shows a deepening gulf between God and mankind that would increase the sense of insecurity. The ground/soil was cursed because of Adam but Cain himself is cursed and driven from the ground/soil (Gen. 4:1–16).

This cursed ground from which Cain is driven is the resource on which almost all human life on earth still depends for its survival. The fact that growing food became problematic as a result of alienation from God creates a profound insecurity that helps to explain inequality in human access to this basic provision throughout history.

When coupled with the self-centeredness of human beings alienated from God this insecurity breeds oppression and violence. Biblically this is the context for the development of power structures, beginning with the family patriarch and ending with warrior kings. In the family of Cain insecurity manifests itself in the building of the first city, in the forging of metal tools, which would have more than likely included weapons, and in the paranoid boasting of Lamech with his obscene concept of retaliation for any injury he might suffer (Gen. 4:23–24).

The very bleak picture that we have of the development of humankind in the line of Cain in Genesis 4 is affirmed when we come to the story of Noah and the flood in Genesis 6. Between these two chapters we have the genealogy of Adam and Eve through Seth. It was the line of Seth that 'began to call on the name of the Lord' and to which the Enoch who walked with God belonged (Gen. 4:26; 5:24). But something happened even among the descendants of Seth that led to the corruption of the godly line so that Noah became the only just man left in his generation.[3] In stark contrast to seeing what he had made at creation as very good, God now saw 'how great man's wickedness on the earth had become, and that every inclination of the thoughts of his heart was only evil all the time' (Gen. 6:5). The crown of God's creation had become comprehensively corrupted. Being rotten to the core humankind spewed out rottenness on each other. The word that is used to describe this manifest rottenness is 'violence' (Gen. 6:11, 13). Wenham comments:

> Animals and men had been intended to fill the earth (1:22, 28); instead, 'violence' . . . fills it . . . 'Violence' denotes any antisocial, un-neighborly activity. Very often it involves the use of brute force, but it may just be the exploitation of the weak by the powerful or the poor by the rich (e.g., Amos 6:1–3), or the naive by the clever (Prov. 16:29) . . . 'Chamas is cold-blooded and unscrupulous infringement of the personal rights of others, motivated by greed and hate and often making use of physical violence and brutality' (*Theological Dictionary of the Old Testament*, ed. G. J. Botterweck and H. Ringgren 4:482).[4]

After the terrible destruction of the flood there is no essential change in the deeply flawed condition of human nature. Every inclination of the human heart continues to be evil from childhood (Gen. 8:21; cf. 6:5). Strikingly, the incorrigibility of mankind now becomes the reason for God's mercy rather than his judgment. So, God makes a covenant with the earth and all its crea-

---

3. The key to what happened is the mysterious narrative of the sons of God being attracted by the daughters of men in Gen. 6:1–8. The very heavy emphasis in the OT on the corrupting influence of unbelieving women who do not belong to the covenant supports the traditional interpretation of this passage. It is also possible that a Middle Eastern myth of divine beings consorting with women could have been used to make the point.

4. Comment on Gen. 6:11 in Gordon J. Wenham, *Genesis 1–15* (WBC; Dallas: Word Books, 1998).

tures. He vows never again to curse the ground (*'ădāmâ*)⁵ and all living creatures in a flood (Gen. 8:21). From now on, and as long as the earth lasts, days
and seasons will follow each other in orderly progression so that the ground
will always yield its fruits for the blessing of all God's creatures.

In Genesis 10 we get the account of the descendants of Noah's sons that
is really the fulfilment of the renewed command to humankind to increase in
number and fill the earth. As people increase in number they spread out over
the face of the earth and as they become more remote from each other they
develop different languages and cultures. When people who share a common
language and culture come to think of themselves as sharing a common origin,
history and place, an ethnic identity is born with its strong sense of solidarity.
This is underlined in the refrain at the end of the genealogy of each of Noah's
sons that speaks of their clans, nations, languages and territories (Gen. 10:5,
20, 31). All this is seen as a perfectly natural outcome of God's command to
multiply and fill the earth.

The sections on Nimrod (Gen. 10:8–12) and the Tower of Babel (11:1–9)
teach us that the process of nation formation that happens when human
beings obey God's command to scatter happens in the context of the continuing sinfulness of humankind. Nimrod is a great warrior, someone who is
addicted to violence. He builds a kingdom with blood and Babylon was one of
the first centres of his empire. Babel is also Babylon. Having found the good
broad valley of the Euphrates and developed building materials that would
enable them to construct large buildings, these descendants of Ham decided
to build a city with a tower reaching up to the heavens. Their motivation was to
make a name for themselves and 'not be scattered over the face of the whole
earth' (Gen. 11:4).

The fundamental insecurity that we found in Cain is still present in the
builders of Babel. They are continuing to look for a safe place without God
and believe that the only way to create such a place is to build a city where
they can defend themselves against the threat of others. They build on the
assumption that complete security will only be gained when they have divine
status. The tower they set out to build has to be so high that it will awe everyone and make the citizens of Babel invincible. To achieve this both human
and material resources have to be drawn into the city rather than dispersed
from it. Godless power is a centripetal force. The city sucks into its vortex

---

5. When God says in Gen. 8:21 'Never again will I curse the ground because of man'
he does not rescind the curse of Gen. 3:17. The curse referred to here is the curse
of a comprehensive flood.

people with military, administrative and all sorts of creative gifts, but also a majority of oppressed people that are needed in order to carry out its grandiose schemes. The security of the few has to be bought with the oppressive sweat of the many. Then the bigger the pretensions the larger are the sum of resources needed in order to achieve them. Since large human resources are required to build the invincible city they can be deployed most effectively in a monolingual context. Therefore, God's command to scatter and diversify linguistically has to be resisted at all costs.

Babel was the first of many attempts by rebellious mankind to make themselves secure by grasping at divinity. In Babel's case the language was confused, the people found themselves unable to communicate, and without communication the ambitious project was doomed to failure. So, the people scattered as God had intended. God's power is a centrifugal force. But the fact that human beings were forced to do what God had intended they should does not mean a change of heart. Human nature remains polluted at its source.

What, then, are the roots of poverty that have been exposed in the book of origins? Alienation from God the Creator is fundamental. Whereas before the fall decisions were taken with and before God, now decisions are taken in independence of God. With Cain this leads to a rejection of the Creator's right to judge his actions. God warns Cain about the danger of not doing what is right but even when he has perpetrated the most heinous crime of fratricide there is no suggestion of a sense of guilt. To be able to murder with impunity is the limit of this narcissism and absolute proof that fallen humanity is endemically preoccupied with self.

Insecurity is a fundamental consequence of this preoccupation. Since our true identity is only found in our unity with God, away from God we exist in a constant crisis of identity. Unable to be content to be made in God's image we feel the need to assert our superiority over others. When Adam is challenged about his blatant disobedience he blames Eve and Eve in her turn blames the serpent. Cain has the audacity to blame God for the insecurity that he feels after killing his own brother! The last thing we can do is admit that we are not secure in ourselves away from God. From the perspective of fallen humanity to walk with God is to walk away from this pathological human longing for self-centred security.

That we have become self-centred creatures does not mean that we have lost our social or relational nature but that we take our self-centredness and insecurity into all our social relations. We still value marriage, family, clan, tribal and ethnic identities. But we struggle to be truly social beings and our relationships too often become means either to satisfy our own ego or to protect us from our fears. This explains our readiness to dominate and to be dominated.

The insecurity of mankind is further increased after the fall as a result of God cursing the ground. The contrast between the Edenic and post Edenic state is not between leisure and labour but between secure and insecure labour. Work in Eden was unfailingly productive with no possibility of a nutritional deficit. Outside Eden there is no such certainty. Producing food from the ground is now fraught with difficulty. Given this insecurity it was inevitable, as humankind increased in number, that food production would become an issue of power and control as well as a struggle against the curse.

The desire to be someone significant coupled with the desire to have a secure supply of things that have been taken from the ground, which includes food as the most basic good, has driven the desire for empire throughout history. The book of origins ends with God bringing to nothing the first attempt at establishing an empire. But this is not the end but merely the beginning of empire building. The world has always been, and still is, full of empire-builders, big and small, and the poor are still the victims of their violence.

God's strategy for overcoming poverty in the history of redemption

God's covenant with Abraham and Israel

The primeval history of Genesis 1 – 11 does not end with Babel, the paradigm of the pretensions and injustice of human society alienated from God, but with the genealogy of Shem. The book of origins ends with Terah leaving Ur of the Chaldeans with his son Abram, which marks the beginning of God's alternative 'empire'. Interestingly the blessing that God promises to Abram was what the builders of Babel aspired after – a numerous people and a great name. The big difference between the two empires was that it was God who would be responsible for the increase and the greatness of the name and that because of that this world 'empire' would be a blessing to all peoples and nations.

The empires founded on the basis of alienation from God and its ensuing insecurity cannot possibly be a blessing to all nations. Such empires are oppressive by definition, even though they always present themselves as a blessing to the people they subdue! Self-aggrandizement and self-interest always lurks behind the propaganda that the empire's rule is actually benign. In contrast God's 'empire' through Abraham's descendants was to be built on obedience to God, which meant that it was going to be built on righteousness and justice. 'For I have chosen him,' God says of Abraham, 'so that he will direct his children and his household after him to keep the way of the LORD by doing what is right and just, so that the LORD will bring about for Abraham what he has promised to him' (Gen. 18:19).

The exodus was an important stage in the fulfilment of God's promise to Abraham. God's purpose in rescuing Israel was to give the nation a piece of earth – the land of Canaan – because nations by definition need a territory to call their own. The law is really God's tenancy agreement with the Israelites. Fundamental is God's continuing claim to ownership – 'the land is mine and you are but aliens and my tenants' (Lev. 25:23). This important statement comes from the jubilee law that was clearly meant to reflect the principle of equitable land distribution, which conditioned Israel's occupation and would hinder the growth of inequality in land-holding. God's directive for the division of the land and the jubilee law show that God wanted all his people to have a fair share of the economic opportunity that the land provided.

The law is an integral package of spiritual, moral and judicial prescriptions that from the economic point of view would ensure a society without poverty. As Deuteronomy says, 'there should be no poor among you, for in the land the LORD your God is giving you to possess as your inheritance, he will richly bless you, if only you fully obey the LORD your God and are careful to follow all these commands I am giving you today' (Deut. 15:4–5). Obeying all the commands, however, would call for an exercise of faith and trust in God that from the point of view of the insecure non-believer would be seen as extremely risky if not foolish behaviour.

Limits were placed on economic production. Work was prohibited every seventh day and every seventh year the land was to be left fallow and the poor and wild animals were allowed to take what grew of itself. In the jubilee year land was to be returned to the families that had received it at the conquest. Every year that crops were grown generous gleanings were to be left for the poor. There was to be debt release for poor creditors every seventh year and loans to poor fellow Israelites were to be interest free. Israelites who sold themselves into debt slavery were to be freed in the seventh year and generously provided for. Every year a tenth of all produce was to be given to God to support the priests and Levites and every third year this tithe was also used to support needy Israelites and immigrants. Three times a year Israelites able to travel were expected to go to the central sanctuary to celebrate, where those that were well provided for were expected to share what they had with the needy so that all could rejoice together (Deut. 16:11, 14). This brief outline of some key laws shows clearly that obeying God's law was both costly and risky. Without trust in God they would be impossible to keep because they made self-interest subservient to divine interest. The works they demanded would be impossible without faith. It was a lack of faith in God that led Israel to adopt economic models that bred inequality and oppression of the poor and resulted in their expulsion from the land.

The new covenant in Jesus

It was as Israel/Judah was hurtling inexorably towards destruction that the prophets announced the future establishment of a new covenant written on the heart and made possible through the vicarious suffering of the Servant Messiah. Jesus claimed to be this Messiah and the economic implications of his teaching are clearly a fulfilment of the old covenant.

We begin the brief consideration of this topic with Jesus' description in the Sermon on the Mount of what it means to belong to the kingdom of heaven (Matt. 5–7). The first beatitude affirms that an active dependence on and trust in God the provider is fundamental to the new covenant. That is what poverty of spirit means. It is the admission that everything we need both spiritually and physically comes from the hand of God. The richer we are the more difficult it becomes to be poor in spirit, so we must learn to mourn – to look outside our comfort zone and take into our lives the spiritual, moral and physical grief of the world alienated from God. Poverty of spirit drives us to God, mourning drives us to God with the evils of the world, and meekness is the attitude that makes it possible to do something about it because of our dependence on God's strength. Moses was described as the meekest man on earth (Num. 12:3). Meekness is the opposite of self-assertion but does not preclude strong assertion of the truth and justice of God. Kingdom people are passionate about the righteousness/justice[6] of God as something that comes to us as a gift from God, is manifest in the individual as personal integrity, and worked out in the public square as social and economic justice. But justice is to be guided by mercy.

When Jesus comes to deal with works of righteousness/justice later in the Sermon on the Mount the first work is showing mercy, understood as giving alms to the poor. People who have the qualities described thus far in the beatitudes must be pure in heart. God is at the centre of their life and by his Spirit in them his life can flow out to others (John 7:37–38). And it flows out as peace in the sense of *šālôm* – the sort of comprehensive relational well-being of the new heavens and earth that is described in Isaiah 65:17–25. This peace means that things are right between human beings and God, between human beings and each other and between human beings and the rest of creation. In the context of this paper it must be said that things are not right between human

6. *Dikaiosynē* is invariably translated 'righteousness' in most English translations of the NT even though there is no other Greek word to convey the idea of 'justice'. Since it contains the concept of justice I have decided to use righteousness/justice when referring to it.

beings because some, like most people in the West/North, enjoy great riches while others are dying of hunger.

Amazingly these people of the kingdom of heaven, who seem to be the sort of kind, generous and loving people that any country would long to have as citizens, can expect to be hated and persecuted. The reason for this is that their existence challenges the validity of the foundations of the kingdoms of this world. They condemn by their attitudes and actions all idolatries that sanction social and economic injustice.

I find it amazing that Jesus, who we are told spent most of his ministry among the poor, includes what can only be described as a blistering attack on consumerism in the Sermon on the Mount. This is the great idol of our age. The constant message of consumerist advertising is that accumulating material treasure is the way to a life worth living. Jesus says a resounding, no! to this message. The treasure that is worth having is immaterial – the proverbial 'pie in the sky when you die'. Moreover the treasure we value shows clearly to everyone what motivates us. People who say they are Christians but spend much of their time and energy gathering around them all the things that the world can offer show clearly where their heart is. This is the message of Matthew 6:19–21. In Matthew 6:24 Jesus drives his point home by saying that God and money – what Jesus calls Mammon – are incompatible, alternative masters. Jesus gives us a stark choice. We must serve either God or money, and 'money' includes everything that money can buy.

What Jesus says about alternative treasures and masters raises the question of how we can know which treasure we are seeking and which master we are serving? The answer is found in the somewhat enigmatic section about 'eyes' in Matthew 6:22–23.

Jesus is clearly not talking about a physical disability when he refers to 'good' and 'bad' eyes in this passage. In the case of 'bad' eyes Jesus' original hearers would have heard him talk about 'evil eyes', which was a perfectly familiar idea to them as Jews with their roots in the Old Testament and rabbinic traditions. For example when hearing Deuteronomy 15:9 read in the synagogue they would have heard the 'do not give an evil eye to your needy brother' that is in the Hebrew text or the 'do not be hard in your eyes' that is in Deuteronomy 15:18. To them to have a hard, evil eye was to refuse to be generous towards the poor and needy. So, the 'bad' eye was a 'mean' eye.

So, if the 'bad' eye is a mean eye is the 'good' eye a generous eye? The word that is translated 'good' (*haplous*) in Matthew 6:22 only occurs here and in the parallel passage in Luke 11:34 but the way other words from the same root are used, points to 'generous' as a possible translation, even without the strong circumstantial evidence of Deuteronomy 15. James 1:5 says that 'if any of you lacks wisdom, he should ask God who gives generously (*haplōs*) to all without finding fault' (cf. Rom. 12:8; 2 Cor. 8:2; 9:11, 13). However, 'generous' is not the prime meaning of *haplous*. The prime meaning is 'simple' or 'single'. It refers to that 'in which there is nothing complicated or confused'; something that operates in the way it should. A simple eye is an eye that responds generously when it sees someone in need. No questions are asked. Things are seen as they really are – the response fits the seeing. God responds to our request for wisdom in the same way. There is nothing complicated about it. He responds 'simply, openly, frankly, sincerely' motivated 'solely by his desire to bless'. In the same way, when teaching about exercising the gifts of the Spirit in Romans 12, Paul says that the gift of contributing to the needs of others is to be done in 'simplicity, sincerity, [with] mental honesty' and 'an openness of heart'[7] leading to generous gifts.

So how do we know that heavenly treasure is what motivates us and that we are serving God, not money? By having simple rather than evil eyes. Having eyes that see the suffering of the poor in all its stark reality and that respond generously without quibbling. It means living simply that others may simply live.

Of course doing this will be as risky as obeying the law under the old covenant had been. So, Jesus goes on to tell us not to worry about things such as food and clothing that we need to sustain our physical life because God knows that we need these things and will provide for us. Rather our focus should be on the kingdom of God and his righteousness/justice. Since God has chosen to focus his rule in Jesus, the twin passions of kingdom people should be Jesus and righteousness/justice. One could almost say Jesus and the poor, because poverty is the clearest evidence that the rule of God is being ignored.

Conclusion

In their search for a secure home away from God human beings come together to make sure that they have adequate provision from the cursed soil. Some of these communities eventually develop into significant cities, powers or even civilizations where the well-being and prosperity of the included is built on the oppression and exploitation of the excluded. All the great empires have also claimed divine sanction and have justified their violence towards their enemies, which are seen as hindering the spread of the blessings of the 'empire', by appeal to a higher ideal that they claim to serve. This is what Augustine of

---

7. Quotes in this paragraph are from J. H. Thayer (ed.), *A Greek-English Lexicon of the NT* (Edinburgh: T & T Clark, ⁴1901), p. 57.

Hippo called the city of this world[8] – the ungodly exercise of power that manifests itself in an empire-building mentality on all levels of society. The dominant expression of this empire in our day is globalized free-market capitalism with its economic and military heart in the USA. The ideology it espouses is 'freedom' and 'democracy' but it is freedom to worship Mammon and the religious expression of this worship is consumerism.

In contrast to this 'city' and its various historical manifestations we have the city of God focused in the Old and New Testaments on his covenant people. Here insecurity is dealt with through trust in God the provider. Israel was redeemed so that they could establish a society founded on the justice of God. Complete trust and obedience would mean that there would be no poor among them. In his mercy God recognized how difficult this was – and is – for sinful people and provided a whole raft of pro-poor laws to ensure that when poverty appeared no-one would have to remain in perpetual poverty. The divinely anticipated failure of Israel proved the need for a covenant and law that would be written on hearts. This new covenant was established through the vicarious death of Jesus that, through faith, made possible the indwelling of the Holy Spirit in our hearts. It was their experience of the Holy Spirit that enabled the first Christians to reject the ideology of the Roman empire and put Jesus and righteousness/justice before all else. That this actually happened historically is proved by the statement describing the early church in Jerusalem that 'there were no needy persons among them' (Acts 4:34), clearly echoing God's expectation of his obedient people in Deuteronomy (Deut. 15:4).

Two key actions for overcoming poverty

Many things need to be done in response to the Bible's teaching on poverty. We shall focus on two key responses.

Rejecting consumerism

The first thing that needs to be done is to challenge rich Christians to make Jesus their treasure and forsake money/Mammon, which is unquestionably the god of our age.

It is now almost thirty years since the publication of Ron Sider's prophetic *Rich Christians in an Age of Hunger*, in which he challenged Western Christians

---

8. In his great work entitled *The City of God* (rev. edn, London: Penguin Classics, 2003).

to be more generous in sharing their surplus wealth with the poor. Sadly, especially in the USA, many focused on excoriating him for his weak grasp of economics and missed his very good grasp of what the Bible teaches. In 2005 he published a small book entitled *The Scandal of the Evangelical Conscience: Why are Christians Living Just Like the Rest of the World?*[9]. The book is based on an analysis of statistics comparing the behaviour of Christians, especially evangelical Christians, and non-Christians in the areas of divorce, material-ism and the poor, sexual disobedience, racism and domestic violence. Where 'Materialism and the Poor' is concerned there is evidence that even though their income has increased enormously, evangelical Christians are giving a smaller percentage of their wealth to the church and to the poor than they did thirty years ago. To quote:

> American Christians live in the richest nation on earth and enjoy an average household income of $42,409. The World Bank reports that 1.2 billion of the world's poorest people try to survive on just one dollar a day . . . if American Christians just tithed, they would have another $143 billion available to empower the poor and spread the gospel. Studies by the United Nations suggest that an additional $70–$80 billion a year would be enough to provide access to essential services like basic health care and education for all the poor of the earth. If they did no more than tithe, American Christians would have the private dollars to foot this entire bill and still have $60–$70 billion more to do evangelism around the world.[10]

We may well ask why is it that the more we have, the more we want to spend on ourselves. Our basic insecurity already discussed explains this tendency. The teaching of Jesus in Luke 12:13–34 clearly underlines this. But as Western Christians we also live in a world that is constantly telling us that we *need* something else, which we never thought was necessary for us to have, in order to enjoy a full and meaningful life on earth. Our concept of need is being constantly expanded through advertising as the ideology of economic growth ensures that we have the means to indulge ourselves more and more. As Alan Storkey says in a powerful essay entitled 'Postmodernism is consumption':

---

9. Grand Rapids: Baker Books.
10. Pp. 21–22. The reason for quoting this passage from Sider is not to engage in yet more US bashing but to emphasize that growth in the wealth of Christians does not mean growth in generosity. There are no statistics available for the UK but I have a strong suspicion that they would be very similar to the US.

For almost all western people no religious exposure, no political conviction, no
educational engagement comes within a tenth of the penetration of consumer
advertising into their lives . . . Let us list a few of the inner appeals which are made,
premised on buying certain goods: confidence, innocence, relaxation, love, security,
power, naturalness, fun, status, comfort, peace, happy families, romantic love,
friendship, excitement, freedom from stress, sex appeal, personal attraction . . . and
many more aspects of a good life are tied to products and services.

He goes on to say that 'The appeals of consumerism are pathetic in that they
are not true' and concludes: 'So we have an invasion which landscapes the
mind, emotions and inner character of millions of people, even though it is
fabricated of lies. This could be the most serious challenge to humankind of
all time. The ability to swallow lies is one of the best indices of our ability to
mess up, and we are now gulping.'[11]

To awaken UK Christians to the deception of the global empire of consumerism is an enormous challenge. It may be the biggest challenge that faces
biblical and theological educators. The students, colleagues and congregations
that listen to us – like us – are constantly bathing in a sea of lies. At the very
least we need to constantly remind ourselves and our audience that eternal life
is about passion for Jesus and righteousness/justice. I believe that bringing
the plight of the poor to the attention of those who listen to us should be an
essential component of our attempt to counter the great lie of consumerism.
The best way to do this is to face up to the difficult challenge of living in simplicity. As Sider discovered over thirty years ago this will not be easy:

In the late 1970s, I attended a national conference of evangelical leaders. My small
group, as I recall, included prominent persons like Carl Henry, the first editor of
Christianity Today; Hudson Armerding, the president of Wheaton College; and Loren
Cunningham, the founder of Youth with a Mission. Several times in our small group,
different persons referred to the issue of a simple lifestyle, urging its importance. Finally
Loren Cunningham said something like the following: 'Yes, I think the evangelical
community is ready to live more simply – if we evangelical leaders will model it.' That
ended the discussion. There were no further recommendations to live more simply.[12]

---

11. C. Bartholomew and Th. Moritz, *Christ and Consumerism: A Critical Analysis of the
     Spirit of the Age* (Carlisle: Paternoster, 2000), pp. 113–114.
12. Ron Sider, *Scandal of the Evangelical Conscience*, p. 22. For a very helpful description
     of what living in simplicity means see also Ron Sider, *Lifestyle in the Eighties: An
     Evangelical Commitment to Simple Lifestyle* (Exeter: Paternoster, 1982).

Grasp the significance of church

The second thing to do is to grasp again the significance of church in God's purpose towards the earth and its peoples in this time of grace. With a lot of talk of the 'emerging' church or of 'new expressions' of church, ecclesiology has become a hot topic once again. This could be one of the latest fads that generally come from the USA and that are soon replaced by yet another 'answer' to all the church's problems. Cell church was certainly all the rage some years ago but hardly anyone mentions it now. It seems to me that much of the talk about the church is focused on survival – on how the Western church has to change in order to keep or attract people in an era of rapid cultural change. I would not suggest that there is no value in all the current writing on this topic as long as there is clarity on the fundamental issues of the unchanging nature and purpose of the church. That, I am glad to say, is the perspective of the growing interest in the church among those that are called to serve the poor.

As far back as 1997 there was a growing conviction in Tearfund that the local church should play a more important role in transforming societies for the better. There are a variety of reasons for this but the terrible genocide in Rwanda is a key factor. Here was a country full of evangelical churches, which had experienced a powerful revival in the twentieth century but where a very large proportion of the population joined in the mass killing of their neighbours. There were glorious exceptions but generally the Rwandan churches' teaching on what the local church is and should be was shown to be woefully lacking.

A second important factor that has come increasingly to the fore is the failure of development agencies of all types to deliver development to the grass roots and the realization that success depends to a large extent on the strength of civil society organizations. In many countries where there is profound poverty – and this is especially true of sub-Saharan Africa – the churches are by now very common civil society organizations. The tragedy is that because of false or incomplete biblical teaching they often don't realize how significant they are.

So, when we came to formulate operating principles for Tearfund, the church was given a high profile. This is what is said in a document that was eventually approved in May 1999:

> God has called the church to be a reconciled community. We define the church
> as communities of people who follow Jesus Christ linked together as part of the
> worldwide people of God. We do not equate the church with denominations,
> structures, institutions or hierarchies. Denominations and parachurch organisations
> have a role, but we believe they must serve local Christian communities where these

exist or have a vision for indigenous local churches where they do not currently exist. The church is central to God's saving purpose. It is the community in which God lives by his Spirit. . .

The New Testament gives little explicit teaching on either evangelistic or developmental methods. Instead it calls upon the church to be a caring, inclusive and distinctive community of reconciliation reaching out in love to the world. When we see the church in this way there is no opposition between evangelism and social action.[13]

In the context of what has been said in this paper about insecurity because of alienation from God leading to exclusion and violence, the fact that the church by definition is a community of reconciliation is deeply significant. By definition, being reconciled with God means reconciliation with those who would normally be seen as enemies. And since our calling into fellowship with God is a sovereign work of God, we have no ultimate say as to who belongs to the reconciled community. That Jesus called a zealot and a tax collector to belong to the apostolic band laid down an early marker of the sort of community that he came to establish.

Jesus' favoured image of the gathering of those that followed him was 'family'. Status was to have no place whatsoever within this 'family'. It was to be a community of equal brothers, mothers and sisters under the authority of the one heavenly Father. Children were to be its most important members and to be great in it meant serving the servants. The Lord himself is the supreme example in that he gave his life to redeem weak and helpless sinners.

Paul's favoured picture of the church is a 'body'. He develops this theme extensively in Romans 12, 1 Corinthians 12 and Ephesians 4, and refers to the church as the body of Christ in a number of other places.[14] In comparing the church to a body Paul highlights its unity and diversity. It is interesting in the light of Jesus' teaching on the essential nature of his community that in both Romans and Ephesians Paul places his discussion of the church as a body in the context of an appeal for humility.[15] Humility is the first step to a

---

13. This emphasis has gathered strength in Tearfund since 1999. One result of Tearfund's most recent strategic review was the following new strapline: 'We are Christians passionate about the local church bringing justice and transforming lives – overcoming global poverty.'

14. Eph. 5:23; Col. 1:18, 24; 3:15.

15. Rom. 12:3; Eph. 4:2–3.

real experience of unity in the context of the church. After all the church is a collection of very different people from diverse backgrounds with a whole range of endowments. Yet there is no difference that is able to keep them apart. Nationality, colour, social and economic status and gender are all irrelevant. In the community of the church 'there is no Greek or Jew, circumcised or uncircumcised, barbarian, Scythian, slave or free, but Christ is all, and is in all'.[16]

I believe that a church that has this New Testament teaching at its heart will be a transforming community that will bring about real and meaningful economic, as well as other forms of change, in the lives of its individual members and society at large. In a paper that I co-wrote[17] for Tearfund in 2004 entitled 'Overcoming Poverty' some of the economic impacts of the true church of Jesus Christ were described as follows:

> Because churches bring people of different class and economic status into sharing communities of love they have tremendous potential for diminishing poverty. This is further enhanced because these reconciling communities, by definition, belong to each other because of the presence of the Holy Spirit, who has reconciled them with the Father through Jesus Christ. This pre-existing spiritual reality makes actual links across space and culture relatively easy and is a major advantage . . . in transforming the lives of the poor.

With global communication now so easy there is great potential for churches to share physical and spiritual resources.

The Bible does not view the poor as helpless and hopeless. They are seen rather as those who lack the power, opportunity and security to work themselves out of poverty. Laws such as the seventh year release of the land (Exod. 23:10–11; Lev. 25:2–7; Deut. 15:1–11), the ban on interest (Exod. 22:25; Lev. 25:35–38; Deut. 23:19–20), the jubilee (Lev. 25:8–55) and others, were all about empowerment, opportunity and security, rather than welfare. There were welfare laws such as the triennial tithe (Deut. 14:28–29; 26:12–15) as well but they were meant to provide a statutory safety net when the structural legislation failed. As the new covenant people of God called in Jesus to fulfil the meaning of Old Testament law, the church is now God's instrument for transforming the lives of rich and poor. It is in the context of the community of the church that theological transformation – the transformation of the

---

16. Col. 3:11.

17. My co-author was Tearfund's Advocacy Director, Andy Atkins, who is now the CEO of Friends of the Earth.

mind – leads to social transformation in the church first and then through the church in society at large. As the 'Overcoming Poverty' paper states:

> Jesus affirms the infinite value of every human being and integrates them into his church of equal sisters and brothers, whatever their social background. In this context of love and mutual respect the poor are able to discover their gifts and vocation and are given the confidence and space to articulate their own needs and influence resource allocations through involvement in state and social institutions at local, national and international levels . . . Coming to know God in Jesus Christ enables the rich to re-evaluate their wealth and to begin to use it not to satisfy their own lusts but to serve God and the needy. This leads to sharing possessions, influence, knowledge and professional skills. The church is the ideal context in which to learn to do this because the poor person is a brother or sister from whom the rich person often learns what it means to walk with God. There is no one without assets in the church.

The paper concludes that 'because of a misguided missionary strategy almost throughout the twentieth century many of the vast number of churches that have been planted by evangelical missions have been rather weak as civil society organisations'. If the thousands, if not millions, of evangelical churches were anything like what the New Testament envisages churches should be, the impact on world poverty would be immense. That is why Tearfund's current ten-year vision is to see 100,000 local churches bringing physical and spiritual transformation to 50 million people in poverty.[18]

© Dewi A. Hughes, 2009

---

18. For one wonderful story of a small church bringing amazing transformation into its Cambodian village see David Evans, *Creating Space for Strangers* (Leicester: IVP, 2004), pp. 84–86. There are many other stories in this book of church bringing transformation.

10. THE BIBLICAL BASIS FOR SOCIAL ETHICS

C. René Padilla

Many years ago I was a member of the Tyndale Fellowship. I keep pleasant memories of a couple of opportunities I had to attend meetings held under its prestigious sponsorship at Tyndale House in Cambridge. It was quite a privilege for me as a PhD student at the University of Manchester to be able to sit at the same table with scholars who had made a name for themselves in the academic world. Now that I have been invited as a speaker, over four decades later, I still feel highly privileged to attend a conference of this Fellowship, but with the added responsibility to read a paper at a plenary meeting. I view this invitation as a great honour indeed.

At the same time, I view this occasion as an opportunity to make a heartfelt plea to a distinguished audience made up of scholars committed to biblical research. In synthesis, my plea is for much more biblical research that, without renouncing loyalty to the historical Christian faith, will make a real difference to the way in which Christians, especially in the wealthy world, listen to what God requires of us: 'To act justly and to love mercy and to walk humbly with [our] God' (Mic. 6:8). My basic assumption here is that one of the most important aspects of the *raison d'être* of theology is to help the people of God to discern the meaning of this ethical injunction in order to live up to it, in the power of the Spirit, in concrete situations and to the glory of God.

Think of the situations that the following data[1] reflect – situations that cry out for responsible responses shaped by justice, mercy, and humility before God on the part of the Church today. Over 1,200 million people today have no access to a public water supply; 1,000 million lack adequate housing; 840 million (95% in the so-called developing countries, 75% in rural areas), 200 million of them children less than five years old, are undernourished; 880 million have no access to basic health care. The world produces over 10% more than all the food required to feed humankind, but an average of 35,000 children die of hunger every day. And yet, between 1990 and 2000, the investment of the wealthy countries in development aid was reduced by 50%.

What do we, as Christians, have to say and what are we to do in this world in which, as Alan Storkey has put it, 'The right to property becomes the right to grossly unequal economic power'?[2] To raise that question is to raise what may be regarded as the key question of Christian social ethics today.

The theology with which I grew up in my Christian home in Colombia and Ecuador did not ask that type of question. To say the least, it was rather limited in its scope. It reflected the kind of teaching that my parents, both of them converts from Roman Catholicism, had received from Protestant missionaries from the United States and Australia. Already in high school I began to realize the inadequacies of that theology when I found myself unable to answer a number of questions posed by Marxist professors. Six years of studies at a Christian college and graduate school in the United States led to my attainment of a BA in philosophy and an MA in theology. When I came back to Latin America with the International Fellowship of Evangelical Students (IFES), however, I felt ill prepared to answer questions posed by Christian students who found themselves challenged by their Marxist peers. I had been trained in the common ways of doing theology in the West![3] It took a few years for me to realize that, if

---

1. These data are taken from P. Gregorio Iriarte, *Análisis crítico de la realidad: Compendio de datos actualizad* (Cochabamba: Grupo Editorial Kipus, [15]2004), and from various web pages, including that of the World Bank.

2. Alan Storkey, *A Christian Social Perspective* (Leicester: IVP, 1979), p. 322.

3. There is no intention here to ignore or minimize the importance of the valuable contributions made in the West in the field of social ethics from a biblical perspective, especially in the last two decades or so. That this is the case is demonstrated here – much of the bibliography intentionally referred to in this essay was written by Western authors. Special mention should be made of John Howard Yoder's ground-breaking work on *The Politics of Jesus*, originally published in 1972.

I was to equip Christian university students to fulfil their vocation as 'salt of the earth' and 'light of the world' upon graduation, I needed to learn and to teach what Gustavo Gutiérrez of Perú has called 'a new way of doing theology' – a theology engaged with socioeconomic and political reality, a theology inseparably united to social ethics. My exploration in the early 1960s into the relation between the Church and the world in the Pauline epistles not only led to a PhD from the University of Manchester, but also laid the basis for a long pilgrimage in search of the social dimensions of the gospel and the role of the Church as the sign of the kingdom in the midst of the kingdoms of this world.

The present paper may be regarded as an effort to synthesize the convictions that have been shaped in me during more than four decades of struggle (first as a student worker with the IFES, and then with the Latin American Theological Fellowship and the Kairos Foundation), for the sake of the gospel, to relate Scripture to life in a world deeply affected by injustice and poverty, exploitation and abuse of power. More than an academic essay on the biblical basis for social ethics, this chapter represents a sharing – from the Majority World – of insights related to that subject and, at the same time, an invitation to biblical scholars in the wealthy world to focus on a new way of doing theology in the service of the kingdom of God in today's global world.

The urgent need of social ethics

My inability to respond to the questions posed by my Marxist professors in high school and, later on, by Christian university students who felt cornered by their peers was closely related to the common way of conceiving Christianity – and indeed of doing theology – in the West. I lacked a Christian social ethics because I grew up in a Christian home and studied at a Christian college that saw God's justice as the basis for the individual's 'justification by faith' in terms of freedom from guilt graciously granted by God to law-breakers rather than as the basis for God's acceptance of the individual as God's child and hence a member of God's covenant community – a community of grace and freedom.[4] In other words, justice had been cut off from *shalom*, without taking into account that, as Christopher D. Marshall has put it:

The fact remains, however, that these contributions are praiseworthy exceptions to the common captivity of Western theology to the privatization of religion.

4. See Mark D. Baker, *Religious No More: Building Communities of Grace and Freedom* (Downers Grove: IVP, 1999).

The central concern of biblical law was the creation of *shalom,* a state of soundness or 'all rightness' within the community. The law provided a pattern for living in covenant, for living in *shalom.* Specific laws were considered just, not because they corresponded in some abstract ethical norm or reflected the will of the king or protected the welfare of the state, but because they sustained *shalom* within the community. This, in view of Israel's origins as liberated slaves, necessarily required provisions for the impoverished and oppressed, which is why so much of biblical legislation is devoted to 'social justice' concerns, such as care for widows, orphans, aliens and the poor, the remission of debts, the manumission of slaves, and the protection of land rights. In this connection, covenant justice could be understood as positive succor for, and intervention on behalf of, the poor and the oppressed.[5]

One of the main criticisms coming from the Majority World of the Western approach to theology has to do with its strong bent toward the kind of individualism which has oftentimes obstructed the development of social ethics. According to the Enlightenment creed, each individual is free to pursue personal happiness without allowing others to invade his or her privacy. That creed found theological support in a doctrine of salvation that emphasized the individual's relationship to God but left aside the social dimensions of the gospel and, consequently emaciated Christian discipleship.

Writing from the perspective of liberation theology, Jon Sobrino (1981) claims that, in general terms, the basic difference between European theology and Latin American theology is derived from the real interest behind each of them. Both are related to the Enlightenment, but while European theology is concerned with the liberation of individual reason from every form of dogmatism and authoritarianism Latin American theology is oriented towards the liberation of people from socioeconomic misery. The former aims at *explaining* reality that threatens faith, where the individual is in need of understanding the meaning of life; the latter aims at *transforming* reality dominated by structural sin, where the masses are unable to satisfy basic bodily needs. The former is concerned, we may add, with orthodoxy; the latter is concerned with orthopraxis.[6]

---

5. Christopher D. Marshall, *Beyond Retribution: A New Testament Vision for Justice, Crime, and Punishment* (Grand Rapids: Wm. B. Eerdmans, 2001), p. 48.

6. Jon Sobrino, *Christology at the Crossroads: A Latin American Approach* (Maryknoll: Orbis Books, 1978). (First published in Spanish in 1976.)

In light of Sobrino's analysis of the common Western approach to theology we should not be surprised at the relative scarcity of contributions made in the Protestant and evangelical West to social ethics, especially from a biblical perspective. In the field of economics, the rampant individualism of Western culture has created 'some of the problems that have plagued the developed countries: special interests that clothe self-serving arguments behind a veil of market ideology'.[7] In the field of theology, it has reduced salvation to an individual and subjective experience, which may include ethics for the private life but is oftentimes totally oblivious of social ethics. How can a church without social ethics speak to the world prophetically? How can she prevent her message from becoming to a large extent a religious version of the ideology of the day?

A dramatic illustration of what may happen to the church in the absence of social ethics rooted in Scripture is what happened in Germany during the Nazi period, from 1933 to 1945. To be sure, the German resistance to Hitler, nobly exemplified by the Confessing Church, must not be forgotten.[8] The fact remains, however, that Hitler succeeded to a large extent in keeping the church 'intact as a subservient instrument, furthering his policy and proclaiming his doctrines'.[9] With this precedent, we should not be surprised by the way in which the large majority of Christians in the United States have been co-opted by the nationalist ideology of the Republican party to support a war waged on the basis of lies – the war in Iraq. The big gulf between private faith and socioeconomic and political life has rendered them totally unable to see the nefarious nature of this armed conflict.

A church without social ethics rooted in the moral vision of Scripture with its emphasis on justice, mercy, and humility before God is in no condition to avoid irrelevance in relation to the great problems that affect humankind. At best it will concentrate on empty ritualism and private morality, but will remain indifferent to the plight of the poor and the rape of God's creation. At worst it will fail to recognize its own captivity to the culture-ideology of consumerism and will be used by the powerful to provide religious legitimization to their unjust socioeconomic and political system and even to war.

---

7. Joseph Stiglitz, 'Development in Defiance of the Washington Consensus', <http://www.guardian.co.uk/commentisfree/2006/apr/13/comment.business>, 13 April 2006.

8. See E. H. Robertson, *Christians Against Hitler* (London: SCM Press, 1962).

9. Ibid., p. 8.

A new way of doing theology

Justo L. González, in a masterpiece that only a church historian of his calibre could write, expounds and compares three streams of theology that have informed Christian thought throughout its history. Without denying that the three types share certain common elements, he claims that each one has emphases and perspectives that make it distinct: *Type A,* centred in Carthage, is represented by Tertullian (born around AD 193). He was probably a lawyer and has been regarded as the father of Latin theology. Strongly influenced by Stoicism, he conceived Christianity as 'superior to any human philosophy, since in it one receives the revelation of the ultimate law of the universe, the law of God'.[10] *Type B,* developed in Alexandria, has Origen (born around 185) as its main exponent. Living in an environment permeated by Platonism, he dedicated himself to the search for 'immutable truths, realities that would not be dependent upon sensory perception, and scriptural interpretations to show that the Bible sets forth a series of unalterable metaphysical and moral principles'.[11] *Type C* had as its centre the geographical area roughly comprising Asia Minor and Syria, with Antioch as the main city. The most outstanding exponent of it was Irenaeus (born around 130). In contrast with Tertullian and Origen, he was not a prolific writer, but he was a pastor and had closer links with the sub-apostolic tradition. His interest was not in immutable truths but in the New Testament events that had taken place in Palestine, Antioch and Asia Minor. Taking salvation history as his starting point, he sought to equip the believers with an ethical basis for a life worthy of the gospel.[12]

González's typology shows how the prominent feature of each type of theology – law in type A, truth in type B, and history in type C – colours the understanding of every theological theme, from creation to consummation, in patristic and in medieval theology, in the Reformation and beyond. He claims that, although type A and type B are better known to Western Christians, type C is the oldest of the three. Originally, the three types were

---

10. Justo L. González, *Christian Thought Revisited: Three Types of Theology* (rev. ed., Maryknoll: Orbis Books, 1999), pp. 6–7.

11. Ibid., p. 11.

12. González, *Faith and Wealth: A History of Early Christian Ideas on the Origin, Significance, and Use of Money* (San Francisco: Harper & Row, 1990). González gives plenty of evidence to demonstrate that in this third type of theology the issues of economics and social justice were a central concern.

regarded as orthodox. After the conversion of Constantine in the fourth century, however, type A, revised with elements of type B, became the standard theology, especially in the West, while type C was generally set aside and ignored in theological creeds.

The relevance of this historical analysis to our subject lies in the fact that today, with the demise of modernity, there is, especially in the Majority World, a rediscovery of type C theology, and that opens the door for a return of social ethics as an essential aspect of the theological task. The 'new way of doing theology' which is being explored by most theologians in the Majority World is not, after all, so *new*! It is rather the unearthing of a pre-Constantine approach to theology – an approach that gives proper weight to the historical nature of biblical revelation, including the incarnation, and understands the church and its mission in light of God's action in history to manifest his kingdom, his power, and his glory in the midst of the kingdoms of this world.

From this point of view, biblical social ethics is neither an optional theological task nor a mere appendix to theology. Rather, it is a theology in search of discernment – in light of Scripture and under the guidance of the Spirit – of the times and of concrete ways in which the church can manifest the relevance of God's justice and peace in the socioeconomic and political realm.

Hermeneutics and social ethics – the hermeneutical task

My initiation in the formal study of biblical hermeneutics took place at Wheaton College over half a century ago. My professor was Dr. A. Berkeley Mickelsen, who (a few years after I took his course) wrote *Interpreting the Bible*.[13] I could hardly have had a more brilliant expositor of the historical-grammatical approach to Bible study. I deeply appreciated his combination of sincere belief in the trustworthiness of Scripture, rigorous scholarship, and warm-hearted commitment to biblical truth.

Since those days, a burning concern to relate biblical teaching to human life in all its dimensions has led me to see the need to go beyond the historical-grammatical approach to Bible study. In a way, this implies a rather different view of the hermeneutical task – an expanded view that keeps the inextricable link between theology and social ethics in the interpretive process. For my beloved professor, 'the task of interpreters is *to find out the meaning of a statement*

---

13. A. Bekeley Mickelsen, *Interpreting the Bible* (Grand Rapids: Wm. B. Eerdmans, 1963).

(command, question) for the author and for the hearers and readers, and thereupon to transmit that meaning to modern readers.[14] Upon returning to Latin America as a staff worker with IFES, the questions posed by university students and others forced me to see that the historical-grammatical approach to hermeneutics was a good start, but it did not go far enough.

In the first place, I could not simply assume that I could extract myself from my own historical context, with all its conditioning socioeconomic, political and cultural factors, in order to interpret the text *objectively* in line with the subject-object scheme inherited from the Enlightenment. I began to see myself and today's church as actually participating in the story of the people of God which begins in the Old Testament and continues to unfold in the New and throughout the whole Christian era up to the present time. I realized that, without discarding the aim to understand the original historical context and the original meaning of the text, the task of interpreters had to be expanded to include, right from the start, the aim of lifestyle transformation according to the moral vision of Scripture. As I stated in the paper I read at the Willowbank Consultation on Gospel and Culture convened in 1979 by the Lausanne Committee's Theology and Education Group and chaired by John Stott: 'The basic problem of biblical hermeneutics is to transpose the biblical message from its original context into the context of the modern readers or hearers so as to produce in them the same impact that the message was intended to produce in the original readers or hearers.'[15]

This approach to biblical hermeneutics enabled me to see the importance of keeping tightly together the study of the meaning of the text in its original historical context, on the one hand, and the critical analysis of the situation in which the message is presently delivered, on the other hand. The point was to let the text illuminate the contemporary situation and, at the same time, to let the contemporary situation illuminate the text – a hermeneutical cycle which would make it possible for the contemporary readers or hearers to perceive present-day reality from a biblical perspective, even as the original readers and hearers could perceive their own reality from the perspective of a worldview rooted in revelation.[16]

---

14. Ibid., p. 5; Mickelsen's emphasis.

15. C. René Padilla, 'Hermeneutics and Culture,', in J. R. W. Stott and Robert T. Coote (eds.), *Gospel and Culture* (Pasadena: William Carey Library, 1979), p. 83.

16. There is a detailed explanation of the hermeneutical cycle in 'Hermeneutics and Culture'.

Since I wrote my Willowbank paper on hermeneutics several scholars have shown the value of sociological analysis in the study of Scripture.[17] Their writings have enabled us to see even more clearly the role that ideas, ideological commitments and constructions of reality played in the formation and transmission of the text. This type of analysis brings out the conflicts that the original readers or hearers of God's word had to face in their own environment. What becomes quite clear is that their struggles were not merely on an intellectual level, but had to do with questions of wealth and power, injustice and oppression – the kind of questions that are the subject matter of social ethics. Social ethics was imbedded in a covenantal worldview rooted in the revelation of God as a God of love and justice, totally at odds with other worldviews.

Evidently, the Bible is a political book in which economic and social issues are not tangential but occupy a central place. The unanimous concern of the biblical writers was to enable their readers to be consistent with God's 'covenant of creational restoration' by placing every aspect of life and all their relationships in their historical context under the sovereignty of God. Accordingly, they usually addressed communities – hardly ever individuals – in the vocative case. Their purpose was to lead the people of God, not merely into the right kind of thinking, but into the right kind of living – living according to God's will for God's covenant people – in contrast with living according to the ideology of the current establishment. Doctrine, therefore, became subservient to a lifestyle marked by justice, mercy and humility before God, as well as by love, forgiveness, reconciliation and non-violence.

The sociological approach to Bible study goes beyond the study of the text in its historical context. In the same vein, the literary analysis of the text goes beyond the grammatical study of it. It enables the interpreters to see the power of language to incisively critique the current socioeconomic and political establishment and to project an alternative to it coherent with the covenantal worldview. It shows how 'prophetic imagination'[18] subverts the world created by its official ideology and creates a new world based on hope in the fulfilment of God's promises. Scripture is full of illustrations of the power of language to deconstruct an oppressive ideological reality and to construct an imagined reality that reflects God's purpose for human life and for all creation.

In order to transpose the biblical message from its original context into the context of the modern readers or hearers so as to produce in them the

---

17. E.g., Ekkehard W. Stegemann and Wolfgang Stegemann, *The Jesus Movement: A Social History of Its First Century* (Minneapolis: Fortress Press, 1999).

18. This phrase is taken from the title of a book on prophecy by Walter Brueggemann.

same impact that it was intended to produce in the original readers or hearers, the reading of the text has to be accompanied with the reading of their contemporary situation in light of the text. While the cultural and social reading of that situation is necessary and helpful, the text enables the interpreters to discern the factors that make the new situation a reproduction of the same social reality in which the text was originated. Thus the text retains its power as a subverting critique of the ideology of the establishment and as a witness to God's liberating alternative in every situation.

The hermeneutical cycle between the study of the text and the analysis of the social context of the readers or hearers of the biblical message makes it possible for the interpreters to articulate a theology which is both faithful to biblical revelation and relevant to their own situation at the same time. Faithful in that it seeks to do justice to the meaning of the message in its original socioeconomic and political context, using for that purpose the tools of exegesis and historical analysis. Relevant in that it addresses the questions arising from the contemporary socioeconomic and political context in light of the moral vision of Scripture.

A corollary of this hermeneutical approach is that, without ignoring the problem posed by the conflict of interpretations, we need to go back to Scripture in order to get a glimpse of the way in which God expects the church to do justice, to love mercy and to live in humility before him in today's world. At the same time, this hermeneutical approach makes it possible for the church to fulfil its prophetic vocation in the world – a God-given task that cannot possibly be carried out without biblically-based social ethics.

Another corollary of this hermeneutical approach is that, without ignoring the fact that in today's world every socioeconomic and political situation has something in common with every other situation, we need to recognize the need of contextual social ethics in every situation. Gone is the time when it was thought that Western theology and Western ethics were the standard for the whole world, equally valid everywhere outside the West as they were in their original context. The time has come to read Scripture in light of every local situation and to read every local situation in light of Scripture.

The Christ-event as the basis for social ethics

One way to approach the question of the biblical basis for social ethics is to take as the starting point the 'Christ-Event', including Christ's life and ministry, his death on the cross, his resurrection, and his exaltation. Each of these salvation events points towards the personal and social dimensions of the mission of the church as the community that has been called to prolong Jesus' mission as salt and light of the world throughout history.

The life and ministry of Jesus and social ethics

As N. T. Wright has cogently argued, historical integrity in talking about Jesus is essential to authentic Christianity: 'we cannot retreat into a private world of "faith" which history cannot touch (what sort of a god would we be "believing" in if we did?)'[19] A cursory analysis of the story narrated in the Gospels against its historical background prevents us from conceiving him as a 'depoliticized' Jesus, isolated from the imperial realities and the power struggles and conflicts that characterized Palestine at that time, under the dominion of the Roman Empire and the ruling authority of the temple and its high priesthood in Jerusalem.

When the historical task is taken seriously, the conclusion is unavoidable that Jesus had a political agenda which stood in sharp contrast with other political agendas open to Jews in his day, such as those of the Sadducees, the sect of Qumran, the Pharisees, and Zealots.[20] He claimed that, in his own person and work as the Servant-Messiah announced by the Old Testament

---

19. N. T. Wright, *Jesus and the Victory of God* (Minneapolis: Fortress Press, 1996), p. 122.

20. For a provocative discussion of Jesus' political context by various scholars, see Ernst Bammel and C. F. D. Moule (eds.), *Jesus and the Politics of His Day* (Cambridge: Cambridge University Press, 1984), and John Howard Yoder, *The Politics of Jesus: Behold the Man! Our Victorious Lamb* (Grand Rapids: Wm. B. Eerdmans, ²1994 [1972]). The least one can say of Yoder's work, a watershed in New Testament ethics, is that it demonstrated that Jesus Christ had a definite political agenda which stood in contrast with other agendas of his own day. Several Latin American theologians have made a lasting contribution to the rediscovery of the political dimension of Jesus' (and, consequently, of the church's) mission, See, for instance, José Míguez-Bonino (ed.), *Jesús: Ni vencido ni monarca celestial* (Buenos Aires: Tierra Nueva, 1977); Leonardo Boff, *Jesus Christ Liberator: A Critical Christology for Our Time* (Maryknoll: Orbis Books, 1978 [Portuguese: 1976]); Jon Sobrino, *Jesucristo Liberador: Lectura histórico-teológica de Jesús de Nazaret* (Madrid: Editorial Trotta, 1991); Hugo Echegaray, *The Practice of Jesus* (Maryknoll: Orbis Books, 1984 [Spanish: 1980]). The same concern for a 'whole Christ' has been present in other areas of the Majority World, as is shown in Vinay Samuel and Chris Sugden (eds.), *Sharing Jesus in the Two-Thirds World: Evangelical Christologies from the Contexts of Poverty, Powerlessness and Religious Pluralism* (Grand Rapids: Wm. B. Eerdmans, 1983).

prophets the kingdom of God was breaking into history – a kingdom of justice and peace to be manifested first in Israel as God's covenant people, and then in the whole world. The coming of the kingdom was the substance of the *euangelion* that he proclaimed, the good news on the basis of which he challenged his hearers to repent and believe and thus become members of the kingdom movement which was gathering around him. His call was not for people to become religious or to withdraw from the world. His call was to pledge allegiance to him as Israel's representative sent by God for the renewal of the chosen nation and the salvation of the world, and to participate with him in the task of implementing his political-agenda – an agenda focused on the kingdom of God and subversive of other political agendas.

What made Jesus' kingdom-agenda especially offensive to the leaders of the Jewish establishment was that it claimed that the fulfilment of God's purpose for Israel – a nation called to be the light of the world in the practice of justice, mercy, and humility before God – had nothing to do with the preservation of Jewish identity or with national liberation; instead, it was being accomplished through his own life and mission. That meant giving up their own agendas and powerful Jewish symbols, such as sabbath-keeping, dietary laws, land and family, and the temple, and accepting God's agenda mediated through his Servant-Messiah and summarized in what we call the Sermon on the Mount (Matt. 5–7).[21] It meant opting for the power of love instead of the love of power, opting for hunger and thirst for justice instead of the love of money, opting for pleasing God instead of the approval of one's neighbour. It meant adopting a kingdom lifestyle that would reproduce the image of the Son of Man who 'did not come to be served, but to serve, and to give his life as a ransom for many' (Mark 10:45).

Jesus' cross and social ethics
The cross represents the culmination of Jesus' surrender in submission to the will of God for the redemption of humankind. God 'made him who had no sin to be sin for us, so that in him we might become the righteousness of God' (2 Cor. 5:21). This is at the very heart of the gospel. The theological significance of Jesus' crucifixion, however, must not be separated from the incidents that preceded that horrid episode. Historically, his crucifixion was the result

---

21. For a commendable effort to explore the implications of the Sermon on the Mount for life in our contemporary world, see Glen H Stassen and David P. Gushee, *Kingdom Ethics: Following Jesus in Contemporary Context* (Downers Grove: IVP, 2003).

of the growing hostility that his ministry – which significantly enough was carried out mainly among the poor – provoked on the part of the high-priestly establishment and the Pharisees. His death was the way to get rid of someone whose prophetic teaching and action was good news to the poor and had thus became a threat to the establishment. And it was the kind of shameful death that Rome reserved for political subversives.

From this perspective, the cross does not only point to the way in which 'While we were still sinners, Christ died for us' (Rom. 5:8), but also represents the cost of faithfulness to God's call to do justice, to love mercy, and to walk humbly before God. During his earthly ministry, when Jesus called people to follow him, he called them to take up the cross, to embrace his vocation, to accept the risk involved in his political alternative – the 'upside-down kingdom' – willing even to die. When he sent his disciples out on their mission he warned them that suffering would be a constituent part of their mission even as it was for his (Matt. 10:22, 24–25). It would not be fortuitous or accidental, but the logical consequence of membership in the community of followers of the way of the Suffering Servant – the community of cross-bearing people, called to live as Jesus himself lived.

The cross was also the means whereby, according to Paul, Christ broke down the wall of separation between Jew and Gentile, thus creating a new humanity, one body (Eph. 2:14–16). The church therefore is called to provide a glimpse, both in its life and in its message, of a new humanity that in anticipation incarnates God's plan – the plan which will be brought to fruition in 'the fullness of time' namely, 'to bring all things in heaven and on earth under one head, even Christ' (Eph. 1:10).

The resurrection of Jesus and social ethics

The resurrection of Jesus is also at the very core of the Christian faith and the Christian life. It was an act of God through which justice was vindicated over against the powers of darkness which were behind Jesus' crucifixion. By raising Jesus from the dead God not only displayed his power but demonstrated that 'the rulers of this age . . . are doomed to perish' (1 Cor. 2:6, NRSV) and that Jesus' way – his kingdom politics – is the right way. It was thus confirmed that the coming of the long-awaited kingdom of justice and peace did not depend on human political schemes, but on God's wisdom and power embodied in his crucified Messiah.

According to God's plan, the church's agenda in relation to the world is derived from Jesus' agenda in relation to Israel in his own day, and the fulfilment of that plan depends on the power with which Jesus was raised from the dead – the power of the resurrection. The resurrection of Jesus is the dawn of a new day in the history of salvation. It has confirmed that his sacrifice succeeded in overcoming not only the powers of darkness but also the fatal consequence of sin, which is death. For those who put their trust in him, therefore, death does not have the last word. Because death has been vanquished, Christian hope in God's final victory has a solid foundation.

The risen Christ is the first fruits of the great harvest, a new humanity. By his resurrection he has begun a new era – a 'new creation' (2 Cor. 5:17); he has introduced into history a principle of life which guarantees the permanent validation of all that the church does through the power of the Spirit for the cause of Jesus Christ and the kingdom of God – the only cause that has a future.

The exaltation of Jesus and social ethics

From the perspective of the New Testament, Jesus Christ has been exalted as Lord of all creation. Having been crucified, he has been raised, and 'God has made [him] . . . both Lord and Messiah' (Acts 2:36). As Lord and Messiah, he has sent the Holy Spirit to make the mission of the church possible. Even after the crucifixion and the resurrection, however, the apostles were still clinging to those nationalist aspirations which had prompted them to follow Jesus from their first encounter and right up to his crucifixion. Jesus' reply to their question, whether the time had come for him to establish an earthly Jewish kingdom (Acts 1:6), sets in relief the combination of factors which are going to come into play in salvation history after the ascension of Jesus Christ: 'It is not for you to know the times or dates the Father has set by his own authority. But you will receive power when the Holy Spirit comes on you; and you will be my witnesses in Jerusalem, and in all Judea and Samaria, and to the ends of the earth' (Acts 1:7–8).

According to Luke these are Jesus' final words before his ascension. They include the fifth account of the 'Great Commission' in which the missiology of the whole book of Acts is summarized in narrative form. Beginning in Jerusalem, the gospel spreads first to the adjacent areas, Judea and Samaria, and then progresses until it arrives in Rome. In the whole process, the church occupies a vital place, but her mission is not merely a human project – it is Jesus' mission being extended in history in the power of the Holy Spirit. As such it is brought to fruition, not only by what the witnesses to Jesus *say*, but also by what they *are* and *do* on behalf of the kingdom which was inaugurated by Jesus Christ.

At Pentecost the enthroned 'Lord and Messiah' sends his Holy Spirit to equip the church for the purpose of forming in all nations communities of disciples with a kingdom moral vision. The universal horizons of the mission are foreshadowed by the presence in Jerusalem of 'God-fearing Jews from every nation under heaven' (Acts 2:5) on the day of Pentecost. The risen Christ, to whom the Spirit bears witness, has been anointed to reign and put his enemies under his feet. With the exaltation of Jesus Christ and the coming of the Holy Spirit at Pentecost, a new era has been inaugurated in salvation history – the era of the Spirit, which is at the same time the era of the church called to prolong Jesus' mission of justice and peace throughout history.

Jesus' promise to his apostles that he would be with them always, 'to the end of the age' (Matt. 28:20) – a promise which accompanied his commission to make disciples of all nations – is fulfilled through the presence of the Spirit and the word, the combination that made possible the existence of the church and the success of her mission as the witness to the politics of the kingdom of God in the midst of the kingdoms of the world.

Finally, Acts 2:41–47 clearly shows that the result of the Pentecost experience is no ghetto-church, devoted to cultivating individualistic religion. On the contrary, it is a community of the Spirit, a community that becomes a centre of attraction, 'having the favour of all the people' (v. 47), because it incarnates the values of the kingdom of God and affirms, by what it is, by what it does, and by what it says, that Jesus Christ has been exalted as Lord over every aspect of life, including economics. It is a missionary community which preaches reconciliation with God and the restoration of all creation by the power of the Spirit. It is a community which provides a glimpse of the birth of a new humanity, and in which can be seen, albeit 'in a mirror, dimly' (1 Cor. 13:12), the fulfilment of God's plan for all humankind.

From a biblical perspective, the basis for Christian social ethics is the story of Jesus of Nazareth, who was anointed by God with the Holy Spirit and with power; who 'went about doing good and healing all who were oppressed by the devil, for God was with him' (Acts 10:38); who died on a cross as a victim of worldly politics; who was raised from the dead and exalted by God as Lord and King of all creation. Without the political meaning of that story, Christians are left without the narrative through which the Spirit of God enables them to live as the servant people 'on whom the ends of the ages have come' (1 Cor. 10:11), called by God to be the salt of the earth and the light of the world.

Social ethics and the subverting of the empire

It is my considered opinion that one of the most urgent theological tasks today is the articulation of a Christian social ethics which will provide guidance for the life and mission of the church in the context of an empire that has institutionalized injustice on a global scale. The appalling figures that I quoted at the beginning of this chapter are only a symptom of the socio-economic and political disorder that characterizes today's world under the *Pax Americana*.

An excellent illustration of the kind of theological work that is needed today in the context of the present world disorder is *Colossians Remixed: Subverting the Empire* by Brian J. Walsh and Sylvia C. Keesmaat – a milestone in the history of biblical commentaries. Serious exegetical work, scholarly knowledge of ancient history, in-depth cultural and political analysis of our contemporary world, and amazingly creative writing are combined to produce in today's readers the same kind of life-transforming impact that Colossians must have produced among its original readers. Already in the Preface the authors clearly express their conviction that 'Paul's letter to the Colossians will only be read with integrity in our time when the radical vision of Christian faith encountered in this text engenders a similarly alternative way of life in our midst'.[22]

The result is a commentary that keeps theology and social ethics closely knit together and succeeds in challenging the readers not merely to an intellectual assent to Christian doctrine but to a life that reflects their submission to the lordship of Jesus Christ in all areas of life. This is accomplished not by discarding the historical-grammatical approach to hermeneutics generally applied in traditional commentaries, but by going beyond it in order to hear Colossians anew in relation to their own cultural context. 'Ours is a cultural, political, social and ecological reading of this text,' the authors say, 'because these are the kind of questions that our friends and our students ask.'[23]

On the one hand, on the basis of careful historical study, the authors make an effort to discern the worldview of Asia Minor in the first century. The usual approach to the study of the letter to the Colossians has given a great deal of attention to the nature of the 'Colossian heresy' – described in 2:8 as 'philosophy and empty deceit, according to human tradition, according to the elemental spirits of the universe, and not according to Christ' – against which the recipients of the letter are warned. In contrast, Walsh and Keesmaat take as their starting point that '*All* Christians [including those living in Colossae] at this time would have found themselves confronted with the worldview of empire'.[24] The conscious awareness of that historical fact makes possible for

---

22. Brian J. Walsh and Sylvia C. Keesmaat, *Colossians Remixed: Subverting the Empire* (Downers Grove: IVP, 2004), p. 8.

23. Ibid.

24. Ibid., p. 58.

them what Hays has called 'an integrative act of the imagination', necessary for 'the task of hermeneutical appropriation'.[25]

According to Walsh and Keesmaat the marks of empire, illustrated by the Roman Empire, are four:

1. Systemic centralization of power.
2. Socioeconomic and military control: an economics of oppression.
3. Powerful myths: the *Pax Romana*.
4. Imperial images that capture the people's imagination.

A deep knowledge of the original context of Colossians, including the historical background of daily life bearing these marks of empire, provides the basis for the authors' explanation of the meaning that certain words and images in Paul's letter, such as 'peace', 'hope', 'gospel', 'image of God', 'the whole world' and 'fruitfulness' probably had for the original readers. It becomes clear that these readers were challenged by the apostle not to live according to the worldview of empire shaped by the story of Rome, but according to 'an alternative imagination' shaped by the story of Israel and the story of Jesus, 'who was crucified by the empire and rose to proclaim God's new rule, manifest in communities that sold all they had so that none would have need'. These stories gripped their imaginations and provided them 'a compelling critique of life in the empire'.[26]

This critique constitutes the core of this socially perceptive reading of Colossians. Such reading, however, is not restricted to the reading of the text in its own historical context, but it is also, on the other hand, the reading of the text in the context of contemporary imperial realities. Quite rightly, the authors claim that we, as biblical interpreters, are not called to repeat, line by line and over and over, a completed script. Rather, we are called to see ourselves as participants in a continuing story – the story of the people of God.

This hermeneutical approach succeeds in keeping theology and social ethics together. There is in it a dialectical interplay between the past and the present – between the meaning of the text for the Colossian Christians living under the Roman Empire and the meaning of the text for Christians living under the American Empire. From this interplay emerges a moral vision which is just as subversive to the worldview of *Pax Americana* in the twenty-first century as it was to the worldview of *Pax Romana* in the first century.

---

25. Richard Hays, *The Moral Vision of the New Testament: Community, Cross, New Creation – A Contemporary Introduction to New Testament Ethics* (San Francisco: Harper, 1996), p. 6.
26. Walsh and Keesmaat, *Colossians Remixed*, p. 64.

What makes this fusion of horizons possible is that the study of the historical past goes hand in hand with the critical analysis of today's cultural context.
On the basis of this analysis the authors discern in today's predominant worldview the same old marks of empire. Read in light of this worldview of empire
Colossians becomes again 'an explosive and subversive tract'.[27]

Walsh's and Keesmaat's commentary is a good demonstration that it is not
possible to have a biblical social ethic without the risk involved in naming the
powers. All throughout it the readers are challenged to discern the 'dynamic analogies' between life in Paul's world under Caesar's rule and life in a world under
the thrall of the Pentagon, the transnational corporations, the international
financial organizations and many other 'contemporary parallels to the rulers
and authorities that put Jesus on the cross'.[28] For the authors, these 'systemic
centralizations of power', which foster the imperial globalization that marks the
world today, 'dictate the social policy of dependent countries, ensuring that it
favours the corporations of the North to the detriment of local people, economies and land'.[29] The myth of *Pax Romana,* based on economic and military
control, is replaced in our day by *Pax Americana* with its myth of progress and
'its clear distinction between good and evil and its self-righteous and aggressive
foreign policy'. The 'Corporate logos and corporate advertising [that] not only
shape the public space in our culture but also permeate our private lives' have
taken the place of the imperial images, including the images of the Caesar, which
'dominated both private and public space in the Roman empire'.[30]

Christians in the first century were called to subvert the empire through an
alternative imagination based on the stories of Israel and Jesus. We are called
to do the same today in our own situation. The question is whether we are prepared to let our lives be moulded not by the idolatrous lies of the empire but
by the biblical story – the story of God's dealings with humankind to create a
world where people embody justice, mercy, and humility before God.

© C. René Padilla, 2009

---

27. Ibid., p. 7.
28. Ibid., p. 8.
29. Ibid., p. 61.
30. Ibid., p. 62–63.

11. PUBLIC EXECUTION: THE ATONEMENT AND WORLD TRANSFORMATION

Anna Robbins

The missing centre

For a few years now, there have been inklings amongst young evangelicals in particular, of an emerging and growing concern for social and political issues. Passion for the poor, for the environment, for Aids and human trafficking seems to be stirring some Christians to action. There is a recovering awareness that historically, evangelicals are activists, and there is an increasing urgency for Christians to take social obligations as seriously as their personal ethics. This is a welcome, if precarious shift in contemporary evangelical thought and action. Welcome, because Christians have clear biblical and theological compulsion for social involvement; precarious because action can too easily become separated from the theological convictions that motivated it in the first place. Indeed, it may even be possible, if not likely, that many activists become involved in social action without ever thinking through the reasons for their commitment. In such a situation, it may not be long before a social movement takes on a life of its own apart from Christian convictions, and when that happens, the movement no longer has a sufficient impetus to drive it forward. As was the case at the turn of the last century, a social gospel with weak theological roots will fizzle out after a generation. Once the energy of youthful enthusiasm wears out, a movement needs to be able to recall the reasons for its existence that call Christians to persistence and commitment beyond the immediate satisfaction of quick results and easy answers.

To be fair, there are some whose convictions do drive their actions, but there are others who believe that we ought to mould our theology around our praxis, in order to catch up with what God is doing in the world. This runs the risk that we shape God after our own understanding, rather than allow God to reveal himself, and then mould our action around that revelation. My own passion for justice resonates with the cries of theologians a century ago, as they lamented the lack of social understanding present in their evangelical churches. They longed for a faith that would release them to make a difference in the world around them, and not finding one in the church, they shaped one that did. The problem was that when ethics drove the gospel rather than the other way around, there was little lasting theological motivation to be socially involved. Thus disconnected, social ethics became Christian in name rather than by distinctive content. Within a generation, many people no longer felt a need to be connected to the church or the gospel for their social involvement. Indeed, it ended up contributing little that was distinct or unique to the social enterprise that could not be gained elsewhere. At the same time, some people in the church, who might have been mobilized for social action, retreated into doctrine, appalled by the lack of content put into practice by the activists. Both sides failed the challenge to keep doctrine and practice together.

We risk the same danger today. At a time when the opportunity for evangelicals to be involved in social and political issues is significant we often fail to see the crucial importance of our doctrine feeding our action. Why should energetic young people, keen to see justice realized in this generation, be limited by the constraints of the church and its theology when they can get on board with Live 8 and fair trade campaigns? Why should we pay much attention to theology at all when it is clear that we can just get on with making a difference for Jesus right now? A thorough and rigorous theology will encourage and direct the activist as well as stir the whole of the church to action. Failure to recognize this runs the risk of evangelicals losing, or never having, a social conscience.

The centrality of the cross

To speak of a centre of faith is not straightforward today.[1] Nevertheless, in terms of how we actually work out our faith in the world, there is always some-

---

1. David Wells, *Above all Earthly Pow'rs: Christ in a Postmodern World* (Cambridge: Eerdmans and Leicester: IVP, 2005), p. 233.

thing that serves as a central organizing principal for the rest. Some believe that the best central theological principal for contemporary social action should be a doctrine of creation. Though aspects of this doctrine are crucial, they are, alone insufficient. We can only understand our little contextual window on creation from a broader revelational perspective. While there is a revelational continuity between the Creator and the creation, 'there is a soteriological discontinuity'.[2] We not only view the creation differently as a result of the person and work of Christ, but we participate in it differently.[3] Because Christ has done what he did, the Christian view of the world *is* discontinuous with non-Christian views of cosmos and ethics.

Thus it is that we have two diametrically opposed visions of life. In the one, there is no centre; in the other, there is and it is Christ. In the one, life is but a succession of random events; in the other, life is lived out under the sovereign rule of Christ. In the one, we are alone in the cosmos; in the other, we are not. In the one, salvation is humanly managed; in the other, it is divinely given. Christianity best flourishes when the sharpness of these opposing visions is preserved, and it becomes sickened when it is not.[4]

If theology is crucial to the task of social ethics, then the cross of Christ[5], as the unique intervention of the Creator in his creation, must be central to this theology. The cross is the moral centre of our faith.[6]

I suggest that it is only a theology of the cross that can sustain a social movement in the long run. We need something deeper than a cultural trend or a wave of guilty conscience to drive forward the kind of social energy the world needs today to really see change take place. The kind of change we need will not happen overnight. It requires a long attention span, and a commitment that can only come from a life-changing encounter with the God of the universe. Thus we are led back to the cross of Christ, and its significance for world transformation.

---

2. Ibid., p. 251.

3. Wells suggests: 'The purpose of God's redemption, then, is that, on the one hand, we should take our place in his world, through Christ, and own him as our Maker and, on the other hand, live in his world by his ethical will . . . Thus it is that creation is connected both with redemption and ethics, with worship and service.' Ibid., pp. 255–256.

4. Ibid., p. 262.

5. I take the phrase 'cross of Christ' to represent the work of Christ, as the fulfilment of his life and teaching, encompassing his death, burial, resurrection and ascension.

6. P. T. Forsyth, *The Work of Christ* (London: Independent Press, 1910), *passim.*

Since the cross is the cornerstone of evangelical faith, our understanding of the cross ought to define the shape of our social ethic. If social ethics are neglected in our churches, it is perhaps because we have a misshapen understanding of the cross. If our social ethics take the place in our faith that the cross alone should hold, then again, perhaps we have lost a grasp of the centrality of the cross to our faith, and failed to understand the transformative implications it has for the whole of life. Just as Christ was lifted up through a public execution for the healing of many, so must he continue to be lifted up in our actions individually, and collectively as the church, through our sacrificial involvement in his world. This is our public execution.[7]

There are those who suggest that as evangelicals we ought to remould our understanding of the cross. They argue that some traditional understandings of the cross have held back, or even stifled, the social impulse in our churches. Their suggestion is that some views of the atonement hinder the social impulse or even create an ethic that is violent and hostile, and are therefore best avoided, regardless of the central place they may traditionally have held among evangelicals.

Those who posit such arguments are right in that they recognize the power of our understanding of the atonement to shape our action. However, sometimes they dismiss too quickly a particular theology of the cross because they see something unpalatable to contemporary tastes in its explication. When this happens, they risk losing something valuable, which that model of the atonement might actually contribute to the Christian life. While focusing on an aspect that they have found to be distasteful, they have missed what might be a compelling impetus for all Christians to act for justice.

Moreover, our disagreements as Christians about the nature of the work of Christ on the cross can prevent us from acting together, and from being reconciled from within. We are sometimes tempted to think that as historical tools, the various models of the atonement (moral influence, ransom, penal substitution, *Christus victor*, etc.) have little relevance to our social ethics today. But John de Gruchy notes how, during the Truth and Reconciliation process in South Africa, some of the problems of understanding issues of guilt and forgiveness, reconciliation and justice, 'derived from differences of interpretation [of the

---

7. I have addressed elsewhere the significance of the subversive death of the atonement in the light of Jean Baudrillard's philosophy. See Anna Robbins, 'Atonement in Contemporary Culture: Christ, Symbolic Exchange and Death', in D. Tidball, D. Hilborn and J. Thacker (eds.), *The Atonement Debate* (Grand Rapids: Zondervan, 2008), pp. 329–344.

cross] within the Christian community and from a lack of understanding of the history of Christian doctrine by Christians and others alike'.[8]

It is simply not true that 'doctrine divides but service unites'. That was the mantra of the ecumenical social movement of a hundred years ago. But those activists reluctantly came to realise that without a doctrinal core, service lacks coherence, and that, in fact, differences over doctrine yield conflict in praxis as well. What we understand about the cross will be reflected in our social ethic, whether we are aware of it or not.

We have an obligation, then, to explore what the atonement means for our social ethics. Regarding the various models of the cross, de Gruchy notes that,

> . . .there can be no adequate, fully satisfying, rational account of how it is that God has reconciled the world. What we have, rather, is a series of bold attempts to weave together a rich range of biblical images and metaphors into a coherent whole that seeks to interpret the grand narrative of redemption, helps faith and experience understand themselves, and informs both worship and witness.[9]

We therefore need to take as close an account of the various models as possible, especially as it is clear that at least some of the metaphors reflected in doctrines of the atonement are intended by New Testament writers to be taken seriously.[10]

Central themes of the atonement

I intend to use the rubric of 'reconciliation' as the overarching theme of the atonement, and its subsets of satisfaction, regeneration and triumph, to begin an exploration of the implications of the atonement for social ethics.[11] Though

---

8. John W. de Gruchy, *Reconciliation: Restoring Justice* (London: SCM, 2002), p. 57.

9. Ibid., p. 63.

10. I. Howard Marshall writes: 'I reiterate the point made by Henri Blocher that the metaphorical language used in the New Testament does convey truth and is to be taken seriously' ('The Theology of the Atonement', in *The Atonement Debate*, p. 50). Cf. Henri Blocher, 'Biblical Metaphors and the Doctrine of the Atonement', *Journal of the Evangelical Theological Society* 47.4 (2004), pp. 629–645.

11. Forsyth, *Work of Christ*. Forsyth describes this as the threefold cord, based on 1 Cor. 1:30. (Thus, the notion of the cross as achieving reconciliation is not simply representative of contemporary concerns, as de Gruchy suggests.)

not exhaustive, these categories do provide us with a helpful framework for considering perhaps the most important elements of the atonement, without dividing the discussion artificially into the categories of traditional atonement models. What I hope to accomplish through this approach is a demonstration that theological elements from various models of the atonement provide biblical and essential elements of a social ethic that is truly transformative. For Christians, a fully-orbed social ethic must be developed from a fully-orbed view of the work of the cross.

Reconciliation as God's justice

It would be difficult to argue biblically against reconciliation as a main theme of Christ's life and work. However, this reconciliation is multifaceted. It involves reconciliation between God and humanity, God and the rest of the cosmos, humans and one another, and humans and creation. We see these ideas encapsulated not exclusively but supremely in 2 Corinthians 5:17 – 6:5, which describes reconciliation as being God's work, in Christ, reconciling the world to himself, and by not counting their sins against them, reconciling human beings to himself. This was made possible by some sort of vicarious exchange, whereby Christ, 'who knew no sin' was made by God 'to be sin' so that 'in him we might become the righteousness of God'. Having been thus reconciled, we are made God's ambassadors, as he has entrusted the message of reconciliation to those who have been reconciled to him. We are to work together with him, so as not to 'accept the grace of God in vain' (6:1). It is not sufficient to be objects of grace – we must also be its agents. This act of reconciliation required a public execution, and bearing this message of reconciliation requires a public execution. It is a matter of communicating what Christ has done, and it is also a matter of acting in such a way to see reconciliation realized, at least to some degree, if not completely, in our lifetime. It is clear that this is not an easy task, and it needs to be worked out in real places and times. It will require 'great endurance, in afflictions, hardships, calamities, beatings, imprisonments, riots, labours, sleepless nights, hunger' (6:4–5).

Being reconciled to God makes us a people of reconciliation. Being reconciled means that we are in a relationship of righteousness before God, and that relationship empowers and ensures the victory of justice in human affairs. This is the vision of Isaiah, who discerned the intimate connection between the character of God and the actions of his people. The quality of the vertical relationship is worked out on a horizontal level. A people reconciled are a righteous people. A righteous people are a people of justice.

But what is it that we are talking about when we speak of reconciliation? How did this reconciliation come about? Why was it necessary, and how is it possible?

It involved, first of all, something for God. There was something about the act of the cross that did something for him, otherwise, why would he require it, or even allow it? Today, we focus so much on what the cross meant for human beings that we often miss this crucial question – what did the cross mean for God?

Can't get no satisfaction (justice defined)

In discussions of the atonement, there is much discussion of the concept of satisfaction, though sadly, much of it is unsatisfactory. Partly, this is because too often, a caricature of the concept is built, usually beginning with a cursory nod towards Anselm's *Cur Deus Homo* and the idea that God's honour was outraged by sin, and thus demanded satisfaction through the substitution of Christ's perfect representation of humanity, punished for our sin, in our place.[12] Although the substitutionary element is significant from a biblical point of view, it is much more difficult to come to terms with satisfaction as a matter of assuaging God's outraged honour. This is particularly so when the concept is treated in some forensic, detached sense.[13] It is also problematic when satisfaction concepts are rejected outright, as sometimes they are. There is a feeling amongst some that to speak of God needing 'satisfaction' in some way is to portray a God who is violent, cold, demanding, and selfish.[14] But if the concept of satisfaction is rejected outright, we miss perhaps the most important idea of the atonement. When we miss this aspect, we end up discussing only what the cross means for us: satisfaction reminds us that the cross means something first and foremost *for GOD*.

P. T. Forsyth was perhaps closer to the mark than Anselm when he suggested that it is primarily God's holiness rather than his honour that has been offended, and requires satisfaction. This certainly seems more representative of the biblical picture.[15] Throughout Old and New Testaments, there is a consistent expression of God's holiness, and his demand that his people be holy. It is represented by, but not limited to a moral legal code. But this is no isolated

---

12. Cf. Colin Gunton, 'One Mediator. . .The Man Jesus Christ', *Pro Ecclesia* XI.2 (2002), p. 150; Marshall, 'Theology of the Atonement', pp. 57–59; Forsyth, *Work of Christ*, pp. 223–225.

13. This point is noted by Hans Boersma, 'Penal Substitution and the Possibility of Unconditional Hospitality', *Scottish Journal of Theology* 57.1 (2004), pp. 80–94.

14. See, for example, J. Denny Weaver, in John Sanders (ed.), *Atonement and Violence: A Theological Conversation* (Nashville: Abingdon, 2006); Joel Green and Mark Baker, *Recovering the Scandal of the Cross* (Carlisle: Paternoster, 2000).

15. Marshall agrees: Marshall, 'Theology of the Atonement', pp. 57–58.

penal system that is disconnected from God's character, or that somehow acts independently upon him. It is instead the requirement of conformity to the will and character of God that is needful in order for God's holiness to be satisfied. Consistently, God's people reject the call to conformity, and go their own way. God's desire for a people to reflect his character is consistently denied. He is not satisfied. He spells out the consequences for his people, because he loves them. There must be consequences, or God's character is without definition. If anything goes, then why should God reveal himself at all?

In a discussion with Von Balthasar, Colin Gunton points out that while there is something 'juristic' going on in the atonement, 'the real concern is with the relation between creator and creature, not considerations of abstract justice'.[16] Satisfaction 'has to do with the divine action in setting right that which has been thrown out of kilter by human sin'. Gunton argues, then, that '[t]he framework of the theology of satisfaction is thus only secondarily human fallenness; the primary focus is the goodness of God and the excellence of creation's crown, since it is through satisfaction that God's intention for humanity can be realised'.[17] Although Anselm might not have stressed God's overwhelming grace in the atonement, we have to recognize that it is grace that flowed from the cross, rather than the cross that procured it.[18] This is because God the Father did not demand a penalty to be exacted from the innocent human Son, but the atonement 'is the act of the triune God in the unity of his personal being'.[19] Citing Anselm, Gunton highlights the unmerited grace that comes through such a triune involvement in history: 'Therefore, since he himself (Jesus Christ) is God, the Son of God, he offered himself to his own honour to himself, as he did to the Father and the Holy Spirit'.[20] Though we might highlight God's holiness rather than his honour, the point is clear: satisfaction is about the Son offering to God a holiness that which could not be achieved by humanity on its own. When God's holiness is satisfied, we are reconciled to him. He deems us righteous in his sight, something he could not do in our sinful separation from him without denying his own perfect nature.

This is not to say that there is no penal aspect involved in reconciliation. Indeed, God's holiness excludes the presence of sin, and more than that, sin

---

16. Colin Gunton, *The Actuality of the Atonement* (London: T&T Clark, 1988), p. 91.

17. Ibid.

18. A well-known phrase of P. T. Forsyth.

19. Gunton, *Actuality*, p. 92.

20. Ibid.; see also Anselm, *Cur Deus Homo*, in *Anselm of Canterbury*, 4 vols., transl. and ed. Jasper Hopkins and Herbert Richardson (Toronto: Edwin Mellen, 1976), II.xviii.

exacts the judgment of holiness. This is not the random anger of a tyrant directed at any who would dare to transgress him. Rather, this is the discerning holy love of a Creator for his creation that must exclude some things in order to have shape and definition. Holiness cannot include sin. Holiness cannot include evil or selfish rebellion. Those things must be discerned and judged as being alien to God's character, in order that reconciliation with his fallen creation may take place. Holiness and sin by nature exclude one another. They can have no fellowship together. We are reminded that 'all have sinned and fall short of the glory of God' (Rom 3:23). If God is to have reconciled fellowship with a world where evil and sin reside, then his holiness must be satisfied in part through a judgment on those things that are not holy. They must be put to eternal death for his holiness to be vindicated, and for sin to be shown its place. 'For the wages of sin is death. . .' (Rom. 6:23). Even in this judgment we are confronted by grace: '. . .the free gift of God is eternal life in Jesus Christ our Lord'. What we could not offer ourselves, the perfect one, Jesus Christ, offered in our place. When God's holiness is satisfied, it becomes possible for his character to be reflected in the created order.[21]

With God's holiness satisfied, we have not only a cosmic affirmation of what is right and pure and good, and a cosmic judgment on evil, sin and alienation but also a revelation of God's just character and the possibility of fellowship again with our Creator because from his satisfied perspective, we have been reconciled. He who could not fellowship with sin 'made him who had no sin to be sin for us, so that in him we might become the righteousness of God' (2 Cor. 5:21). When we are completely reconciled with our Creator, we are deemed to be righteous before him. Being reconciled to God gives us the potential to be reconciled to one another. As we live out our righteous status before God, in our context, in our world, we become agents of transforming justice, seeking right relations between ourselves and others, and others and God. Such theological affirmations begin to put in place some of the key aspects of a biblical social ethic.

Ethical implications of satisfaction

It is not surprising that today we find we have little patience with aspects of the atonement that we think do not apparently or readily address our specific contexts. We are consumers of the cross as we are of theology, and are consistent in our demands that the cross meets our needs, our wants, our desires.

---

21. I established this previously in 'Atonement in Contemporary Culture'.

All of these ideas regarding God's satisfaction, his holiness, his justice, seem potentially cerebral and conceptual rather than engaging with our reality. But if we have no patience for such concepts, we focus only on what the cross means for us, and miss the ethical implications of what the cross means for God. And such ethical implications are of crucial significance.

God's satisfaction in consumer culture

That God is satisfied through the vicarious self-giving act of Christ on the cross places him, and potentially his church, outside of the realm of consumer culture.[22] Because his holiness is satisfied, the church, as his body, has full fellowship with him. In a culture that is not only dominated, but also defined by consumerism, satisfaction is an almost unrecognizable category. Perpetuation of the culture depends on the continuous generation of dissatisfaction, of unfulfilled desire. The only way of being able to act in a counter-cultural fashion is to be reconciled to the one who is satisfied, and therefore stands outside the realm of commodity and commercial exchange. The church is able to make counter-cultural moves inasmuch as we identify with the satisfaction of God in Christ, and recognize that we have no desire unfulfilled in our perfect, reconciled relationship with God that can be met with the goods and commodities made by human hands.

One of the biggest ethical challenges today is to live and act as a people who are not defined and driven by possessions and things. The pressure for people both rich and poor is to acquire more goods. The result is unfathomable inequality: some have no clean water to drink while others have homes abroad; some will not eat today, while others will spend on lunch what might feed a small village elsewhere. To be reconciled to a God who is satisfied is to be a people who are satisfied. This is not a simple satisfaction that rests easy with the problems of the world. Rather it is one of inner contentment that suggests there is nothing we can own, nothing we can buy, no commodity we can exchange that will bring the fulfilment of righteousness that we have in Jesus Christ.[23] It was not something we could do for ourselves. It is an external, imputed righteousness that brings contentment, and frees us to act for others rather than ourselves.

When we witness what the cross means for God, we are reminded anew of the great cost of the atonement. The cost was God's own Son, a self-giving that leaves us in awe of the wondrous grace of Christ. The cost of God's satisfaction was so high, that it leads us to a response of gratitude for what was accomplished

---

22. See Robbins, 'Atonement', p. 336–339.

23. This is, perhaps what Paul meant when he indicated he had learned to be content with whatever he had (Phil. 4:11).

out of God's great love. We see at once the depth of our sin that has so violated his holy character, and we have a glimpse of the pain our rebellion has caused him, reflected through his judgment. And we are overwhelmed by the height of love that has overcome our separation from him. This has at least three distinct implications for our ethics. One, it compels us to a response of gratitude; two, it enables us to make ethical judgments – to distinguish between sin and righteousness, between good and evil. And thirdly, it creates in us a humble passion for God's holiness that compels us to act justly and walk humbly with our God.

Response of gratitude

When we recognize how hurtful our sin has been to God, that his judgment upon it is real, and that he took that judgment upon himself in order for his holiness to be satisfied, we are moved with a deep sense of gratitude. In a response of thanks we want to live lives that reflect our love in return, as we seek no longer to outrage his holiness, but to live as his people. This response is characteristic of the moral influence theory of the cross, championed historically by Abelard, but recognized more widely as an aspect of the atonement from a New Testament perspective.[24] That repentance is more than a feeling of regret; a turn towards a new life is closer to the mark. A response of gratitude is not all that motivates our ethics, but it should be part of what does.

Making ethical judgments

When God reveals his holy character, and the cost of sinful rebellion against it, we recognize from the penalty of Christ's death that good and bad, right and wrong, are real concepts that cannot be embodied by a simple moral code. It becomes abundantly clear that God distinguishes right from wrong, and the moral responsibility bestowed on humanity at creation is given a new power. Because God has judged sin, and been satisfied by the perfect offering of the Son, we too are able to judge right from wrong and good from evil. We are able to recognize that our own outrage against injustice reflects the image of God in us, as we distinguish between that which offends his character, and witnesses against his goodness in this world, and that which honours him and testifies to his goodness.

We need immediately, however, to state some qualifications here. There may be some who take this to imply that Christians may enact any sort of behaviour on God's behalf, suggesting that it lies with them to avenge his holiness

---

24. A similar idea is argued by T. W. Manson in *Ethics and the Gospel* (London: SCM, 1960).

when it is violated. There may be others who suggest that it is their task to enact judgments, even of violence, against those who offend God's holiness. There are some who even suggest that this is a natural outworking of a penal substitutionary view of the cross.

However, such conclusions cannot be reached as a result of any understanding of the cross that includes a grasp of God's satisfaction. God has been satisfied by the perfect sacrifice of his Son. He will not be satisfied further by any human activity, no matter how passionate. He *is* satisfied. He did what we could not, and cannot do. And so we act in this world, but we do so with much humility. When we act in the world we must always remember that God is satisfied, and he is satisfied by the sacrifice of the Son, not by our ethical offerings. The fact that we are reconciled to God and are in a relationship of righteousness with him, carries with it the obligation to work for justice towards our neighbour, not to enact violence on God's behalf. Even our actions towards justice are under God's judgment of perfect love. This keeps us humble as we are reminded that even though we are righteous before him, our actions are still prone to the effects of the fall. We are yet sinful human beings and our efforts towards justice are ever marked by mixed motives of self-sacrifice and self-service.[25]

Yet, we do testify to the goodness of God, and his passion for justice. As he is satisfied we need not fear that we need to get our actions right all of the time or that God will lash out randomly in anger. But because his satisfaction is perfect in Christ, we approach the ethical task with humility. As Karl Barth pointed out, when we pursue the ethical life with passion, our ideals can too easily become our idols.[26] Many Christian social movements have gone off the rails because ideologies came to replace theologies. It is the work of the cross that supremely enables us to say 'Yes' here and 'No' there.[27] We must make judgments as we strive for justice, but we overcome those judgments with the furious love of Christ. Love is what God's justice looks like.

Passion for holiness

The passion for holiness has been described by Barth as a 'zeal for God's honour'. It longs to see God's kingdom come and his will be done. For the evangelical, it has often been interpreted in personal terms alone. But when we recognize that the satisfaction of the cross and the reconciliation achieved

---

25. This is reflective of the ethical thought of Reinhold Niebuhr.

26. Karl Barth, *The Christian Life: Church Dogmatics,* vol. IV, pt. 4: Lecture Fragments, transl. G. Bromiley (London: T&T Clark, 2004), p. 225.

27. Ibid., pp. 207; 270–271.

was a cosmic act, our passion for holiness goes beyond personal ethics to an entire way of life with implications for social and political involvement. We long to see obstacles to faith removed by improving the social order and thus contributing to a testimony of God's goodness in the world. We labour against the principalities and powers that keep people subject to evil systems just as much as we work to uphold a personal ethic that speaks to the world of a holy people. If offences such as abortion, sexual immorality and blasphemy outrage us, so should the Aids epidemic, environmental degradation and crippling poverty not only break our hearts, but challenge us to work against them in the name of God's holiness.

Regeneration – justice empowered

And so, having considered something of what the cross means for God, and some implications for our ethics, we move to consider what the atonement means for us, and consequently for world transformation. When we consider the atonement as regeneration, we are focusing on the implications of the cross for humanity. If looking at the theme of satisfaction helped us to define justice, then the theme of regeneration helps us to understand how the atonement makes justice possible in human existence, despite our sinful pretensions.

Regeneration is the language of the new creation. The new creation consists of a new people, a new community, and amazingly, a new cosmos. All that is subject to sin and decay, has, in Christ, not simply been encouraged to be better. It has been made over again. It is here that we are reminded that Jesus did not just bring a new set of ideas to inspire humanity. He did not just demonstrate something on the cross that we are to emulate, as if that were so easily possible. Rather, he achieved something unique, once and for all. It is not new ideas about God that people need – but rather 'it is life and power we need'.[28]

New people
We are made into a new people through the mediating work of Christ, and through the sanctifying work of the Holy Spirit. The latter is dependent on the former.[29] Jesus is not a being halfway between God and humanity, as the Gnostics might posit. As one who is fully God and fully human, he is uniquely,

---

28. Forsyth, *Work of the Cross*, p. 216.

29. 1 Tim 2:5–6; Heb 7:24–28.

incarnationally placed to be the perfect mediator, to stand in the gap between a sinful humanity and a holy God.[30] Through the reconciling work of the cross, Jesus Christ brings humanity's perfect obedience to God and God's prefect forgiveness to humanity.

Through Christ's mediation, humanity is a new creation. As we learn from a ransom theory of the atonement, humanity was enslaved to Satan's rule, and through Christ's mediating act, a blood price was exacted and humanity freed. Through the blood of the cross, true mediation between God and humanity was accomplished, and a new creation began that is a new ethical reality. In the words of John de Gruchy:

> . . .it is impossible to remain faithful to the New Testament and not recognise the centrality of Jesus' self-giving on the cross, the 'shedding of his blood', as the pivotal moment in the history of salvation. Or in acknowledging Jesus' call to his followers to 'take up their cross' if they are to be his disciples and thus become participants in the work of reconciliation. What we are talking about is nothing other than the vicarious offering of one's life for the sake of others without which Christianity would become a mere moral code.[31]

Yet we cannot separate the mediating sacrifice from the mediating resurrection. The mediating work of the atonement is a work of hope and vindication. Satan, sin, evil, death, do not have the last word. The resurrection is the guarantor of regeneration as a new people:

> Because Jesus Christ rose from the dead, because and as he is himself present on all sides as the living Son of God and Son of Man, God is and always will be the God who is known anew to the world. The true man who lived and lives here as the man of God and therefore in direct unity with God as the God of man, did not and does not live for himself, but as the 'first-born of all creation' (Col. 1:15), as the last Adam who in order is the first (1 Cor 15:45) he lived and lives for all men in the place of all.[32]

All of this has significant implications for our ethics. At creation, humanity was endowed with moral responsibility. This was, in part, what it meant to bear the image of God. As God's under-stewards, people were given the responsibility to look after one another, and the environment, in order

---

30. Gunton, 'One Mediator', pp. 148–149, 150.

31. de Gruchy, *Reconciliation*, pp. 58–59.

32. Barth, *Christian Life*, p. 124–125.

that it might flourish and bring glory to God the Creator. God made them accountable, moral, beings. Certain things were expected and required of them, and in return God would give all that they needed. But the first humans, like all others after them, neglected this moral responsibility, and found themselves so estranged from God that their moral capability was corrupted to the core. The image of God remained, but was thoroughly damaged. Regeneration in Christ renews our moral responsibility. We are still accountable to God for ourselves, one another, and the planet. But through Christ's mediation and the sanctifying work of the Holy Spirit, there is the possibility that at least some of God's expectations might actually be met through our efforts, inasmuch as the people of God are available to him to do his kingdom work through us.

New community
The new covenant people are not merely regenerated individuals. Rather, they are built into a society, by the work of the Holy Spirit. Because we are reconciled to God, and are a new people, the breach between sinful humanity and a holy God is overcome such that his Spirit can dwell within us, forging a new community. This community is filled with expectation, and empowered to live the life of discipleship, worship and witness. Without the reconciling, mediating work of Christ through the atonement, such power would not be available to the Christian community, and any hope of justice in this world would be lost. As it is, the people of God are not only empowered for good works, but are called to them, as a matter of urgency. Moreover, many of those who cry for justice are now brothers and sisters of the community, and the family obligation to speak out for those who cannot speak for themselves is clear. A new community within the new creation has new eyes for seeing, and new hands for helping. Indeed, they become through the mediation of the Spirit, the eyes and hands of Christ in the world.

New world
Christ's work on the cross has cosmic dimensions. It is not only a matter of the regenerated believer, or of the regenerated community, but of the regeneration of the entire creation. This work of regenerating a new world is God's ongoing work of salvation. For us it is a call to be involved in his transforming plan. It is a new call, to be kingdom agents, as we are sent out as Christ's ambassadors of reconciliation. This is a powerful image for Christians to take to heart. The entire creation groans in eager longing for its redemption. We are part of that creation, and stewards of the created order entrusted to us. The work of atonement compels the regenerated community to serve as

ambassadors in the messy work of reconciliation between individuals and communities, and for the creation. The atonement is the fulfilment of world transformation; regeneration is its witness day by day. Moral responsibility is restored, there is a new vocation to serve the new covenant, and the cosmos is freed from slavery to sin and death. It is in this context that the people of God engage in the task of world transformation. It reflects the work and heart of God, and is the very mission of the church.

Triumph (justice fulfilled)

It is clear, however, that the world does not seem to be regenerated, even through the witness of the new community. The world is in as much need of transformation as ever, and even what claims to be the new community sometimes seems to be in worse shape than the old one. Nevertheless, the work of the atonement gives us perspective on this problem. It helps us to see our call to social transformation in light of God's victory, and to appreciate the tension of the kingdom inaugurated but awaiting consummation. We engage the ethical task, therefore, as those who know the fulfilment of justice, but who understand its temporal limitations. We know that justice fulfilled is a costly victory that requires his people to take up the cross and follow him. We do this as a people of hope.

The triumphal aspect of the atonement is usually associated with the *Christus Victor* model of the cross. It is associated with the theologian Gustav Aulén, but it is older than his twentieth-century perspective. It has roots with Ireneaus' recapitulation theory, and is closely related to the ransom view of the atonement. This is not to be seen as a legal transaction, as in Anselm's penal substitution theory, but rather as a drama of divine victory.[33] The model has some biblical support, to be sure. The idea that Jesus had victory over the principalities and powers, over Satan and his enemies, both in his death, and in his resurrection, is apparent in the Gospels, and is specifically mentioned in Colossians 2:15: 'Having disarmed the powers and authorities, he made a public spectacle of them, triumphing over them. . .' That humanity was liberated from Satan's oppression and freed from slavery to sin and death is central to our concept of reconciliation. To be reconciled to God is to be freed from bondage. And if the Son shall make you free, you shall be free indeed (John 8:36).

---

33. Cf. Gunton, *Actuality*, p. 54–55.

Although this is not all that is to be said about the cross, it nevertheless has something to teach us about justice. Here we find past, present, and future lenses. If God has reconciled the world to himself, as Aulén suggests, by overcoming the powers of evil and the 'tyrants' under whom people suffer, then why are so many in the world today yet suffering, and have yet to be liberated? The answer is to be found in the now but not yet tension of the kingdom of God. In Christ, the kingdom has come to earth. In his life and work, his death and resurrection, the kingdom has been realized. But it has not been fully consummated, and will not be until his return. We look back to a time when we were without hope, and we look forward to a fulfilment of hope. The promise of victory that is ours in Christ leads us to hope for liberation here and now, though we recognize it will be achieved to greater and lesser degrees through our efforts. This recognition does not nullify the effort – indeed, it spurs it onwards. As a people of victory, we live now in light of the fulfilment of the victory to come.

This theological reality has yielded at least two contrasting approaches. Some have delivered an approach to social ethics that is less than humble, as they believe they will establish Christ's kingdom on earth through their efforts. This was the view of the social gospel. Others have neglected a social ethic altogether, waiting for the fulfilment of victory in the afterlife. Neither view is sufficient. The first approach looks to the past, at what Christ has achieved, believing it lies completely within the realm of human effort to establish the kingdom of God on earth. This is what characterized Walter Rauschenbusch's 'Christianizing' society project.[34] The second approach looks to the future when there will be no more crying or pain and Christ will wipe every tear from every eye. Both forget that there is a present in which we are left with the tension that so much is assured, but we don't see it yet. Because of what Christ has done, we know that liberation has the last word over oppression. And we work in light of its perfect fulfilment, even when it is not apparent to the human eye. Because of Christ's victory, we learn to look backwards and forwards at once, and live now in light of them both. This entails an active pursuing of transformation in the world. Christians

> live solely by hope and therefore by the promise that human right, worth, freedom,
> peace and joy are not a chimera but have already been actualized by God in Jesus
> Christ and will finally and ultimately be revealed in their actualizations. They have to
> be witnesses, shining lights of hope, to all [humans]. They have to make the promise

---

34. See Walter Rauschenbusch, *Christianizing the Social Order* (New York: Pilgrim, 1912).

known to them in its direct wording and sense as a call to faith. There arises here the missionary task of the Christian community in the narrower sense, a task in which each individual Christian will naturally have a part.[35]

Atonement and transformation

There is much more that could be said about both the atonement and social ethics than has been said here. Nevertheless, I hope that we have considered enough aspects to be able to draw some conclusions about the implications of atonement for world transformation.

Transformation is cosmic
Understanding the cosmic dimensions of the atonement cannot allow us to isolate transformation to one aspect of life alone. Christ's work on the cross brings about spiritual transformation through a reconciled relationship with God, but that has physical implications for an embodied, physical world. How we work out our salvation through discipleship is evidence of the spiritual transformation that has taken place within. If there is no external fruit borne, we may doubt the spiritual reality. Moreover, God's reconciliation with his creation extends beyond humanity. We are accountable to God for our treatment of others, and of the planet.

Transformation is a work of God
God is the one who initiates, executes, and completes transformation. He is the author of new creation, and will bring about its fulfilment. We are to be humble about our efforts to bring about social transformation, but we are to also recognize, that through the work of his Spirit, God invites us to partner with him in his transforming work, to demonstrate his justice to the world – a justice that is outraged by oppression, that is characterized by love, and that seeks to work out in creation the reconciliation that was achieved through the cross.

The members of the body of Christ are both objects and agents of transformation
As those who are incorporated by the Spirit, members of the church are those who have been reconciled by the work of Christ. They are reconciled to God, and become agents of his transformation, sent out as ambassadors of recon-

---

35. Barth, *Christian Life*, pp. 270–271.

ciliation. As those who are in a restored relationship of righteousness with God, members of the church are to be his agents of justice, saying 'yes' and 'no' to aspects of the social order, and engaging in counter-cultural transformation. As God has been satisfied through the atonement, they stand with him potentially outside the realm of commodified consumer culture.

Transformation will be incomplete until the consummation of the kingdom

We ought not to delude ourselves into thinking that we can achieve full transformation in this lifetime. Just as we could not save ourselves, and required Jesus the mediator to achieve the impossible, so we are still marked by sin and pride. Our best efforts will not bring about the complete transformation of the world. But we are nevertheless called and empowered to make the effort towards transformation, and to do so with hope of its fulfilment beyond human effort.

Transformation in this world is possible

When we are tempted by disillusionment to surrender the pursuit of transforming justice in this world, the atonement reminds us that because of Christ's work, transformation is possible. Through regeneration, creation groans for its fulfilment, but fulfilment is coming. Triumph is guaranteed. The fact that transformation will be limited in each generation does not nullify our obligation to work towards justice. The assurance that transformation is possible, and is coming, encourages us in our efforts.

God has, in Christ, affected a work of reconciliation with far-reaching repercussions. Because he is satisfied, his people are regenerated, and the world awaits final victory of his justice. But waiting is an activity. As those reconciled to God in Christ, we are also to work towards our reconciliation with each other, and with the planet. All of this means being rightly related to one another. We cannot wish for a different task, or to be taken from this vale of tears to some other world. Herein lies our origin, our being, our task, our call.

Conclusion

We have explored some aspects of the atonement that are central to understanding the meaning of the cross. We have considered initially how satisfaction, regeneration and triumph as aspects of reconciliation help us to develop a fully-orbed social ethic that encourages us towards world transformation. While not focusing exclusively on diverse models of the cross, aspects of penal substitution, ransom, moral influence and *Christus victor* have been considered.

All of them reflect something of what we would wish to convey through a biblical understanding of reconciliation. It is important, therefore, that we do not exclude any particular view of the cross if we are to understand what sort of ethic is motivated by theological reflection on the atonement. Just as our understanding of what Christ accomplished is diminished when we exclude one element or the other, so our ability to engage in social transformation is placed in jeopardy when we neglect particular aspects that at first glance appear unpalatable to the contemporary social impetus. Conversely, when we allow a fully-orbed view to reflect the many biblical facets of the atonement, we may find we are left with a rigorous social ethic that can raise up the church to face the tough challenges of injustice in the world today, and that may also endure beyond this generation.

> So let us not grow weary in doing what is right, for we will reap at harvest time, if we do not give up (Gal. 6:9, NRSV).

© Anna Robbins, 2009

12. ESCHATOLOGY AND THE TRANSFORMATION OF THE WORLD: CONTRADICTION, CONTINUITY, CONFLATION AND THE ENDURANCE OF HOPE

Tim Chester

'Christianity is eschatology.' So said Jürgen Moltmann in the 'Meditation on Hope' which opens his famous *Theology of Hope*. This axiom proves to be the starting point not only for *Theology of Hope*, but Moltmann's whole theological programme.

> From first to last, and not merely in the epilogue, Christianity is eschatology, is hope, forward looking and forward moving, and therefore also revolutionising and transforming the present. The eschatological is not one element *of* Christianity, but it is the medium of Christian faith as such . . . Hence eschatology cannot really be only a part of Christian doctrine. Rather, the eschatological outlook is the characteristic of all Christian proclamation, of every Christian existence and of the whole church.[1]

As Christianity became intertwined with the state, Moltmann argues, it replaced its orientation to the future with a support of the status quo. The future was relegated to a vague beyond in eternity. This, says Moltmann of the last days, 'robbed them of their directive, uplifting and critical significance for all the days which are spent here, this side of the end, in history'. Messianic

---

1. Jürgen Moltmann, *Theology of Hope: On the Ground and the Implication of a Christian Eschatology* (London: SCM, 1965; ET 1967), p. 16.

hope 'emigrated as it were from the church and turned in one distorted form or another against the church'.[2] Moltmann in contrast asserts that eschatology is not an irrelevant appendix at the end of dogmatics, bearing no relation to its central themes, but the framework or starting point for Christian theology and not just theology, but Christian mission as well.

Which brings us to a second axiom that Moltmann sets out in *Theology of Hope*: 'The theologian is not concerned merely to supply a different *interpretation* of the world, of history and of human nature, but to *transform* them in expectation of a divine transformation.'[3] This is clearly an allusion to Karl Marx. In his *Theses on Feuerbach* Marx famously said: 'The philosophers have only interpreted the world in various ways; the point, however, is to change it.'[4] Compare this with another statement by Moltmann and the echo is clearer still: '"The theology of hope" . . . does not merely want to interpret the world differently. It wants to change it.'[5] For Marx the role of philosophy is to change it. For Moltmann theology takes the place of philosophy, but the principle is the same: the task of theology is to transform the world.

Christianity is eschatology. The theologian's concern is the transformation of the world. Put the two together and what we get is the task of eschatology is to transform the world. By this Moltmann claims more than that eschatology is simply the account of how God will transform the world at some point in the future. He is claiming that the doctrine of eschatology should promote world transformation in the present. Resurrection hope is not a sterile, impotent hope for a future beyond, but a hope which is 'revolutionising and transforming the present'. Moltmann's theology can be seen as the exposition of how eschatology serves the task of social transformation.

The presupposition that a role of eschatology is to transform the world (and often it is seen as *the* role of eschatology) has become programmatic not only for Moltmann's theology, but for much modern theology. We should note that this is a reversal of the traditional direction in which influence is traced. In the past the emphasis has fallen on the present influencing the future. What we do in the present or in time affects what happens in the future or in eternity. Now the emphasis falls on hope for the future affecting what we do in the present.

---

2. Ibid., p. 16.

3. Ibid., p. 84.

4. Karl Marx, *Theses on Feuerbach* (1845), in *Selected Writings*, ed. Lawrence H. Simon (Indianapolis: Hackett Publishing, 2000), p. 101.

5. Jürgen Moltmann, *The Spirit of Life: A Universal Affirmation* (London: SCM, 1991; ET 1992), p. 110.

I do not, however, want to take issue in this essay with the assertion that eschatology serves the transforming work of Christian mission. I agree that eschatology contributes to world transformation. 'We continually remember before our God and Father,' says Paul to the Thessalonians, 'your work produced by faith, your labour prompted by love, and your endurance inspired by hope in our Lord Jesus Christ' (1 Thess. 1:3). The work of faith and the labour of love are sustained through the inspiration of hope. But we must question some of the ways in which this link is conceived. The manner in which hope sustains work and labour must be carefully drawn – otherwise hope will betray us. Too often eschatology is co-opted for programmes of social change in ways that are theologically unsatisfactory. We will consider three ways of connecting eschatology and world transformation under the headings of contradiction, continuity and conflation.

Contradiction

This is the route taken by Moltmann himself. The form that future hope takes in the present is *promise*.[6] The promise does more than *disclose* history; it *opens up* history to a new reality.[7] 'The promised future is already present in the promise itself; and mobilizes people concerned through the hope it awakens.'[8] 'The *promissio* of the universal future leads of necessity to the universal *missio* of the church to the nations.'[9] The promise leads to change by bringing its recipients into contradiction with the present. What Moltmann calls 'the exodus church' experiences an 'unrest' which is 'implicit to itself'.[10] This unrest is created by the promise and as such it 'is not a universal human presupposition for the Christian understanding of God, but is a mark of the pilgrim people of God and a goal of the Christian mission to all men'.[11]

---

6. Moltmann, *Theology of Hope*, p. 87.
7. See Jürgen Moltmann, *Hope and Planning* (London: SCM, 1971), p. 18; *Experiences in Theology: Ways and Forms of Christian Theology* (Minneapolis: Fortress Press, 2000, ET 2000), pp. 54, 93–95, 98, 102.
8. Jürgen Moltmann, *In the End – The Beginning: The Life of Hope* (Minneapolis: Fortress Press, 2004), p. 3.
9. Moltmann, *Theology of Hope*, p. 225.
10. Jürgen Moltmann, *The Church in the Power of the Spirit: A Contribution to Messianic Ecclesiology* (London: SCM, 1975, ET 1977), p. 3.
11. Moltmann, *Theology of Hope*, p. 276; see also *Experiences of God* (London: SCM, 1980), p. 12.

The truth of a statement is judged by its conformity to reality. Moltmann maintains, however, this is not the case with statements of Christian hope. Hope does not conform to reality, but contradicts it. It speaks not of present existence, but of new possibilities of existence – of a new creation. The promise of Christian hope is for a new future unlike the present.[12] It is for this reason that eschatology is frequently expressed in negative terms because 'eschatology . . . must formulate its statements of hope in contradiction to our present experience of suffering, evil and death'.[13] This, too, is how Christians can speak with relevance to contemporary society. 'Atheists and Christians find themselves in solidarity in the contradiction that is disclosed. For unbelief, this contradiction becomes the occasion to put God in the wrong. For faith, it becomes the occasion to put reality, as it presents itself, in the wrong.'[14]

The contradiction between present and future corresponds to the contradiction of the cross and resurrection. The sin, death, suffering and hatred of the cross are contradicted by the righteousness, life, glory and peace of the resurrection.[15] As such, the resurrection is more than merely consolation in suffering. It is 'the protest of the divine promise *against* suffering'.[16] Moltmann emphasizes the identity of the crucified one with the risen one in the Easter appearances. In this way the resurrection functions as promise: the contradiction of the godlessness of the cross by the resurrection points to a time when all godlessness will be contradicted by an analogous act of new creation. We can only hold on to this truth as we hold on to the *contradiction* of the cross–resurrection *and* the *continuity* of the cross–resurrection in the identity of the crucified one with the risen one. This leads to what Moltmann calls 'an open dialectic';[17] a dialectic which will find its resolution only in the eschaton.

This eschatological *contradiction* allows no harmony with the present. Instead it brings Christians into conflict with present reality. 'Present and future, experience and hope, stand in contradiction to each other in Christian eschatology, with the result that man is not brought into harmony and agreement with the given situation, but drawn into the conflict between hope and experience.'[18]

---

12. Ibid., p. 18.

13. Ibid., p. 19.

14. Moltmann, *Hope and Planning*, p. 16.

15. Moltmann, *Theology of Hope*, p. 18.

16. Ibid., p. 21.

17. Ibid., p. 201.

18. Ibid., p. 18; *The Future of Creation* (London: SCM, 1979), p. 104; *The Coming of God: Christian Eschatology* (London: SCM, 1995, ET 1996), p. 139; *Experiences in Theology:*

The Christian is no longer content with the status quo, but only with change that corresponds to hope. 'If there were no God, then perhaps one could accept violence and injustice, because that was the way things were. But if there is a God and this God is just, then one can no longer accept them.'[19] In this way eschatology provides a powerful incentive for world transformation.

The reality that the contradiction of present experience takes in the world is the kingdom of God. The kingdom becomes this-worldly as it 'becomes the antithesis and contradiction of a godless and god-forsaken world'.[20] The form the kingdom takes in the world is the suffering experienced by believers as its contradiction is imposed upon them.[21] And if the contradiction of hope is the incentive for mission, the possibilities opened up by the resurrection make it possible to bring about change and the promise gives direction to that change:

> If the promise of the kingdom of God shows us a universal eschatological future horizon spanning all things – 'that God may be all in all' – then it is impossible for the man of hope to adopt an attitude of religious and cultic resignation from the world. On the contrary, he is compelled to accept the world in all meekness, subject as it is to death and the powers of annihilation, and guide all things towards their new being.[22]

So the openness to the future engendered by the promise has both a subjective side and an objective side. Subjectively it creates in people hope for the future and places them in contradiction with the present. Objectively the promise betokens the transforming and liberating power of God's rule and 'thus sets an open stage for history, and fills it with missionary enterprise and the responsible exercise of hope, accepting the suffering that is involved in the contradiction of reality, and setting out towards the promised future'.[23] The Christian is not to be concerned with the maintenance of the status quo, but with discovering possibilities for change which correspond to the promise.

So Moltmann emphasizes the radical contradiction of present existence by the promise of God. He does this by insisting the future is entirely new.

Ways and Forms of Christian Theology (Minneapolis: Fortress Press, 2000, ET 2000), pp. 100–101.

19. Moltmann, *Creating a Just Future* (London: SCM, 1989), p. 7.
20. Moltmann, *Theology of Hope*, p. 222.
21. Ibid., p. 222.
22. Ibid., p. 224.
23. Ibid., p. 86; see also *Experiences in Theology*, pp. 100–101.

Only the *ex nihilo* acts of resurrection and of new creation can truly correspond to the promise. He reinforces this by emphasizing that the Latin word used for parousia is *adventus* (coming) rather than *futurum,* which has the sense of that which develops out of the present.[24] God's future is coming towards the present rather than developing (becoming) out of the present. The parousia comes as something new – not as the culmination of an historical process.

The problem with Moltmann's approach is that any transformation in history is, by Moltmann's own criteria, contradicted by the promise. No transformation in history can be affirmed if the present itself is wholly contradicted by the future – hardly a sound basis for a transforming involvement in history! Langdon Gilkey argues that Moltmann's position on the utterly new of the future works against his own political and revolutionary interests: 'In any political understanding of history and even more in an effective revolutionary one, the relevant idea for the future cannot be understood as *utterly* new, as a *creatio ex nihilo* out of the future, as totally unrelated to the latent forces or conditions of the past and present.'[25]

Moltmann seems to argue that the radical contradiction of the present by the promise implies that change must be radical and revolutionary. Yet even radical change cannot be affirmed if the promise totally contradicts the present. Schuurman says: 'Since all possible consequences of Christian striving for justice will be annihilated as a prelude to another *creatio ex nihilo,* it is impossible to affirm the significance of such striving for the eschaton.'[26] In what sense can there be possibilities in the present if that present is contradicted by the promise? How can the promise create potentialities while at the

24. See Jürgen Moltmann, *Church in the Power of the Spirit,* p. 130; *God in Creation: An Ecological Doctrine of Creation,* The Gifford Lectures 1984–1985 (London: SCM, 1985; ET 1985), pp. 132–135; *The Way of Jesus Christ: Christology in Messianic Dimensions* (London: SCM, 1989; ET 1990), p. 206; *Coming of God,* p. 22–29; 'Theology as Eschatology', in F. Herzog (ed.), *The Future of Hope: Theology as Eschatology,* (New York: Herder and Herder, 1970), pp. 11–16; *The Experiment Hope* (London: SCM, 1975), p. 52; *Future of Creation,* pp. 29–31, 55; *History and the Triune God* (London: SCM, 1991), p. 95.

25. Langdon Gilkey, *Reaping the Whirlwind: A Christian Interpretation of History* (New York: Seabury, 1976), p. 235; see also R. H. Preston, 'Reflections on Theologies of Social Change', in R. H. Preston (ed.), *Theology and Change: Essays in Memory of Alan Richardson* (London: SCM, 1975), p. 156.

26. Douglas J. Schuurman, 'Creation, Eschaton, and Ethics: An Analysis of Theology and Ethics in Jürgen Moltmann', *Calvin Theological Journal* 22 (1987), p. 57.

same time contradicting them? What relationship can these possibilities have to a future that is utterly new and *ex nihilo*?

To these criticisms Moltmann expresses surprise. He maintains that he only intended to criticize 'the negative and dangerous aspects of the modern world, that is, the repressive structures of society and the increasing crisis aspect of modern civilisation'.[27] He did not intend, he adds, to imply the negation of all relationships. Yet in his discussion of the contradiction of reality by the promise, his statements express the unqualified totality of the contradiction. Walsh doubts whether Moltmann can affirm the present at all despite his attempts to do so: the theology of hope is 'ultimately devoid of any meaningful affirmation of the present'.[28]

If the future is utterly new then without some form of mediation it is irrelevant. If the promise contradicts reality, then it must also contradict actions in that reality. If history is discontinuous with eschatology, then so is action in history. If the present has the potential to be annihilated, then so have actions in that present. Some form of mediating categories is needed to bridge the gulf between the present and the future if hope is going to be related to mission.

These criticisms suggest a fuller discussion of the presence of the kingdom is needed. The presence of the future kingdom could be the mediating category which Moltmann lacks. In history God rules through his word and his Spirit, although in a hidden and resisted way. Moltmann himself can say, 'the coming kingdom is present in history as liberating rule'.[29] These ideas, however, receive no sustained treatment and figure little in his understanding of mission.[30] Or again, if Moltmann had expressed the absolute contradiction between present and future in terms of the contradiction between the old age and the new age then, by affirming the presence of the new age in history ahead of the eschaton, he could have maintained the contradiction while at the same time having a more positive attitude to the present.

In his later work Moltmann has increasingly stressed the importance of 'anticipations' as a mediating category. He concludes *The Way of Jesus Christ* with a call for '*life in anticipation* of the Coming One'.[31] The future is present

---

27. Moltmann, 'Towards the Next Step on the Dialogue', in *The Future of Hope*, p. 156.

28. Brian J. Walsh, 'Theology of Hope and the Doctrine of Creation: An Appraisal of Jürgen Moltmann', *Evangelical Quarterly* 59 (1987), p. 59.

29. Moltmann, *Church in the Power of the Spirit*, p. 191.

30. Ibid., pp. 190–192; *Way of Jesus Christ*, pp. 97–99.

31. Moltmann, *Way of Jesus Christ*, p. 340; see also, for example, *Church in the Power of the Spirit*, pp. 193–195; *Future of Creation*, pp. 45–48.

now when it is anticipated. In this sense anticipation is the form in which the possibilities created by the promise are realized in history.

The real problem, however, is the way that Moltmann conflates creation and the fall. For Moltmann death precedes sin rather than sin preceding death. He says: 'behind sin is death'.[32] He even speaks of an 'imperfect creation'.[33] In *The Coming of God* Moltmann rejects the view that 'death is the result of original sin', replacing it with the assertion that death is 'a characteristic of frail, temporal creation which will be overcome through the new creation of things for eternal life'.[34] In what must be an intentional reversal of the biblical order, Moltmann describes sin as 'the wages of death'.[35]

Moltmann acknowledges that what he calls the Augustinian position – that human death is the consequence of human sin – was the dominant view of the Church until nineteenth-century Liberal Protestantism. But he rejects this view.[36] He does not view sin in objective terms, but in subjective terms as 'distress of conscience' or 'self-alienation'. It is a psychological problem rather than an offence against God. This is why Moltmann is so ambiguous on atonement.[37] For him sin is a symptom, but not the root problem and because it is not the root problem, it requires no solution through atonement. The underlying problem is 'the intruding Nothingness',[38] the 'apocalyptic pressure of affliction of everything that wants to live and has to die'.[39] 'Everything which exists is *burdened with transitoriness*, but burdened in hope because it wants to be free.'[40] This affects Moltmann's conception of salvation. 'Creation, new creation and resurrection are external works of God against chaos, nothingness and death.'[41] This puts the emphasis of salvation upon ontological transitoriness rather than the problems of sin and judgment.

---

32. Moltmann, *Future of Creation*, p. 164.

33. Moltmann, *Coming of God*, p. 91.

34. Ibid., p. 78.

35. Ibid., p. 94.

36. Ibid., pp. 85–90.

37. See Tim Chester, *Mission and the Coming of God: Eschatology, the Trinity and Mission in the Theology of Jürgen Moltmann and Contemporary Evangelicalism* (Paternoster, 2006), ch. 5.

38. Moltmann, *Future of Creation*, p. 163; *Spirit of Life*, p. 213.

39. Moltmann, *Future of Creation*, p. 164; see also *Church in the Power of the Spirit*, p. 34.

40. Jürgen Moltmann, *Religion, Revolution and the Future* (New York: Charles Scribner's Sons, 1969), p. 217; see also p. 36.

41. Moltmann, *The Crucified God: The Cross of Christ as the Foundation and Criticism of Christian Theology* (London: SCM, 1973; ET 1974), pp. 192–193.

This is why Moltmann regards the new creation as *ex nihilo*, as the new creation is set against the fundamental tendency of reality towards nothingness. The problems of sin, alienation and guilt are simply an expression of this underlying ontological instability. As a result Moltmann says that the new in the new creation is 'not only new as compared with sin, but also as compared with creation'.[42] To support his view Moltmann refers to Romans 8 and the 'frustration' and 'bondage to decay' of creation. As Walsh points out, however, 'Romans 8:19f portrays the groaning of creation in terms of Adam's sin, not the inherent structure of creatureliness'.[43]

As a result of the conflation of creation and fall, Moltmann has no basis for distinguishing between sin and creation. So he repeatedly speaks of the promise being in contradiction with 'reality' – not in contradiction with sin or reality marred by sin, but with reality itself. Moltmann has little place for *re*-generation, *re*-newal or *re*-creation.[44] Salvation is not the renewal of creation, but an act *ex nihilo*. This means it represents the negation of creation and therefore, despite Moltmann's protestations, action within history.

Continuity

A second approach to transformation and eschatology has been to emphasize the continuity between the present and the future. Continuity exists at what we might call a 'moral level' in the form of eschatological rewards. While the New Testament sees our eschatological fate as dependent solely upon our relationship to Christ, it also seems to indicate some form of eschatological reward. But the debate over eschatology and world transformation has centred on the issue of what we might call 'ontological continuity'. A number of advocates of social action, especially among evangelicals, have sought to extend ontological continuity beyond the resurrection of the body to embrace human activity and social change. If salvation is cosmic in scope, they have argued, then work done in the world will be redeemed along with creation. This continuity gives our actions eternal significance – our mission work, our attempt to further a distinctively Christian culture, will have value not only for this world but even for the world to come.[45]

---

42. Moltmann, 'Theology as Eschatology', p. 29.
43. Brian J. Walsh, 'Theology of Hope', p. 64.
44. See, for example, Moltmann, *Spirit of Life*, p. 145.
45. A. A. Hoekema, *The Bible and the Future* (Exeter: Paternoster, 1978), pp. 39–40; see also p. 287.

Those who have the assurance of this continuity find in it a strong incentive to social and cultural involvement. (The Grand Rapids Report)[46]

The affirmation of this neglected biblical teaching must then serve as an incentive to social involvement. (Peter Kuzmic)[47]

In the light of the present and coming kingdom, Christians can invest their lives in the building of a historical order in the certainty that neither they nor their efforts are meaningless or lost. (Vinay Samuel and Chris Sugden)[48]

The argument for continuity is based on texts such as 1 Corinthians 3:10–15, Revelation 14:13; 21:24, 26, along with the pattern set by Christ's physical resurrection.[49] Christian hope is not for release from physical existence, but the transformation of that existence into resurrected bodies in a new creation. If this involves continuity for the body, then why not also for the rest of creation? And why not for our stewardship of that creation? And so our stewardship of creation in both its ecological and social dimensions, it is argued, finds its fulfilment in the eschatological renewal of creation.

Peter Kuzmic argues that in 'much of evangelical eschatology' there is an emphasis on a radical break between this present earth and the new creation. This 'total discontinuity' sees the earth as unredeemable and the new creation as 'a kind of *creatio ex nihilo*'. This, argues Kuzmic, represents 'a neglect or misunderstanding of the biblical doctrine of creation and the New Testament teaching on the present aspect of the kingdom of God'.[50] While there is an

---

46. *Evangelism and Social Responsibility*, the conference report of the Consultation on the Relationship between Evangelical and Social Responsibility, Grand Rapids 1982 (Exeter: Paternoster, 1982), p. 42.

47. Peter Kuzmic, 'History and Eschatology: Evangelical Views', in Bruce Nicholls (ed.), *In Word and Deed* (Exeter: Paternoster, 1985), p. 152.

48. Vinay Samuel and Chris Sugden, 'God's Intention for the World', in Vinay Samuel and Chris Sugden (eds.) *The Church in Response to Human Need* (Oxford: Regnum, 1987), p. 146.

49. See Peter Beyerhaus, 'A Biblical Encounter with Some Contemporary Philosophical and Theological Systems', in Nicholls (ed.), *Word and Deed*, p. 181; A. A. Hoekema, *The Bible and the Future,* p. 280; Vinay Samuel and Chris Sugden, 'Evangelism and Social Responsibility,' in Nicholls (ed.), *Word and Deed*, p. 152; 'God's Intention for the World', p. 145.

50. Kuzmic, 'History and Eschatology', p. 151.

emphasis upon discontinuity in the Bible, there is 'some continuity as well'. As such, 'we are to work for a better world already here and now, knowing that everything that is noble, beautiful, true and righteous in this world will somehow be preserved and perfected in the new world to come'.[51] Kuzmic believes that eschatological continuity is one way of correcting the failure to relate history and eschatology which underlies evangelical non-involvement in social issues.[52]

Miroslav Volf undertook his doctoral research under the supervision of Moltmann in Tübingen and shares Moltmann's concern to use eschatology in the service of social transformation. Volf, however, places a much greater emphasis on the continuity between pre- and post-eschaton existence to avoid the problems created by Moltmann's radical contradiction of history by the new creation. So Volf's view of history is not wholly negative. The new creation will always relativize history,[53] but the 'normativeness of new creation enables us to evaluate (*and appreciate*) present achievements'.[54] Judging history in the light of the new creation will not necessarily produce a wholly negative judgment on a given situation, even though each situation falls short of the new creation. At times we will discern progress; at other times deterioration. Volf speaks of 'a "kaleidoscope" theology of social life, according to which social arrangements shift in various ways under various influences (divine, human or demonic) without necessarily following an evolutionist or involutionist pattern'.[55] The continuity between transformation in history and the new creation, argues Volf, means that eschatology gives significance to human work. Volf sees work as a cooperation with God in the transformation of creation, not just its preservation.[56]

This use of eschatological continuity to promote social transformation has, however, been criticized by Stephen Williams. Williams neither denies the importance of social involvement, nor that hope has a proper effect upon Christian social activity. Neither, indeed, does he question the *fact* of eschatological continuity. What he questions is its *significance* as a motive in social action.

---

51. Ibid.
52. Ibid., p. 155.
53. Miroslav Volf, 'Democracy and the Crisis of the Socialist Project: Towards a Post-Revolutionary Theology of Liberation', *Transformation* 7.4 (1990), p. 16.
54. Miroslav Volf, *Work in the Spirit: Toward a Theology of Work* (New York: OUP, 1991), p. 84; emphasis added.
55. Ibid.
56. Ibid., p. 89–102.

Williams argues that a continuist position adds little to the motive of love in Christian social ethics. Indeed a continuist position 'may only reveal how impoverished our love is – a love whose energies are somewhat dissipated either by ignorance of or disbelief in "eternal consequences"'.[57] Christian social action does not need these incentives to be effective in love. What action, he asks, would be undertaken by a continuist that would not be undertaken by a discontinuist motivated by love? Or what qualitative difference would the action of a continuist have compared to that of a discontinuist? This argument, however, fails to recognize the importance of eschatological *rewards* in the New Testament. 'Treasure in heaven' may not be the same kind of incentive as that held by continuists. It is arguably less altruistic than a continuist position since its eternal significance lies in the effect upon the subject of the activity (personal reward), whereas with the continuist position the eternal significance lies in its effect upon the object of the activity. But the New Testament unashamedly encourages us to look to the eternal consequences, in whatever form, of our acts of love.

More significant is the question Williams raises about how meaningful it is to speak of human achievements being taken up into the new creation. What form will such achievements take in the new creation? How can we know whether a particular scientific or cultural achievement will merit inclusion and upon what criterion? 'At best the incentive seems to be that of a possibility, not that of a promise'[58] and a work sustained by possibility is not the same as a work sustained by hope in the New Testament sense of the word. Williams acknowledges that we do not need to know *how* God will effect the transformation of our actions for them to operate as incentives. But 'the deeper our agnosticism goes . . . the more we should be inclined to ask whether we are on the right track as regards incentives for social responsibility'.[59]

Williams goes further: if one maintains a non-universalist position, as most evangelicals would, then the continuity incentive is seriously limited. What continuity can there be when the beneficiaries of those actions are not part of the new creation? How can an action to improve the social conditions of a particular individual, or community, have eschatological significance, if that individual, or community, do not themselves enter the eschatological kingdom? It may well have significance for the agent of the action in the sense

57. Stephen Williams, 'Hope, Love and Social Action', *Evangel*, 4.3 (1986), p. 3.

58. Stephen Williams, 'The Partition of Love and Hope: Eschatology and Social Responsibility', *Transformation* 7.3 (1991), p. 26.

59. Ibid.

which we have described as moral continuity (eternal reward). But there can only be what we have called ontological continuity if we resort to some form of abstraction. The continuity of an action could only be realized apart from the concrete expression of that activity in history. Any continuity thus conceived looks more like the moral continuity of eschatological rewards than the ontological continuity proposed by the continuists.

In response to Williams' question about the difference continuity might make in practice to a person's actions, Miroslav Volf says 'such belief gives human beings important inspiration for cultural, social and ecological action, even when such action is not appreciated by one's neighbour'. People in such a position, Volf believes, can 'draw inspiration and strength from the belief that their noble efforts are not lost'.[60] The problem is that when Volf describes how we might think of eschatological continuity, his three suggestions all involve a person making a *public* contribution to humanity. First, he says we should think of 'the cumulative work of the whole human race'; the human 'project' in which 'one generation stands on the shoulders of another, so that the accomplishments of each generation build upon those of the previous one'.[61] Second, while not every single human product will be integrated into the world to come, 'the worldly home of human beings' to which they contribute, will as a whole be integrated. Third, Volf argues that human activity contributes to the identity of human beings and, while that activity itself may not be continuous, the identity it creates is not lost on resurrected personality. These three ways may indeed help us to think of continuity correctly, yet it is hard to see what comfort these are to those whose work is unappreciated. How are succeeding generations to build upon work that is 'unappreciated' and 'lost'? What effect can unappreciated work have on human identity? Volf cannot have it both ways. Either continuity involves what he describes and gives little incentive to those whose work is unappreciated. Or continuity inspires those whose work is unappreciated and it involves considerably more than Volf describes or, one suspects, can reasonably defend.

Will the novels of Jane Austen be in the libraries of the new creation? Will works of art be on display?[62] And if such cultural achievements are to be purged of any trace of human sin does this mean certain lines will be cut

---

60. Miroslav Volf, 'On Loving with Hope: Eschatology and Social Responsibility', *Transformation* 7.3 (1991), p. 30.

61. Ibid., p. 31.

62. See Richard Mouw, *When the Kings Come Marching In: Israel and the New Jerusalem* (Grand Rapids: Eerdmans, 1983), pp. 19–20 for a suggestion along these lines.

from a Shakespeare play or certain notes edited from a Beethoven symphony? What does this do to the overall integrity of the work? And in the area of scientific achievement will we have light bulbs in the city where God himself is the light? It might be replied that such questions are simply frivolous: continuity will take place on a more abstract level. It is the spirit of cultural achievements, the love behind social activity, the commitment to the greater good and the advancement of human knowledge – purged of all impure motives – that will be continuous. Yet again this appears to be more akin to moral continuity than the ontological continuity most continuists propose. It is no longer even dependent on a renewed (as opposed to a replaced) earth. It seems the more specific one tries to be in pinning down the nature of continuity the more abstract one is forced to be! And yet the more abstract one is, the less concrete becomes the motive for social or cultural action at a practical level.

God's purposes in creation involve humanity as stewards of that creation. Humanity has a central role in God's creational purposes. If the new creation is the fulfilment of those purposes then it must also involve the fulfilment of humanity's participation, by the grace of God, in those purposes. This, however, raises an important point which is overlooked in the debate, namely, that *fulfilment is not the same as continuity*. Certainly it may well involve continuity, as the biblical texts cited above seem to indicate. Nevertheless our knowledge of post-eschaton existence and the way in which God will transform reality into the new creation is so limited that it is very difficult to give any substance to continuity as a motive for action.

Conflation

Consider this analogy given by Nicholas Wolterstorff:

> Every human endeavour that is not coerced requires, as a minimum, the hope that its goal will be achieved. Optimism is not required – optimism being understood as the expectation that one will achieve what one endeavours. The ambulance attendant who endeavours to resuscitate the person pulled down by the waves at the beach may not expect to succeed in his endeavour; he may expect that he will not succeed. He may not be at all optimistic. Yet as long as he sees some hope, he tries – as long as there's a chance. If he thinks there is no hope, he gives up and stops trying.[63]

---

63. Nicholas Wolterstorff, 'Seeking Justice in Hope', in Miroslav Volf and William H.

The logic is clear. We will not work for the transformation of the world unless we have hope. Christian hope, rooted in the resurrection of Jesus overcoming all that the cross represented, provides just such hope – the hope we need to get involved in social change. And so calls for social involvement are littered with the language of hope. The cry goes up: 'We can make a difference: the gospel gives us hope for change.'

The danger which such language, however, is that it conflates ultimate hope and penultimate possibilities. The language of eschatology is used to describe hope for change in history through social involvement. Ultimate hope is reduced to proximate expectation. It is not always clear how conscious this is, especially at a popular level. A less charitable heading for this section might be 'confusion'. Ultimate hope and penultimate possibility are confused as the language of biblical hope is employed to enthuse social activism. Hope becomes hype.[64] In other words, the expectation of historical change – which can be a powerful motive for action – is not the same as the eschatological hope of the New Testament. Even with the transforming presence and power of the kingdom in history, hope for imminent change within history remains at best a possibility. However valid and important such hope might be, it remains distinct from the certain hope of eschatological transformation created by the divine revelation of promise.

What makes Wolterstorff an interesting point of departure is that he seems aware of the problem. He explores in some detail the definition of hope in Aquinas in which Aquinas understands hope, in Wolterstorff's phrase, 'as a supernatural mode of union with God'. 'Christian hope is not hope for what might transpire in history, but hope for a state of *eudaimonia* (happiness) that transcends history.' The result for Aquinas is, laments Wolterstorff, that hope 'has nothing in particular to do with the struggle for justice in history'.[65]

Wolterstorff in contrast argues that Christian hope is hope for change within history as well as for consummation. He does this by identifying three storylines in the Bible: the storylines of creation, redemption and consummation. The point is that redemption is an independent story to the story of consummation. It is the story of God undoing injustice through the reign of

Katerberg (eds.), *The Future of Hope: Christian Tradition Amid Modernity and Postmodernity* (Eerdmans, 2004), p. 77.

64. Stephen Williams, 'The Limits of Hope and the Logic of Love: On the Basis of Christian Social Responsibility', *Tyndale Bulletin* 40.2 (1989), p. 267.

65. Wolterstorff, 'Seeking Justice in Hope', p. 79.

Christ in history. Christian hope, therefore, according to Wolterstorff, encompasses hope for the overcoming of injustice within history.

One could criticize Wolterstorff's reduction of redemption to overcoming the problem of human injustice, ignoring the biblical theme of Christ overcoming the problem of divine justice through the justification of the unjust. More pertinent to our present concerns is the question of whether redemption and consummation represent separate stories. Whether creation would have been brought to consummation had humanity not sinned, so that consummation goes beyond or is independent from redemption, is open to debate. What is clear is that in biblical terms both creation and redemption are stories that end in consummation. Consummation is not a third story, but the climax of creation and redemption. Thus Christian hope is hope for the consummation of history (including the eradication of injustice). This is evident from the language of hope in the New Testament. New Testament hope is sure and certain: it does not disappoint. It differs from hope for change within history for this hope does disappoint. Change in history is provisional: subject to reversals. Christian hope is certain.

Wolterstorff's motives are clear from his opening analogy. All human endeavour requires some level of hope. We do not embark on activities unless we consider there to be some possibility of success even if we are pessimistic about that success. It is a very powerful analogy. But even powerful analogies can be misleading. It is true that I will want to know someone is still alive before I try to resuscitate them. But how does this scale up to social change or world transformation? Suppose I am involved in a community reconciliation project. According to Wolterstorff's analogy, I want to be confident my work might produce some change in order to engage fully in it. I need some hope of success. But to what category does this hope belong? It cannot be the biblical hope of eschatological transformation. I cannot be sure and certain my community project will succeed. I cannot claim it will usher in God's kingdom. I might have a reasonable hope of community reconciliation, but it is not a certain hope. I may be disappointed. Even if I succeed in the short-term, I have no guarantees that change will be sustainable.

Wolterstorff fears that without hope Christians will not seek justice. This may be correct, but we need to be clear about the kind of hope we have in mind. He encourages us to identify the hand of God in history (the example he gives is that of the defeat of apartheid in South Africa). But it would be better to describe this theological virtue as faith: faith in the sovereign God who rules over this world and who intervenes in history in response to the prayers of his people. Hope for social change in history may be important for those who engage in such activities. But the New Testament category that generates such proximate expectations is not eschatological hope, but faith. It is not eschatology that is serving transformation in such cases, but faith in a sovereign God who has not abandoned his creation, but continues to reign over it in his merciful providence.

Does this matter? It does because otherwise hope will disappoint. Williams is concerned that, unless a distinction is made between hope for historical change and the certain hope of eschatological transformation, 'one may give false hope to the suffering'.[66] Preston warns of the danger of presenting 'impossibilities as possibilities'.[67] Movements for social change in history can suffer frustration, setbacks and ultimately failure. Hope can collapse into despair. Attempts to employ hope to prevent the death of social activism in this way run the risk of killing it altogether.

The incentive for social transformation is established on other grounds – faith in God and love for others. The role of eschatological hope is to sustain that labour. We are back to 1 Thessalonians 1:3: 'We continually remember before our God and Father your work produced by faith, your labour prompted by love, and your endurance inspired by hope in our Lord Jesus Christ.' Adapting Wolterstorff's analogy, Christian hope is more like the hope the ambulance attendant has that at the end of a hard day's work he will hear his boss say: 'Well done, good and faithful servant . . . Enter into the joy of your master' (Matt. 25:21, ESV).

Conclusion: the endurance of hope

Much of the discussion of eschatology in relation to mission is shaped by a fear of it acting as a disincentive to social involvement. There has been a high degree of sensitivity to the Marxist critique of Christian hope as opium for the people. The attempt has been made, therefore, to make eschatology function as a basis for social involvement. Eschatology, however, remains ambiguous in its relationship to social involvement. Ultimately even Moltmann himself acknowledges this in *The Coming of God*: 'Every hope is equivocal. It can fill the present with new power, but it can also draw power away from the present. It

---

66. Stephen Williams, 'On Giving Hope in a Suffering World: Response to Moltmann', in Nigel Cameron (ed.), *Issues in Faith and History* (Edinburgh: Rutherford House, 1989), p. 7.

67. Preston, 'Reflections on Theologies of Social Change', p. 161.

can lead to resistance – and also to spiritual escape.'[68] Hope for eschatological transformation appears to act as an incentive to change in history for some and a disincentive for others. It is hard to avoid the suspicion, however, that one's presuppositions about social transformation count more than one's eschatology.

Moltmann's adaptation of Marx's assertion that philosophy must serve the cause of world transformation demonstrates this. The point is that the commitment to social transformation is presupposed and therefore prior to the discussion of eschatology. For Moltmann Christian hope must not be 'the opium of the people', but 'the power and ferment of emancipation here and now'.[69] His fear of a quietistic and escapist hope leads him to neglect the New Testament association of hope with patience, endurance and long-suffering. Yet this need not be a quietistic long-suffering. It can also be the endurance and long-suffering of love which patiently labours even in the face of disappointment.

Our criticisms are not meant to suggest that eschatology has no place in social transformation; nor to suggest that attempts by Moltmann and others to relate eschatology and missiology have been wholly in vain. Despite our criticism, it is our conviction that eschatology is an important feature of trans-formational missiology. Given that such a motive can be established on other grounds, hope can have an important and creative role to play. In particular, hope has the potential to sustain the long-suffering endurance of love. An emphasis upon future blessing need not function as 'opium for the people', but can reinforce one's commitment to social involvement. We want to assert that a form of other-worldliness – not in the sense of belief in a wholly new, ethereal future, but in the sense of patient hope for a radically new future beyond history – can in fact promote this-worldly activity.

In his introductory 'meditation on hope' with which we began Moltmann cites Calvin. The passage which Moltmann cites is as follows:

> Eternal life is promised to us, but it is promised to the dead; we are told of the resurrection of the blessed, but meantime we are involved in corruption; we are declared to be just, and sin dwells within us; we hear that we are blessed, but meantime we are overwhelmed by untold miseries; we are promised an abundance of all good things, but we are often hungry and thirsty; God proclaims that he will come to us immediately, but seems to be deaf to our cries. What would happen to us if we

---

68. Moltmann, *Coming of God*, p. 153.
69. Moltmann, *Religion, Revolution and the Future*, p. 79.

did not rely on hope, and if our minds did not emerge above the world out of the midst of darkness through the shining Word of God and by his Spirit?[70]

'Calvin', says Moltmann, 'perceived very plainly the discrepancy involved in the resurrection hope.' 'Present and future, experience and hope, stand in contradiction to each other in Christian eschatology, with the result that man is not brought into harmony and agreement with the given situation, but is drawn into conflict between hope and experience.'[71] To a certain extent this is true of Calvin. Yet Moltmann's fundamental contradiction between present and future is for Calvin only an apparent contradiction because with the eye of faith we perceive that united with Christ we already share the glory of the future. Calvin says, 'these two things *apparently contradict* each other, but yet they *agree perfectly* when we are concerned with faith.'[72] Moltmann's real contradiction leaves him, as we have seen, without adequate mediating categories between the present and future. For Calvin, however, the present and future are linked by our union with Christ. Through his resurrection and ascension Christ now enjoys the glory of heaven and we through our union with him share this by faith. Our resurrection life is now hidden under our present experience of the cross. This means that, whereas in *Theology of Hope* the accent is on faith and hope expressing themselves in an agitation for change, for Calvin they are frequently linked with *patience*. 'Hope,' Calvin contends, 'is sustained only by patience. The salvation of believers, therefore, is fulfilled only by patience.'[73]

Yet for Calvin eschatology did not lead in practice to the quietism which many seem to fear will be the correlate of an emphasis on patience.[74] For Calvin the patience of hope is always connected with the work of faith and labour of love. The faith that arises from hope 'is an earnest faith, full of power, so that it shirks no task when our neighbours are in need of help'.[75] In Calvin's mind it is not those whose affections are rooted in this earth

70. John Calvin, *Commentary on Hebrews 11:1*. Citations from Calvin's commentaries are taken from *Calvin's Commentaries*, The New Testament, 12 vols., eds. D. W. and T. F. Torrance (Edinburgh: St Andrew's Press, 1959–66, 1972).

71. Moltmann, *Religion, Revolution and the Future*, p. 18.

72. Calvin, *Comm. on Hebrews 11:1*; emphasis added.

73. Calvin, *Comm. on Romans 8:25*; see also, for example, *Comm. on 1 Thessalonians 1:3*.

74. David E. Holwerda, 'Eschatology and History: A Look at Calvin's Eschatological Vision', in Donald K. McKim (ed.), *Readings in Calvin's Theology* (Grand Rapids: Baker, 1984), p. 312.

75. Calvin, *Comm. on 1 Thessalonians 1:3*.

who exercise love for others to the full. Rather it is those who, through their union with Christ in his death, deny themselves and mortify the flesh, and who, through their union with Christ in his resurrection, have set their hearts on things above so that they are liberated from the pursuit of their own interests in this life and can truly persevere in love. T. F. Torrance says that 'Calvin's eschatology was activist, stressing the mighty acts of God in Christ and *therefore* the work of the church in obedience and joy, in thankful assurance of victory waiting for the final act of redemption'.[76] Confident in a better life ahead, the believer is able to remain steadfast in good works.[77]

There is in the life of the believer a pattern of suffering followed by glory which corresponds through our union with Christ to the pattern of his cross and resurrection. In the present the mark of Christian discipleship is the cross. To follow Jesus is to deny ourselves and take up our cross: to live a life of service, sacrifice and love. Through the Spirit we do experience resurrection power – the life of the future – in the present. But, and this is crucial, this experience of resurrection is that which enables us to follow the way of the cross. It is, as it were, power to enable us to be weak and life to enable us to die.

Luther distinguished between a theology of glory which seeks the revelation of God in the power and glory of his actions and a theology of the cross which sees the ultimate revelation of God in the cross. At the cross we see by faith power in weakness, victory in failure and glory in shame. I want to suggest we should apply the same pattern to eschatology. We must reject an eschatology of glory which seeks the glory and victory of the resurrection without accepting the reality of the cross in the present (the mistake made by James and John in Mark 10:35–45). Instead we must embrace an eschatology of the cross which looks forward to glory and victory, while seeing them as present now, in a hidden form, as shame and weakness. This is true for personal discipleship and it is true for world transformation. The redemption of the world is a future reality. History still exists under the shadow of the cross. According to Calvin, the fault of the disciples was to hold what we have called an eschatology of glory. Their fault was 'to confuse the completeness of Christ's kingdom with its beginning, and to wish to acquire on earth what should be sought in heaven'.[78] Calvin comments, 'It is enough that the faithful

---

76. T. F. Torrance, *Kingdom and Church* (Edinburgh: Oliver and Boyd, 1956), p. 91.

77. Calvin, *Comm. on 1 Corinthians 15:58*; see also *Comm. on 2 Peter 3:12*.

78. Calvin, *Comm. on Matthew 24:3*.

receive a taste of these good things now, that they may cherish the hope of their full enjoyment in the future.'[79]

The cross judges any claim to the establishment of that which will rightly happen only after the eschaton. An eschatology of the cross will function as an eschatological proviso, guarding against what we might call 'overly-realized eschatologies'. It will protect us also from de-historized, or spiritualized, eschatologies of an eternal present which lay claim to the experience of the resurrection at the expense of, or by by-passing, the transformation of the world from the experience of the cross (what we might call 'eschatologies of escape'). Thus it is that Calvin speaks of hope not only sustaining faith, but also restraining it.[80] In other words, the very fact that we hope means we have not yet received our full redemption (Rom. 8:24–25) and, as such, hope guards faith against falling into an eschatology of glory. Faith must be accompanied by patient endurance.

© Tim Chester, 2009

---

79. Calvin, *Comm. on Matthew 24:4*.

80. John Calvin, *The Institutes of Christian Religion* (The Library of Christian Classics, vols. XX and XXI), transl. F. L. Battles, ed. J. T. McNeill (Philadelphia: Westminster Press and London: SCM, 1961), 3.2.42.

13. EVANGELICALS AND SOCIETY: THE STORY OF AN ON-OFF RELATIONSHIP

David W. Smith

Close to where these words are being written, near the heart of the old city of Glasgow, there is an extraordinary burial ground known as the Necropolis. It rises up behind the ancient cathedral and contains hundreds of impressive monuments in stone to the great and the good who, one hopes, contributed to Glasgow's growth and well-being over the past centuries. At the highest point on this hill stands an impressive statue of John Knox, erected by the city burghers in 1825 as Irish Catholic immigrants were pouring into the West of Scotland. Knox holds the Bible aloft, extending it toward the city below as though reminding people caught in the throes of the industrial revolution that (to quote Glasgow's traditional motto), prosperity comes through 'the preaching of God's word and the praising of his name'.

A century later, when industrialization and urbanization had done their work, the city modified this motto to become less a prayer, more a wish: 'Let Glasgow Prosper'. The understanding of human well-being was thus severed from its religious roots, so abandoning people to unconstrained materialism. In the run up to Christmas 2006, the huge and still expanding shopping mall in the centre of Glasgow ran a high profile publicity campaign, in which the seven deadly sins were turned into virtues 'because Glasgow loves shopping'. The social consequences of this idolatry are sadly evident in the streets below the Necropolis by both day and night.

Meantime, while those who came to exercise political power disowned the religiously inspired social vision of John Knox, many who claimed spiritual descent from the reformer continued to stress the vital importance of preaching and worship while detaching these activities from the well-being of the city as a whole. That is to say, a once unified vision of what constitutes human and societal flourishing in a modern, urban world was lost as the Reformation dream of a 'holy commonwealth' was carved into separate and isolated segments. Concerns about 'prosperity' were delegated to the politicians who inhabited the vast, cathedral-like city chambers, while believers turned their attention to acts of piety and devotion, effectively sealed off from the wider culture. This 'great divorce', which continues to affect attitudes toward worship, preaching and mission, constitutes one of the central issues requiring ongoing historical, biblical and theological reflection.

The Reformed vision

The concern of this book is with evangelicalism and socio-political responsibility but, as the previous paragraphs remind us, this movement developed historically from the Protestant tradition. This being the case, it is worth recalling the kind of social vision which animated a man like John Calvin, whose influence on Knox was immense. Calvin has been described as a 'constructive revolutionary' and a detailed study of his sermons in Geneva suggests that they dealt little with 'another world and happiness there', but rather focused on the necessity of glorifying God in the here and now: 'They cry scorn against all injustice, whether it be ecclesiastical, bureaucratic, legal, or in the market place.'[1] W. Fred Graham asks us to reflect on the likely reaction of Genevan merchants in the reformer's congregation who might be tempted to divorce their economic activities from the ethics of the Bible, to a passage like this:

> There would be those who would rather that the wheat spoil in the granary so that it will be eaten by vermin, so that it can be sold when there is want (for they only wish to starve the poor people) . . . See the wheat collected; how well our Lord has poured out his grace and his benediction so that the poor world would be nourished. But the speculator will gather it in granaries and lock it up securely, till finally the cry of famine is heard and that's no longer possible. What will happen? It will be spoiled and

---

1. W. Fred Graham, *The Constructive Revolutionary: John Calvin and His Socio-Economic Impact* (Atlanta: John Knox Press, 1978), p. 19.

rotten. How true it is that our Lord is mocked by those who want to have much profit
. . . These people entomb the grace of God, as if they warred against his bounty and
against the paternal love which he displays toward everyone.[2]

This is clearly radical preaching with a prophetic concern for social justice and
it serves to illustrate the thesis of Nicholas Wolsterstorff that the Reformation,
especially in its Calvinist expression, introduced a fresh vision of Christianity
in its relationship to the social world in which the fundamental structures
of that world were 'held up to judgement' and 'sentenced to be reformed'.[3]
Wolsterstorff identifies this Reformed vision as *world-transformative* Christianity
in contrast to what he calls *avertive* forms of religion, the latter involving the
attempt to escape from what are perceived to be the inferior realms of the
social and political worlds, in order to cultivate spiritual purity and 'attain closer
contact with a reality outside oneself which is higher, better, more real'.[4]

The world-transformative impulse of the Calvinist vision of a whole world
renewed by the preaching of the gospel can be traced across time and space
wherever the Genevan reformer's teaching took hold. This is especially true
of Scotland where, according to John McNeill, the Reformation put down
deeper roots among ordinary people than anywhere else in Europe, excluding
Switzerland.[5] Having caught sight of Calvin's utopian vision of the transformation that the gospel might bring in a world facing rapid and far-reaching
social and cultural changes, Knox and his colleagues set about reforming
the whole life of the Scottish people, designing a system of education that
included placing a schoolmaster in every town, radically transforming the
universities, and introducing legislation which curbed the power of oppressive
landlords and proposed practical measures to relieve poverty.

Of course, there were many streams within the movement we identify as the
Reformation and it is often overlooked that Protestant Christianity took shape
in central Europe in ways that moved beyond the top-down social and political
reforms which Calvin attempted in Geneva. For example, among the Czech
people the Reformation was preceded in the fourteenth century by a series
of remarkable social experiments under the leadership of Jan Milic (1325–75),

---

2. Ibid., p. 56.
3. Nicholas Wolsterstorff, *Until Justice and Peace Embrace* (Grand Rapids: Eerdmans,
   1983), p. 3.
4. Ibid., p. 5.
5. John T. McNeill, *The History and Character of Calvinism* (New York: Oxford
   University Press, 1954), p. 307.

including the establishment of a foundation in the centre of Prague named 'New Jerusalem' as a haven for converted prostitutes. In the next generation Jan Hus challenged the fundamental assumptions of Christendom, contrasting Jesus, whom he called 'the poor king of the poor', with the wealth and glory of the papacy and laying the foundation for the socially radical movement that was later to bear his name. A modern Czech theologian sums up the distinctive legacy of this stream of the Reformation as consisting in its 'emphatic insistence that a true and serious reform of the church must have its social-ethical and social-critical dimensions'. He adds that the *semper reformanda* 'must never be applied only to the realm of doctrine and ecclesiastical theory, but also to the life-style and practical engagement of the church, the personal life of the Christian as well as the institutional life of church and society'.[6]

In seventeenth-century England this same socially transformative form of Christianity can be seen at work in the English Puritan movement. Wolsterstorff illustrates this by quoting a sermon preached by Thomas Case before the House of Commons in 1641:

> Reformation must be universal . . . reform all places, all persons and callings; reform the benches of judgement, the inferior magistrates . . . Reform the universities, reform the cities, reform the countries, reform inferior schools of learning, reform the Sabbath, reform the ordinances, the worship of God . . . You have more work to do than I can speak . . . Every plant which my heavenly father hath not planted shall be rooted up.[7]

Clearly, we have entered a different world from that of the Middle Ages in which social structures were treated as fixed and immovable. By contrast, the Puritan treats social arrangements as human constructions, created in time by fallen people and so requiring modification and reform in the light of the revelation of the will of God given through the gospel of Jesus Christ. This is indeed a revolutionary change in which the structures of human society, and not merely the 'persons who exist within these structures', must be changed to be brought in line with the will of a just, holy and gracious God.[8]

This was the soil from which the movement we know as Evangelicalism emerged in the eighteenth century and our task in the remainder of this chapter will be to reflect on what happened to the world-transformative impulse bequeathed to the movement by the Reformation.

----

6. Jan Milic Lochman, *Christ and Prometheus?* (Geneva: WCC Publications, 1988), p. 11.

7. Quoted by Wolsterstorff, *Until Justice and Peace Embrace*, pp. 8–9.

8. Ibid.

Evangelicalism as world-transformative religion

I have argued elsewhere that the evangelical movement which emerged from
the Great Awakening in the eighteenth century was a form of world-transformative Christianity and that it constituted 'a remarkable example of religion
as a powerful agent for political and social change'.[9] This claim can be demonstrated in all kinds of ways, but consider the poetry of the hymn writer, William
Cowper, friend and colleague of John Newton. In a long, and once extremely
popular, poem called 'The Task', published in 1785, Cowper comments on the
growth of urban centres with the same sense of horror and anxiety which we
might today experience in the slums of Nairobi, Rio de Janeiro or Mumbai.
He turns his attention specifically to 'opulent, enlarged and still increasing'
London and, after a devastating analysis of the evils of the city, pens the well
known anti-urban line: 'God made the country, and man made the town.'
However, this critique of London is based on a profound insight into the *sources*
of the wealth being flaunted within the metropolis and the price being paid for
this development on the other side of the globe. Cowper writes of the city:

> It is not seemly, nor of good report,
> That she is slack in discipline; more prompt
> To avenge than to prevent the breach of law;
> That she is rigid in denouncing death
> On petty robbers, and indulges life
> And liberty, and ofttimes honour too,
> To peculators of the public gold;
> That thieves at home must hang; but he that puts
> Into his overgorged and bloated purse
> The wealth of Indian provinces, escapes.[10]

Within the space of a few lines Cowper has managed to critique the bias of
the criminal justice system, defend the rights of the poor and oppressed, and
expose the hypocrisy and rapacious greed of capitalists who had begun the
plunder of lands and peoples on the other side of the globe.

Clearly, we are still dealing with world-transformative religion here. Indeed,

---

9. David W. Smith, *Transforming the World? The Social Impact of British Evangelicalism*
    (Carlisle: Paternoster Press, 1998 [digital edition, 2005]), p. 2.

10. William Cowper, 'The Task', in *The Poetical Works of William Cowper* (London:
    Frederick Warne, n.d.), p. 235.

it can be argued that the Calvinist concern with the reformation of human society was reinforced in early evangelicalism by the appearance of a particular eschatology which fostered the strong hope that the triumph of the gospel was about to bring far-reaching social transformation. Such hopefulness can be traced back to Calvin himself who exhorted Christians to 'hope boldly' in the confidence that, despite all opposition, Christ would one day 'surpass our opinion and our hope'.[11] Such confidence in the power of the gospel increased during the seventeenth century, so that a Puritan like Thomas Brooks could anticipate a time when 'in this world holiness shall be more general, and more eminent, than ever it hath been since Adam fell in Paradise'.[12] What Iain Murray called the 'Puritan Hope' was developed in the writings of the American theologian Jonathan Edwards into an eschatological system which enabled the early evangelicals to interpret the revival they were experiencing and the immense changes taking place in an industrializing society as signs of the times, pointing unerringly toward the dawn of the long-promised millennial golden age. Edwards anticipated that what he called the 'latter-day glory' would be 'unspeakably great' and would result in the renewal of the whole of human society. It is worth quoting him at some length:

> A time shall come wherein religion and true Christianity shall in every respect be *uppermost* in the world; wherein God will cause his church to arise and 'shake herself from the dust', and put on her beautiful garments, and sit down on a throne; and the poor shall be raised from the dust, and the beggar from the dunghill, and shall be set among princes, and made to inherit the throne of God's *glory;* a time wherein vital piety shall take possession of thrones and palaces, and those that are in the most exalted stations shall be eminent in holiness (Isa.xlix.23.) . . . A time of wonderful *union* and the most universal peace, love, and sweet harmony; wherein the nations shall 'beat their swords into plowshares' &c. and God will 'cause wars to cease to the ends of the earth. . .' A time wherein the earth shall be abundantly fruitful; . . . A time wherein the world shall be delivered from that multitude of sore calamities which before prevailed (Ezek.xlvii.20.) and there shall be an universal blessing of God upon mankind, in soul and body, and in all their concerns, and all manner of tokens of God's presence and favour . . .[13]

---

11. Quoted in Iain Murray, *The Puritan Hope: A Study in Revival and the Interpretation of Prophecy* (London: Banner of Truth, 1971), p. xii.

12. Ibid., p. xiii.

13. Jonathan Edwards, *An Humble Attempt to Promote Explicit Agreement in Extraordinary Prayer, for the Revival of Religion and the Advancement of God's Kingdom on Earth* [1748], in *The Works of Jonathan Edwards*, vol. II (London: Westley and Davis, 1834), pp. 287–288.

It is significant that Edwards' work was published in Britain in 1789, edited by the Baptist pastor John Sutcliff in the village of Olney in Bedfordshire, the very place in which the Anglican Cowper had written the lines quoted above but four years earlier. The hope that *this* world would witness a moral, social and political transformation as the outcome of the mission of the people of God was common among early evangelicals and it appeared to them to be the clear implication of the teaching of the prophetic scriptures.

Parting of the ways

At some point in the nineteenth century the world-transformative impulse of evangelical Christianity which we have briefly described above, went into decline and was eventually eclipsed through the emergence of a new form of evangelicalism that returned to the *avertive* type of religion which had been rejected within the Reformed tradition. The story of how this change came about is a complex one, but we may identify a number of factors which contributed to the creation of another-worldly, dualistic type of evangelicalism.

On the one hand, there were *external* influences, most notably the impact of the French Revolution, which gave birth to a new social conservatism and a growing sense of fear, sometimes of sheer terror, so that even the discussion of social changes became suspect since it came to be believed that such debates could be the first step toward chaos and anarchy. Many Nonconformists initially welcomed the news of radical social changes from across the English Channel, even hailing the Revolution in France as yet another indication that the 'latter-day glory' was indeed breaking into human history. In Scotland, for example, Robert Haldane could write that he 'rejoiced in the experiment that was making in France' and prayed that it might result in a new age characterized by 'the universal abolition of slavery, of war, and of many other miseries that mankind were exposed to'.[14] Haldane's biographer, writing in the middle of the nineteenth century, recalls his subject's social radicalism with evident embarrassment, commenting that he was 'for a time somewhat dazzled with the delusive prospect of a new order of things', and noting that the 'adherents of the Established Churches, both in England and Scotland, and a great

---

14. Alexander Haldane, *The Lives of Robert Haldane of Airthrey, and of his brother, James Alexander Haldane* (London: Hamilton Adams, 1852), pp. 86–87.

majority of the landed aristocracy, were united with the holders of office *in deprecating all political discussion*.[15]

What we witness here is the opening of a division within the broad stream of evangelical Christianity concerning the legitimacy of demands for social and political change, or what Hugh McLeod has called the beginning of 'Europe's age of religious polarisation'.[16] Such tensions had been present at an earlier stage in British Christian history, as is evident from the description John Bunyan reports as being applied to his congregation by the guardians of state and religious power; they were viewed as 'a turbulent, seditious, and factious people'. Bunyan of course paid a great price for preaching the gospel in a manner that appeared to be socially subversive, being arrested in 1660 for holding 'unlawful meetings' and spending the next twelve years of his life in prison.[17] A century-and-a-half later the upheaval in France revived memories of those earlier turbulent times and, as positions hardened across growing social divides, both the early pan-evangelical unity, and the radiant sense of hope, to which reference has been made above, became distant memories.

A second cause of the decline of world-transformative evangelicalism therefore, relates to the increase of class divisions and social tensions within an industrializing, modernizing society. As the statement of Haldane's biographer quoted above suggests, Christians within the established churches, many of whom had experienced evangelical conversion, came to understand their faith in terms of personal transformation, while refusing even to entertain debate concerning the possibility of socio-political change. William Wilberforce's immensely influential book, *A Practical View of the Prevailing Religious System of Professed Christians in the Higher and Middle Classes of This Country, Contrasted with Real Christianity* (1797), was designed to appeal to privileged and powerful people by presenting evangelical religion in a form that challenged ostentatious displays of wealth, while justifying the continuance of a hierarchical social system. Hugh McLeod describes this book as the 'manifesto of the new evangelicalism' and comments that it defended a highly stratified social order and summoned both rich and poor to accept the

---

15. Ibid., p. 83. Italics added.

16. Hugh McLeod, *Religion and the People of Western Europe, 1789–1970* (Oxford: Oxford University Press, 1981), p. 15.

17. The description of Bunyan's congregation is derived from the Bedford preacher himself and it forms the title of Christopher Hill's study of Bunyan: *A Turbulent, Seditious, and Factious People: John Bunyan and His Church* (Oxford: Oxford University Press, 1988). See especially pp. 90–110.

given-ness of the British constitution 'and the consolations of a highly dog-
matic form of Christianity'.[18] Wilberforce appealed to professing Christians
in the privileged classes to 'accept the duty to serve, if not actually to save,
their country . . . not by political interference, but by that sure and radical
benefit of restoring the influence of true religion and raising the standard
of morality'. In other words, Britain might be preserved from revolutionary
changes if only the upper classes would seek and find the spiritual power
capable of enabling them to change their patterns of behaviour, using their
wealth in 'moderation' and withdrawing from 'the competition of vanity'.[19]
As the US senator Mark Hatfield observes in his appreciative introduction
to an American edition of Wilberforce's book, there is an area of the great
anti-slavery campaigner's life and theology that demands critical examination:
'In his view, the end of a society of classes would come only with the second
coming of Christ, not with a manifestation of the kingdom on earth.' Hatfield
adds that large swathes of the biblical teaching on justice 'were left largely
untouched by the Clapham Society . . . that God is a God who exercises his
justice on earth (Jeremiah 9:24)'.[20]

   While Wilberforce interpreted evangelical conversion in ways that might
result in a transformation of the 'manners' of people in possession of wealth
and privilege, aristocratic philanthropists like Hannah More applied this
new, *avertive* form of evangelicalism to rural peasants suffering from extreme
poverty, and even starvation, by stressing the sanctity of the class system and
the comforts of heaven. William Dale Morris cites the following exhortations
of Hannah More, offered to poor women in the Mendip villages at the start of
the nineteenth century, as evidence that this period witnessed what he calls the
most blatant use of Christianity 'as an antidote to social unrest':

> Let me remind you that probably that very scarcity has been permitted by an all-wise
> and gracious Providence to unite all ranks of people together, to show the poor how
> immediately they are dependent upon the rich, and to show both rich and poor that
> they are all dependent upon Himself. It has also enabled you to see more clearly the
> advantages you derive from the government and constitution of this country – to
> observe the benefits flowing from the distinction of rank and fortune, which has
> enabled the high so liberally to assist the low: for I leave you to judge what would

---

18. MacLeod, *Religion and the People of Western Europe*, p. 108.

19. William Wilberforce, *Real Christianity* [Revised American edition of *A Practical View*]
    (Basingstoke: Pickering & Inglis, 1982), p. 130.

20. Ibid., Mark Hatfield, 'Introduction', p. xxvii.

have been the state of the poor of this country in this long distressing scarcity had it not been for your superiors.[21]

While the British upper classes, described by Wilberforce as 'those who matter', were turning toward an *avertive* form of evangelicalism, the rising middle class embraced Christianity but interpreted the religion in a manner that provided them with theological and ethical foundations for their demands for cultural change and far-reaching social reforms. McLeod observes that the first half of the nineteenth century was 'a formative period in the development of the identity and values both of the working class and the middle class' and that the latter were in the process of 'busily distancing themselves from everything that seemed rough, uncultured and vulgar'.[22] This 'distancing' found expression in physical space in the rapidly expanding urban centres, leaving its mark even today on cities like London, Sheffield, Manchester and Edinburgh. In Glasgow, where we began this chapter, the growth of a prosperous middle class wedded to evangelical Christianity, led to demands for new church buildings characterized by the elegance and comfort felt to be appropriate to the status and dignity of this segment of society. Callum Brown observes that middle-class evangelicalism appeared to complement economic individualism and he notes that church extension into Glasgow's new West End 'permitted social segregation and the self-elevation of middle-class groups'.[23] One may still survey the extraordinary profusion of spectacular nineteenth-century church buildings which remain in Glasgow's West End today, even though most of them are now converted into luxury accommodation, or trendy restaurants and night clubs. It is easy to lament their plight as evidence of spiritual decline, but knowledge of the origin of such churches may cause us to wonder whether the seeds of secularization were not sown here from the very beginning? As McLeod observes, in the early years of the nineteenth century, 'poorer members of affluent

---

21. William Dale Morris, *The Christian Origins of Social Revolt* (London: George Allen & Unwin, 1949), pp. 156–157. On another occasion Hannah More offered the wretched victims of slow starvation the comfort 'of knowing the advantage you have had over many villages in your having suffered no scarcity of religious instruction'.

22. Hugh McLeod, *Religion and the Working Class in Nineteenth-Century Britain* (London: MacMillan, 1984), p. 59.

23. Callum Brown, 'Religion and the Development of an Urban Society: Glasgow 1780–1914', unpublished PhD thesis, University of Glasgow, 1981, vol. II, p. 336.

congregations were being priced out, frozen out, or goaded into leaving by
sermons extolling the British constitution'.[24]

Prophetic voices

As we have noted, the *world-transformative* tradition of Christianity stemming
from the Calvinist Reformation was eclipsed by the rise of *avertive* evangelicalism as large numbers of the aristocracy experienced a form of religious
conversion that brought about personal, ethical renewal, while buttressing the
social status quo. However, the older tradition remained alive, and throughout
the nineteenth century considerable numbers of preachers and a growing
army of urban missionaries understood their faith as providing the inspiration
and dynamic to bring into existence a new kind of society, one that would be
characterized by social justice and far greater economic equality. This counter-
cultural movement was fed from two sources: an awareness of the traditions
of social theology flowing from the Reformed and Puritan traditions, on the
one hand, and the actual experience of the downside of the industrial revolution on the part of evangelicals whose compassion compelled them to work
with the urban poor and oppressed, on the other.

In many cases these two factors were combined in the same person, as
Ian Shaw has shown in his important study of high Calvinist preachers in
this period. Indeed, it is significant that even as the 'new evangelicals' were
modifying Calvinist traditions in theology, perhaps aware of the revolutionary
implications of Genevan doctrine, many Nonconformist ministers working
in contexts of extreme urban deprivation and poverty, based their social criticisms on an explicitly Calvinist theological foundation. The most obvious and
familiar example is found in the extraordinary ministry of Charles Haddon
Spurgeon, who saw himself as following in the tradition of the Reformers
and Puritans and retained both a postmillennial hope which underpinned his
expectation of radical social changes, and a prophetic approach to preaching
and ministry which led him to denounce both domestic evils and imperialist
wars. However, Shaw notes that scores of lesser known ministers worked tire-
lessly in the cities of industrial Britain and raised their voices on behalf of the
poor and oppressed. For example, William Gadsby of Manchester strikes a
completely different note from that which we have heard from Hannah More
in a similar context: 'It is extreme distress that makes the poor people cry for

---

24. Ibid., p. 59.

redress of their grievances, and I believe that in time the Lord will hear their cries, whether anyone else will or not.'[25]

John Wesley may have rejected aspects of the Calvinism of his Puritan ancestors but he clung to their world transformative faith and left a substantial legacy for many who looked to him for inspiration in the industrial cities of the nineteenth century. The plea of Wesley's true successors was often heard among the more radical voices and they could sound far more angry and threatening than the likes of William Gadsby. For example, Joseph Rayner Stephens, a Wesleyan minister who, in the aftermath of the passing of the infamous Poor Law of 1834, became an active Chartist, warned an audience in Glasgow that such humiliating legislation would be liable to result in the very revolution that the upper classes so much feared:

> If they will not learn to act as law prescribes and God ordains, so that every man shall by his labour find comfortable food and clothing – not only for himself, but for his wife and babes – then we swear by the love of our brothers, by our God who made us all for happiness, by the earth He gave us for our support, by the Heaven He designs for those who love each other here, and by the hell which is the portion of those who, violating His book, have consigned their fellowmen. . . to hunger, nakedness and death . . . we shall wrap in one awful sheet of devouring flame, which no arm can resist, the manufactories of the cotton tyrants, and the places of those who raised them by rapine and murder.[26]

While few evangelicals were willing to use language as inflammatory as this, very many felt and expressed a righteous anger concerning the structural injustices that condemned millions of people to destitution in a society that continued to trumpet its Christian character. In Edinburgh, for example, Thomas Guthrie (whose statue graces the famous Princes Street and identifies him as 'The friend of the poor and oppressed') claimed that the urban poor were doubly deprived of justice since the squalor in which they lived compelled them to seek for survival by any means possible, and they were then convicted of crimes which were traceable to the heartlessness and greed of respectable society. Where, Guthrie asked in exasperation, is the justice in that? The Scottish Calvinist's language is more restrained than that of Stephens quoted above, but his warnings of the possibility of insurrection and revolution are no less clear

---

25. Ian Shaw, *High Calvinists in Action – 1810–1860* (Oxford: Oxford University Press, 2002), p. 135.

26. Quoted in Morris, *Christian Origins of Social Revolt*, p. 170.

and urgent: the upper classes should realize that their interests are inextricably intertwined with those of the poor and that God has decreed that 'those who neglect the interests of others shall themselves suffer in the end'.[27]

I have elsewhere drawn attention to the witness of Edward Miall, whose ministry I believe to have been perhaps the outstanding example of *world-transformative* evangelicalism in the nineteenth century.[28] Certainly, few books written in this period can match his 1849 work *The British Churches in Relation to the British People* in terms of sharp critical analysis and prophetic courage, and this radical critique of a bourgeois Christianity co-opted to serve the narrow class interests of the privileged and powerful remains relevant today. Miall lamented the tragedy of churches which, instead of offering a challenge to the structures and divisions that polarized the wider society, had allowed themselves to become split along precisely the social fault lines created by modernization and capitalism, thus achieving numerical success by ignoring the precepts of Christ.[29] Here is a purple passage from Miall's analysis of Victorian Christianity in which, without using the terms, he exposes the apostasy that awaits *avertive* evangelicalism:

> Religion as embodied in the written word of God, and in that more emphatic living Word which was 'made flesh and dwelt among us', uniformly champions the cause of the weak, the friendless, the oppressed – religion, embodied in modern organisations, preaches up the rights of the powerful and dwells mainly upon the obligations of the powerless . . . Once her favourite occupation was to move as an angel of love among outcasts, to breathe hope into the spirits of the desponding, to wipe away tears as they rolled down the cheeks of the neglected – and when among the great, her theme of discourse was the vanity of perishable honours and possessions . . . In our day, she is more at home with the comfortable than with the wretched.[30]

---

27. Thomas Guthrie, *The City: Its Sins and its Sorrows* (Edinburgh: Adam & Charles Black, 1851), p. 118.

28. David W. Smith, 'A Victorian Prophet Without Honour: Edward Miall and the Critique of Nineteenth-century British Christianity', in Stephen Clark (ed.), *Tales of Two Cities: Christianity and Politics* (Leicester: IVP, 2005), pp. 152–183.

29. I owe this phrase to H. Richard Niebuhr who opens his study of denominationalism with these memorable words: 'Christendom has often achieved apparent success by ignoring the precepts of its founder.' *The Social Sources of Denominationalism* (New York: Meridian Books, 1929), p. 3.

30. Edward Miall, *The British Churches in Relation to the British People* (London: Arthur Hall, Virtue, 1849), pp. 203–204.

It should be noted at this point that the kind of searching, prophetic critiques which we have cited above did not apply to all middle- or upper-class Christians in this period. Indeed, as the nineteenth century wore on and awareness of the extent of the social and economic divisions in British cities increased, there were numerous examples of evangelicals who determined that their faith should dictate the practice of business ethics in relation to issues such as the level of wages paid to workers, as well as the conditions in which employees lived and laboured. George Cadbury, for example, escaped from a dualistic theology which confined religion to the spiritual realm, to develop a model of social responsibility in the industrial and commercial sphere which still strikes us as important. Cadbury, remarkably for his time, supported the concept of a legally enforceable minimum wage and built the famous Bourneville Village on the outskirts of Birmingham to provide his workforce with ideal working conditions and pleasant housing (including the all-important gardens). Bourneville contained libraries, recreation areas, swimming pools, medical and dental facilities, convalescent homes, and offered programmes for the continuing education of the workforce. George Cadbury condemned extremes of wealth and poverty, saw gambling as a curse, and even donated £50 a week to support engineering workers during a lock-out in 1897. He understood his Quaker evangelicalism as 'something really practical that brought joy and peace with it' and he delighted in witnessing previously sad and depressed people being given fresh opportunities in life through which they found dignity and 'were filled with all peace and joy in believing'. His remarkable industrial experiment challenged the reigning theories of market economics and 'showed how wages might be raised in a modern industry and how something like Jerusalem might be builded not *among* dark Satanic mills, but *in* mills that were no longer dark or Satanic'.[31]

Less than conquerors

In the year 1849 two men arrived separately in London, both of whom were to encounter at first hand the immense social problems caused by extreme poverty, and both of whom were to devote the rest of their lives to addressing such issues. Karl Marx and William Booth were moved and

31. H. G .Wood, 'George Cadbury (1839–1922)', in Hugh Martin (ed), *Christian Social Reformers of the Nineteenth Century* (London: SCM Press, 1927), p. 186.

scandalized by what they discovered in the East End, where the thousands of people who lived in indescribable squalor came to be known as the 'submerged tenth', or the 'residuum'. Commenting on the matchmaking industry, Marx observed that Dante would have found the worst horrors of his inferno surpassed by the sights and sounds in these factories, and then set about developing his revolutionary social theory. Interestingly, William Booth made a similar reference to Dante but then announced his intention to establish an alternative match factory in which workers' health would be safeguarded and they would be paid a living wage. Ann Woodhall comments that the reaction of the two men underlines the contrasts between them: 'Marx eruditely detailing conditions... as part of his overall attack on capitalism and Booth rushing to produce a practical solution to a specific problem.'[32]

William Booth was a true child of John Wesley and he departed from Wesleyan Methodism because of its betrayal of its founders' world transformative faith. Like John Wesley he never lost his passion for evangelism and continued to employ language which suggested that the 'salvation of souls' remained a high priority in urban mission. But, like so many other urban evangelists, both in Europe and the United States, he came to realize that there were physical, social and cultural factors that militated against a positive reception of the good news which he proclaimed to the poor. In a moving passage, Booth asks what hope there can be for the 'bastard of a harlot, born in a brothel, suckled on gin, and familiar from earliest infancy with all the bestialities of debauch, violated before she is twelve, and driven onto the streets by her mother'?[33] His conclusion is that such a poor woman has little chance in this life, never mind the next! Encounters like these led Booth and his companions to recognize that evangelism simply could not be divorced from social action, as Norris Magnuson explains:

> Entering the slums in pursuit of the evangelism that remained their chief concern, they gained there an almost unparalleled knowledge of the conditions in which the poor had to live. Encountering that kind of need, they responded with energy and growing sympathy and indignation. The extensive first-hand experience of rescue workers in the slums taught them both the worth of the poor and the heaviness of

---

32. Ann M. Woodhall, *What Price the Poor? William Booth, Karl Marx and the London Residuum* (Aldershot: Ashgate Press, 2005), p. 2.
33. William Booth, *In Darkest England and the Way Out* (London: Salvation Army, [1890]), p. 47.

the environmental pressures that weighed upon them. It taught them also that society bulwarked the prosperous and oppressed the helpless.[34]

This last claim is demonstrated dramatically in William Booth's famous 1890 book, *In Darkest England and the Way Out,* which together with the works by Miall and Guthrie mentioned earlier, seem to me to constitute key texts in evangelical social theology in this period. Booth wrote with a prophetic passion which at times results in language not far removed from the angry denunciations of Joseph Stephens we have encountered earlier. He confesses that the sight of helpless and vulnerable people being trampled by 'beasts of prey in human shape' has led him to doubt the existence of God. In an extraordinary passage he indicts the owners of firms which 'reduce sweating to a fine art', defraud workers of their wages, rob widows and orphans, and then deflect criticism of their actions by making professions 'of public spirit and philanthropy'. Booth's verdict is devastating: '. . . these men are nowadays sent to parliament to make laws for the people. The old prophets sent them to hell – but we have changed all that. They send their victims to hell, and are rewarded by all that wealth can do to make their lives comfortable.'[35]

While the members of the Salvation Army were immersing themselves in urban mission, many middle class evangelicals were moving in a direction that consolidated the *avertive,* dualistic form of evangelicalism that became so significant in the nineteenth century. Whereas, as we have seen, it had earlier been assumed that a class-based, hierarchical society was divinely sanctioned, and so represented a Christian civilization, by the end of the century it was becoming impossible to retain such views, both because of the growth of 'modern thought' and because the demands of a developing capitalist culture increasingly seemed to overwhelm Christian ethical principles. Consequently, as Douglas Frank has shown, middle-class evangelicals became increasingly uneasy and disoriented. Those who attended the proliferating conventions which offered to provide a way to discover a 'victorious life' confessed to sins such as 'an ugly temper', 'giving way to grudges against others', and being unloving 'toward people who are very trying'. Franks notes that in the late nineteenth century the old Protestant ethical values were increasingly displaced by 'consumptive virtues' such as impulsive buying, ostentatious display, and a much freer use of money:

---

34. Norris Magnusson, *Salvation in the Slums: Evangelical Social Work, 1865–1920* (Metuchen: Scarecrow Press, 1977), p. 178.
35. Booth, *In Darkest England,* p. 14.

The economy increasingly demanded that people buy the goods it was so fruitfully producing, and the message 'live it up while you can' began to compete with the image of a sober, virtuous life represented by a former generation of Calvinist faithful. This dissonance . . . added its strain to the lives of conscientious Christian people. In addition, increasingly frenetic competition made for a blurring of the lines between honest and dishonest business dealings.[36]

In this atmosphere the teaching of a number of North American visitors, such as Robert and Hannah Pearsall Smith, offering release from worry and constant spiritual defeat, and the promise of a 'victorious and happy life' was eagerly embraced. The social background of the majority of those who attended the early Keswick Conventions is clear from the 'besetting sins' which were confessed there: 'a tattling tongue, angry looks, viciousness on the croquet lawn, impatience with servants'. Women found strength on those days when they 'felt poorly' and men were able to stop worrying about 'the next bank failure'.[37]

What this meant was that at a point of major change within the wider culture, middle-class evangelicals increasingly turned *inward*, seeking an experience of individual peace and well-being which enabled them to rediscover happiness, while bypassing the crucial issues of discipleship in a modernizing, capitalist society and leaving the questions raised by the prophetic voices we have listened to unanswered. Not surprisingly, there were tensions between these groups, illustrated by Catherine Booth's response to a gentleman who, in reaction to her critique of middle-class Christianity, claimed that there was great love for Jesus in his church: 'Yes', she replied, 'for their idealistic Saviour, but suppose Jesus was to come to your chapel as He went about Palestine, with a carpenter's coat on . . . all over perspiration and dust. . ., where would your chapel steward put him to sit?'

One man who knew the answer to that question from personal experience was the Scottish social activist and founder of the Independent Labour Party, Keir Hardie. His childhood was blighted by extreme poverty and the desperate struggle of his mother to feed and clothe the family. As a young man Hardie was employed by a local baker noted for religious zeal, but when he arrived a

---

36. Thomas Frank, *Less Than Conquerors: How Evangelicals Entered the Twentieth Century* (Grand Rapids: Eerdmans, 1986), pp. 139–140.

37. Ibid., p. 142. On the shape of holiness in the evangelical tradition see my *Against the Stream: Christianity and Mission in an Age of Globalization* (Leicester: IVP, 2003), pp. 27–43.

few minutes late for work one winter's morning, he was summoned upstairs where the family were seated for a sumptuous breakfast and was read a lecture on the sin of sloth and warned that any repetition would lead to instant dismissal. A few weeks later, while caring for his ailing, famished brother, Hardie again arrived moments late and was discharged on the spot with two weeks' wages withheld as a punishment. Such experiences fired a burning passion for justice, while also leading him to explore the life and teachings of Jesus for himself. He joined a small, sectarian group known as the Evangelical Union and, according to Fenner Brockway, came to appreciate 'the truths of the teaching of Christianity', revering above all the life and example of Jesus.[38] At the end of a truly remarkable life, during which he was tireless in challenging injustice, became a key figure in founding the Independent Labour Party, entered Parliament himself and campaigned against a host of social evils, Hardie confessed that if he could begin again he would devote all his energies 'to the advocacy of the Gospel of Christ'.[39]

Evangelical social theology in a globalized world

The story of the loss and recovery of the evangelical social conscience during the twentieth century has been told elsewhere and cannot be dealt with here.[40] During the first half of that century large segments of the evangelical movement in Britain and North America appeared to lose contact with the historic roots of the tradition and turned in a direction that resulted in the redefinition of their faith as an almost wholly *avertive* form of religion.

Evangelicals in Britain and North America came to identify a world transformative faith with what they believed to be the Trojan horse of liberalism and turned toward forms of mission that concentrated solely on individual salvation and the planting of churches. In the mercy and wisdom of God these efforts were to bear considerable fruit and played a significant part in

---

38. Fenner Brockway, 'James Keir Hardie (1865–1915)', in *Christian Social Reformers of the Nineteenth Century*, p. 231. Brockway was himself a Labour Member of Parliament who had known Hardie personally.

39. Ibid., p. 239.

40. See, for example, my *Transforming the World? The Social Impact of British Evangelicalism* (Carlisle: Paternoster Press, 1998), especially pp. 73–102. Timothy Chester has described the recovery of social concern in detail in *Awakening to a World of Need: The Recovery of Evangelical Social Concern* (Leicester: IVP, 1993).

the growth of Christianity across the southern hemisphere, but the absence of anything remotely like an adequate social theology often left new Christians voiceless in contexts in which violence and injustice needed to be challenged. In time this would result in accusations that the entire missionary enterprise was 'a religious counterpart of the capitalist movement' and the suspicion grew that there was a 'secret alliance between the world missionary movement and the internationalist capitalist enterprise'.[41]

After the mid-point of the twentieth century the tide began to turn against *avertive* evangelicalism as a new generation of leaders came to recognize the tragic consequences of the betrayal of a tradition that had once possessed such a prophetic cutting edge and a radiant hope of social transformation. At the Berlin Congress on Evangelism in 1966 the reduced understanding of mission as consisting almost exclusively in evangelistic proclamation prevailed, but a few voices recalled earlier, *world-transformative* perspectives. One of these belonged to Paul Rees, vice-president of World Vision, who bravely cited examples of situations in which failure to *practice* the faith had fatally undermined the credibility of its proclamation. He argued that when deeds contradict the message then the 'victims of our discriminations' become frustrated and cynical about the claims we make for the gospel. Rees asserted that the message of Christ is never preached in a social vacuum, because witness is related, whether we recognize it or not, 'to the whole of life and the total fabric of society'.[42]

From this small, largely unnoticed beginning, the turning tide rose rapidly, fed by new streams flowing into discussions of these matters from Christians in the emerging heartlands of the Christian religion across the southern hemisphere. From their perspective, the almost exclusive focus on individual salvation looked like a truncated gospel shaped less by the teaching of the Bible than by modern, Western culture with its dualistic separation of religion from politics, and its concentration on the individual over against the community. The Lausanne Congress of 1974, with its declaration that Christians must

---

41. These are the words of Orlando Costas in *Christ Outside the Gate: Mission Beyond Christendom* (New York: Orbis Books, 1984), pp. 58, 69. Costas's later work, *Liberating News: A Theology of Contextual Evangelization* (Grand Rapids: Eerdmans, 1989) uses rather more measured language and offers a thoughtful, creative and significant contribution toward the development of a biblical theology of integral mission.

42. Paul Rees, 'Evangelism and Social Concern', in Carl F. H. Henry and W. Stanley Moonyham (eds.), *One Race, One Gospel, One Task. Volume 1, World Congress on Evangelism, Berlin, 1966* (Minneapolis: World Wide Publications, 1967), pp. 307–308.

share God's concern 'for the liberation of men from every kind of oppression' and its affirmation that 'evangelism and socio-political involvement are both part of our Christian duty', was a watershed which moved the tradition back toward its *world-transformative* beginnings. As René Padilla was to say after the Congress:

> In the final analysis, the greatest accomplishment of the Congress was to clarify the
> meaning and nature of the Christian mission. Over against an unbiblical isolation
> of the proclamation of the Gospel from the total mission of the Church, there
> emerged a concept of evangelism in which the proclamation was seen as inextricably
> connected with social responsibility, discipleship, and church renewal . . . [T]he
> Lausanne meeting turned out to be an updating of the evangelical agenda, made
> possible by a renunciation of fierce pragmatism and a return to biblical theology.
> Evangelism remained intact, but was no longer understood as ecclesiocentric
> activism, but rather as God's means of placing the totality of life under the lordship
> of Jesus Christ.[43]

Padilla's confident statement probably overestimated the achievements of the Lausanne Congress since the new perspective he so well describes (and to which he made a significant contribution) was to remain contested territory. In the light of our survey of the debates that took place between Christians throughout the nineteenth century, this ongoing discussion should not surprise us. When religious faith becomes ideological and is used (often without the knowledge of those who profess it) as a justification of vested social and economic interests, its defences are not easily or speedily broken down. As a result, there have been continuing battles over the relationship between evangelism and social responsibility and the apparent gains achieved at the Lausanne Congress have needed to be defended, and sometimes even recovered.

Conclusion

The situation faced by evangelical Christianity at the start of the third millennium is, I wish to suggest, significantly different from that which confronted the Victorian churches, or even that which existed at the time of the Lausanne Congress. There are multiple factors that have created a new context in which

---

43. René Padilla (ed.), 'Introduction', *The New Face of Evangelicalism* (London: Hodder & Stoughton, 1976), p. 14.

discussion of the subject we are dealing with in this volume simply cannot be an optional extra for the Christian community, but actually takes us to the very heart of what it means to confess and follow Jesus Christ in the world today.

Among these factors we might mention the rise of political Islam and the considerable challenge which aspects of its social ethics offer to contemporary Christians. The late Lesslie Newbigin, whose work contributed massively to the renewed search for a faithful social theology, made the following significant claim in his final public address:

> I have said that this so-called Western, modern, scientific, free market culture is the most powerful in the world at the present time. There is one serious challenger at the present time – Islam. Islam, with a courage that should put us Christians to shame, is openly challenging the claim that the free market and all its ideology is what rules the world, claiming as we do that God is in control.

Newbigin went on to say that the twenty-first century would witness *three* worldviews competing for the allegiance of the human family: 'the gospel, the free market, and Islam.'[44] May it not be the case that as Christians awaken to the missiological challenge posed by the free market, they may discover previously unrecognized common ground with Muslims and, in that process, find a basis on which missionary dialogue can be initiated?

Which brings us to the second major factor shaping our world demanding a missionary response based on adequate theological foundations, namely, the peculiar form that modern capitalism is taking at the present time. There is not space to discuss this development here, but the cancerous growth of the ideology of the market might suggest that Christians are today facing the biggest challenge to faithfulness and obedience that our world has seen since John of Patmos caught sight of the Christ who rules over death and Hades (Rev. 1:18).[45] The social and economic polarizations which occurred in an industrialized society in nineteenth-century Britain are now writ large on a global scale with consequences in the lives of billions of people which almost defy analysis and comprehension. The world's dismal shanty towns now house

---

44. Lesslie Newbigin, *Signs Amid the Rubble: The Purposes of God in Human History* (Grand Rapids: Eerdmans, 2003), pp. 118–119.

45. See for example, Thomas Frank, *One Market Under God: Extreme Capitalism, Market Populism and the End of Economic Democracy* (London: Secker & Warburg, 2001); Zygmunt Bauman, *Wasted Lives: Modernity and its Outcasts* (Cambridge: Polity Press, 2004).

(if that word is adequate) a billion people and a staggering 78.2% of the urban populations in the cities of the Global South live in such contexts.[46] Statistics like these serve to highlight the conclusions of Jane Collier and Rafael Esteban that the economic system that now rules the world has become a form of *ideology*, even a *culture* in its own right, which must be challenged by the gospel which names Christ as Lord.[47]

There is a final factor shaping our world today which has a direct bearing on the quest for a social theology, and this is the growth and character of Christianity across its new heartlands in the southern hemisphere. Much of what has been written in this chapter, and much of the debate concerning the relationship between the gospel and social action, is in truth a local, even rather *parochial* discussion, shaped by the experience of rich Christians in what is called the 'developed' world. However, the future shape of theology and mission will be determined elsewhere, precisely in the contexts of poverty and human suffering we have alluded to above, because this is where the vast majority of Christians will be found living in the coming century. The implications of this are simply enormous, but one of these relates directly to the theme of this book because in contexts characterized by oppression and poverty, believers are simply unable to afford the kind of theoretical debates about justice and oppression to which reference has been made above.

What exactly this will mean in regard to the mission of the people of God in the age of globalization remains to be seen. But it looks likely that, one way or another, evangelical Christianity is likely to take a *world-transformative* shape in a world ruled by an ideology that runs counter to the gospel of the risen Lord.

© David W. Smith, 2009

---

46. See Mike Davis, *Planet of Slums* (London: Verso, 2006), p. 23.

47. Jane Collier and Rafael Esteban, *From Complicity to Encounter: The Church and the Culture of Economism* (Harrisburg: Trinity Press International, 1998).

14. AN APPEAL TO MORAL IMAGINATION AND COMMERCIAL ACUMEN: TRANSFORMING BUSINESS AS A SOLUTION TO POVERTY

Peter S. Heslam

I have a dream. When I am old I would like to take my great-grandchildren to a museum to see what poverty was like before it was eradicated and dispatched to the annals of history. The year 2005 could be highlighted as a significant milestone in such an exhibition. Although, contrary to the hopes and expectations of many, there were no major development breakthroughs at the global economic summits held that year, the plight of the world's poor reached a new level of public consciousness, aided by the attention given to it by the global media. Four events conspired to sustain this attention throughout most of that year. First, a series of devastating natural disasters – a tsunami in South Asia, an earthquake in Pakistan, a series of hurricanes in the Gulf of Mexico and a drought in Niger – reaped havoc amongst large numbers of poor people; second, Live 8 concerts were held around the world to mark the twentieth anniversary of Live Aid, attracting the largest audience in rock history; third, the Commission for Africa published its long-awaited report, the contents of which received massive media coverage[1]; fourth, a huge and well-organized conglomeration of NGOs, campaign groups, trade unions, celebrities and faith groups were mobilized

---

1. *Our Common Interest: Report of the Commission for Africa* (London: Commission for Africa, 2005). Available at <http://www.commissionforafrica.org>.

under the banner 'Make Poverty History'.

These circumstances have contributed to a situation in which poverty, which has always been with us, has reached a new high on the world's political agenda. There is a danger, however, that the potential of the private sector – of business – to help tackle the problem of poverty is downplayed or overlooked. After fifty years and more than a trillion dollars spent on international development, almost half of the world's population still lives on less than US$2 per day. Yet flourishing and responsible international business, along with well-regulated foreign direct investment, can deliver the kind of economic growth that lifts people out of poverty, giving them hope for the future and a vision of dignity and well-being that can be realized through their own honest endeavour. The recent experience of low-income countries such as India and China confirms that the private sector provides the most effective means to alleviate poverty. This has been true for every rich country, and it's true for every poor one now.

Under the impact of globalization, business is becoming a predominant form of global culture in which millions of people across the world interact with each other on a daily basis. Indeed, there has never been a time when so many people in the world have belonged to the same community of work. The business sector is thereby vested with unprecedented opportunities to be an agent of positive social, material and spiritual transformation in the contemporary world.

Business alone is not enough, of course. Both the Africa Commission and the Make Poverty History Campaign stress the importance of well-targeted aid, debt cancellation and the reform of global trading rules. However, at least two additional factors are required to achieve prosperity: first, the social institutions that characterize all free societies, such as property rights and the rule of law; second, the cultivation and exercise of virtue beyond the requirements of the law. These elements have strong biblical foundations, and provide the context in which business can flourish.

Basic conditions such as these aside, there is simply no other way to banish poverty long-term than through the vigorous growth of enterprise. Why then is this so often ignored or denied? One reason is the negative attitude towards business that is generally found amongst the churches, which have played a key role in highlighting the plight of the world's poor. In as much as Western culture has been radically influenced by Christianity over the past two thousand years, this attitude can also be found in wider culture, though the traffic in attitudes flows in both directions – there is good evidence that the church's attitude grew out of its wider cultural context during the early centuries of its history.[2] However, insofar as the contemporary blind spot towards the potential of business is attributable to Christian teaching, this chapter seeks to make the case that at least part of the remedy is the development of a theology of business, and that such a theology has greater prospects, both in theory and in practice, if it is based on the theological paradigm of *transformation* rather than the one on which it has been based ever since the advent of liberation theology in the 1960s, which is *liberation*.

Christian attitudes to business

To set this task in a theological framework this chapter will use Richard Niebuhr's characterization, or 'typology', of Christian perspectives on contemporary culture in his book *Christ and Culture*.[3] Although this typology involves inevitable simplification, it remains a useful analytical tool. For this reason, the Church of England Bishop of Lincoln John Saxbee has referred to Niebuhr's book as 'the key text for studies in religion and culture during the second half of the 20th century'.[4] Similarly, the US theologian Stanley Hauerwas writes:

> Reinhold Niebuhr may remain better known than H. Richard Niebuhr, but it
> is arguable that H. Richard Niebuhr's work has had a more lasting impact on
> contemporary theology . . . H. Richard Niebuhr published 'only' six books, but his
> influence on American theology was immense. He became the teacher of teachers
> who would determine the main directions in theology and ethics in the second half
> of the twentieth century.[5]

---

2. For an evaluation of the key teachings on wealth and poverty of the patristic period, see Peter S. Heslam, 'Can Christianity Give a Positive Value to Wealth? An Engagement with the Early Church Fathers' at <http://transformingbusiness.net>.

3. Richard Niebuhr, *Christ and Culture* (New York: HarperCollins, 2002 [1951]).

4. *Church Times*, 28 May 2004.

5. Stanley Hauerwas, 'H. Richard Niebuhr', in David F. Ford (ed.) with Rachel Muers, *The Modern Theologians: An Introduction to Christian Theology Since 1918* (Oxford: Blackwell, ³2005), pp. 194–203 (pp. 194–195). For a more detailed account of Niebuhr's impact, see William Werpehowski, *American Protestant Ethics and the Legacy of H. Richard Niebuhr* (Washington: Georgetown University Press, 2003). Notable critiques of Niebuhr's scheme include Peter R Gathje, 'A Contested Classic: Critics Ask: Whose Christ? Which Culture? – Christ and Culture', in *Christian Century*, 19

When Niebuhr's typology is applied to attitudes towards business, the following types emerge:

Type One: Christ against business
Type Two: Christ subsumed by business
Type Three: Christ subsumes business
Type Four: Christ and business in paradox
Type Five: Christ transforms business

While there is merit and deficiency in all five of these types, this chapter allows space only for a discussion of the first and last.[6]

Christ against business

With this type, the impact of the fall on business is stressed to such an extent that Christ is seen in opposition to business. The only option for Christians, therefore, is to dissociate themselves as much as possible from the corruption of the business world and to focus instead on the new order established by Christ. As already indicated, this attitude has a venerable history that goes back to some of the early Church Fathers and their cultural context. Tertullian (c. 160–225), for instance, argued that trade can hardly be considered a servant of God, and that the acquisition of goods was motivated by covetousness, which is a form of idolatry. In the same vein, Jerome (c. 345–420) wrote: 'Avoid, as you would the plague, the clergyman who is also a man of business.'

June 2002 (available at <http://www.findarticles.com>); George Marsden, 'Christianity and Cultures: Transforming Niebuhr's Categories', in *Insights: The Faculty Journal of Austin Seminary* (1999), available at <http://www.religion-online. org>; John Howard Yoder, 'How H Richard Niebuhr Reasoned: A Critique of Christ and Culture', in Glen H. Stassen, D. M. Yeager and John Howard Yoder (eds.), *Authentic Transformation: A New Vision of Christ and Culture* (Nashville: Abingdon, 1996), pp. 31–89; T. J. Gorringe, *Furthering Humanity: A Theology of Culture* (Aldershot: Ashgate, 2004), pp. 12–16.

6. For fuller applications of Niebuhr's scheme to economic institutions, see Ronald Preston, *Religion and the Persistence of Capitalism* (London: SCM, 1979), pp. 7–9; David Krueger, *The Business Corporation and Productive Justice* (Nashville: Abingdon Press, 1997), pp. 30–34; Louke van Wensveen Siker, 'Christ and Business: A Typology for Christian Business Ethics', *Journal of Business Ethics* 8 (1989), pp. 883–888.

Today this sentiment pervades academic theology, which has been profoundly influenced by liberation theology.[7] It can also be found in many forms
of popular spirituality, from the contemplative to the charismatic. Indeed, I
have met business people from various spiritual traditions who have told me
of encounters they have had with fellow believers who assume that business
is so compromised a profession that they cannot imagine why anyone would
remain in it except for its material rewards.

Christ the transformer of business

With this final type, business is affirmed as an arena of Christ's transforming
work. Culture, it maintains, is under divine rule and represents corrupted good,
rather than evil. While all human achievements are vulnerable to error, perversion and evil, human beings have the capacity to embody within their work God's
ordering and creativity. Culture needs constant conversion, therefore, rather
than outright rejection and replacement. The process is one of transformation,
involving both personal and social change. Given the possibility of such change,
those belonging to this type tend to focus more on the strengthening and pro-
motion of good practice than on negative campaigning against the failures of
business, their concern being to work *with* business, rather than to antagonize
it. They endeavour to take a holistic approach, paying attention to the material
as well as the spiritual, the individual as well as the communal. While they often
express concern for economic injustice, they also express hope in the possibility
of real change and improvements that are beneficial for all concerned.

As already indicated, Type One is the most dominant attitude in the church.
It coincides with a general antipathy towards business which pervades both
intellectual and popular culture, stimulated in part by sensation-seeking media
portrayals of reprehensible behaviour amongst the business elite. It is par-

---

7. See, for example, Timothy Gorringe, 'The Principalities and Powers: A Framework
   for Thinking about Globalization', in Peter S. Heslam (ed.), *Globalization and the Good*
   (London: SPCK, 2004), pp. 79–91. Many theologians influenced by feminist and
   Radical Orthodox theology conform to this type. See, for instance, Cynthia Moe-
   Lobeda, 'Offering Resistance to Globalization: Insights from Luther', in *Globalization
   and the Good*, pp. 95–104. John Milbank, one of the foremost representatives of
   Radical Orthodoxy, is sharply critical of business and market economics, arguing that
   capitalism is a heresy. See his monumental and highly influential *Theology and Social
   Theory: Beyond Secular Reason* (Oxford: Blackwell, ²2005 [1990]). For a robust critique of
   Radical Orthodoxy see Christopher J. Insole, *The Politics of Human Frailty: A Theological
   Defence of Political Liberalism* (London: SCM, 2004).

ticularly important, therefore, that the weaknesses of Type One are exposed. I shall pay attention only to two of these before turning to two features that commend Type Five.

Why Type One will not do

Focus on distribution
In recent years most mainline denominations have produced a number of official statements on the economy. These documents generally express an admirable solidarity with those in poverty and a commitment to letting their voice be heard. They generally help raise awareness about poverty, encourage debate, and shape opinion amongst church leaders. In general, however, they fail to give adequate recognition to the fact that, as business is the means of wealth creation, it has a key role in poverty alleviation.

Three documents stand out as exceptions to this trend. The first is one which, though without official ecclesiastical status, involved input from economists and business leaders, rather than merely from theologians and ethicists: the *Oxford Declaration on Christian Faith and Economics*. One of its passages reads:

> We recognize that poverty results from and is sustained by both constraints on the production of wealth and on the inequitable distribution of wealth and income.
> We acknowledge the tendency we have had to reduce the causes of poverty to one at the expense of the other. We affirm the need to analyse and explain the conditions that promote the creation of wealth, as well as those that determine the distribution of wealth.[8]

A second notable exception is the papal encyclical *Centesimus Annus*, issued in 1991. In it, Pope John Paul II advocates 'a society of free work, of enterprise and of participation' and insists on 'the positive value of the market and

---

8. The declaration was first published in *Transformation* (April/June 1990), pp. 1–8. It was later published, with analysis and comment, in Herbert Schlossberg, Vinay Samuel and Ronald J. Sider (eds.), *Christianity and Economics in the Post-Cold War Era: The Oxford Declaration and Beyond* (Grand Rapids: Eerdmans, 1994) and in Max L. Stackhouse, Dennis P. McCann and Shirley J. Roels (eds.), *On Moral Business: Classical and Contemporary Resources for Ethics in Economic Life* (Grand Rapids: Eerdmans, 1995), pp. 472–482. The citation is from section 36.

enterprise'.[9] He even highlights the advantages of the free market and provides a qualified endorsement of capitalism, if by that term is meant 'an economic system which recognizes the fundamental and positive role of business, the market, private property and the resulting responsibility for the means of production, as well as free human creativity in the economic sector'.[10] When poor countries are able to produce goods and services for the global market, the Pope argues, they have the best chance of escaping poverty:

> Even in recent years it was thought that the poorest countries would develop by isolating themselves from the world market and by depending only on their own resources. Recent experience has shown that countries which did this have suffered stagnation and recession, while the countries which experienced development were those which succeeded in taking part in the general interrelated economic activities at the international level . . . It would appear that, on the level of individual nations and of international relations, the *free market* is the most efficient instrument for utilizing resources and effectively responding to needs.[11]

A third exception is *Prosperity with a Purpose*, published by Churches Together in Britain and Ireland (CTBI).[12] As with the two documents just mentioned, it contains plenty of qualifications but its endorsement of the market is unmistakeable. The church representatives responsible for producing it clearly wish to distance themselves and their churches from the censorious attitudes that such statements have tended to convey:

> A purely negative appraisal of economic activity is unacceptable and an injustice to those engaged in it. Economic activity is instead something to celebrate. When it raises the standard of living of the population while relieving the lot of the poor, it is part of God's will for humanity. There is a need to redress a perceived imbalance in the way Christians have regarded the creation of wealth by economic activity. They should recognize that it is one of the chief engines of progress and greater well-being in the modern age, both directly and indirectly; and thank God for it.[13]

---

9. *Centesimus Annus*, sections 35 and 43.

10. *Centesimus Annus*, sections 40 and 42.

11. *Centesimus Annus*, sections 33 and 34. Pope John Paul II's endorsement of the free market is qualified in part by his insistence on the role of the state in regulating the economy.

12. *Prosperity with a Purpose: Christians and the Ethics of Affluence* (London: CTBI, 2005).

13. *Prosperity with a Purpose*, pp. 15–16.

Exceptions aside, most official church statements assume that the creation of wealth and the mechanisms of production are of little moral importance compared to the ethical imperative to address the inequities of distribution.

Productive justice is, however, no less important than distributive justice. Indeed, the ethical demands of distribution cannot be considered in isolation from the ethical demands of production, not least because without wealth production there cannot be any wealth distribution. For this reason, contemporary theologies and spiritualities that focus on identifying with the poor and reading the gospel through their eyes need to be careful that they do not misrepresent the attitudes of many people trapped in poverty and do not misunderstand what is in their best interests. These interests have to include the ability to take part in the wealth-creating processes of production – they cannot be reduced to benefiting from more equitable distribution. It is perhaps significant in this regard that a major survey of attitudes to globalization across the world found that support for free markets is higher in many African countries than in the developed world as a whole.[14]

It is remarkable, therefore, how little has changed since the fall of communism; theological opinion within most mainstream churches still tends to regard capitalism as a system built only on greed, acquisitiveness, materialism, consumerism, economic 'rationality' and individualism. Within this critique, there is little constructive discussion of the role and function of business and how theology might apply to it. Developed as it is in isolation from business, most contemporary theology is deemed irrelevant by the vast numbers of people who spend most of their lives working in the commercial sector, or being closely associated with it.

Business theology stifled

Secondly, the mistrust that inevitably accompanies the notion of Christ against business serves to stifle a full-orbed theology of business. Some have sought to justify such mistrust by appealing not only to the teachings of the Church Fathers but to the New Testament, citing such passages as James 5:1–6 and the teachings of Jesus. In many cases, however, the origins of this attitude are far

---

14. Taking all the countries surveyed, support for free-market economic systems is greater in high-income rather than low-income countries, but only marginally so (66% compared to 63%). Nigeria (80%) and the Ivory Coast (79%) were the developing countries showing the greatest support in Africa. Vietnam (90%) showed the greatest support overall. See The Pew Global Attitudes Project, *Views of a Changing Word*, 2003, pp. 103–105 (<http://www.people-press.org>).

more recent, lying in the period between the two world wars of the twentieth century.[15]

To British intellectuals and other members of the higher social classes at this time, a career in business was a dull and contemptible way of life. 'Successful business is devastatingly uninteresting' is the way one of C. P. Snow's characters puts it.[16] C. S. Lewis expressed utter disdain for the car manufacturer William Morris (Viscount Nuffield), Oxford's biggest employer at the time and one of the University's most generous benefactors. Comparing Cambridge – to where he moved in 1954 to take up a professorial chair – to Oxford, where he spent most of his career, he wrote to an American pen-friend Mrs Allen: 'Cambridge is charming. No Lord Nuffield (drat that man!) has come to turn it into a huge industrial city, and one can still feel the country-town under the academic surface. In that way it is more like what Oxford was in my young days.'[17] And he once wrote with distain about the current 'Managerial Age':

> The greatest evil is not now done in those sordid 'dens of crime' that Dickens loved to paint . . . But it is conceived and ordered (moved, seconded, carried, and minuted) in clean, carpeted, warmed, and well-lighted offices, by quiet men with

---

15. Precedents can, however, be found in the Victorian novel. See, for instance, the prejudice expressed towards those involved in trade in Elizabeth Gaskell's novel *North and South,* 2 vols. (London: Chapman & Hall, 1855). The heroine, Margaret Hale, attempts to defend John Thornton, a wealthy manufacturer, against the snobbism of her mother but unwittingly her words are full of irony: 'And as for Mr Thornton being in trade, why he can't help that now, poor fellow. I don't suppose his education would fit him for much else' (I, 114). Later Margaret exclaims: 'I don't like shoppy people . . . I like all people whose occupations have to do with land; I like soldiers and sailors, and the learned professions, as they call them. I'm sure you don't want me to admire butchers and bakers, and candlestick-makers, do you mamma?' Eventually, however, Margaret becomes conscious of her own snobbery. Another example of Victorian anti-business sentiment is Mr Bulstrode, the 'evangelical' though hypocritical banker in George Eliot's *Middlemarch: A Study of a Provincial Life,* 4 vols. (London: William Blackwood, 1871–3).

16. See C. P. Snow's *The Masters* (London: Macmillan, 1951), p. 93. This novel is part of Snow's *Strangers and Brothers* series which was published between 1940 and 1974 but depicts English life between 1930 and 1960.

17. The letter is dated 26 November 1955. Cited in Lancelyn Green and Walter Hooper, *C. S. Lewis: A Biography* (Glasgow: Collins, 1974), p. 286.

white collars and cut fingernails and smooth-shaven cheeks who do not need to raise their voice.[18]

In a similar vein, J. B. Priestly reproached 'the shoddy, greedy, profit grabbing, joint-stock company industrial system we'd allowed to dominate us' as the real villain in English society.[19] H. G. Wells, likewise, dismissed entrepreneurs as belonging to:

the urban variation of the peasant type, for whom urban property, money, and visible triumph over one's neighbour are the criteria for success. The first exploitation of the gifts of invention and science was very largely instinctive, unintelligent exploitation. And to this day the typical face of the big industrialist and the big financier has a boorish quality.[20]

Even children's literature was influenced by this phenomenon. See, for instance, the attitudes expressed by George Banks, the London banker, in P. L. Travers' *Mary Poppins*.[21]

This situation appears not to have pertained in the US, or at least not to the same degree. Abraham Flexner, an American observer of British university education, noted in 1930:

Practical courses in salesmanship are conspicuous by their absence. The teaching staff are not unfamiliar with American developments, but they are out of sympathy with them. They do not pretend to be practical men capable of advising business concerns; no member of the business or commerce faculty at Manchester has any remunerative connection with industry . . . they have also found that successful businessmen have nothing to tell their students.[22]

---

18. From the Preface to C. S. Lewis, *The Screwtape Letters* (rev. edn, New York: Macmillan, 1961), p. x. Further reflections by Lewis on commerce and industry can be found in his 'Good Work and Good Works', in *The World's Last Night and Other Essays* (New York: Harcourt, 1987 [1960]), pp. 71–81.

19. J. B. Priestly, *English Journey: Being a Rambling but Truthful Account of What One Man Saw and Heard and Felt and Thought During a Journey Through England During the Autumn of the Year 1933* (London: Penguin, 1977 [1934]), p. 66.

20. H. G. Wells, *The Work, Wealth and Happiness of Mankind* (London: Heinemann, 1932), p. 318.

21. First published in London by Peter Davies in 1934.

22. Cited in John Micklethwait and Adrian Wooldridge, *The Company: A Short History of*

The contrast between the British attitude to William Morris (1877–1963) and the American attitude to his older contemporary and fellow car manufacturer Henry Ford (1863–1947) is particularly striking. Whereas Ford became something of a folk-hero, attracting both fame and controversy, Morris often received, as he did from C.S. Lewis, the cold shoulder.[23]

It was commonplace, during this period, for industry to be accused of polluting the countryside, debasing culture, and eliminating peace and quiet. Not surprisingly, therefore, pre-Second World War Britain produced no more than a handful of university departments of business and accounting, and those that did appear took pains to resist contact with the business world. Inevitably, British companies were thereby denied both able recruits and up-to-date expertise. Some rebelled, of course, against the prejudices of their parents. Ian MacLaurin (Baron MacLaurin of Knebworth), formerly chairman of Tesco and Vodaphone, who was born in 1937, writes in his autobiography about the snobbish anti-trade sentiments of his mother.[24] But amongst those graduating from Cambridge University in 1937–8, fewer sons followed their fathers into business than into any other vocation.[25] In general, business was left to recruit people who had failed to make it into university or the traditional professions.[26]

Negative attitudes to business that were shaped in the interbellum have manifested a die-hard quality. The obituary columns of newspapers have shown a relative disinterest in lives spent in business.[27] When historians refer

---

    a Revolutionary Idea (London: Weidenfeld & Nicolson, 2003), p. 87. No source given.

23. Neil McKendrick, 'General Introduction' to R. J. Overy, *William Morris, Viscount Nuffield* (London: Europa Publications, 1976), p. vii.

24. Ian MacLaurin, *Tiger by the Tail: A Life in Business from Tesco to Test Cricket* (London: Macmillan, 1999).

25. *University Education and Business: A Report by a Committee Appointed by the Cambridge University Appointments Board*, published in 1946. Cited in Michael Sanderson, *The Universities and British Industry, 1850–1970* (London: Routledge and Kegan Paul, 1972), p. 283.

26. See Martin J. Wiener, *English Culture and the Decline of the Industrial Spirit, 1850–1980* (Cambridge: CUP, 1981).

27. Roy Lewis and Rosemary Stewart studied the obituaries in *The Times* for three months in 1957 and noted that out of 203 obituaries only 12 featured businessmen (whereas 34 featured military professionals) and that these 12 were comparatively short. See their book *The Boss: The Life and Times of the British Business Man* (London: Phoenix, ²1961), p. 29.

to William Morris it is generally to the Victorian writer, designer and social-ist activist, who targeted his products to the rich, rather than his namesake and fellow Oxfordian who sought to make cars for all.[28] Likewise, entries for business people in the monumental sixty-one volume *Oxford Dictionary of National Biography* are disproportionately fewer than for other major pro-fessions.[29]

Contemporary anti-business sentiment is focused largely on multina-tionals. National elites see them as threats to their rightful authority; con-servative populists condemn them as agents of cosmopolitanism; socialists anathematize them as 'the highest stage of capitalism'; extremes on both left and right blame them for the loss of Western jobs to workers in the east. The political power of multinationals, real or imagined, is often seen as particularly objectionable, responsible for the loss of democratic freedoms.[30]

Such opprobrium towards multinationals appears to be intensifying, partly in reaction to the reckless lending practices of some major banks. It has fed into the hands of so-called anti-globalization protestors. They burst onto the global media stage around the turn of the millennium, when some of their more anarchistic elements resorted to violence at major demonstrations in Seattle, Washington and London. Challenging what they regarded as the awesome power of multinationals, they cast a number of well-known and successful companies in a sharply negative light. Multinationals, they claimed, represented a new form of imperialism. Their sheer size and strength allowed them to penetrate traditional societies and thus to contaminate them with their perverted values. The effects include increasing inequality, social fragmenta-tion and environmental degradation.

In response, big corporations and business journalists have sought to show how multinationals adapt their products to local taste and how their chief thrust on world markets is for ideas rather than cheap labour. Their concern, they insist, is to combine global scale with local knowledge. They also point out that multinationals are considerably less powerful and more socially and environmentally responsible than their critics claim and that they have helped to increase productivity, thereby raising living standards for ordinary people.

28. McKendrick, 'General Introduction', p. xxxix.

29. Edited by H. C. G. Matthew and Brian Harrison (Oxford: OUP, 2004).

30. The irrelevance of traditional categories of 'right' and 'left' within this debate is noted in Peter S. Heslam, *Globalization: Unravelling the New Capitalism* (Cambridge: Grove Books, 2002), pp. 4–5.

Because of this, they maintain, they should be regarded as a force for good in the world.[31]

It is within this debate, which is often highly polarized, that a theology of business has so much to offer. It can provide a basis from which what is good about contemporary global business enterprise can be affirmed and what is bad can be challenged – on the grounds, for instance, of the basic goodness, fallenness and redemption of the created order, as we shall see below. Instead, contemporary business is more frequently regarded as part of the problem, rather than as part of the solution to poverty. The upshot is that the moral vocation of the business sphere, as distinct from those of the family, education or the state is simply ignored. This is a significant failure for the church, which needs to help the institutions of contemporary life, including business, to find and fulfil their various callings and charisms. As long as it maintains an attitude of contempt or suspicion, the church will be unable to articulate what it expects of these institutions. It will be left with a mode of theological and ethical discourse that is largely irrelevant.

The theological resources available to us for a substantive Christian engagement with the ethics and purpose of business are perilously thin at a time when the business sphere has become so pervasive and influential in contemporary culture. This is a lamentable situation for the church to find itself in, not only because, as the economist Michael Hudson puts it, 'civilization's economic institutions are the product of religious organization', but also because so much of its teaching, not least on the need to steward the earth and serve the poor, could be made relevant and attractive to business. As it is, the current situation resembles that of the Church of England in the early 17th century in Richard Tawney's famous quip: 'The social teaching of the Church had ceased to count, because the Church itself had ceased to think'.[32] Left in this state of

---

31. See 'How Big are Multinational Companies?' by Paul de Grauwe and Filip Camerman at <http://www.econ.kuleuven.ac.be>. The defensive tone of the argument is reflected in the titles of Johan Norberg, *In Defence of Global Capitalism* (Stockholm: Timbro, 2001) and Jagdish Bhagwati, *In Defence of Globalization* (Oxford: OUP, 2004). See also Steve Hilton and Giles Gibbons, *Good Business: Your World Needs You* (London: Texere, 2002); John Lloyd, *The Protest Ethic: How the Anti-Globalization Movement Challenges Social Democracy* (London: Demos, 2001); Michael Mosbacher, *Marketing the Revolution: The New Anti-Capitalism and the Attack upon Corporate Brands* (London: The Social Affairs Unit, 2002); and Martin Wolf, *Why Globalization Works* (New Haven: Yale University Press, 2004).

32. Richard H. Tawney, *Religion and the Rise of Capitalism: A Historical Study* (London: Penguin, [1926] 1937), p. 188.

affairs, the church is more likely to help make poverty permanent than to help make it history.

Why Type Five will do

Whereas Type One will not do, Type Five will do. The choice of words is deliberate. It is not that Type One has to be dismissed entirely; there will be situations such as corruption in business, in which, Christ's 'no!' can and should be heard. Likewise, in the case of Type Five, 'transformation' is not so all-encompassing that it is the only paradigm with which business can adequately be addressed. It is, rather, one that is sorely needed in developing a theology of business that resonates both with those in poverty and with those in business. There are two key reasons why this is so.

It takes account of the impact of business

In thinking about the contribution business can make to the positive transformation of society, it is helpful to go back to the Latin roots of the word 'company'. These lie in the two words *cum* and *panis*, which when compounded mean 'breaking bread together'. The word 'corporation', moreover, comes from the Latin *corpus*, meaning body, and the original meaning of 'commerce' suggested intimacy in communication and relationship, reflected in Shakespeare's use of the term to denote sexual intercourse. These meanings are deeply suggestive of the way in which contemporary business can be a transforming agent in society, helping to build credible, meaningful and inclusive patterns of community. They even suggest that in doing so they manifest a form of sacramentality. This certainly corresponds with the experience of many Christian business people who find that their workplaces provide a relational context for exercising their gifts that is deeper and more effective than those provided by their churches.

A single example from history is sufficient to highlight the transformative potential of an inclusive approach to business. Liberation theology assumes that the task of social revolution is the preserve of those excluded or oppressed by the wealth-creating processes of contemporary economies. The history of Marks & Spencer suggests, however, that business itself can be a vehicle of such revolution, by way of its inclusivity. By the mid-1920s, the four brothers-in-law who ran the company, which had begun penny bazaars in Manchester in 1884 and variety stores in 1915, had turned the company into a major chain of variety stores. At this point they could have decided to sit back and enjoy their considerable wealth. Instead, after visits made by Simon Marks to US retailers in 1924, they decided to re-think the overall purpose of Marks

& Spencer. This, they decided, was not retailing but 'social revolution'. The company would seek to subvert the class structure of Victorian England by making goods of upper-class quality available to the working and lower middle classes, at prices they could easily afford. This vision influenced the company's decision to concentrate on clothing, as in the England of the time, what people wore was the most visible sign of class distinctions.

Instead, therefore, of seeing business as the power from which we must be liberated, it may be more fruitful if we were to hold business organizations in a similar regard to the way we hold our churches, neighbourhoods, voluntary organizations, schools and hospitals. We may even grow to love business, though to do so we would need to make concerted efforts to understand it and become more familiar with its constraints and opportunities, for as St Augustine wrote: 'you cannot love what you do not know'. This need for understanding is well expressed by two Roman Catholic writers, who call for 'intellectual caution by religious thinkers when speaking about anything as complex as modern business. The theologizing is bound to be better if there is a comprehensive understanding of what it is businessmen and women do.'[33]

If we were to do this we would still find plenty wrong with business. But the attitude of trust that would spring from such love would mean that any judgments and moral demands we make are far more likely to be heeded and acted on by those within the business sphere. The prophetic, in other words, needs to be balanced with the pastoral. To fail in this would be to allow the role of the church to be banished yet further from the mainstream of society. As Ronald Cole-Turner writes: 'It is altogether too likely that the church will marginalize itself in the role of chaplain, picking up the pieces, caring for the bruised, mopping up the damage, but never engaging the engines of transformation themselves, steering, persuading and transforming the transformers.'[34]

Without developing a transformative theology of business, it is doubtful, indeed, whether the church will be able to construct a viable vision for the strengthening and renewal of civil society, as business has become the chief agent of social transformation. It is also the social form distinctive of an increasing amount of cooperative activity outside the family, government and

---

33. Oliver F. Williams and John W. Houck (eds.), *The Judeo-Christian Vision and the Modern Corporation* (Notre Dame: University of Notre Dame Press, 1982), p. 23.

34. Ronald Cole-Turner, 'Science, Technology, and the Mission of Theology in a New Century', in Max L. Stackhouse with Don S. Browning (eds.), *The Spirit and the Modern Authorities* (Harrisburg: Trinity Press International, 2001), pp. 139–65 (p. 143).

personal friendships. It is true, of course, that estimations as to which sector of society is the most pervasive and influential have often been exaggerated, with damaging effects. For Hegel it was the state; for Marx, the commune; for Lenin and Hitler, the political party. Earlier estimations have included the church, the feudal lords, and the monarchy. Each of these suggestions reflects the historical context in which they were forged. Today, however, there can be little doubt that it is business that has become the pre-eminent social sphere in most of the Western world.

Within this world, nation-states are generally on the defensive, churches are in numerical decline, trade unions have lost muscle and vitality, families are disintegrating and education (particularly higher education) and health care are under intense financial pressure. In the meantime, however, the business sphere has been going from strength to strength, despite the serious difficulties that have followed the credit crisis of 2008–09. Most employed people in the West now work in business and business supplies most of the world's products and services.[35] In the space of just a couple of decades, the role of business in Western society has changed out of all recognition. Areas of social life that were once assumed to be 'public' are increasingly regarded as the preserve of business – schools and hospitals included. Given such a seismic change in circumstances, it could be argued that anyone intent on maximizing their social impact would be better pursuing a career in business, rather than running for political office, climbing the academic or medical career ladder, joining the armed forces or becoming a cleric![36]

Whatever the pros and cons of this situation, it does seem generally to hold true that where opportunities to form businesses are constricted or the skills needed to sustain them are deficient, societies stagnate and remain materially deprived. The converse is also true – many countries in Asia, most notably India and China, are undergoing vigorous development in circumstances in which the amount of red tape surrounding the formation of businesses has been considerably reduced.[37] The US and Canada now have more inter-corporate

---

35. According to the National Audit Office, there are around four million companies in the UK, 99% of them being relatively small (employing less than fifty people).

36. Micklethwait and Wooldridge, *The Company*, p. 10.

37. Registering property in Norway requires one step, but 16 in Algeria. To incorporate a business takes two days in Canada, but 153 in Mozambique. In Haiti it takes 203 days longer than in Australia. In Sierra Leone it costs 1,268% of average income, compared with nothing in Denmark. To register in Ethiopia, a would-be entrepreneur must deposit the equivalent of 18 years' average income in a bank

trade with Asia than with Europe, reflecting the fact that the focus of global commerce is shifting from the Atlantic community to an emerging Asian community of nations. And despite the ongoing vigour of liberation theology in Latin America, the larger nations of that region are turning to a renewal of democratic patterns of governance, with an increased role for business.

Business is clearly a social institution to which more and more of the world is becoming committed. The biblical message needs, therefore, to be dynamically reconceived in social and economic environments far removed from those of biblical times. This task is at least as important to the future of humanity as today's theologies of sexuality and biomedical ethics. The biblical, doctrinal, ethical and interpretive resources of the churches have more to offer contemporary culture by means of a focus on business than has yet been seen to be the case. A rediscovery of these resources is the first requirement of all Christians and church communities that wish to speak with social and ethical relevance in today's rapidly changing culture.[38] The second requirement is to listen carefully and humbly to people in business, who are immersed in that culture and often face ethical dilemmas from which theological ethicists are generally protected. Otherwise there is a danger that the church's teachers will become like the lecturer in liberation theology encountered by the Harvard business academic Laura Nash. When asked whether he had ever engaged in a discussion with managers of multinational corporations with responsibilities in developing countries, he answered with surprise, 'Why should I do *that*?' He was quite certain that he understood the psychology of business people, which was bound by selfishness and greed and lacked theological grounding.[39]

Footnote 36 (*Continued*)

account, which is then frozen. In Lagos, Nigeria's commercial capital, recording a property sale involves 21 procedures and takes 274 days. These and other regulatory and bureaucratic obstacles to prosperity can be found in the World Bank's *Doing Business* reports. See <http://www.doingbusiness.org>.

38. Max L. Stackhouse and Dennis P. McCann, 'Post-Communist Manifesto: Public Theology after the Collapse of Socialism', *Christian Century*, 16 January 1991, pp. 1, 44–47. Reprinted in Stackhouse, McCann and Roels, *On Moral Business*, pp. 949–954.

39. Laura Nash, 'How the Church has Failed Business', in *The Conference Board Review* (2007), at <http://www.conference-board.org>. Nash and her colleague Scotty McLennan came across many examples of this attitude in the extensive surveys and interviews they carried in preparation for their co-authored book *Church on Sunday, Work on Monday: The Challenge of Fusing Christian Values with Business Life* (San Francisco: Jossey-Bass, 2001).

It takes account of the biblical story

A second key advantage of the transformative paradigm is that it takes account of the biblical story of creation, fall, redemption and consummation. It is thereby able to avoid extreme positions that either denounce business as irretrievably corrupt or embrace it as synonymous with God's kingdom. Unlike a liberational perspective, a transformational one advocates the reform, rather than replacement, of the means of production. The market economy, existing as it does under the sovereignty of God, is fundamentally good rather than bad, and Christians are called to participate in it, affirming and strengthening what is good, mitigating the effects of the fall, furthering the effects of redemption and anticipating the coming new order.

A transformational perspective allows business to be seen, therefore, as one of the foundational spheres of human life that provide the moral framework for human flourishing. This sphere is constituted and shaped, at least in the current era, by market-orientated institutions and practices – in a similar way to which, in the political sphere, at least in high-income countries, democratically oriented institutions and practices are predominant. It should, therefore, be accorded the kind of qualified ethical affirmation given to it in the papal encyclical *Centesimus Annus*, noted earlier. This is not to suggest that the market principle, any more than the democratic principle, can be read back in the pages of Scripture in an effort to gain blanket biblical endorsement. But it does imply commitment to and concern for the institution of business, striving to provide moral guidance, inspiration, challenge, support and friendship for those who work within it.

The positive impact of such action would be felt on many levels, contributing to the reform not only of business but of society at large. As Michael Schluter and John Ashcroft argue: 'Reform seeks to create an environment in which it is easier to live righteously. It is both reasonable and right to mould society so as to minimize the conflict between Christ and culture . . . Transforming society is about getting relationships right.'[40] It would, moreover, help to maximize the potential of business to help extend the kingdom of God. This kingdom is breaking into the created and fallen world through the redeeming work of Christ, even in instances in which Christ is not named. In words from the Second Vatican Council: 'Earthly progress must be carefully distinguished from the growth of Christ's kingdom. Nevertheless, to the extent that the former can contribute to the better ordering of human society,

---

40. Michael Schluter and John Ashcroft (eds.), *Jubilee Manifesto: A Framework, Agenda and Strategy for Christian Social Reform* (Leicester: IVP, 2005), pp. 26–28.

it is of vital concern to the Kingdom of God'.[41] Whether the extension of God's kingdom through business occurs in explicit or implicit ways, Christian mission and development agencies are gradually becoming aware of this potential. Some are beginning to encourage business professionals to use their commercial skills to bring both spiritual and material uplift to needy countries. This new model of mission reflects the fact that business is becoming a transcendent global culture. Through their involvement in it, business people are finding that otherwise impenetrable societies are opening up to Christian witness *and* experiencing increasing economic well-being.

Again, this global business culture has great potential for ill as well as for good. It can be used to dominate, exploit and demean, as neo-Marxist post-colonial intellectuals are often swift to point out.[42] The principle of reciprocity must always be maintained, therefore, as a safeguard against abuse. In other words, the transformers need the consent of those whose lives they propose to transform. It is arguable, however, that markets based on free exchange provide a rudimentary form of reciprocity. Many people in poor countries are finding, moreover, that business, though having the potential to exploit, can be a vehicle of social justice, dignity and freedom from oppression. Indeed, a recent Globescan survey commissioned by the Commission for Africa found that most Africans lay primary responsibility for the problems in their countries at the door not of global business, nor of the former colonial powers, but of their own national governments.[43] The critical question is not, therefore, whether globalization is good or bad but what *kind* of globalization is good? Whether it turns out in practice to be largely good or largely bad depends, at least to some extent, on how radically and creatively people with the appropriate skills follow Christ into the global marketplace, seeking to pervade every area of business with his truth, liberty and justice. As Lord Bishop Richard Harries writes:

> We need a new vision of capitalism existing for all God's children. Such a vision and
> the determination to bring it about is the work of Christian discipleship in the social,

41. *Gaudium et Spes* (1965), section 39.

42. See, for instance, Michael Hardt and Antonio Negri, *Empire* (Cambridge, Mass: Harvard University Press, 2000), especially sections 3.4 and 3.6.

43. The results showed that 49% blamed their own politicians; 16% blamed former colonial powers; and 11% blamed other rich countries. In other words, three times more Africans blamed their own countries than former colonial powers. See the Commission for Africa's *Our Common Interest*, p. 41.

economic, and political spheres. The risen Lord, whom Christians seek to serve, calls us to follow him not only in our personal lives but by denying ourselves, taking up our cross and following him into the companies, markets, exchanges and parliaments of the world. If we do this we are bound to come up against vested interests, and deeply ingrained forces of institutional self-interest as well as personal selfishness. But in suffering with Christ on behalf of the poor we will enter more fully into the joy of the resurrected life.[44]

For the call to seek first the kingdom of God (Matt. 6:33) is not just for ministers and professional missionaries, leaving business people merely to support them financially. Rather, in the twenty-first century, business holds a vital key to unlock societies to the freedoms and joys of the kingdom of God. Countries that have closed the door to traditional missionaries are competing with each other to attract professional entrepreneurs who can help grow their economies. Taking the opportunities for Christian witness that are naturally available in commerce is a vital and strategic means of co-operating in God's mission to the world.

This mission involves bringing salvation, healing and *shalom* to every sphere of society. The impact of the fall is waiting to be undone. Because of the cross and resurrection, evil can be overturned and the scourge of poverty can be addressed. History is replete with examples of how Christians have picked up this challenge – through the political and economic framework of the Roman Empire, the trade relations of the Age of Exploration, the invention of the printing press, even through the colonial apparatus, and, most recently, through global business enterprise.

Christian business people working in the global economy are uniquely placed to bring transformation to the circumstances of the world's poor. As they do so, they are ensuring that globalization works as a blessing, rather than as a curse. They are helping to realize globalization's potential to bring social uplift, serve the common good, and even help protect the environment. While the emphasis in liberation theology on seeing the world from the perspective of the poor is to be cherished, its economic dogmatisms, and those of other Type One attitudes, have to be set aside for the sake of a rigorous and theologically balanced engagement with the transformative role of business in today's world. Without this, it is not obvious that the church will have a sufficiently compelling vision to allow it to 'make a difference' in contemporary

---

44. Richard Harries, *Is there a Gospel for the Rich?: The Christian in a Capitalist World* (London: Mowbray, 1992), pp. 175–6.

culture. For a reconstruction of its theology will require a major shift in orientation and tone. But such a reconstruction is an important first step in realizing the dream of making poverty history.